THE PUBLIC SECTOR IN CANADA
Programs, Finance, and Policy

THE PUBLIC SECTOR IN CANADA

Programs, Finance, and Policy

JOHN C. STRICK
University of Windsor

THOMPSON EDUCATIONAL PUBLISHING, INC.
Toronto

Thompson Educational Publishing, Inc.
14 Ripley Avenue, Suite 104, Toronto, Ontario M6S 3N9
Tel: (416) 766-2763 / Fax: (416) 766-0398
Email: publisher@thompsonbooks.com

Canadian Cataloguing in Publication Data

Strick, J.C., 1937-
   The public sector in Canada : programs, finance and policy

Includes bibliographical references and index.
ISBN 1-55077-101-9

1. Canada - Economic policy. 2. Industrial policy - Canada. 3. Government business enterprises - Canada. 1. Title.

HC115.S885 1999   338.971   C98-932640-3

Copyediting: Elizabeth Phinney
Cover design: Elan Designs
We acknowledge the support of the Government of Canada through the Book Publishing Industry Development Program for our publishing activities.
Printed in Canada.
1 2 3 4 5   06 05 04 03 02 01 00 99

Table of Contents

Preface   7

PART ONE
GOVERNMENT IN THE
ECONOMY / 9

**1. Introduction: The Role of
Government**   11
Social Goals and Government
   Activities   12
Resource Allocation   13
Redistribution of Income   14
Economic Stability and Growth   15
Other Objectives   16
Summary   17

**2. Economic Efficiency in Resource
Allocation**   19
Imperfections in Competition   19
Externalities   22
Public Goods and Services   24
Summary   26

**3. Government Resource Allocation
Programs**   31
Health Care Services   31
Education   35
National Defence   37
Transportation and Communications   38
Environmental Protection and
   Conservation   39
Other Resource-Absorbing Activities   41
Summary   41

4. Income Redistribution and Security   43
Income Distribution and Poverty   43
Anti-Poverty Programs   46
Income-Security Programs   51
Summary   55

PART TWO
PUBLIC SECTOR GROWTH AND
MANAGEMENT / 57

**5. Growth and Composition of Public
Sector Expenditures**   59
Factors Influencing Public Sector
   Growth   59
Government Expenditure Growth
   Theories   62
Government Expenditure Trends
   and Patterns   64
Expenditures of Public Enterprises   69
Tax Expenditures   72
Summary   73

**6. Alternative Program Delivery
Systems**   75
Traditional Delivery Systems   75
Alternative Means of Delivering
   Services   76
Summary   82

**7. Budgeting and Financial
Management**   85
The Financial Structure of the
   Canadian Government   85
The Budget Cycle   89
Features of the Budgetary System   91
Features of Provincial and Local
   Government Budgeting   101
Summary   102

PART THREE
FINANCING THE PUBLIC SECTOR / 111

8. Introduction to Taxation	113
Tax Bases	113
Principles of Taxation	116
Tax Incidence, Tax Shifting, and Economic Effects	119
Historical Development of Taxation in Canada	121
Summary	125
9. The Federal Tax Structure	127
Tax Revenue Features	127
Personal Income Tax	127
Corporate Income Tax	142
Other Business Taxes	143
Consumption-Based Taxes	144
Payroll Taxes	152
Other Revenue Sources	152
The Underground Economy and Tax Evasion	153
Summary	154
10. Provincial and Local Government Finance	155
Provincial Taxation	155
Provincial Non-Tax Revenue	161
Local Government Revenues	162
Summary	165
11. Non-Tax Sources of Revenue	167
Miscellaneous Revenue Sources	167
User Charges	168
Gaming	171
Summary	176
12. Debt Finance	179
Borrowing	179
Public Debt in Canada	183
Issues and Concerns of Borrowing and Debt	186
The Federal Debt Treadmill	190
Provincial Deficits, Debt, and Struggle for Control	192
Debt Retirement	194
Comparison with Other Countries	196
Summary	196

PART FOUR
INTERGOVERNMENTAL FISCAL RELATIONS / 199

13. Historical Development	201
Historical Development of Fiscal Relations	202
Federal-Provincial Fiscal Arrangements: 1941-2002	205
Summary	216
14. Intergovernmental Transfers	219
Federal Transfers to Provinces	219
Transfers to Local Governments	227
Summary	229
15. Constitutional Reform and Related Issues	231
Early Developments	231
The Quebec Issue	232
Constitution Act, 1982	233
The Meech Lake Accord	235
The Charlottetown Accord	237
Confrontation over Natural Resources	240
Co-ordination of Economic and Social Policies	243
Summary	245

PART FIVE
FISCAL POLICY / 247

16. The Budget as An Instrument of Fiscal Policy	249
The Budget Accounts	250
Fiscal Impulse Measures	252
Goals of Fiscal Policy	254
Summary	261
17. Application of Fiscal Policy in Canada	263
Background	264
Fiscal Policy 1955-1974	266
Fiscal Policy 1975-1998	268
Implications for Future Counter-Cyclical Fiscal Policy	278
Summary	280
Index	285

Preface

This book covers most aspects of the economics of the public sector in Canada. Its design and structure permits its use as a textbook or a primary supplementary source in a variety of courses on government economic and social policies for which students require little background in economic theory.

The book is divided into five parts, each reflecting a major segment of public sector economics and policies.

Part I consists of four chapters on government expenditure policy in Canada. It covers the role of government in compensating for market failures in the allocation of resources and the redistribution of income. The major resource-absorbing programs of government are analyzed, including health care, education, defence, transportation and communications, and environmental regulation, along with the various programs in income security and maintenance such as Old Age Security, the Canada Pension Plan, and Employment Insurance.

Part II examines the growth and management of government spending. The growth and composition of federal, provincial, and local expenditures are analyzed, with brief reference to public expenditure growth theories. A complete chapter is devoted to alternative program delivery systems which governments in Canada have turned to in attempts to restrain spending and improve the efficiency and effectiveness of providing goods and services to the public. The chapter on budgeting and financial management in government also looks at recent budgetary developments designed for more effective control of government spending.

Part III consists of five chapters on financing the public sector. Following an introductory chapter on principles and concepts in taxation, the federal, provincial, and local government tax systems are analyzed. A separate chapter is devoted to non-tax sources of revenues, with the focus on user charges and gaming, including the controversies over governments' proliferation of lotteries and casinos. This part concludes with an extensive chapter on debt finance in Canada and the long string of federal and provincial budgetary deficits and rapidly rising debt.

Part IV describes and analyzes intergovernmental fiscal relations in Canada in three rather lengthy chapters. One chapter traces the historical development of federal-provincial relations in Canada, a second examines various aspects of intergovernmental transfers, and the final chapter is devoted to constitutional reform and related issues. This last chapter focuses on events leading to, and the failure of, the Meech Lake and Charlottetown Accords and the issue of Quebec separatism, plus confrontations between provinces and Ottawa over natural resources and other matters.

Part V covers economic stabilization policy which utilizes the government budget to combat recession, unemployment, and inflation. Following a brief theoretical explanation of traditional Keynesian fiscal policy and the budget as an instrument of this policy, a major chapter traces the federal government's use of fiscal policy since World War II. The analysis then concentrates on the problems in applying the Keynesian formula as reflected in the continuous and increasing federal budgetary deficits over the past twenty years. This part concludes with an evaluation of the current state of traditional stabilization policy and its potential for the future.

The book contains only the minimum economic theory necessary. Economic principles and concepts are clearly explained, making the book comprehensible for students with little or no background in economics.

This book would be an appropriate textbook for a course in Canadian public sector economics or Canadian public finance. For courses dealing with selective issues of the Canadian public sector or economic policy, one or more of the five parts of the book may be appropriate. These would include courses on Canadian taxation, the economics of public expenditures, fiscal federalism, stabilization policy, public administration, or a general course on Canadian public policy.

PART ONE

GOVERNMENT IN THE ECONOMY

CHAPTER 1

Introduction: The Role of Government

The importance of government in the modern economy is enormous though difficult to measure. It is a producer, owner, regulator, subsidizer, and income redistributor, as well as a protector of the consumer and society. There is perhaps no line of economic activity that is not to some degree influenced by government, for it has permeated practically every aspect of economic life.

As an owner and producer, government is involved in the provision of goods and services that are not provided by private interests or are deemed to be provided in insufficient quantity. As a regulator and supervisor of private entrepreneurship, government issues licences, permits, and patents and has passed legislation governing such aspects of production as quality, content, packaging, advertising, safety standards, competitive practices, and occasionally pricing policies. Certain production activities are prohibited, others are limited, and still others are assisted through subsidies, tariffs, and marketing services.

Government is also concerned with the way in which goods and services — the proceeds of production — are distributed among members of society. Considerable government activity is directed towards redistributing income from wealthier groups to poorer groups through taxes and expenditures. In this process, the government has assumed an obligation to ensure that the less-privileged members of society, people of lesser means and the disabled and elderly, are provided with at least a minimum standard of living. Benefits to low-income groups may take the form of direct money payments, the provision of goods and services, or through regulation. Some redistribution programs involve direct transfers, such as old age pensions, Employment Insurance, disabled persons' allowances, Workers' Compensation, and welfare payments to families with little or no income. Other programs have redistributional effects through their impact on real income; they include subsidized housing, rent controls, supply management, and medical and hospitalization programs. These various expenditure programs are financed primarily through the tax system, which, to the degree that it is progressive, tends to impose a relatively greater burden on higher-income groups and consequently also has a redistributive effect.

Other areas of government involvement in the economy include the protection of people and property through the administration of justice and national defence, regulating international trade, managing the monetary system, and attempting to promote economic growth and stability.

In addition, the government exerts considerable indirect influence on the economy through rules and regulations established to provide a framework for the orderly conduct of economic activity in the private sector of the economy.

In meeting its obligations, the government acts as an employer, as a producer of goods and services, as a purchaser of materials, and as a redistributor of income, thus assuming considerable direct significance in the economy. The most comprehensive and widely employed measure of government influence in the economy in general is the ratio of total government expenditure to gross domestic product (GDP), which is the value of all goods and services produced in a country in a given year. This ratio tends to overestimate the importance of government as a producer of goods and services because its spending includes transfer payments as well as direct expenditures on goods and services. On the other hand, this measure tends to underestimate the overall impact of government on the economy since the effects of government regulations on activities comprising GDP far exceed the amount government actually spends in administering these regulations. The measure, however, is useful in that it serves to indicate the proportion of the total expenditure stream in the economy that is affected directly by government through its spending on goods and services and its transfer payments to individuals and to business and social organizations. These expenditures by all level of government combined — federal, provincial, and local — were approximately 46 percent of GDP in 1996. (The composition and growth of government expenditure are analyzed in detail in chapter 5).

Social Goals and Government Activities

Every society faces the basic economic problem of allocating its available resources among competing uses and of distributing the proceeds of production among its members. Given the scarcity of resources, it is not possible to meet all of the demands for goods and services. If the goal of society is to achieve some optimal level of social services, resources must be used to provide those goods and services that society desires most, and they must be used as efficiently as possible in the process. Furthermore, optimal social welfare implies that the returns from production — income — which give an indi-

vidual command over goods and services, should be distributed in an equitable manner.

In a market economy, prices determine the use of resources and the distribution of income. If the system is perfectly competitive, the prices of goods and services and the factors of production are determined by supply and demand. Resources are allocated to the production of those goods and services that consumers want and for which they are prepared to pay. The income of consumers — their ability to pay for goods and services — is in turn determined by the prices they can command for their productive services in the factor market. This system, characterized by consumer and producer sovereignty and referred to as the free enterprise system, will theoretically, under certain conditions, assure an efficient use of resources to provide all goods and services most desired by society. In practice, however, the price system suffers serious limitations in performing this function. Not even Adam Smith would unqualifyingly advocate an undisturbed market mechanism as the complete solution to the problem of resource allocation and income distribution, and few economists today would propose that what is determined the marketplace will necessarily be optimal for the welfare of society.

Government participates in the economy to assist the market mechanism to achieve objectives of society. In fact, government activities are usually divided into three main categories reflecting those objectives: (1) activities designed to promote the efficient allocation of resources; (2) activities designed to redistribute income and wealth in accordance with standards of equity determined by national consensus; and (3) activities designed to maintain a stable rate of economic activity and promote economic growth.[1] The focus of these objectives is the effective and efficient use of resources and the fair distribution of the proceeds from resource use. Although government and society will have other goals — the preservation of individual freedoms, national unity, and cultural aspirations are examples in Canada — the economic study of the public sector has traditionally centred on the three basic socioeconomic objectives of government.

Resource Allocation

In economic theory, an optimum allocation of resources — a Pareto optimum — is described as a situation in which, given the availability of resources, the state of technology, and the distribution of income, one individual cannot be made better off without making another individual worse off. A Pareto optimum,[2] in simple terms, is a situation in which prices equal the marginal costs of production, factors such as labour are paid the value of their contributions to production, there are no excess profits, and all factors are employed. In effect, maximum efficiency is achieved in the use of resources.

For the market mechanism to achieve a Pareto optimum, certain conditions in the market are required. First, the market must have perfect competition, characterized by perfect knowledge, homogeneous products, large number of buyers and sellers, and perfect mobility of resources. Second, there must be no external economies or diseconomies in production and consumption. Finally, all the goods and services for which there is an effective demand must possess the properties of excludability and rivalry in consumption.

In the perfectly competitive market model, prices and output are determine by the interactions of supply and demand, and each firm in the market takes the price as given. There are a sufficiently large number of buyers and sellers, so one cannot influence the price of a particular product or service. Perfect competition also assumes that each individual consumer has a complete knowledge of products and services available and of their attributes; that each producer is familiar with and aware of the availability of the factors of produc-

tion; and these factors can be readily shifted from one use to another. In equilibrium in perfect competition, each firm will produce so that its price just equals its marginal cost and its minimum average cost. The firm will enjoy normal profits. (Normal profit is the opportunity cost of the entrepreneur who owns the firm; it is a return just sufficient to keep the entrepreneur in business and is included in the average cost curve in the model of the firm.)

The absence of externalities in consumption and production implies that all benefits of consumption accrue directly to the buyer and that all costs are included in the firm's costs of production. In other words, the price of a commodity as determined by supply and demand will reflect the benefits of supplying an additional unit of the commodity and will cover all costs involved in its production.

Goods and services must be exclusive and rival in consumption if they are to be bought and sold in the marketplace. Goods and services that are exclusive can be withheld from consumers who are not prepared to pay for them. Goods are rival when consumption by one individual reduces the amount available to others. Goods and services that possess these features are known as private goods. In contrast, other goods and services are consumed collectively and consumption by one person does not reduce their availability to others. These are known as public goods, and no market for them can exist.

The conditions for Pareto optimality are not completely fulfilled in the economies of today's world. Few, if any, products and services are bought and sold in a perfectly competitive market; rather, the markets for most have a variety of imperfections that distort the allocation of resources away from Pareto optimality. Most lines of consumption and production produce varying degrees of external benefits and costs. And certain goods and services are public in nature and will not be provided by the marketplace despite society's desire for them. Such situations, discussed in greater detail in the next chapter, reflect market failures in resource allocation and are cited as providing justification for government involvement or interference in the economy to improve efficiency in the use of resources in order to move it closer to Pareto optimality.

Redistribution of Income

One of the goals generally attributed to society is a fair distribution of income and wealth among its members. Opinions vary on what is fair, but it is generally agreed that severe inequalities in income levels are not acceptable. History has shown that the market system usually produces a distribution of severe inequality. An equitable distribution of incomes is, however, difficult to define and involves value judgements on the part of society and those elected to govern.

The distribution of income in a country, including the degree of equality, is influenced by many factors including individuals' capabilities, educational opportunities, property holdings and laws of inheritance, the scarcity or abundance of specific resources, and the homogeneity of resources. Factors are not homogeneous, and certain factors will always be scarce. Some individuals are more capable and ambitious than others, have a greater entrepreneurial spirit to initiate a successful enterprise, or can command factors in scarce supply. Indeed, one of the foundations of the free enterprise system is individualism — the freedom to pioneer and take risks for motives of higher income, more power, or prestige.

Some people may have lower incomes because of ill health, lack of skills, old age, or social barriers that make it difficult for them to develop their potential. Some occupations are seasonal and comparatively low paying, such as farming and fishing. Certain regions of a country may lack an economic base conducive to high incomes and lag in economic development and growth. The incidence of low incomes bordering on poverty is generally concentrated in rural areas and among the elderly and undereducated.

Government takes measures to counter some of these situations by redistributing income. It is worth noting, however, that it is often difficult to establish a clear distinction between government income-redistribution programs and government resource-reallocation programs. Some programs serve both objectives. Medicare, for example, yields external benefits to society, but at the same time, if it benefits the poor relatively more than the wealthy, it reduces the income gap between the two groups.

Canadian governments have recognized their obligation to redistribute income and wealth to attain a greater degree of equality and to reduce the incidence of poverty. The means to this end at the federal and provincial levels are a number of welfare and income-maintenance programs, including Old Age Security payments, the Canada Pension Plan, programs such as widow's allowances and pensions for the blind and disabled, and subsidies and quotas in agriculture to maintain and stabilize farm incomes — as well as programs to increase and improve education, provide technical training and labour retraining, and assist labour mobility. In addition, there are Employment Insurance and Workers' Compensation plus minimum wage regulations and rent controls. Another government approach is transfer programs that provide real goods and services, such as subsidized housing, medical care, hospitalization, and education. Since these programs usually benefit the poor relatively more than the wealthy, some income redistribution is realized. The various redistribution programs are financed by a tax system that attempts to use progressive income tax rates and various exemptions in consumption-based taxes to place a greater burden on higher-income groups than on low-income groups.

The Canadian government has also made a commitment to try to reduce regional economic disparities. Differences between provinces in terms of resource endowment, population, proximity to markets, investment opportunities, and so on lead to different degrees of economic development, industrialization and industry structure, employment, and income levels. In the Atlantic provinces, average per capita income is only half of that in more prosperous regions, such as Ontario and Alberta. To reduce this inequality, the federal government has introduced a variety of policies, including the payment of subsidies and tax concessions to encourage industry to develop in these areas, worker retraining and mobility programs, equalization grants to the governments of the poorer provinces to enable them to provide their residents with public services comparable to those of other provinces, and the establishment of special programs and funds to develop opportunities for employment at an adequate wage.

One of the difficulties with an objective of achieving greater equity in income distribution is the existence of factors that tend to limit redistribution. Attempts to divide total income more evenly among members of society may reduce the amount to be divided. Excessive taxation of the upper-income groups and business in order to finance transfers and goods and services benefiting lower-income groups may stifle incentives to work, to invest, to maintain maximum efficiency in production and distribution, and to engage in risky business ventures. The result would be a waste of resources; economic growth, capital accumulation, and consequently future production and employment would be lower than they otherwise might have been, decreasing the total income available for distribution among society's members. Government may, therefore, have to strike a compromise between the objective of a more equitable distribution of income and the objective of efficiency in the use of resources and economic growth.

Economic Stability and Growth

Over the last half-century or so, the Canadian government, like most modern governments, has accepted an obligation for economic stabilization and the attainment of the general goals of high levels of employment, reasonably stable prices, and an adequate rate of economic growth. This function of government is a relatively new one, dating from the Depression of the 1930s.

History has shown that the market economy is characterized by fluctuations in economic activity, with periods of rapid expansion and rising prices, periods of economic decline and unemployment, and periods of stagnation characterized by slow economic growth, rising unemployment, and inflation. Classical economics viewed these fluctuations as temporary maladjustments that the forces of the market would remedy. It became apparent with the Depression, however, that prolonged periods of economic stagnation and high levels of unemployment could occur, with the market system unable to prevent them or to remedy them speedily once they set in. It was in this depressed economic climate that J.M. Keynes wrote his *General Theory of Employment, Interest and Money* in which he built the foundation for macroeconomics and discretionary fiscal policy. Refining Keynesian theory, economists in the United States, such as Alvin Hansen, argued for increased government participation in the economy to influence the rate of economic activity and prevent fluctuations. With Keynes, they said that the stable operation of the market economy required government action.

Keynesian fiscal policy became traditional policy. It consists of discretionary adjustments to government tax and expenditure policies to influence aggregate demand. During a period of economic decline, government increases expenditure and reduces taxes. The resulting deficit in the budget indicates that government is putting more purchasing power into the economy than it is taking out, producing a net increase in aggregate demand and providing a stimulus for increased output of goods and services and, therefore, increased employment.

Periods of excessive economic expansion generally produce rapidly rising prices or inflation and require just the opposite policy. Inflation may be caused by excessive demand or rapidly rising costs of production. Government can temper aggregate demand by reducing its own demand through a decrease in its expenditure. Similarly, increased taxes may reduce private demand by reducing purchasing power in the hands of the pubic and leaving people with fewer funds to spend on consumption and investment.

Governments employ monetary policy in conjunction with discretionary fiscal policy in attempts to stabilize the economy and promote economic growth. Indeed, in recent years, with budget flexibility hampered by continuous large annual deficits, monetary policy has become the primary stabilization instrument. Monetary policy includes varying the money supply and regulating interest rates. High interest rates and a reduction in the growth rate of the money supply may be used for contractionary effects to combat inflation, with just the opposite policy in periods of economic decline.

Alternative or in addition to fiscal and monetary policy during a period of inflation, government may use more direct controls, such as wage and price regulation. The governments of most democracies have been reluctant to interfere in economic activity to this extent and have tended to rely on the more indirect means of tax and expenditure policy. In the past, Canada, the United States, and the countries of Western Europe have resorted to rigid, direct controls only in periods of emergency, such as crises in national security (i.e., World War II). In the post-war period, a number of countries, including Canada, experimented with temporary wage and price regulations in the face of serious inflation.

The Canadian government's first use of discretionary fiscal policy occurred during the latter stages of the Depression. It was not until 1945, however, that it officially and openly declared an obligation for fiscal policy. Since that time the country has experienced periods of decline and prosperity, and the government's fiscal policy has varied in both its intensity and its degree of success. Indeed in recent years the use of government budgetary policy for economic stabilization has become questionable. The Canadian government budget was in a deficit position from 1975 to 1997, regardless of the state of the economy, producing a huge public debt. A number of provinces have passed balanced-budget legislation, preventing budget deficits and the accumulation of debt. These issues will be discussed in later chapters.

Other Objectives

In addition to the three basic socio-economic objectives outlined above, governments may use their spending, taxing, and regulatory powers to promote various other social and cultural goals. In Canada, the federal government has historically used these powers to bring the country's various regions together to establish, maintain, and enhance an integrated economy and a national identity. This has been particularly true of federal transportation and communications policies. The National Policy of 1879 included the construction of a transcontinental railway to bring the regions together and a tariff wall to promote the development of Canadian industry. The creation of the Canadian Broadcasting Corporation (CBC) was followed by various regulations, including specification of broadcast content, to foster Canadian programming and culture.

The government has also used regulation and direct participation to attempt to increase Canadian ownership and control of the country's industry. These efforts have included the pursuit of a national energy policy involving the co-operation and participation of government and the private sector in developing the country's energy resources in the interests of Canada. One such enterprise was Petro Canada, established by the federal government in 1976 as a Crown corporation to participate in the exploration for oil and gas and the refining and marketing of petroleum products. (Petro Canada has since been privatized.)

Government involvement in the provision of goods and services that are essentially private in nature may stem from a desire to maintain or develop certain industries to diversify the economy's industrial base and to create employment opportunities. This activity may involve the establishment of government enterprise (such as Air Canada) or the takeover — nationalization — of existing private enterprise. The objective of nationalizing an industry may be to redirect its operation in the public interest. On the other hand, government may nationalize failing private enterprises to prevent the industry from terminating operations and laying off workers. Examples of the latter goal include the federal government's purchase of Canadair Ltd. and de Havilland Aircraft of Canada Ltd. during the mid-1970s. Assisted by large federal grants, these two corporations operated as Crown corporations until their sale to private interests during the privatization movement of the late 1980s. (The operations and administration of Crown corporations is further examined in chapter 5.)

The Canadian government's efforts in nation building include its policy of promoting the use of both English and French throughout Canada. Other nation-building measures are demonstrated in relations with the provinces. Jurisdictional disputes over areas of authority are not uncommon; generally they arise when the federal government's view of a policy in the national interest conflicts with the narrower regional interests of the provinces. Some recent disputes have centred

around energy, telecommunications, offshore mineral rights, and constitutional reform.

It has not been uncommon for special regional social and cultural objectives and for political philosophies to guide the expenditure and tax policies of provincial governments. For example, the CCF (Co-operative Commonwealth Federation, which was the forerunner of the New Democratic Party) came to power in Saskatchewan in 1944 promoting a form of socialism. Its policies included the improvement of social security measures and greater government involvement in economic planning and in the production and distribution sectors of the economy through the establishment of Crown corporations and co-operative ventures with private interests. Many of these ventures were later terminated and some government-owned corporations were sold when right-wing governments, which placed greater emphasis on the marketplace for directing activities in the economy, came to power.

The province of Quebec has traditionally sought to protect and promote its French language, culture, and identity on the Anglo-dominated North American continent. This objective has been pursued through a variety of measures, including some of the province's economic, social, and educational policies and a movement to separate from the rest of Canada.

Summary

Most government activity in the economy can be classified under one or more of the three major objectives of government: to secure adjustments in resource allocation, to achieve equity in income distribution, and to promote economic stability and growth. The market system, which operates under its own constraints and limitations, is unable to achieve these goals to the satisfaction of society. Canadian governments at all levels are heavily involved in assisting the economy to achieve these objectives. Their activities include promoting competition, combatting external diseconomies such as pollution, providing public services, redistributing income through taxes, transfers, and a variety of income-maintenance programs, and applying fiscal and monetary policies to combat unemployment and inflation and to promote economic growth.

The various government objectives frequently conflict, and there is the question regarding the most effective methods of achieving them. Economic analysis can contribute to establishing compromises and solutions to these issues, but they must be resolved within the political and administrative decision-making structure and processes. In essence, the study of public finance must include elements of politics and public administration as well as economics.

NOTES

[1] This classification of government activities, found in a number of textbooks in public finance, was first presented in the classic, R.A. Musgrave, *The Theory of Public Finance* (New York: McGraw-Hill, 1959).

[2] The term "Pareto optimum" is named after the economist Vilfredo Pareto (1848-1923), who first put forward the conditions or criteria for economic efficiency in the economy. These efficiency conditions, defined for consumption and production, are explained in most intermediate textbooks in microeconomics, as well as in various public finance textbooks. See, for example, David N. Hyman and John C. Strick, *Public Finance in Canada* (Toronto: Harcourt Brace, 1995), pp.74-85.

CHAPTER 2

Economic Efficiency in Resource Allocation

As outlined in chapter 1, one of the goals of society is the achievement of economic efficiency in the allocation and use of a country's resources. An optimum allocation of resources is described as a Pareto optimum.

In a market economy, certain conditions must be satisfied if the market is to attain this optimum level. These conditions are described as: perfect competition, the absence of externalities, and rivalry and excludability of goods and services. The extent to which these conditions are not met in the market economy of a country will attest to the degree to which the market fails to achieve a Pareto optimum. While it is highly unlikely that any nation can hope to achieve this theoretical standard for economic efficiency, any degree of correction by government for market failures should produce an improvement in efficiency. A more efficient use of resources will provide a higher standard of living for society in terms of the production and consumption of goods and services desired by society.

The market failures which society and government must address consist of imperfections in competition, the existence of external economies and diseconomies in production and consumption, and the desire by society for public goods and services which are characterized by non-rivalry and non-excludability in consumption. Each of these failures in the market is examined in this chapter, together with a description and analysis of government actions in Canada in response to the failures.

Imperfections in Competition

Government has accepted a responsibility to reduce imperfections in the economy or to mitigate their consequences. Among these imperfections are lack of knowledge on the part of the consumer and on the part of factors of production, factor immobility, and monopoly control. Government attempts to correct these problems through a variety of activities and services.

Consumer Services

If consumers are to obtain the greatest satisfaction from their limited resources, they must be familiar with the goods and services available to them. But in any economy characterized by variability and multiplicity of products that are technologically sophisticated and promoted by large-scale advertising and a host of other sales techniques, the consumer is open to exploitation. The government attempts to establish safeguards and regulations to protect consumers and to improve their knowledge of goods and services.

At the federal level in Canada, this function is undertaken primarily by Industry Canada through its marketplace program, designed to protect the consumer and promote an efficient marketplace. Laws and regulations protecting the consumer are also administered by numerous other departments and agencies. The provinces have counterpart bureaus and agencies.

Governments in Canada attempt to protect consumers against fraud, deception, and unsafe products. Regulations have been established governing the accuracy of weights and measures and the character of advertising; labelling requirements stipulate the information that must be shown on packages and containers. Factory-inspection spot checks are made on certain goods before they are sold. Standards are established for the construction of buildings, automobiles, and a host of consumer durables. The department is also a focal point for consumer complaints and inquiries. It assists consumers with their problems and distributes information on a wide range of consumer subjects.

Industry Canada also works in close liaison with other agencies administering consumer-protection legislation. Among these is the Department of Transport, which regulates the safety of air and rail facilities. Another is the Department of National Health and Welfare, which is charged with supervising the manufacture and distribution of food and drug products. New drugs are tested and must be approved before they can be marketed; food-processing plants are inspected, and foods are tested for their nutritional value.

Factor Services

Unemployed workers may be unaware of available jobs or lack the skills necessary for the work available. Government attempts to correct these imperfections in the labour market. The federal government tries to bring together employers and prospective employees through regional offices called employment centres. These centres provide information to employers concerning the labour market and information to workers about job opportunities. In addition, they offer counselling to workers and serve as contacts for workers for government training programs.

Unemployed workers are also assisted through various government-established (or supported) labour training and mobility programs, including occupational training for the unskilled, retraining for changing job qualifications, and relocation grants covering some costs of moving from one area to another in search of employment. The federal government has been transferring responsibility for the administration of employment measures to the provinces, and this transfer is expected to be completed by the year 2000.

Government is also engaged in ensuring that workers are not subjected to undue hazards in the performance of their work. Provincial Workers' Compensation Boards, for example, conduct continual investigations into safety conditions in factories, mines, and other places of employment. And federal and provincial government combine to establish a system of providing workers and employers uniform information about hazardous materials present in the workplace.

Monopoly Regulation

The most significant type of imperfection in the real world market economy is unquestionably the existence of monopoly or elements of it. Indeed, practically every line of production and distribution is characterized by some degree of monopoly, ranging from the extreme of pure monopoly through oligopoly to monopolistic competition.

Theoretically, the monopoly element results in inefficiency in the use of resources by making output smaller and prices higher than they would be under competitive conditions. Competition, in most cases, leads to the largest possible output at the lowest price, directs resources to their most productive channels, and encourages technological change and high productivity as producers attempt to gain an advantage over competitors. Government has accepted a responsibility to prevent the creation of monopolies in many situations, as well as to reduce the degree of monopoly and restore prices and output to more competitive levels.

The Canadian government has attempted to regulate monopoly and anti-competition practices through legislation since 1889, when it passed *An Act for the Prevention and Suppression of Combinations in Restraint of Trade*. This law and its successors, most of which were called the *Combines Investigation Act*, proved difficult to enforce and were thus often ineffective. In recent years, the government has attempted to strengthen its competition policy through the *Competition Act*, which established a Bureau of Competition Policy and a Competition Tribunal. Under it, restrictive agreements such as price fixing and restricting the entrance of competitors are unlawful, as are practices such as misleading advertising and unfair forms of promotional games and contests. Mergers and other business practices are examined by the Bureau of Competition Policy to determine whether they are in the public interest or whether they promote or impede economic efficiency. Many kinds of charges are heard by the Competition Tribunal, which can order the dissolution of mergers and cartels, terminate patents and copyrights, and impose heavy penalties. Even for the few matters treated under the criminal law, individuals have the right to initiate civil suits to recover damages incurred as a result of violations of the legislation.

Natural monopolies, such as public utilities and some forms of transportation and communication, present different problems. These are firms which claim large economies of scale. The interests of efficiency dictate that one large firm is more desirable than a number of small competing firms. In lieu of competition, government regulation may be required to ensure that the firm does not use its monopoly position to exploit consumers, manipulate prices, and earn large excess profits. To change prices, rate structures, or services provided, the monopoly is required to obtain the permission of the regulatory agency. Canada has such agencies at the federal, provincial, and municipal levels, primarily to regulate public utilities. Examples include the regulation of hydro-electric

power, cable television, and local telephone services.

At the other extreme, government may become involved where ruinous competition threatens the stability and viability of essential industries such as agriculture. In such cases government employs supply management to interfere with the market mechanism and prevent major cyclical fluctuations in production, prices and farm incomes. This has been the role of farm marketing boards in Canada.

In the cases of both natural monopoly and ruinous competition, government regulation may have an adverse impact on resource use, producing inefficiencies in operations and consequent high costs of production. The argument is that producers who do not face competition but have assured profit levels or rates of return have few incentives to maintain maximum efficiency.[1]

An alternative to government regulation of private industry production and prices is public ownership of industries that tend to be natural monopolies. Provincial and municipal government own and operate many utilities. Government ownership, however, does not necessarily assure operating efficiency, as will be shown in a later chapter.

Monopoly regulation also extends to the factor market. Unions tend to be monopoly sellers of labour services. Both federal and provincial laws give workers the legal authority to bargain collectively on wages and working conditions. Legislation governs bargaining procedures as well as procedures to be followed in the event of an impasse. Unions have the right to strike by temporarily withdrawing labour services, but government has the power to intervene and force the continuation of labour services that are deemed necessary for the public interest.

Externalities

The existence of externalities in consumption and production accounts for a considerable proportion of government activity in the economy. It has generally been accepted that where external economies and diseconomies exist, government participation is justified to alter the use or allocation of resources in the interest of social welfare and efficiency. Government may channel more resources into areas of production and consumption that experience external economies; where there are external diseconomies, it may initiate actions to reduce them or discourage resource use there. A diagrammatic analysis of externalities is presented in the appendix to this chapter.

External Economies

Benefits that accrue to society in addition to those received directly by the individual engaged in the production or consumption of a commodity or service are called external economies. Education is frequently viewed as a service with external economies in consumption. When an individual obtains an education, he or she benefits personally, but society as a whole also benefits in terms of increased productive potential. Under the price system, individuals buy education in accordance with the benefits they expect to receive personally and with their financial means; in making their purchase decisions, they do not consider the additional benefits that may accrue to society. Government, on the other hand, is concerned with social benefits and endeavours to provide education facilities in excess of what the market would provide, either by subsidizing private educational institutions or by assuming direct responsibility for education.

A similar rationale can be applied to government provision of health care and other services. The funding of health services is a major government activity, justified partially on the grounds of the social benefits they

yield. Similarly, research activities to improve technology and productivity and develop new products and services have the potential of yielding benefits to society and so are financially supported by government.

External Diseconomies

Costs that accrue to society from consumption and production in addition to the direct costs of the individual consumer and producer are called external diseconomies. Recently, considerable attention has been focussed on such diseconomies, particularly pollution. Pollution of the environment is not generally included in the private costs of production — and is thus not reflected in the market price of goods and services — yet its costs to society are high. Harm to health resulting from water and air pollution, contamination of fish and waterfowl from the dumping of production waste into lakes and streams, and similar destruction of some resources in the use of others are common in modern industrialized economies. Examples abound in Canada. Fishing has been banned in a number of lakes and streams because of mercury contamination, resulting in the loss of food for some Native peoples, of sport fishing, and of occupation for commercial fishers. The Great Lakes are being threatened by pollution discharged into the air from surrounding industry and returned in the form of acid rain. Many logging firms make only minor attempts at reforestation after stripping an area, and firms engaged in open-pit mining may leave unsightly landscapes.

It has been argued that externalities are caused by the lack of property rights and can be corrected by the marketplace through the assignments of such rights. Water, for example, is a resource viewed as "common property." No one has exclusive property rights over such resources, so there is a tendency to abuse and waste these resources. Firms can dump industrial wastes into streams and lakes without paying to do so. The assignment to one firm of property rights to the stream or lake would exclude other firms from using it unless they paid for its use, including the right to pollute it. Payment for the right to pollute would result in the internalization of the external diseconomy since the cost of pollution would be included in the price of the goods and services sold by the polluting firms. Such payments, however, would cause the offending firm to consider carefully whether pollution is worthwhile in comparison to steps that could be taken to avoid pollution.[2]

Diseconomies in consumption are also common. Excessive consumption of alcohol is likely to lead to increased rates of traffic accidents, crime, and absenteeism from work — costs to society over and above the costs to consumer. The consumption of tobacco and drugs produces social costs in their hazards to general health and work effectiveness.

In cases of external diseconomies in both consumption and production, the government has assumed an obligation to intervene with varying degrees of supervision and control. With respect to consumption, the federal government has passed legislation prohibiting the use of drugs, such as heroin and marijuana, that society deems to have high social costs. Attempts are made to curtail the consumption of alcohol and tobacco. High excise taxes on these products are designed to increase their price and discourage their purchase. Smoking is banned in many public buildings and facilities. Cigarette and hard-liquor advertisements are banned on television, and producers are forced to stipulate on cigarette and tobacco packages that the product may be detrimental to health.

Government policies to combat external diseconomies in production may include the establishment of standards, payment of subsidies, imposition of taxes, charges for effluents, or some combination of these. For example, government may set pollution-emission standards, backed by penalties, that force the industry to curb pollution through the use of anti-pollution devices or changes in the production process. Subsidies can be applied to help industry defray the costs of pollution-control devices. Government can also impose taxes on commodities whose production causes pollution; such taxes have the effect of raising prices, reducing consumption and production, and, therefore, lowering the amount of pollution generated. Effluent charges that vary with the type and quantity of pollution can cause polluting firms to try to curb emissions through pollution-control devices or changes in production methods. Both the federal and provincial governments have legislated pollution controls, with penalties ranging from fines to prison sentences. In addition, tax concessions have been granted to encourage firms to introduce pollution-control measures. Environmental legislation has often not been rigorously enforced, however, perhaps partly because of public apathy, partly because of pressure from vested interest groups, and partly because of the technological complexity of the problem.

Much has been said and written about external diseconomies, such as pollution, and the role of government in controlling them. Theoretically, government action to control external diseconomies in production does not contradict the operation of the market mechanism. Indeed, government action is intended as a corrective for market failure. The basic problem is that the market pricing mechanism fails to include the total costs of production. For example, the emission of sulphur dioxide in the production of copper and nickel is a basic source of acid rain, yet the damage or cost resulting from those emissions has not been included in the costs of production by the nickel and copper industry. Instead, the cost has been reflected in pollution and thus borne by all society, both present and future generations. In a sense, production with external costs has been subsidized in the past, the subsidy being the deterioration of the environment, so that goods could be produced at a reasonable price to consumers.

Legislation forcing manufacturers to introduce pollution-control devices results in additional costs to the manufacturer and higher prices of manufactured goods. But these costs should have been included and passed on the consumer in the form of higher commodity prices to begin with. By forcing firms to internalize the external costs, government regulations can be viewed as assisting the market mechanism to perform its function. Those benefiting from the use of a commodity when they purchase it will cover the entire cost, instead of passing part of it on to the rest of society. Higher costs and prices may lead to reduced sales or termination of production, but, it is argued, this is the law of the marketplace, which leads to the production of those goods and services that people desire and are prepared to pay for.

Others argue, however, that this solution is oversimplified, that certain realities of the economy must be taken into consideration. If industry is forced to reduce output or possibly even close because of excessively high costs of pollution-control equipment, the result is a loss of jobs, representing a cost to society. If industry is forced to raise prices to cover increased costs, it runs the danger of losing its competitive position in foreign trade (assuming other countries do not follow similar antipollution policies). The result will be costs to society in terms of reduced employment in the domestic market.

It appears, therefore, that there is a trade-off between a clean environment and other economic goals, such as employment and economic expansion. Society may have to decide how much unemployment and how great an increase in prices it is prepared to accept in order to reduce pollution. The government cannot ignore the realities of this trade-off and should attempt some compromise to minimize the external diseconomies subject to the constraints of other goals. One policy that could be followed would be to use subsidies, grants, and tax concessions to help industries cover the initial costs of large investments in anti-pollution equipment, thereby distributing some of the initial cost to society, rather than expecting the producers and consumers involved to carry the full burden.

Public concern over external diseconomies in production has been increasing in recent years. To a large extent, the past disregard stemmed from public emphasis on maximizing material wealth and status without due regard to the quality of life. A gradual awakening to the tremendous costs that result from the neglect of external diseconomies has focussed increasing attention on these costs. Ensuing public pressure has produced more government supervision of the production process, which is reflected in the strengthening of environmental protection legislation.

Public Goods and Services

Government has assumed responsibility for providing a number of important goods and services that are public in nature. As already noted, unlike private goods, public goods are non-excludable and non-rival in consumption. When a good or service is non-excludable, people cannot be kept from enjoying its benefits even if they do not pay for it. When a good is non-rival, one person's consumption does not reduce or affect another person's consumption of it. The marginal cost of an additional person's consumption is zero, so it is not desirable to exclude anyone or to ration the good. Goods and services that possess these features are called *pure public goods*. Since they are consumed collectively, the market will not provide them. Examples include national defence and a pest-control program. In both cases, benefits accrue to all individuals residing in an area regardless of whether they pay for the service, and there is no additional cost if additional individuals benefit from it. Society may desire pure public goods and services, but resources will be channelled to their provision only if government undertakes to do so because it is neither feasible nor economical for the private sector to provide them.

In addition to pure public goods, there are goods and services that can be viewed as *impure* or *quasi-public*. These are goods to which exclusion can be applied, although they may be non-rival to a degree. Provision by the private sector would be inefficient and impractical, necessitating large administrative costs to collect fees or charges from consumers. It is, for example, more efficient for government than for the market to provide highways, bridges, streets, sidewalks, parks and recreational facilities, sewage facilities, and protection or security services. Government provides such services free of direct charge, finances them from taxation revenues, and avoids the high costs of administering user fees.

Government may also provide goods and services that are not public or even quasi-public but could be provided by private enterprise once markets are established. This situation frequently occurs when private interests are reluctant to enter a specific field because risks are so high and initial outlays so heavy that returns are very uncertain and cannot be expected for several years. Government may, therefore, take the initiative in the provision of the good or service. For example, transcontinental air services were begun in 1937 when the federal government established Trans Canada Airlines (now Air Canada); Polymer Corporation was created during World War II to produce synthetic rubber; Atomic Energy of Canada Limited was established to research and develop nuclear energy. Private interests later entered some of these areas, but governments, in many cases, continued their operations in direct competition with private enterprise. Government investments are, of course, subject to market risks similar to those of private investments and may not always be successful (although government enterprises may have recourse to public funds through government loans and parliamentary appropriations should they encounter financial difficulties).

Fundamental to the market system is the principle of consumer sovereignty, which means that consumers are free to choose how they will spend their incomes given the goods and services available to them. In addition to instances in which government interferes with consumer sovereignty because of externalities, there are situations in which it compels individuals to consume a private good or service or to consume a greater quantity than they desire. This interference with consumer preferences applies in the case of *merit goods*, which are particular commodities that the government deems to bestow a greater amount of benefit to individual consumers than do the individuals themselves. In other words, in the paternalistic view of government, the commodity is sufficiently meritorious that it should be consumed, or more should be consumed than the amount purchased in the marketplace. Examples include elementary education and automobile seat belts, which are made mandatory by government. Other examples include the performing arts, since government financial support makes theatre, concerts, and so on more readily available to consumers than they would be without subsidies.

The provision of public, quasi-public, and merit goods and services does not necessarily involve direct government employment of resources. Government can choose to make such goods available by directly employing labour and using materials to produce them, or by arranging for private firms to produce them for the government through contract. In both cases, resources are channelled from private use to public use, but only in the first method does government directly employ factors of production.

Summary

Real world economies are characterized by numerous inefficiencies and market failures which prevent an economy from achieving a Pareto optimum in the allocation of resources. Market imperfections include imperfect knowledge on the part of consumers, producers, and factors of production, and the existence of monopoly. Externalities in consumption and production result in market production of goods and services which is either excessive or insufficient. Furthermore, the market will simply not produce pure public goods. In each of these cases, there is justification for government intervention in the economy to correct market failures and attempt to move the economy towards a more efficient allocation or use of resources, and in the process to improve the economic well-being of society. In Canada, all three levels of government actively apply a variety of policies in an attempt to achieve this goal.

NOTES

1 For an examination of regulation in Canada — including regulatory agencies, processes, objectives, and effects — see John C. Strick, *The Economics of Government Regulation: Theory and Canadian Practice*, 2nd ed. (Toronto: Thompson Educational Publishing, 1994).

2 The issue of property rights and externalities, which is discussed in a number of textbooks in public sector economies, was first presented in R. Coase, "The Problem of Social Cost," *Journal of Law and Economics*, 3 (1960).

EXTERNALITIES AND PUBLIC GOODS: A DIAGRAMMATIC ANALYSIS

In the market model of supply and demand, the supply (S) and demand (D) curves show the relationship between price and quantity. The demand curve illustrates the amount of a commodity that will be taken off the market at various prices by consumers. The price a consumer is willing to pay for a unit of the commodity measures the additional benefit or utility that he or she receives from its consumption. The demand curve, therefore, can be viewed as the marginal private benefit (MPB) curve in consumption. The supply curve reflects the costs of producing the commodity; it is derived from the firm's marginal private cost (MPC) curve and represents the cost associated with the production of an additional unit of the commodity. The equilibrium market price (OQ) and quantity (OP) are determined where S = D or MPC = MPB, which is point E in Figure A2-1.

External Economies

External economies are benefits accruing to third parties, those other than the consumers and producers of a commodity. In Figure A2-1, the marginal external benefit (MEB) is the additional benefit received by third parties as a result of the production and consumption of additional units of the commodity. The marginal society benefit (MSB) is sum of the marginal private and external benefits: MSB = MPB + MEB. Assume that no external diseconomies exist so that MPC is equal to marginal social cost (MSC).

In the absence of externalities, the market equilibrium price (OP) and quantity (OQ) will be the efficient levels in perfect competition. With the existence of external economies, however, market equilibrium is no longer efficient. At output OQ, marginal social benefit exceeds marginal social cost by EF. Net benefit to society can be increased by increasing output from OQ to OR, where MSC = MSB at G. The total net gain to society from this increase in output is represented by the area EFG. The condition for private equilibrium is MPC =

MPB, but the condition for social equilibrium is MSC = MSB.

Thus, Figure A2-1 illustrates that in presence of external economies, the market will not produce enough output to maximize benefits to society. A private firm will not expand output to OR, the efficient amount for society, because to sell that amount, it would have to reduce price to OB and incur a loss equal to GH per unit, or a total loss equal to AGHR.

To ensure that the social optimum amount of the commodity is produced, the government can pay a subsidy to the firm to cover its loss or, alternatively, assume direct responsibility for production. If it follows the latter policy, the government may provide OR of the commodity free of charge and finance the total cost (OAGR) from tax revenues, or it may charge a nominal fee equal to OB and finance the remainder of the cost from tax revenues.

Suppose, in addition, the good in question was also viewed as a merit good. In this case, the government views the good as one for which the consumer undervalues the benefits to himself. If the MPB curve in the model represents the consumer's valuation of benefits, the government's valuation of benefits to the consumer would be represented by a higher MPB curve, and combined with the external benefits, MSB would be positioned higher in the quadrant.

External Diseconomies

External diseconomies are costs accruing to third parties, those other than the consumers and producers of a commodity. The marginal external cost (MEC) illustrated in Figure A2-2 is the additional cost to third parties as a result of the consumption or production of additional units of the commodity. Assume that the external cost is pollution that results from production and that the amount of pollution associated with each additional unit of production is constant, as shown by MEC. The marginal social cost (MSC) is the sum

FIGURE A2-1: External Economies

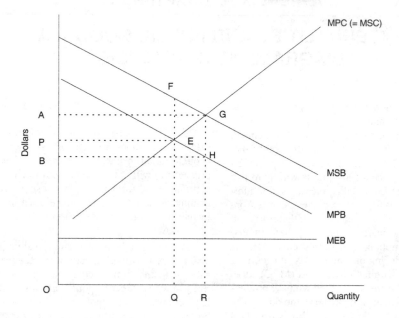

FIGURE A2-2: External Diseconomies

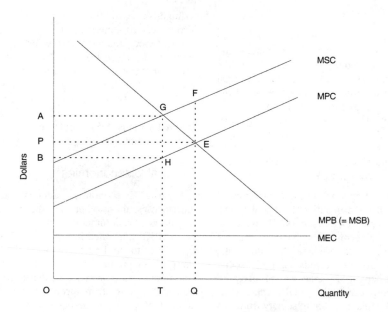

FIGURE A2-3: Derivation of Demand Curves for
Private and Public Goods

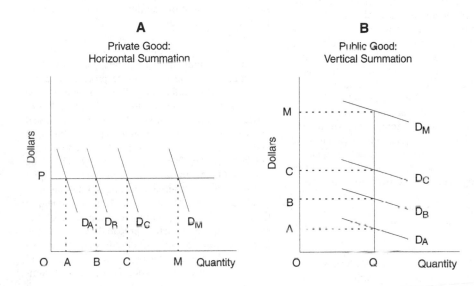

A

Private Good:
Horizontal Summation

B

Public Good:
Vertical Summation

of the private and external costs: MSC = MPC + MEC. Assume that there are no external benefits so that MPB = MSB.

In the absence of externalities, the market price (OP) and quantity (OQ) will be the optimal levels in perfect competition. When an external diseconomy exists, however, the marginal social cost exceeds the marginal social benefit by EF. This cost is not priced in the marketplace and is not included in the manufacturers' cost of production, but it is a cost to society and represents a net loss of welfare or benefits. Net benefit to society can be increased by reducing output from OQ to OT, where MSC = MSB at G. The total net gain to society is equal to EFG, which is the difference between the total cost of producing TQ (= TGFQ) minus the total benefit received from TQ (= TGEQ).

To achieve the socially optimal level of output (OT), the government can impose a tax on the commodity equal to FE per unit at output OQ. The tax becomes a cost to the firm, raising the costs of

production from MPC to MSC and resulting in a loss to the firm equal to FE per unit of output. The firm will, therefore, scale back output to point G, where the price per unit is just sufficient to cover the cost of the unit produced. At output OT, the tax will be GH per unit, with total taxes paid equal to AGHB. The tax succeeds in reducing output and consequently the amount of pollution but does not eliminate this diseconomy entirely. The cost of the pollution remaining is represented by AGHB.

Alternatively, the government can legislate antipollution laws, forcing the firm to purchase pollution-control equipment or alter its methods of production. The resulting increased costs to the firm will be reflected in a leftward shift of the MPC curve and a decrease in production. To the extent that pollution is reduced by the firm's action of incurring costs to prevent pollution, it is said that the firm has internalized the external diseconomy.

Pure Public Goods

Pure public goods and services are characterized by the properties of non-excludability and non-rivalry in consumption. They are consumed collectively, and the consumption of one person does not reduce the amounts available to others.

The difference between private goods and public goods is illustrated by the nature of the demand curves for the goods. The market demand curve for a private goods consists of the horizontal summation of all of the individual demand curves for the good. In Part A of Figure A2-3, D_A, D_B, and D_C are the respective demand curves for individuals A, B, and C. For example, D_A shows the amount individual A is prepared to purchase at various prices. Given price OP, A desires quantity OA, B quantity OB, and C quantity OC. The three consumers together are prepared to purchase an mount OM = OA + OB + OC at price OP. The market demand curve for the private good is the sum of the quantities demanded at given prices or $D_M = \Sigma Q_D$.

In the case of a private good, each individual consumes different quantities at any given price. In the case of a pure public good, on the other hand, each individual pays a different price for a given quantity. A pure public good is non-exclusive, which means that all individuals consume the same amount. It is also non-rival, which means that consumption by one individual does not impede consumption by others. Part B of Figure A2-3 illustrates the situation. D_A, D_B, and D_C are the marginal benefit curves or demand curves of individuals A, B, and C respectively. D_A, for example, shows the amount of additional benefit A receives from consuming a unit of the good at the margin and, therefore, the amount that person is prepared to pay for each unit given the total amount produced. If production of the public good is OQ — for example, the level of police protection represented by OQ number of police personnel — the total amount is available to each individual. Because the good is non-rival, the amount consumed by A does not reduce the amounts available to B and C. Because it is non-excludable, B and C cannot be excluded from consuming OQ. Thus, the amount OQ is there to be consumed in equal amounts by all consumers. At output OQ, the marginal benefit to A equals OA; to B, it is OB; and to C, it is OC. These marginal values reflect the amount each individual is prepared to pay for the public good, so collectively they will pay an amount OM per unit for OQ output. The demand curve for a pure public good is the vertical summation of the individual marginal benefits at each level of output. For output OQ, OM = OA + OB + OC, and $D_M = \Sigma MB$.

CHAPTER 3

Government Resource Allocation Programs

Governments in Canada are engaged in a number of programs and activities that provide public and quasi-public goods and services or are justified on the basis of externalities. The previous chapter identified the public nature of transportation facilities, the external economies that accrue from health and education, and the external diseconomies of pollution. Part of the resources of the economy are allocated or directed to government programs in these areas as reflected by government expenditures.

Table 3-1 illustrates the major resource using programs of government and the amount spent on each in 1994-95. These programs absorbed a total of $153 billion, or almost 42 percent of total government spending of $358 billion in that year.[1] This chapter provides some detail on the structure, operations, and the financing of these programs.

Health Care Services

Medicare

Health care in Canada is provided primarily under a system of public, universal medical insurance — medicare — that covers both hospital care and physicians' services. Health care is mainly under the jurisdiction of the provincial governments, with some financial assistance from the federal government. The public purse finances about 70 percent of health care spending in Canada, with the remainder financed directly by individuals or through private insurance plans.[2]

The medicare system evolved over a number of years. In 1957, the federal government, following the lead of Saskatchewan and British Columbia, passed the *Hospital Insurance and Diagnostic Services Act*, by which Ottawa agreed to contribute approximately 50 percent of hospital costs to provinces that introduced and administered a program whereby hospital care would be provided free of direct charge to Canadians. In 1966, the Medical Care Act extended Ottawa's contribution to include programs covering physicians' services. These two Acts were consolidated in 1984 with the passage of the *Canada Health Act*[3] which ensured the continuation of basic health services to all Canadians under a prepaid national health insurance system.

Under the *Canada Health Act*, the provincial health programs are required to adhere to five basic criteria in order to qualify for federal assistance. These conditions are: (1) public administration — programs are required to be administered by a public authority on a non-profit basis; (2) comprehensiveness — programs must include essential hospital and doctor's services; (3) universal coverage — the services must be provided to all insurable Canadians; (4) portability — a province's plan must cover services to its residents who may be temporarily out of the province or out of the country; and (5) accessibility — programs must ensure access to health services on a uniform basis to all insured residents without the hindrance of user fee's or extra billing by health practitioners for insured services.

TABLE 3-1: Resource Allocation Programs: All Governments 1994-95

Program	$million
Health	47,100
Education	43,920
Protection of Persons and Property	24,477
Transportation and Communications	15,689
Resource Conservation and Management	14,119
Environment	8,040
Total	**$153,345**

Source: Statistics Canada, Public Sector Finance, 1995-1996, cat. 68-212-XPB, p.168.

The insured hospital services cover care on an inpatient or outpatient basis and include accommodation, nursing, laboratory and other diagnostic procedures, surgical procedures and supplies, radiotherapy and physiotherapy, and various treatments necessary for preventing illness and maintaining the health of patients. Non-hospital medical practitioners' services include visits to a doctor's office or clinic, treatments by the practitioner, and diagnostic services at a clinic.

In addition to hospital care and physician's services, the provinces provide a wide variety of public and community health programs. These include maternal and child health care, health programs in schools and homes, family planning, nutrition services, mental health services, alcohol and drug education and rehabilitation, community sanitation, and health inspections.

Health services not covered by the public health system may be covered by private health insurance, such as the extended health benefits provided by Green Shield Prepaid Services Inc., or by non-profit organizations such as Ontario Blue Cross. Benefits such as semi-private and private ward care in hospitals, ambulance services, prescription drugs, nursing home care, dental and optical care, and out-of-country medical care are available through private insurance companies. Coverage may be purchased through an employer

as a group-benefit plan, as part of a home insurance package, or directly.

Provincial health plans may cover some of these extended health services for special groups in society, such as providing drugs free of charge or for a nominal charge for the elderly, the handicapped, and for families and individuals in receipt of welfare benefits.

Administration of hospitals varies among provinces. In some provinces all hospitals are public or government operated, while in Ontario and Quebec, there exist both public and private hospitals. The provincial governments grant hospitals annual budgets to provide their various services. The hospitals are administered by appointed public community boards or boards of management. Most of the hospital personnel, including nurses and technicians, are salaried. Most physicians, however, are paid on a fee-for-service basis, both for their services within hospitals and in their offices or clinics. The fees are negotiated between the provincial government and the professional medical associations of each province such as the Ontario Medical Association or the New Brunswick Medical Society.

Some provinces have introduced community health centres, offering specialized services to various groups such as the disabled. A centre's staff usually includes general practitioners, nurses, social workers, nutritionists and other specialists, all of whom are salaried. It is claimed that these centres provide effective, readily available, and less expensive care than that provided through regular facilities.

Financing Public Health Care[4]

When it was first introduced in 1957, public health care was jointly financed on a 50-50 cost-sharing basis by the federal and provincial governments. Each province operated its own health care plan, but was required to adhere to the five criteria outlined earlier in order to receive the federal cash grant or contribution. In 1977, under a new arrangement called Established Program Financing (EPF), the federal grant was replaced by a combination of tax transfers and cash payments. The tax transfers took the form of increased tax room in the personal income tax whereby Ottawa reduced its tax rates to permit the provinces to increase their tax rates. Under this scheme the federal share was no longer dictated by the cost of health care, since the tax points allotted the provinces were fixed, and increases in the cash component were tied to the growth of the economy. Beginning in the 1996-97 fiscal year, the various federal transfers to the provinces for health, post-secondary education, and social services (EPF and the Canada Assistance Plan) were combined into a single block transfer, consisting of the existing tax and cash transfers, called the Canada Health and Social Transfer. The federal criteria contained in the Canada Health Act, however, continues to be applied.

The federal government's involvement in health care, a constitutional provincial responsibility, and in particular its methods of financing, has been a major source of aggravation for some provinces. Provincial governments have argued that federal changes and unilateral reductions in financial contributions have made it difficult for the provinces to continue to provide adequate levels of care while adhering to the federal criteria for health programs. The federal reductions however were prompted by the soaring costs of provincial health care programs, which caused Ottawa to seek some control over its contributions. The EPF arrangement effectively cut the ties between increasing health care costs and federal financing. Further limits on the federal contribution were imposed in the early 1990s when the federal government, faced with large expenditures and huge budgetary deficits, decided to freeze the EPF cash payments to the provinces. Consequently, as the costs of health care services in Canada continued to grow during the 1980s and 1990s, the federal share began to shrink. Health cash transfers fell from $8.3 billion in 1992-93 to $7.1 billion in 1995-96.

The provinces finance their share of public health primarily with general tax revenues. In Alberta and British Columbia, health care is partly funded from health care premiums, while some other provinces such as Ontario, Manitoba, Quebec, and Newfoundland levy special payroll taxes to help finance health care.

Medicare In Crises

Between 1975 and 1993 provincial spending (including federal transfers) on health care increased from $8.7 billion to $44.9 billion. Health expenditures absorb approximately 26 percent of provincial government budgets. At over 10 percent of the country's GDP, Canada's spending on health is the second highest in the world (the United States is the highest at 14 percent).[5] In the early 1990s, faced with large budgetary deficits, the provinces sought to restrain and even reduce government expenditures, including health care spending. Hospital budgets were cut back, forcing the closing of hospital beds and hospitals and the amalgamation of hospitals. In Ontario, during the five-year period from 1991 to 1996, over 8,000 hospital beds were closed, the equivalent of about 30 fairly large hospitals. Many hospitals were converted to community health centres. Patients were encouraged to have services performed on an outpatient basis and the length of stays in hospitals were reduced. Limits were imposed by many hospitals on the number of individual procedures (i.e., cataract operations) they would perform each year.

The provinces also sought to control doctors' charges to medicare by negotiating or imposing billing caps. Most provinces imposed ceilings on their overall budgets for physicians services. In Ontario, for example, if total doctors' billings exceed the budget, each doctor loses a portion of each fee, effectively imposing limits on physicians incomes. In 1992 the provinces agreed to reduce the enrollment in Canada's medical schools. More recently some provinces proposed a degree of management of the location of doctors in an attempt to direct more doctors to poorly served rural areas and away from large cities where physicians tend to concentrate.

In recent years, numerous services have been removed from provincial health-plan coverage or have been subjected to reduced coverage. These include chiropractic services, children's dental services, eye examinations, and reduced out-of-country benefits. Some provinces have increased the deductibles and co-payments of their drug benefit programs, forcing patients to absorb a larger portion of the costs of the drugs they use.

The soaring costs of health services has brought the very issue of the affordability of a continued public health care system in Canada into question. Same provinces have proposed the application of user fees and the establishment of private clinics.

User fees, it is argued, would serve to achieve an efficient level of health care, ration services, and keep in check the demands and therefore the costs of services. Private clinics would serve to ease the load on the public health care system. The federal government, however, has adamantly refused to permit user fees and introduced a policy which would reduce federal grants to any province adopting user fees or permitting extra billing by doctors. Ottawa claims that user fees or extra billing would lead to a two-tiered system, one for the wealthy and one for the poor. Those who could not afford the extra costs would be denied access to adequate medical services and this would be contrary to the principle of accessibility contained in the Canada Health Act. Private clinics are viewed as a move towards the privatization of health care. With increased privatization of health care facilities and health insurance it is feared that middle- and higher-income voters may be less willing to see their tax dollars allocated to the public system. As doctors and patients flood into the private clinics, those unable to afford the fees or private insurance premiums will be left with an underfunded and inferior system.

A major restructuring is required for Canada's health care system. It is debatable whether health care in Canada, absorbing a higher percentage of GDP than in all other countries except the United States, is underfunded. Countries such as Britain, France, Germany, Sweden, and Japan spend about 25 percent less per capita on health care than Canada and provide comparable or superior health care. Britain employs a combination of public and private health care. In Germany there exists a public health care system from which people may opt out in favour of private care and pay private health premiums. The competing private system serves to take the strain off the public system, thereby enabling it to function. In the United States there is a trend to increased use of primary care clinics known as HMOs (health maintenance organizations) to restrain the costs of health care. In an HMO, doctors are no longer paid on a fee-for-service basis. Instead, the HMO will contract with an insurer to provide comprehensive health care for a specified number of patients (fixed fee per patient). Since the HMO's profit is the difference between the capitation payments it receives and the cost of its services, there is a financial incentive to minimize the cost of medical care. Competition between HMOs for patients should theoretically serve to maintain an adequate quality of service.

Other reforms could focus on improvements in the efficiency of hospitals, more effective control over drug costs, allowing patients more input in their care to reduce doctor-generated demand for services (i.e., laboratory tests), and increased use of community health centres.

Education

The provincial governments in Canada are constitutionally vested with jurisdiction over education. The federal government is responsible for the education of Indian and Inuit people. Government funds supply almost all of the revenues for elementary, secondary, and post-secondary education, including vocational training.

The public sector involvement in education stems from the nature of the service. As outlined earlier, education is viewed as a service with external economies or spill-over benefits, where the benefits of an education accrue not only to the recipient, but to society as well. If left to the marketplace to be provided as a private service, individuals would spend too little on education to achieve the socially optimal level because they equate prices paid with benefits each individual receives and ignore the spill-over benefits. Government support of education theoretically extends the service towards its optimal level for society.

In addition, education is considered to be a merit good; one which the government views as bestowing to the recipient a larger benefit then the recipient places on the good. As in the case of external economies, an insufficient amount of education would be demanded in the marketplace. Elementary education is therefore made compulsory, providing every-

one with at least a minimum level of educational training.

Educational Systems

Most provinces provide for tax-supported public and separate school systems and, together with a scattering of private schools, provide elementary and secondary education. The separate school systems are religion based and are primarily Roman Catholic, along with some Protestant and multidenominational schools. The organization and financing of the elementary and secondary educational systems vary to a degree among the provinces but some common characteristics can be noted.[6]

A province is divided into a number of school districts or divisions, each administered by a local school board of elected trustees. School boards are responsible for managing the schools in their districts, appointing teachers, preparing budgets, and managing the finances. The sources of their finances consist of provincial government grants, property taxes, and various miscellaneous revenues. In the provinces of Prince Edward Island and New Brunswick, provincial grants fund nearly 100 percent of elementary and secondary education. In the remaining provinces, the proportion of education funded by grants ranges from about 90 percent in Newfoundland to approximately 40 percent in Ontario. Most of the remaining funds come from local property taxes in these provinces. There are some differences in the grant programs between provinces. Many provinces employ flat grants to cover school operating expenditures. These provide a fixed amount per student to a school board with an equalization component built into the formula. Equalization attempts to compensate for differences in the revenue base of school districts. Adjustments in the grants to the poorer school districts enable them to provide an adequate level of services without having to levy relatively higher local taxes than does the school board with the better property tax base. Capital expenditures in a school district are usually covered either by a provincial capital grant or borrowing by local school boards. In the latter case, provincial grants cover the debt charges on the borrowed funds along with the annual repayments.

Post-secondary education is commonly described as university and community college education leading to a degree or a diploma. Other education following formal school training consists of vocational training which provides a career trade and may include industry apprenticeship programs, training in private technical or business programs, and various other forms of job-oriented training.

Universities and community colleges are established by the provincial governments and administered by a provincially appointed board of directors. They are funded by provincial grants, tuition and residence fees, private contributions or gifts, and other miscellaneous sources of revenue such as returns on investments. Provincial government grants for operating expenses take the form of block grants or grants calculated using an enrollment formula. Capital expenditures are generally enrollment driven. Of total university income, about 70 percent comes from government and approximately 10 to 12 percent comes from fees. When total operating expenditures of universities are examined, it is shown that operating grants account for less than 75 percent of these expenditures with tuition fees covering almost 25 percent. Since the mid-1980s, as governments have sought to restrain their budgets and reduce their deficits, fees have accounted for an increasing share of operating expenditures rising from about 16 percent to the current level.

Education, including post-secondary education, began to suffer a financial crunch in the 1990s similar to health care as provincial governments sought to contain or reduce their expenditures to balance their budgets. Provincial/local education expenditures fell from $42.8 billion in 1992-93 to $42.0 billion in

1994-95. At the same time, federal contributions to the provinces for education support declined from $2.9 billion to $2.4 billion. Faced with the financial squeeze, some provinces liberalized the controls they had imposed on university tuition fee increases. Universities began to increase fees and restructure their organization and programs in attempts to balance their budgets.

Federal Finance

Since World War II, the federal government has contributed to the funding of post-secondary education under a variety of programs. Early federal contributions to universities consisted of per capita subsidies. Beginning in 1967, the federal government entered into a cost-sharing agreement with the provinces whereby Ottawa would cover one-half of the operating expenditures of post-secondary institutions in the form of tax points and grants. In 1977, the federal government negotiated the established programs financing (EPF) arrangement with the provinces. Under EPF, Ottawa provided additional personal income tax room or points to the provinces plus cash payments in lieu of specific purpose grants for three established shared-cost programs, namely hospital insurance, medicare, and post-secondary education. The federal contribution for post-secondary education was therefore no longer tied to the costs of education, and the revenue from the tax points, which were permanently transferred to the provinces, became part of general provincial government revenues. In 1996 the EPF arrangement was replaced with the Canada Health and Social Transfer (CHST), a single block transfer to the provinces covering post-secondary education, health, and the Canada Assistance Plan. In 1998 the federal government proposed a Canada Millennium Scholarship Foundation, with an initial endowment of $2.5 billion, to provide 100,000 scholarships annually to post-secondary education students. Awards will be available in the year 2000.

Both the public and private sectors are involved in vocational training. The federal government provides approximately 60 percent of funding for vocational training in Canada, the provinces account for 30 percent, and the private sector for 10 percent. The provinces have been assuming increased responsibility for this function, however, and since the early 1970s the provincial share of funding has doubled. Vocational training is designed to prepare people for the workplace by providing them with job-related skills, retraining those who have lost their jobs, and providing greater employment security and increased potential for promotion. It is an investment in human capital with benefits to individual workers in the form of increased prospects for employment, better jobs and higher incomes, and benefits to society in terms of increased productivity and economic growth.

National Defence

A basic function of government is the protection of persons and property in which all three levels of government in Canada are involved. This function includes police law enforcement, the judicial system, correctional services, regulatory services, and national defence. Of approximately $25 billion currently spent on this function, national defence consumes around $11 billion. National defence is a federal responsibility and constitutes about 6 percent of total federal budgetary expenditures.

National defence has the characteristics of a pure public good. Defence services are both non-excludable and non-rival, and because of these features, the market will not provide them. Therefore the resources of an economy will be channelled to national defence only if the government undertakes to do so.

National defence involves the protection of Canadian sovereignty, continental defence in co-operation with the United States (the

North Atlantic Alliance), commitments to defend Europe through the North Atlantic Treaty Organization (NATO), and various international peacekeeping activities and humanitarian assistance. Canadian military forces also assist civil authorities, and help in search and rescue operations, political crises, and emergency situations such as natural disasters (i.e., floods).

The Canadian military consists of three main components, namely maritime command, land forces command, and air command, with various support forces. In 1996-97 the military personnel numbered about 70,000, with an additional civilian labour force of approximately 30,000. About one-quarter of the budget of the Department of National Defence is allocated to capital acquisitions (armaments, vehicles, and other equipment) with the remainder directed to personnel costs, supplies, and the operation of defence bases.

Canada has played a leading role in peacekeeping missions around the world. In 1996 Canada was involved in fourteen peacekeeping missions with a total cost of over one-half billion dollars. Canada has also co-operated with the United Nations in providing humanitarian relief operations in numerous countries.

During the 1980s the government set out to refurbish Canada's defence capabilities. In a 1987 white paper, it announced a major modernization program including a fleet of nuclear submarines and a new fleet of anti-submarine patrol aircraft to protect Canada's coast line and maintain its sovereignty in its Arctic regions. The program also called for additional fighter-interceptor aircraft, new all-terrain vehicles and battle tanks for the land forces, and modernization of the armed forces' communications system. Government expenditure cutbacks, however, dictated by continued unacceptably high budgetary deficits, forced scaling back of these plans.

Most of the planned purchases of military hardware were cancelled, and total national defence expenditures were reduced from over $12 billion in 1990 to less than $11 billion by 1996. The cancellation included a $5 billion contract for fifty coastal patrol and search and rescue helicopters from a European manufacturer. Cancellation of the contract (which had been negotiated by the Conservative government) by the newly Liberal government, as part of an election campaign pledge in 1993, forced the government to pay the manufacturer almost one-half billion dollars in penalties. In a controversial decision in 1997, the same Liberal government decided to purchase 15 similar search and rescue helicopters from the same manufacturer, prompting charges against the government of playing costly political games at the expense of the Canadian taxpayer. In 1998 Ottawa announced the purchase of four modern, slightly used submarines at a cost of almost $1 billion.

Transportation and Communications

Transportation and communication facilities are essential to the development and functioning of an economy, particularly a country as geographically large and diversified as Canada. They serve to bring the various regions together both economically and socially.

Transportation

Transportation has been used in Canada as an instrument of national policy. Indeed the cornerstone of the famed National Policy of 1879 was the construction of a transcontinental railway, the Canadian Pacific Railway (CPR), a private venture but with considerable federal government financial assistance. Government funding was also directed to the construction of roads, bridges, canals, and harbours. In 1920 the federal government took control of a number of failing railroads and formed Canadian National Railways, a Crown corporation providing another trans-

continental railway in competition with the CPR. The development of air travel prompted the federal government to establish Trans Canada Airlines (currently Air Canada) and construct and operate the necessary airport facilities to handle air traffic. Two major projects completed in the 1950s were the Trans Canada Highway and the St. Lawrence Seaway. As the population and the economy grew, transportation facilities were expanded and modernized, with the completion of new major projects such as the causeway connecting Prince Edward Island with the mainland.

Over one-half of federal spending on transportation consists of transfers, such as the transfers to VIA Rail, to support passenger rail service; to Marine Atlantic, to operate freight and ferry service; and to the railroads, as rail freight subsidies. The remainder is spent by Transport Canada to operate airports, the Canadian Coast Guard, ice breaking and search and rescue operations, and for highway programs.

Provincial governments are responsible for the road, highway, and bridge networks across the province, and local governments build and maintain the road, street, and sidewalk grids within their boundaries with assistance from the province.

Government ownership and operation of transportation facilities such as roads, bridges, streets, and sidewalks stems from their nature as quasi-public goods. These are goods which, while largely excludable and rival, would incur high administrative costs to collect fees and charges from consumers. It would be impractical and inefficient for the private sector to provide these facilities, other than major throughways or bridges where high traffic volume makes private ownership feasible and economical. Even in these instances, however, it has been commonplace for governments to construct and operate toll transportation facilities.

In addition to constructing, operating, and maintaining transportation facilities, governments in Canada have historically been actively involved in the regulation of transportation.[7] Facilities regulated included the railways, airlines, trucking, and shipping and navigation. The objectives of regulation included insuring the continuity of basic services, providing service to remote and sparsely populated areas, and ensuring a satisfactory level of safety standards. Regulation was also undertaken to ensure that transportation services were provided at reasonable or fair prices. The various components of the transportation industry lend themselves to monopoly, either on a national or regional basis, with potential for excessive rates and profits.

Beginning in the 1980s, government in Canada embarked on a policy of deregulating the transportation sector and promoting competition. It was anticipated that a competitive industry would be self-regulating and provide improved services to the public. Ottawa deregulated the airlines, opening that sector to competition, and the provincial governments deregulated the trucking industry. Entry into the industry, rates, and domestic routes were no longer subjected to government scrutiny and approval. Regulation of the industry was restricted primarily to safety standards.

Communications

The government's role in communication involves both ownership of facilities and regulation of private sector operations. The Canadian Broadcasting Corporation (CBC), a federally owned Crown corporation, receives about $1 billion annually in grants. The CBC, along with the Film Development Corporation, are invested with the function of promoting Canadian culture. Some of the provinces are also involved in ownership of media facilities such as television stations and help fund film and television program production. Canada Post is a federal Crown corporation responsible for mail delivery and is subsidized by the government.

The federal government, through its agency the Canadian Radio-Television and Telecommunications Commission (CRTC), regulates the telephone industry under its jurisdiction, broadcast radio and television, and cable and pay television.[8] Accepting the claim of the telephone and cable industries that they were natural monopolies, Ottawa restricted entry into these industries, and regulated rates and service, including program content in the radio and television sectors. At the provincial level, the provinces of Alberta, Saskatchewan, and Manitoba owned and operated the telephone systems in the province until recently, when Alberta and Manitoba privatized their systems.

With the development of satellite communications, the federal government began to construct and orbit communications satellites (i.e., the Anik series of satellites). Ottawa established Teleglobe Canada as a crown corporation to operate and oversee satellite and cable communications overseas. It also entered into partnership with Canada's telephone companies to create Telesat Canada to operate the country's domestic satellite communications system, one of the first in the world. The deregulation movement of the 1980s witnessed the privatization of Teleglobe by sale to a private communications company and the liberalization of competition in the long-distance tele-communications market.

Environmental Protection and Conservation

Pollution Control

Pollution of the environment caused by production and consumption activities is an external diseconomy. The nature of external diseconomies and various examples were discussed earlier in chapter 2. As pointed out, environmental pollution consists of the contamination of air, water, or land, rendering their use hazardous to living beings. The latter part of the twentieth century has witnessed a gradual awakening by society to the hazards of pollution, and governments have responded with a proliferation of pollution prevention and control policies.

In Canada all three levels of government are engaged in pollution control. Government regulations to protect the environment are contained in a variety of statutes and regulatory agency decisions.[9] The main federal legislation is the Canadian Environmental Protection Act, administered by Environment Canada. Similar legislation exists at the provincial government level. The laws and regulations cover such issues as air and water quality standards, pollution emissions from industry and vehicles, the transport of hazardous products, storage and disposal of wastes, the use of chemical substances, and the safety of workers handling hazardous products. In 1993 Environment Canada established the National Pollutant Release Inventory which requires over 2,500 business firms to calculate their annual emissions of toxic substances and to release that information to the public. The objective of this reporting requirement is to help governments set priorities for regulation while encouraging companies to take some initiative to reduce pollution.

Government pollution regulations are backed by sanctions to ensure compliance. Sanctions include the cancellation of operating licences, an escalating scale of monetary penalties in accordance with the severity of pollution, and in the most severe cases even prison terms for those responsible for the pollution. In recognition that pollution prevention measures in some industries could be so expensive as to adversely affect a firm's competitive position in the domestic or international market, governments have offered tax concessions and subsidies to financially assist firms to develop and employ pollution control devices.

While the enactment and administration of pollution legislation is a very important function of government, it is not a costly one. The major cost of pollution prevention and reduction is incurred by industry through compliance with the regulations. It has been estimated that the ratio of compliance costs to administrative costs has been approximately twenty to one. In other words, for every $1 governments incur to administer pollution control regulations, industry spends $20 to comply with those regulations.

Expenditures on the environment by all levels of government in Canada totalled over $8 billion in 1995-96. Approximately 85 percent of this amount was spent by local governments, primarily on water purification and supply, sewage collection and disposal, and garbage and waste collection and disposal. Local government capital projects such as water and sewage treatment facilities, however, are heavily subsidized by the provincial government.

Resource Conservation and Management

While governments in Canada are interested in promoting the development of the country's natural resources, they are also concerned with the manner in which these resources are used. Policies for the long-term preservation of resources are designed to prevent overuse, waste, and mismanagement of Canada's energy, mineral, forest, fish, and wildlife resources. The National Energy Board regulates various aspects of the oil, gas, and hydro-electric power industries. The federal Department of Fisheries and Oceans oversees the management and use of fish resources on Canada's coasts and inland waters. Recent examples of conservation policies was the reduction of salmon fishing and the ban on cod fishing in coastal waters when the reserves of these two fish reached critically low levels. Canada's forest resources are closely supervised by the federal and provincial governments to prevent overutilization and to ensure reforestation practices. Governments require that hunters and fishermen be licenced and quotas are set for the amount of game that can be taken. Endangered species of wildlife are protected as are the habitats of some of these species.

Other Resource-Absorbing Activities

In addition to the programs and activities already discussed, government in Canada provides numerous private-type goods and services. They are frequently provided by government-owned and -operated business-type enterprises. These enterprises are established to achieve social and economic policy objectives, are incorporated, and are frequently in competition with private sector corporations. The use of the corporate form, as opposed to regular government departments or bureaus, provides greater flexibility in operation and fewer political constraints.

The federal government provides a number of such services through various classes of Crown corporations. The proprietary Crown corporations are business-type enterprises of a commercial, industrial, or financial nature which were established for the purposes of achieving government policy objectives. Air Canada, and Canadian National Railway (before they were privatized) were created to provide transcontinental transportation services to help unify the country. The Canadian Broadcasting Corporation (CBC) has a mandate to express and promote the Canadian identity. Atomic Energy of Canada was created in 1952 to develop domestic uses of atomic energy.

Numerous business-type enterprises are also owned and operated by the provincial governments, and operate on a huge scale. These include enterprises providing hydro-electric power, such as Ontario Hydro, Quebec Hydro, Saskatchewan Power Corporation, and similar public hydro-electric power enterprises in every province. Government enterprises provide insurance services, such as in Manitoba (Manitoba Public Insurance Corp.) and British Columbia (Insurance Corporation of British Columbia). Provincial agencies operate public housing projects, and liquor sales outlets.

Local government authorities operate numerous enterprises providing services to the public, financed by direct sales or user charges. These include water supply systems, recreational facilities, local airports, parking facilities, and transit systems.

Most of these government business enterprise operations engage in activities which have private good features rather than public good or quasi-public good features. They therefore could be provided by the private sector, with the resources owned and controlled by private entrepreneurs. Some of the reasons for government involvement in these activities, along with reasons for choosing the corporate form for providing them, are outlined in chapter 5.

Summary

The main government programs in Canada that involve government employment or redirection of the country's resources are in the areas of health care, education, national defence, transportation and communications, and environmental protection. Health care, education, and defence account for most of the government expenditures on resource-use programs.

Medicare, a universal public health care program, is administered by the provinces and financed jointly by the provincial and federal governments. Education is a provincial responsibility with financial assistance from Ottawa. Transportation, communications, and environmental protection are shared by the governments, while national defence is under the exclusive jurisdiction of the federal government.

Health care and education absorb a large proportion of provincial government expenditures, and of federal transfers to the provinces. In recent years, however, as governments sought to control spending and reduce their budgetary deficits, both functions have suffered financially, which has affected both the quantity and quality of services. Hospitals have been closed or amalgamated and doctors' incomes have been limited, but the federal government has insisted that the essential features of medicare be maintained and has opposed the application of user fees to help finance the system. Similarly, reduced funding has forced the restructuring of education in many provinces. University tuition fees have increased as provincial governments lifted limitations on these fees.

The proportion of the federal budget devoted to national defence has fallen drastically in the post-World War II period. Canada is a member of NATO, and has taken a leadership role in international peace-keeping missions. Canada's military hardware, however, has suffered from cut-backs in spending.

The government's activities in communications, environmental protection, and natural resources has been primarily of a regulatory nature. Pollution of the environment has become a major concern to society, and governments have responded with more rigorous controls and stronger sanctions against offenders.

NOTES

1   Statistics Canada, *Public Sector Finance*, 1995-96, cat. 68-212-XPB (Ottawa: 1996), p.168.

2   Health Canada, *National Health Expenditures in Canada, 1975-1993*, cat. H21-99/1993 (Ottawa: Supply and Services, 1994), p.15.

3   For an overview of the Canada Health Act and details of the medicare program in each province, see Health Canada, *Canada Health Act Annual Review*, cat. H1-4/1994 (Ottawa: Supply and Services).

4   Details of health care expenditures are presented in A.Y. Cuyler, *Health Care Expenditures in Canada: Myth and Reality: Past and Future*, Canadian Tax Paper No. 82 (Toronto: Canadian Tax Foundation, 1988); and Health Canada, *National Health Expenditures in Canada, 1975-1993*.

5   Health Canada, *National Health Expenditures, 1975-1993*, p.6.

6   An overview of the organization and an analysis of financing education in Canada is presented in Harry Kitchen and Douglas Auld, *Financing Education and Training in Canada* (Toronto: Canadian Tax Foundation, 1995), Tax Paper No. 99. See also, Statistics Canada, *Education in Canada*, 1995, cat. 81-229-XPB.

7   For an analysis of Canadian government regulation of transportation, particularly the air carrier industry, see J. C. Strick, *The Economics of Government Regulation* (Toronto: Thompson Educational Publishing, 1995), ch.8.

8   Regulation of the telephone and television industries in Canada is discussed in *ibid*, ch.9, 10.

9   See *ibid*, ch.12.

CHAPTER 4

Income Redistribution and Security

The provision of an adequate level of income for all Canadians, along with security of that income, has been a primary objective of government in recent years. As outlined in chapter 1, the state of distribution of income and wealth in society is determined by a variety of factors, including individual capabilities and initiatives, educational opportunities, inheritances, the scarcity or abundance of specific resources and the ownership of these resources. These factors generally produce a considerable disparity between the highest and the lowest income groups in society, frequently leaving the lowest group in a state of poverty. Through its various income transfer programs, government has attempted to alleviate poverty and provide low-income families with a basic, acceptable standard of living.

In addition, government has attempted to ensure the stability or security of incomes of individuals and families. Income security programs provide direct financial benefits to those experiencing reductions in income due to unemployment, illness, old age, or other causes.

This chapter examines the state of income distribution in Canada and the issue of poverty and describes the various government policies designed to alleviate poverty and to maintain a degree of income security.[1] The main programs and the amounts spent by governments in Canada on these programs are illustrated in Table 4-1.

Income Distribution and Poverty

Measuring Income Distribution

A commonly employed method of measuring income distribution is to divide a country's families into income groups, with each group containing the same number of families, and calculating the percentage of the country's total income earned by each group. In Table 4-2, families in Canada are divided into five equal group (quintiles).

The first column shows the percentage of income accruing to each group before government transfers (earned income). In 1995 the lowest quintile earned only 2.1 percent of total income while the highest group earned 44.6 percent. The second column shows the distribution of income including government money transfers. The share of the lowest quintile rises to 6.4 percent while that of the highest quintile falls to 40.2 percent. The average total money income (after transfers) of families in the lowest quintile was $17,608, of which government transfers accounted for $12,426 or 59 percent, illustrating the dependence of this group on transfers. These transfers are financed by taxation, and to the degree that taxes are progressive, the tax burden falls more heavily on higher-income groups than on the lower-income groups. The third column shows the distribution of income between the five groups after federal and provincial income taxes. These taxes further reduce the gap between the lowest- and highest-income groups but have a much

TABLE 4-1: Income Redistribution and Security Programs

Federal 1995-96	$million
Old Age Security, Guaranteed Income Supplement and Spousal Allowance	21, 034
Employment Insurance	13,476
Canada Pension Plan	16,419
Canada Assistance Plan	7,190
Child Tax Benefit	5,215
Veterans Pensions	1,140
Total	**43,461**
Percentage of Federal Expenditures	**25.4**

Provincial/Local 1991-92	
Social welfare	20,250
Other Social Services	10,463
Total	**$30,713**
Percentage of Provincial/Local Expenditures	**15.2**

Source: Canada, *Public Accounts of Canada, 1996*, Part 1, cat. P51-1/1996-2-1E (Ottawa: Public Works and Government Services, 1996), p1.3 and Statistics Canada, *Public Sector Finance 1995-1996*, cat. 68-212-XPB (Ottawa: 1996), p.194.

TABLE 4-2: Income Distribution in Canada and Effect of Transfers and Taxes, 1995

Families	Income Before Transfers		Total Money Income[a]		Income After Tax[b]	
	Income Share	Average Income	Income Share	Average Income	Income Share	Average Income
Lowest quintile	2.1	5,182	6.4	17,608	7.7	17,058
Second quintile	10.1	24,578	12.0	33,229	13.3	29,410
Third quintile	17.6	42,631	17.4	48,113	18.0	39,903
Fourth quintile	25.6	62,207	32.9	66,129	23.7	52,405
Highest quintile	44.6	108,309	40.2	111,140	37.3	82,646
Total[c]	100.0	48,584	100.0	55,247	100.0	44,286
Gini Coefficient[d]	0.428		0.341		0.298	

[a] Total money income received from all sources including government transfers.
[b] Total money income minus federal and provincial income taxes paid.
[c] Because of rounding, some totals may not be 100 percent.
[d] A Gini coefficient of zero means uniform income for all units (perfect income equality), while a coefficient of one means one unit receives all of the income (perfect inequality). A decrease in the Gini coefficient represents a decrease in income inequality.

Source: Statistics Canada, *Income After Tax Distributions by Size in Canada, 1995*, cat. 13-210-XPB (Ottawa: 1995), pp.23, 26.

smaller equalization impact than do transfer payments.

Also shown in the table is the Gini coefficient, a summary measure of income inequality. The value of the Gini coefficient can range from zero to one. A coefficient of zero means uniform income for all groups (perfect income equality among the five groups); a coefficient of one means the highest income group receives all of the income (perfect inequality). In 1995 the Gini coefficient fell by .087 after transfers are taken into account, and fell by .043 after income taxes, indicating that transfers had more than twice the impact of reducing the inequality gap in comparison to personal income taxes.

An examination of the state of distribution of income before and after transfers in Canada over time shows little change towards greater equality between the family groups, despite the increase in the average rate of transfer payments (measured as transfer payments as a percentage of total money income). For example, the average rate of transfer payment to the lowest quintile increased from 45 percent in 1980 to 59 percent in 1995. In effect, according to the quintile measure of income distribution, the impact of government redistribution policies and programs on the inequality gap has remained more or less constant. Reducing the inequality gap, however, has not been an announced government policy objective. Government redistribution policy has been to raise the absolute level of income of the lowest income group to one providing an acceptable standard of living rather than to concentrate on the relative level of income of this group and the size of the inequality gap.

Measures and Incidence of Poverty

The Canadian government does not provide an official definition or measure of poverty or establish poverty lines. Statistics Canada calculates and publishes a set of measures called low-income cut-offs (LICOs), and these have been used as poverty levels. LICOs are determined from surveys of income and expenditure patterns in the country. From the surveys, Statistics Canada determines the percentage of its gross income an average Canadian family spends on three basic necessities, namely food, clothing, and shelter. The income limits (LICOs) were selected on the basis that families with incomes below these limits spent 54.7 percent (in 1992) or more of their income on the three categories. Families below the limits are considered, by Statistics Canada, to be in straitened circumstances."[2]

The LICOs vary by area and by size of family, and are adjusted for price changes each year by the annual increase in the Consumer Price Index. It is more costly to live in a large city than in a rural area, and of course for a large family as compared to a single individual. In 1995 the LICOs ranged from a low of $11,661 for a single individual living in a rural area, to $16,716 for a two person family living in a small town of less than 30,000 people, to $27,235 for a family of four in a large urban area, to a high of $42,978 for a family of seven persons or more living in a large city. Using these levels as measures of poverty shows that, in 1995, 17.8 percent of the Canadian population or about 5.2 million people were poor.

Statistics Canada does not present LICOs as measures of poverty but rather as measures for determining the incidence of low incomes in Canada. An acceptable measure of poverty should be related to actual costs of basic necessities, such as a reasonable diet, clothing, shelter, health care, and required transportation. Such a basic needs approach was applied by the Fraser Institute of Vancouver for determining poverty lines in 1988. For example, it was calculated that, for a family of four residing in a community between 100,000 and 499,999 persons, the poverty line was $13,140, which yielded a poverty rate of 2.5 percent.[3] In comparison, the LICO data produced a poverty line of $22,371 and a poverty rate of 10 percent.

The Canadian Council on Social Development has employed a much higher income line in its definition of poverty. The Council's poverty line was determined to be one-half of average family gross income. This measure showed 22 percent of Canadian families living in poverty in 1992.

It is important to recognize that different definitions and methodologies of measuring poverty produce wide variations in the results. There is also a considerable degree of subjectivity in attempting to estimate basic needs or acceptable standards of living. Furthermore, individuals may find themselves in different circumstances which may affect their standards of living. Take the example of two elderly persons living on the same amount of pension income. One individual may own a home and enjoy good health and family assistance, while the second may rent housing, suffer poor health, have special needs, and no family support. The first may be able to enjoy a comfortable living on a given income while that same level of income is inadequate to sustain the second person to a similar degree of comfort.

Applying Statistics Canada's set of LICO measures, the most commonly used, some indications of the incidence of poverty (i.e., who are the poor) and trends can be ascertained. The highest incidence of poverty is found in rural areas. Among the groups in society where the incidence of poverty tends to be the highest are the poorly educated, children under the age of eighteen, and the elderly. The trends show, however, that the elderly have made the most impressive inroads in poverty reduction. In 1980, 34 percent of persons sixty-five years of age and over had incomes below the designated low-income cut-off, but by 1995 only about 19 percent of this group were below the low-income limit.

Anti-Poverty Programs

All three levels of government in Canada financially contribute to and administer an array of programs designed to assist low-income families and alleviate poverty. These include provincial social welfare, the Guaranteed Income Supplement to Old Age Security, the child tax benefit program, housing subsidies and rent controls, minimum wage laws, and special programs for Canada's Native population. Programs such as social welfare, the Income Supplement, and housing subsidies are income related and eligibility rests on a means test to establish that beneficiaries meet financial need requirements. There exist, in addition, universal income maintenance and other programs such as Old Age Security, the Canada Pension Plan, education and vocational training, Employment Insurance, and health care, which benefit all income groups including the poor and help raise money and real income levels of the latter. This section will focus on the former group of programs specifically designed to assist low-income groups. Income maintenance programs are discussed later in this chapter.

Provincial Social Welfare

The provincial governments are constitutionally vested with the responsibility of administering social welfare programs. These include family benefits that provide income to those unable to work for long periods; to the disabled; to people with long-term health and physical problems classified as permanently unemployable; to single-parent families and children; and to the elderly not yet eligible for a federal pension. There are also programs that provide assistance in the form of subsidies to child day-care centres; young offenders programs; nursing homes; assistance to Native people; and work activity programs designed to improve the employability of persons. The administration of these programs varies among provinces. Some provinces share the cost and administrative responsibility of certain programs with the municipal governments. For example, in Ontario and Manitoba, municipalities pay about 20 percent of general welfare costs, while certain specific family and child programs are funded entirely by the province.

Eligibility for social welfare is related to income and fixed and liquid assets and provinces impose a needs test for qualification. Only those whose needs or basic requirements exceed their incomes qualify for assistance. The rates of assistance vary among provinces. In 1993 the annual basic social assistance in Ontario was the highest of all the provinces, ranging from about $8,000 for a single employable person to $11,000 for a disabled person, to almost $19,000 for a couple with two children (These rates were reduced following the election of the Harris Conservative government in 1995.) New Brunswick offered the lowest rates of assistance, with corresponding amounts of $3,000, $6,200 and $9,500 (rounded figures).

The cost of provincial social welfare programs was shared by the provinces and the federal government under a program called the Canada Assistance Plan (CAP). It was established in 1966 to co-ordinate federal financial contributions to the provinces for a variety of provincially administered welfare programs. CAP was originally an open-ended shared-cost program in which the federal government contributed one-half of the cost of the services provided under the Plan. In return for the federal funding, Ottawa set standards or conditions for the operation of the programs. Among these were the conditions that the provinces provide assistance to all those judged to be in need and that no residence requirements be imposed, along with federal set limits on liquid assets held by recipients.

Beginning in 1990, in an attempt to control its growing expenditures and a large budget deficit, the federal government imposed a 5 percent limit on the annual increase in CAP contributions to the wealthier provinces of

Ontario, Alberta, and British Columbia. A further change in financing social assistance was announced by Ottawa in 1995. Beginning in the fiscal year 1996-97, federal transfer payments under CAP would be replaced with a new block transfer, combined with the block transfers for health and education. The combined block transfer was called the Canada Health and Social Transfer. Under the new block transfer system, Ottawa payments were no longer tied to costs, and at the same time the degree of federal control over the programs was reduced.

In the fiscal year 1995-96 the federal government paid a total of $7.2 billion to the provinces and territories under CAP. The amount of the block transfer to the provinces under the Canada Health and Social Transfer for the fiscal year 1997-98 was estimated to be $12.5 billion, down from $19.3 billion in 1994-95.[4]

The end of CAP and federal standards witnessed some major changes and restructuring of welfare assistance in some provinces, particularly in Ontario. CAP had prohibited work-for-welfare or workfare, a system under which welfare recipients are required to perform assigned tasks in community projects or participate in training programs. The governments of several provinces including Ontario, Quebec, Alberta, and New Brunswick began to experiment with workfare programs. Ontario also began, in 1997, a major restructuring of responsibilities for government programs between the province and its municipalities. The province would take over education funding from local governments but turn over to them more responsibility for welfare, transit, community public health and ambulance service, social housing, and other programs.

Guaranteed Income Supplement

The Guaranteed Income Supplement (GIS) is a payment to needy elderly people in receipt of Old Age Security (OAS). It was introduced in 1967 as a supplement to OAS and is geared to income through a means test. A person aged sixty-five or over with no other income is eligible for the full GIS which was $476 per month at the beginning of 1997. A married person whose spouse is sixty-five years or over and in receipt of OAS was eligible for a monthly supplement of $310. If OAS recipients have outside income, the GIS is reduced $0.50 for every dollar of outside income. The GIS is terminated after a threshold amount of outside income is reached, which was $11,069 for a single individual and $14,448 for a married couple in 1995. The GIS and the threshold amounts are adjusted by a cost-of-living factor to an annual maximum of 2 percent.

In addition, there is an income-geared spousal allowance for spouses, aged sixty to sixty-four years, of recipients of OAS. The allowance also applies to needy widowed individuals between the ages of sixty and sixty-four years. In early 1997 the maximum monthly spousal allowance and widowed allowance was $710 and $784 respectively. These amounts are reduced as a recipient's income increases and are eliminated when family income reaches the threshold amounts of $26,784 and $15,168 respectively.

In the fiscal year 1995-96 the federal government paid out $16,024 million for OAS, $4,694 million for the GIS, and $436 million for spousal allowances, for a total of over $21 billion, or about 12 percent of total federal budgetary expenditures.

The federal 1996 budget contained a proposal to merge Old Age Security and the Guaranteed Income Supplement into a new Seniors Benefit program to go into effect in the year 2001. The new program was targeted to those most in need, and at the same time slow the growth in costs of public pensions. Everyone over the age of sixty years would receive the benefit, and those with income of up to $40,000 would be made better off than under the old program. The amount of the payment would be geared to income and would start at $11,420 for single seniors with no other income, and decrease to $350 for seniors with income of $50,000. The benefits will be tax free.[5]

Child Tax Benefit

In 1945 the federal government had introduced the family allowance program designed to assist families with children. It was a universal program, with benefits paid to all families with children irrespective of income levels. In 1989 family recipients with incomes above a threshold level were required to repay family allowance benefits received, thereby ending its universality feature. In 1993 the family allowance program was replaced with the child tax benefit program.

The child tax benefit program is not part of the tax system, since payments are not subject to tax and it is not part of any tax credit scheme. Its only relation to the tax system is that eligibility for benefits and the amount of payment to a family with children in any given year is determined by the amount of income reported on that family's personal income tax return of the previous year. The rates in 1997 were $1,020 for the first two children, plus $1,095 for each additional child, plus $213 for each child under the age of seven years. The payment was reduced by 2.5 percent of net family income over $25,921 if there was only one child and by 5 percent if there was more than one child. It was annually indexed for inflation in excess of 3 percent. There was also a working income supplement of 8 percent of net family income in excess of $3,750 to a maximum of $500, which was reduced by 10 percent of net family income over $20,921.

The 1997 budget proposed to combine the child tax benefit programs and the working income supplement for families with incomes of less than $20,921 into an enriched Canada Child Tax Benefit program beginning July 1998. The maximum benefit for families with net incomes below $20,921 was set at $1,625 for one-child families, $3,050 for two-child families, increasing by $1,425 for each additional child. Benefits are reduced as net income rises above $20,921 so that families with incomes above $25,921 will receive the same benefits as they did in 1997 under the Child Tax Benefit.[6]

Housing Subsidies and Rent Controls

The cost of shelter absorbs a large portion of low-income family income. Government programs that reduce the cost of housing for these families play an important role in raising the real income levels of the poor. Subsidized housing programs include public and co-operative housing, mortgage loans and guarantee of loans, rent subsidies and rent controls. All three levels of government are involved in these programs.

The federal and provincial governments, through public housing projects, have funded the capital costs of housing units and have provided these units to low-income families at below market rents. Co-operative housing has been provided through non-profit incorporated associations which attempt to build communities of affordable housing with attention to housing families with special needs, such as the handicapped, single-parent families, and the elderly. Members of the co-operative housing community do not own the units, but rent them on a geared-to-income basis. Operating costs and therefore rents are kept low by membership participation in the operation and maintenance of the housing units.

A Native housing program provides subsidies to Native-sponsored non-profit housing organizations to build and operate rental housing projects.

The agency responsible for administering federal government housing policy is the Central Mortgage and Housing Corporation (CMHC). It provides funds for housing and rent subsidies under a number of programs, but its primary activity is mortgage insurance, whereby it insures mortgage loans made by approved lenders for new and existing homeowner housing and rental housing and dwellings built by co-operative and non-profit associations. It also finances public and co-operative housing projects at low interest rates. In the fiscal year 1995-96 CMHC expenditures exceeded $2 billion.

Most provinces have established provincial housing agencies with functions similar to CMHC. While they may implement their own programs, for the most part they participate in shared-cost programs with the federal agency. The programs are administered by non-profit organizations including church groups, co-operatives, or municipal government housing authorities.

All provinces have engaged in rent controls in an attempt to provide affordable housing for lower-income groups. Rent controls are essentially price ceilings and may take the form of a rent freeze or a limit on the amount that rents are permitted to increase annually. Governments have frequently applied rent controls in periods of inflation or periods of housing shortages when excess demand over supply for housing place upward pressure on rents. A large number of those who rent houses and apartments are low-income families who cannot afford to purchase homes. Higher rents could reduce the real income of these groups by forcing them to allocate a larger proportion of their budgets for rent with a smaller portion left for other goods and services. Where rent controls were established, higher-priced rental units were usually exempt since they were beyond the means of low-income groups. Such a policy, applied in Ontario, created a dual market for rental units; a controlled market and an uncontrolled market.

Minimum Wage Laws

As part of their programs to assist the working poor, provincial governments attempt to force employers to pay a decent wage by enacting minimum wage laws. Minimum wages are price floors for labour where wages are set above the otherwise market wage. The established minimum wage varies among provinces and in 1995 ranged from a low of $4.75 per hour in Newfoundland to $7.00 per hour in British Columbia.

There is considerable controversy over the use of minimum wage policy. While it tends to increase the earned income of low productivity and unskilled workers, it is argued that this policy also contributes to unemployment by pricing low-skilled workers out of the labour market. Employers frequently argue they would be prepared to hire low-productivity and unskilled workers for various menial jobs or tasks where low productivity justifies correspondingly low wages, but they cannot afford to hire them at the established higher minimum wage. Workers willing to work at these tasks are instead relegated to the ranks of the unemployed. Therefore, while the minimum wage does lead to higher earned incomes for those unskilled workers who are employed, it reduces the number of potential jobs for other workers, particularly students and young workers who are just entering the market and have not had an opportunity to acquire the necessary skills. The minimum wage may help to raise the level of income of some families, but reduce the income level of other families because of its disemployment effects. With regard to the latter, minimum wages may lower the average number of workers per family, either because a working member loses his/her job or because a family member who may have found employment in the absence of the minimum wage is now unable to find a job.

Other Programs to Assist the Needy

In addition to the programs described in the preceding pages, there are several other government policies and programs designed to assist low-income individuals and families. The war veterans program administers about $2 billion to provide for pensions and health care for war veterans, along with special allowances, loans, and grants to those in need. The Indian and Inuit Affairs program provides over $3 billion of financial aid, health, social and community services for Canada's Native population.

Benefits in the form of tax savings are also provided for low-income and select groups. A disability tax credit equal to $720 can be claimed by the disabled. The elderly whose income is less than the base amount of $25,921 can claim an age tax credit of $592. All families with incomes of less than $25,921 may claim a tax credit for sales taxes paid through the federal goods and service tax. In addition, the provinces permit tax credits for the retail sales tax and for property taxes paid by low-income households. These tax benefits, frequently referred to as tax expenditures, are discussed in detail in the chapters on taxation.

Limits to Income Redistribution

One of the difficulties with an objective of achieving greater equity in income distribution is the existence of factors that tend to limit redistribution. Attempts to divide total income more evenly among members of society may reduce the amount to be divided. Excessive taxation of the upper-income groups and business in order to finance transfers and good and services benefitting lower-income groups may stifle incentives to work, to invest, to maintain maximum efficiency in production and distribution, and to engage in risky business ventures. The result would be a waste of resources; economic growth, capital accumulation, and consequently future production and employment would be lower than they otherwise might have been, decreasing the total income available for distribution among society's members.

Government may, therefore, have to strike a compromise between the objective of a more equitable distribution of income and the objective of efficiency in the use of resources and economic growth.

Income-Security Programs

Income security covers those programs which provide direct financial benefits to individuals and families and are designed to maintain incomes at some minimum level in the event of loss of income. Consequently when people retire, lose their jobs, become disabled, are injured in the workplace, or when the principal breadwinner in a household is lost, families have some assurance that they will continue to be provided with a decent standard of living. The main income security programs administered by governments in Canada are Old Age Security, the Canada and Quebec Pension Plans, Employment Insurance, Workers' Compensation, Veterans Benefits, various benefits found in provincial welfare programs such as widow's allowances, and Registered Retirement Savings Plans provided through the tax system. This section will focus on the most significant of these programs which are: Old Age Security, the Canada Pension Plan, Employment Insurance, and Registered Retirement Savings Plans.

Old Age Security

The Old Age Pension Act of 1929 first introduced government pensions for the elderly as a shared-cost program between Ottawa and the provinces. Pensions were paid to persons seventy years of age or over who passed a means test. In 1952 the federal government assumed full responsibility for old age pensions with the passage of the Old Age Security Act which provided pensions to all Canadian residents seventy years of age or older. Changes to the Act gradually reduced the eligibility age for Old Age Security (OAS) to sixty-five years by 1970. Enhanced benefits for the elderly were provided with the introduction of the Guaranteed Income

Supplement for recipients of OAS and the Spousal Allowances (both were discussed earlier in this chapter).

The universality principle of OAS was breached in 1989 with the introduction of the social benefits repayment scheme or recapture tax. All persons with at least ten years Canadian residency are still eligible for OAS at the age of sixty-five years. Recipients who have an income in excess of a set base amount, however, are required to repay the pension to the federal government. The base income was set at $50,000 in 1989 and indexed annually by the amount that the Consumer Price Index exceeds 3 percent. For 1996 the base amount was $53,215 and any OAS recipient with income above this amount was required to repay the pension at a rate of 15 percent of the amount by which income exceeded the base. For example, an old age pensioner with an income of $60,000 would be required to repay an amount calculated as $60,000 - $53,215 = $6,785 x 15% = $1,007. High-income pensioners are consequently excluded from the benefits of OAS.

OAS payments are indexed by the increase in the Consumer Price Index and are adjusted accordingly every three months. At the beginning of 1997 the OAS monthly pension was $400.

In 1996 there were about 3.6 million recipients of OAS pensions. Total OAS payments amounted to approximately $16 billion, with an additional $4.7 billion paid in guaranteed income supplements and one-half a billion dollars in spousal allowance. In the ten-year period since 1985 the number of OAS recipients increased by about 40 percent while the total cost of the OAS program doubled. The ageing of the population and the full indexation of benefits to inflation have combined to make OAS one of the largest and fastest growing components of federal government spending.

As mentioned earlier, effective in the year 2001, Old Age Security will be merged with the Guaranteed Income Supplement into a new Seniors Benefit program.

Canada Pension Plan

In 1966 the federal government implemented the Canada Pension Plan (CPP) to supplement private plans. It operates in all of Canada, except Quebec, which administers its own and similar Quebec Pension Plan. While the CPP was created by federal legislation, it operates under the joint control of Ottawa and the participating provinces. Changes to the plan, such as the amount of contributions by Canadians, require the agreement of at least two-thirds of the provinces representing two-thirds of the population (excluding the province of Quebec).

Both the Canada and Quebec pension plans are financed by compulsory contributions from employees, employers, and the self-employed, and from returns earned on investment of any surplus in the fund. For 1998 CPP contributions through payroll deductions were 6.4 percent of pensionable earnings paid equally by the employee and the employer, as well as the self-employed. The maximum pensionable earnings was $36,900 a year, with a $3,500 yearly exemption, resulting in maximum annual contributions of $1,069 by an employee, an equal amount by an employer, and twice this amount or $2,138 for the self-employed.

The amount of pension received by a contributor is based on the average of pensionable earnings in the previous five years and the maximum payment is 25 percent of this average. The maximum annual pension in 1997 was set at $8,840.

In addition to retirement monthly pensions, the CPP makes supplementary payments to surviving spouses (about 50 percent of the deceased member's pension) and to orphans, disabled contributors, and dependent children of disabled contributors. There is also a lump-sum death benefit (maximum $2,500) paid to the estate of a qualified contributor.

Contributors are eligible to collect their full CPP benefits when they reach the age of 65 years and retire. Early retirees, however, may choose to being collecting CPP benefits upon reaching the age of sixty years but, if they do, they receive less than their full pension.

Private pension plans are fully funded pension systems generally established in the workplace. A participating worker contributes monthly to the pension fund (with the employer usually contributing an equal amount). The administrator of the pension fund invests in financial obligations, seeking to obtain reasonable rates of return to contribute to the build-up of the fund. When the worker retires, he or she receives a pension based on the amount of contributions plus the return earned on the investments by the pension fund. Unlike this fully funded pension system, the CPP was established as a pay-as-you go pension plan. The CPP finances pensions for retired contributors in any given year by contributions paid by currently employed workers. These workers in turn expect that contributions of future generations of workers will finance their CPP benefits. The system did provide for a contingency reserve or surplus which over time was expected to equal two years of benefits and to cover periods of shortfall when payouts exceeded contributions. These excess funds were made available for loans to the provincial governments at interest rates approximating those on long-term federal bonds.

When the CPP was first introduced and before many people qualified for pensions, the set contribution rates quickly produced a large surplus. By the late 1980s, however, as the number of people eligible for benefits rapidly increased, benefits began to catch up to contributions. The federal and provincial governments approved a twenty-five-year schedule of contribution increases to keep the system solvent. The combined employee-employer contributions were increased by 20 percent per year to reach 5.6 percent by 1996, 8.1 percent by the year 2006, and 10.1 percent by 2016. The rate increases proved insufficient. By 1993 the CPP was forced to dip into its surplus for the first time in its history. By 1996 the CPP was taking in $12 billion in annual contributions and paying out $17 billion, threatening the exhaustion of the fund's surplus of $40 billion and the solvency of the CPP.

In light of these developments, Ottawa and the provinces approved a new schedule of rates in 1997 designed to keep the CPP solvent by accelerating rate increases over the next six years. The new schedule raised the rates steeply from 5.85 percent of pensionable earnings in 1997 to 9.9 percent by the year 2003 and beyond. This represented an increase from $969 to $1,635 by the year 2003, and then to $1,730 by the year 2030. At the same time benefits were reduced by almost 10 percent over the long term, primarily through reductions in disability and death benefits. It was estimated that the revised schedule of rates and benefits would produce an accumulated surplus of $110 billion in ten years, which was expected to carry the plan through the period of the expected large influx of retirees with the retirement of the so-called "baby boom" generation (the large numbers born in the early post-World War II period) in the early twenty-first century. Along with the new rate schedule the governments agreed that the surplus fund would be invested in other financial securities and stocks, in addition to government bonds, in an attempt to increase the returns on investment of the surplus.

Private Pension and Retirement Savings Plans

In addition to the government administered pension plans (OAS and CPP), the government provides incentives through personal income tax for private pension and retirement savings plans. Amounts contributed by an employee to a pension plan provided by the employer are deductible, up to a maximum of $3,500, from income in the calculation of personal income tax. In addition to these employer-sponsored pension plans, workers are encouraged to save for old age by contributing to a Registered Retirement Savings Plan (RRSP). An RRSP is a government-approved tax deferral program. It permits workers to deduct, from income subject to tax, amounts contributed to their Plan. These amounts earn interest, dividends, and so on, which are not subject to tax until withdrawn at retirement, or earlier. Since the tax savings in the Plan are continually revested, savings through an RRSP therefore grow more rapidly than regular savings on which returns are taxable.

For 1997 a taxpayer was permitted to contribute up to 18 percent of the previous year's (1996) earned income into an RRSP, up to a maximum of $13,500. If the taxpayer also belonged to an employer-sponsored pension plan, the annual RRSP contribution limit is reduced by a pension adjustment for the preceding year. The pension adjustment is calculated by the employer and represents the value of pension benefits accruing to the employee in that year.

Employment Insurance

Employment Insurance (EI) is a program designed to maintain the income of workers who temporarily lose their jobs. It was first introduced by the federal government in 1941 as the Unemployment Insurance program. The name was changed to Employment Insurance on July 1, 1996. The EI program features financing by premiums paid by employees and employers and eligibility based on number of hours worked before becoming unemployed

For 1998 the EI premium for workers was $2.70 per $100 of insurable earnings, and $3.78 (1.4 times the employee rate) for employers. The maximum insurable earnings was set at $39,000, establishing an annual maximum contribution of $1,053 for employees and $1,474 for employers.

Eligibility for benefits is based on the number of hours worked. A minimum of 420 to 700 hours (which is the equivalent of twelve to twenty weeks of thirty-five hours each) is required, depending on the unemployment rate in the claimant's region. The benefit rate is 55 percent of insured earnings of the claimant up to a maximum of $413 a week. In an attempt to curb abuses of the program, repeat users receive progressively smaller benefits. Under a so-called intensity rule, benefits are reduced 1 percent for every twenty weeks claimed since July 1996, but the benefit rate of 55 percent cannot be reduced below 50 percent of insurable earnings. To encourage the unemployed to seek part-time work while looking for a job, claimants can earn $50 a week or 25 percent of benefits, whichever is greater, without losing any benefits.

The number of weeks that benefits are payable is fourteen to forty-five, depending on the number of hours of insurable employment and the rate of unemployment in the claimant's region.

Benefits in the EI program include a family supplement. Claimants with children and a family income under $25,921, who also receive the Child Tax Benefit, are entitled to the supplement, an amount up to 65 percent of insurable earnings. The maximum benefit, however, remains $413 a week for all claimants. Other special benefits include maternity and illness benefits but a minimum of seven hundred hours of work is required to qualify.

High-income EI recipients are required to repay part of their benefits through a tax imposed under the Employment Insurance Act and collected by Revenue Canada as part of personal income tax administration. This so-called "clawback tax" begins when a recipient's income reaches $48,250 and is applied at a rate of 30 percent of the amount that a recipient's net income exceeds $48,750.

Numerous changes were made in the Employment Insurance program between 1993 and 1996 in addition to the name change. The program had been severely criticized in the past as being too generous and too costly. A number of empirical studies of the effect of the program on various aspects of employment and unemployment indicated that the system contributed to the unemployment rate in Canada and the duration of unemployment.[7] Employment Insurance tended to create a "moral hazard" problem, meaning that a person who is insured has a reduced incentive to avoid what he is insured against. Workers tended to more frequently quit their jobs, to stay unemployed for longer periods, and to be less prepared to accept less desirable jobs than would be the case if there was no insurance. Changes to the program in the 1990s raised the requirements for a worker to qualify for insurance and introduced penalties for repeat users and incentives for unemployed workers to accept part-time employment while seeking full-time employment or while waiting to be recalled from lay-off.

In 1998, the EI program's finances became the subject of a major controversy in Parliament. EI contributions are not paid into a special fund but are part of the main budgetary accounts. As unemployment fell in the last few years, revenues from EI premiums began to outstrip payouts. By 1998, the accumulated surplus in the EI program had risen to $20 billion ($7 billion in 1998 alone). This surplus contributed to the elimination of the federal budget deficit.

The Employment Insurance Act, however, requires that premiums be set at a level to keep the account in balance through the business cycle. It was not designed to be just another tax. Finance Minister Paul Martin, in late 1998, proposed to change the rules to let premium levels remain higher than actually required to fund the EI program. He claimed that the excess EI revenues provided the government with a cushion in uncertain economic times, along with flexibility to finance new programs, reduce debt and reduce other taxes. The opposition parties in the House of Commons, together with labour unions and businesses, objected to the proposed change in the legislation and pressed the government to reduce EI premiums. They claimed that the payroll burden from unnecessarily high premiums was hampering business and contributing to unemployment.

Agricultural Marketing Boards and Subsidies

Governments have attempted to stabilize widely fluctuating incomes common to agriculture, to ensure a fair rate of return to farmers, and to provide farmers with a degree of income security through the creation of marketing boards and payment of direct subsidies. Marketing boards have been applied to such agricultural products as grain, fruit, eggs, poultry, hogs, and dairy products. A marketing board consists of a group of producers formed under the authority of government for the purpose of regulating and marketing their product. They perform a function similar to that of a cartel and intervene in the functioning of the market by engaging in supply management through the imposition of quotas on producers. Restrictions in supply have the effect of maintaining and stabilizing prices at a higher level than the equilibrium price and providing farmers with some stability in farm income. The higher prices so established in essence serve as a subsidy to the producers. In some areas of agriculture such as milk production, the federal Canadian Dairy Commission not only sets quotas for each producer, but also pays a direct subsidy for each litre produced under the quota. This policy is designed to ensure the milk producer a stable and adequate price over cost and a secure income, along with stable sources and prices of milk for consumers.

Summary

Income distribution in Canada is characterized by a large gap between the lowest and highest income groups. The government employs the tax and transfer system and regulation in an attempt to raise the level of well-being of the lowest groups. Provincial social welfare programs, rent controls, and minimum wage legislation combine with federal housing subsidies, child benefit programs, and supplements to the Old Age Security for this purpose.

Governments are also engaged in providing Canadians with income security and maintenance in the event of job loss, retirement, or disability. The primary income security programs include Old Age Security, the Canada and Quebec Pension Plans, Employment Insurance and Workers' Compensation. Income tax provisions such as deductions for retirement plans and registered retirement savings plans encourage and assist workers to accumulate income for the period of their retirement from the workforce.

Controversies and problems surround some of these programs. The CPP was instituted as a pay-as-you-go pension scheme. In recent years, as payouts have begun to exceed contributions, the federal and provincial governments have been forced to initiate large increases in premiums to keep the plan solvent.

The OAS program provided universal benefits to the elderly until 1989 when benefits to higher-income individuals were required to be repaid, thereby eliminating the principle of universality of benefits.

Employment Insurance has, in some parts of country which have experienced chronic unemployment, become more of a welfare program than a program maintaining workers' incomes in periods of short-term unemployment. The federal government has attempted to restore the program to its original intent. A potential effect of generous unemployment payments, and for which there is some empirical evidence, is that they may contribute to the unemployment rate and the length of individual unemployment.

NOTES

1 The main sources of information for this chapter are: Human Resources Development Canada, *Basic Factors on Social Security Programs* (Ottawa: Supply and Services, 1998), cat. H21-106 1994E; Human Resources Development Canada, *Canada Pension Plan, Old Age Security*, Statistical Bulletin, December 1996; July 1997; Canada, *Public Accounts of Canada, 1996*, vol. II, cat. P51-1/1996-2-1E (Ottawa: Public Works and Government Services, 1996); and Canadian Tax Foundation, *Finances of the Nation 1997* (Toronto: Canadian Tax Foundation, 1997), ch.9.

2 Statistics Canada, *Income Distributions by Size in Canada, 1995*, cat. 13-207-XPB.

3 Christopher A. Sarlo, *Poverty In Canada* (Vancouver: The Fraser Institute, 1992), p.3.

4 Canada, Department of Finance *Budget 1996, The Seniors Benefit*, March 6, 1996, cat. F1-23/1996-4E.

5 Canada, Department of Finance *Budget 1996, The Seniors Benefit*, March 6, 1996, cat. F1-23/1996-4E.

6 Canada, Department of Finance *Budget 1997, Budget Plan*, February 18, 1997, pp.105-108.

7 It has been estimated that the Employment Insurance program has produced a 1 percent increase in the unemployment rate in the country and increased the average duration of job search by about 20 percent. See Miles Corak, "Is Unemployment Insurance Addictive? Evidence from the Benefits Durations of Repeat Users," *Industrial and Labor Relations Review* 47, 1 (October 1993): 62-72.

PART TWO

PUBLIC SECTOR GROWTH
AND MANAGEMENT

Growth and Composition of Public Sector Expenditures

A general trend in most countries has been for the public sector to grow more rapidly than the private sector and to absorb an increasingly larger relative share of total resources. Various factors have contributed to this trend;[1] the most significant for Canada are outlined in this chapter, which also describes some theories of public sector growth and provides Canadian data on the composition of government spending at each level of government. Some data on the expenditures of government enterprises and on tax expenditures is also presented.

Factors Influencing Public Sector Growth

Wars and Military Expenditures

Government expenditures usually rise dramatically during a country's involvement in war. Canada experienced this sort of growth during the two World Wars, although it is questionable whether they had a displacement effect on the long-run trend of government expenditures. Canadian government spending as a percentage of GDP rose from 22 percent prior to World War II to approximately 50 percent during the war, but by 1950 had declined to the pre-war level. Defence expenditures in Canada have steadily declined since the Korean War in 1953 and today account for only about 6 percent of federal government spending. The comparable figure is 25 percent in the U.S., whose high military expenditures coincide with its assumed leadership obligations in the Western world.

Social Conscience

In Canada, as in many Western democratic societies, there has been a gradual awakening of what may be termed the *social conscience.* Society has come to accept increasing obligations to assist the underprivileged and those who are unable to provide for themselves. In general, a large percentage of the increase in government expenditure in Canada during the last half of this century has been for programs designed to redistribute income more equitably. Spending for this purpose has often been on direct transfers to individuals or on goods and services in programs designed to benefit the lower-income groups relatively more than the higher-income groups. The most prominent expenditures have been for social service and health care programs, including Old Age Security (OAS), the Canada Pension Plan, Employment Insurance, and medicare.

Technological Change

Rapidly changing technology has produced highly sophisticated, capital-intensive means of production requiring an educated and skilled labour force, which, in turn, has contributed to technological development and increased productivity. Society has recognized that technological progress and education are important to the development of a country and its standard of living and that education and labour training yield considerable benefits to all of society. It was primarily because of such recognition that government assumed responsibility for education and vocational training, which account for a significant proportion of government spending.

Changing technology also has provided modern society with an increased supply of sophisticated private goods, which has brought about a corresponding increase in demand for public goods. For example, the increased production and use of automobiles has required more and better roads and highways; the development of larger and faster airplanes has meant larger and more modern air terminals. Thus, the private and public sectors of the economy are interdependent and complementary in the provision of goods and services.

Population Growth and Urbanization

The demand for public goods and services generally grows with the population. Moreover, population growth in this century has been accompanied by an urbanization movement that has brought large increases in the demand for social goods and services, which are most appropriately provided by government. These items include transportation facilities, sanitation, water supply, police and fire protection, and housing, which in Canada primarily fall to the responsibility of the provincial and municipal governments. Not only has the demand for the quantity of these goods and services increased; as people become more affluent in terms of improvements in the quality of private goods, they also expect an improvement in the quality of public goods.

Keynesian Theory

The Keynesian revolution in economic thought fostered increased government involvement in directing and influencing economic activity, which has required increased government spending. Since the Depression of the 1930s, governments in many Western countries, including Canada, have made efforts to fine tune the economy to prevent or reduce the severity of cycles in economic activity and to promote economic growth. Increased government spending for public works, public investment projects, and assistance to industry are examples of governments' efforts to provide employment and to stimulate the economy.

More recently in Canada, government has been attempting to shape and influence industrial development. Nowhere was this more evident than in the energy and natural resources industries, where billions of dollars were expended on nuclear energy development and on joint investment ventures with the private sector in petroleum exploration, extraction, and distribution. During the period of economic decline and inflation of the early 1980s, the Canadian government became active in assisting companies in financial difficulty (for example, Chrysler Corp., Dome Petroleum) through loan guarantees. Grants to industries that locate in designated areas of chronic high unemployment were also initiated.

It could also be argued that the Keynesian formula for deficit finance during recession impacted on government spending in a manner which Keynes had not envisaged. Beginning in the 1970s, the federal government, and later the provinces as well, began to resort to deficits even in periods of economic prosperity. Deficit finance, in lieu of tax increases, appeared to be politically expedient and likely fostered expenditure increases that otherwise may not have been made.

Productivity and Costs

The rising relative cost of public goods and services also may have contributed to the increasing relative size of the public sector. Between 1947 and 1988, the gross domestic product implicit price index rose from 18.8 to 134.3 (1982 = 100), while the price index for government's current expenditures on goods and services (a component of GDP) increased from 10.5 to 142.8.

Some contend that lower efficiency and productivity in the public sector have contributed to this differential. If wages and salaries rise by the same amount in both sectors but productivity in the public sector lags, then unit costs and consequently prices of public goods and services rise relative to unit costs and prices in the private sector. It is argued, though not conclusively, that the lower rate of productivity change in the public sector is partly because of the nature of the services provided and partly because of differences in the behaviour of private suppliers and government bureaus.[2]

It is certain, however, that much government activity involves the provision of services and that productivity in service industries generally lags behind productivity in goods-producing industries. Furthermore, services, particularly public services such as health care and education, are highly labour intensive, and periodically public service wages and salaries have tended to rise more rapidly than wages and salaries in the private sector, thus contributing to the relative rise of unit costs in the public sector.

Government Political Philosophy

The growth of government can also be influenced by the philosophy of the particular political party in power over the longer term. The party elected to power reflects the mood and values of the electorate at the time. In Great Britain following World War II for example, the growth of government relative to the economy increased during the tenure of the Labour Party, which emphasized social programs and the increased participation of government in the economy through the nationalization of various industries. During the 1980s, under the tenure of the Conservative government led by Margaret Thatcher, restraint on social spending and the privatization of a number of government-owned corporations contributed to a decline in the size of government relative to GDP. Similarly, during the conservative regime of Republican President Ronald Reagan, from 1980 to 1988,

the United States government embarked on a program for reducing the size (through government expenditure reduction, except for defence) and influence (through deregulation) of the government sector.

In Canada, as mentioned in the previous chapter, the election of socialist-leaning governments — the Co-operative Commonwealth Federation (CCF) and the New Democratic Party (NDP) — in Saskatchewan, Manitoba, and British Columbia brought increased provincial involvement in economic activity and the establishment of new government enterprises or Crown corporations. These governments initiated public health programs, government-run automobile insurance, and other socioeconomic activities that were the forerunners of similar programs adopted by the federal government and other provinces. In turn, the election to power of more conservative governments usually produced announcements of retrenchment in government involvement in economic activities. A good example was the election in 1995 of the Conservative Harris government in Ontario, which proceeded to revise some of the expenditure-laden policies of the previous NDP government of Bob Rae and to eliminate a continuing huge budgetary deficit incurred by that government.

The Political Process and Bureaucratic Considerations

The increasing size of the public sector can be considered a reflection of the operations of the political process (a point implicit in some of the previous discussion of this chapter). Some attempts to explain government expenditure growth focussed on the nature of collective decision making — choice — and on bureaucratic behaviour. A number of public-choice theories and models in the literature on public finance concentrate on the supply side of government spending — the motivations and actions of the suppliers of government goods and services.[3] Theories developed in this area focus on the self-interest behaviour of political parties, elected representatives, and bureaucrats.

Anthony Downs, for example, theorized that political parties will present to the electorate a budget based on a mix of programs that they believe will maximize their votes and thus their chances of re-election. Whether it will produce an efficient supply of government services cannot be assured, however, for, according to Downs, the social function of political parties is a by-product of their self-interest motive. The mix could lead to an oversupply or an under-supply of government services.

The vote-trading or "log-rolling" model features elected legislators' exchange of votes to obtain support for projects for their constituencies that otherwise might not receive the support necessary for passage by the legislature. In other words, member A of the legislature agrees to support a project for the constituency of member B if B agrees to support A's project. If the benefits from each project are local but are financed by all taxpayers, expenditures can be carried to the point at which the benefits from the marginal expenditure are far less than the costs to society in the form of taxes. The result is an oversupply of government services and an inefficient use of resources.

William Niskanen focussed on the behaviour of bureaucrats, arguing that they are motivated by the desire to accumulate power and the prestige that derives from administering a major government department or section of a department. Bureaucrats may thus be motivated to expand the size of the budget and the output of their administrative units, which can lead to the expansion and growth of government beyond the optimum level.

It is clear that if political parties believe they can be elected more readily by offering to do more for society, they will behave accordingly, but keeping election promises usually entails considerable increases in government expenditure. While this may be interpreted as reflecting social demands for government services, these demands perhaps would not be as high if greater attention were drawn to the costs of proposed services and the relationship between taxes and government-provided goods and services. Unfortunately, election promises generally concentrate on what the government will offer the public, with little said about the method of financing or who will bear the burden. Voters consequently believe the fiscal illusion that they will benefit from activities and other individuals will bear the burden of financing them.

More recently in Canada, facing public alarm over continuous budgetary deficits and a rapidly rising public debt, political parties which have proposed expenditure retrenchment have tended to find favour with the electorate. Whether this is the beginning of a trend or a short-run development remains to be seen.

Government Expenditure Growth Theories

A number of attempts have been made to develop a theory of public sector growth in a mixed economy.[4] In particular, these attempts have focussed on the growth trends and the time patterns of changes in government spending. A general theory of public sector growth would not only serve to explain past behaviour but would also permit predictions to be made about the future growth and size of government.

One of the earliest such attempts was Wagner's Law, developed by German economist Adolph Wagner (1890), who found a functional relationship between a growing economy and government spending. According to Wagner's Law, the relationship is elastic in that a change in GDP produces a more than proportionate change in government spending. He attributed this elasticity of government spending to the income elasticity of demand for social goods and services. As income in the economy increases, demands for government-provided goods, services, and law and order increases in a greater proportion.

Most studies of government expenditure growth in industrialized countries during this century substantiate the existence of a functional relationship as described by Wagner's Law. The relationship has indeed been elastic: as GDP increased, government expenditures increased in a greater proportion. It has been difficult to determine, however, what factors have contributed most significantly to this relationship. For example, R.A. Musgrave theorized about the possible effects of economic and sociocultural factors and concludes that the combined contribution of these factors to the relationship between government expenditure and GDP over the course of a country's growth was theoretically indeterminate.[5]

Although Wagner's Law has been shown to hold true for many industrialized countries, evidence of its application to developing and underdeveloped economies is inconclusive. Some analysts hypothesize that the relationship of government expenditure to per capita income may in fact be inelastic in the early stages of a country's development, reflecting the provision of society's basic needs by the private sector rather than government; elastic during the industrialized stage, reflecting the need for government-provided capital, infrastructure, and complementary services; and inelastic again in the post-industrialized stage, reflecting government's sufficient provision of social goods and services and society's preference for a greater proportion of consumer goods and services.[6]

Other theories have focussed on the time pattern of expenditure growth — the shape of the trend path of government spending relative to GDP over a long period of time. In the early 1960s, Peacock and Wiseman put forward their theory of displacement, inspection, and concentration. Their observations of the historical growth of government spending in the United Kingdom showed the growth to be

steplike, each step indicating a surge in the government expenditure to GDP ratio. They contended that these surges resulted from major social or economic disturbances, such as wars and economic depressions. Each disturbance caused the existing growth path of government expenditure to be replaced by a new, higher-level growth path to reflect the higher expenditure/GDP ratio. After the disturbance ended, the higher level of expenditure was maintained by government involvement in new activities and by a higher tax tolerance level (established when taxes were increased to finance the increased government spending during the disturbance). According to this theory, therefore, disturbances cause a displacement of resources from the private sector to the public sector. This displacement becomes permanent because the disturbance forces the attention of society and government to economic and social problems that were previously neglected; government consequently acquires new obligations that require increased expenditures.

Attempts have been made to apply the Peacock-Wiseman theory to Canada to determine the effect of major disturbances such as wars. The general conclusion is that wars have not had a permanent displacement effect on the long-run growth trend of Canadian government expenditure.[7] For example, at the end of World War II, the government expenditure/GDP ratio in Canada was approximately 50 percent. By 1950, it had been reduced to less than 25 percent, practically equal to the ratio that had existed just prior to the war.

None of the theories developed to explain government sector growth has been accepted as a general theory. They have tended to be applicable to particular periods and to particular countries but have not been universally applicable. They have contributed, however, to the understanding and analysis of the factors that influence and affect government expenditure growth.

Thus, although analysis reveals that Canadian government expenditure as a percentage of GDP increased from 15 percent in the 1920s to almost 48 percent in the 1990s, it is difficult to determine if this rising trend will continue into the future.

A controversial related issue is whether there is a critical limit to the size of government in relation to the economy. There has been speculation that a limit does exist, and once it is surpassed, forces may be set in motion to reduce the size of government.[8] The limitations to government expenditure growth, according to this hypothesis, are related to taxation. In their theory, Peacock and Wiseman referred to a tax-tolerance level that constrained government spending during periods between economic and social disturbances. Taxes are never popular, and governments must maintain an awareness of the potential effects of major tax increases. Opposition to high taxes may be reflected in greater efforts at tax avoidance; in taxpayers' "voting with their feet" and moving to jurisdictions where taxes are lower; in the flight from the country of wealth; in governments being voted out of office; in adverse effects on incentives to work, invest, take risks, and so on, which would stifle economic growth; in the growth of an underground economy to evade taxes, or in the organization of groups of taxpayers and consumers to voice opposition to new taxes, as occurred when the federal government proposed its new Goods and Services Tax (GST) in 1989. Taxes deemed to be unfair, or fear of higher tax rates, may even prompt "tax revolts." In September 1990, the governing council of the village of Elstow, Saskatchewan, fully supported by residents, declared that, as a municipal government, it would neither collect nor pay the unpopular federal GST when it came into effect in January 1991.[9] It was contended that the proposed tax was unfair and inflationary and that its rates would likely spiral in the future. During the late 1970s and 1980s, tax revolts were triggered by the unpopularity of high property taxes in several U.S. states. Irate taxpayers in jurisdictions that permit voter-initiated referendums were able to force enactment of a number of tax-limitation statutes. The electorate was not deterred by arguments that tax limitations would lead to a reduction in government services.

An indication of how Canadian and U.S. governments have perceived public tax-tolerance levels in recent years is the fact that the federal governments in both countries were reluctant to raise taxes by the necessary amount to balance their budgets. During the 1980s and into the 1990s, they continued to incur large annual budgetary deficits, attempting to reduce them by emphasizing expenditure reduction and control rather than tax increases. (The Canadian government's efforts to reduce its deficit are described in later chapters).

Government Expenditure Trends and Patterns[10]

Total government expenditure in Canada has increased considerably over the past eight decades as illustrated in Table 5-1. Disregarding the massive increase during World War II, the trend was a persistent increase in government expenditure as a percentage of GDP until, in 1980, it stood at 40.3 percent. A major increase in total government spending, combined with a small increase in GDP, caused this figure to jump to 46.8 percent by 1985. Since 1990 it has fluctuated between 46 and 48 percent. A similar trend can be found in many other Western countries.[11] Table 5-2 shows the trend in government expenditure as a percentage of GDP for the G-7 countries based on OECD data. The statistics show that government in Canada is larger than in the United States and Japan but smaller than in France and Italy.

Table 5-3 presents an economic classification of total government expenditure for selected years from 1926 to 1996. It can be observed that there have been some changes in the composition of expenditures, particularly during World War II. Currently, approximately 45 percent of government expenditure

TABLE 5-1: Government Expenditures as Percentage of Gross Domestic Product for Selected Years 1926-1996

	Expenditures (percentage of GDP[a])
1926	15.7
1929	16.1
1933	27.4
1939	21.4
1944	20.5
1947	24.3
1950	21.3
1960	28.8
1970	34.9
~0	40.3
198b	46.8
1990	47.1
1995	47.9
1996	46.1

[a] Expressed as a percentage of gross national product to the year 1947.

Source: Statistics Canada, National Income and Expenditure Accounts, 1926 to 1974, cat. 13-001; and Canada, Department of Finance, Economic Reference Tables, Aug. 1966, cat. F1-26/1996E; and Fiscal Reference Tables, October 1997, cat. F1-26/1997E.

TABLE 5-2: International Comparison of Total Government Expenditures as Percentage of Gross Domestic Product or Gross National Product for Selected Years 1970-1996[a]

	Percentage of GDP or GNP			
	1970	1980	1990	1996
Canada	33.5	38.8	46.0	44.7
France	38.5	46.1	49.8	54.5
Germany	38.3	47.9	45.1	49.0
Italy	33.0	42.1	53.4	52.9
Japan	19.0	32.0	31.3	36.2
United Kingdom	36.7	43.0	39.9	41.9
United States	30.0	31.4	32.8	33.3

[a] Based on OECD data.

Source: Canada, Department of Finance, Fiscal Reference Tables, October 1997, cat. F1-26/1997E, p.55.

TABLE 5-3: Shares of Government Expenditure by Economic Classification for Selected Years 1926-1996

	Goods and services	Transfers to persons	Transfers to business	Gross capital formation	Interest on public debt	Other
	(percentage of total)					
1926	48.1	9.1	0.2	13.1	28.5	0.9
1939	47.0	18.8	1.4	12.3	22.8	0.6
1944	82.4	4.3	4.5	1.6	7.1	0.1
1950	47.3	25.1	1.8	12.2	13.3	0.4
1965	50.0	21.5	3.0	14.7	10.1	0.7
1975	48.6	24.9	6.9	9.2	9.6	0.9
1985	42.7	26.7	5.2	5.7	18.0	0.2
1995	40.6	31.1	2.7	4.8	20.5	0.4
1996	40.4	31.5	2.4	4.6	20.4	0.8

Source: Statistics Canada, *National Income and Expenditure Accounts, 1926-1974*, cat. 13-531; and Department of Finance, *Fiscal Reference Tables*, October 1997, cat. F1-26/1997E, p.38.

is devoted to goods and services and capital formation, with the remainder going to transfer payments in the form of payments to persons and to business (including subsidies and capital assistance) and interest payments. Transfers to persons have increased in importance in recent years, rising from about 25 percent of total government spending in 1975 to more than 31 percent by 1996.

Table 5-4 illustrates the share of expenditure functions among the federal and provincial, territorial and local governments for the fiscal year 1994-95. Intergovernment transfers are included only in expenditures of the receiving government, so the data reflects the cost of the services administered by each level of government. The table shows that the provincial/local level did more than 60 percent of government spending in 1994-95. The functions in which the federal government spends considerably more than the provincial/local governments are protection of persons and property, social services, foreign affairs, and debt charges. Provincial/local government account for most of the services

in health care, education, the environment, and recreation and culture.

An alternative method of analyzing government expenditures on various functions is to include intergovernmental transfers only in the expenditures of the donor government. This treatment of expenditures measures the share of government activities financed by each level of government. Regardless of how intergovernmental transfers are treated, however, the historical trend has been towards decentralization of government in Canada, with provincial/local governments assuming an increasingly larger share.

Tables 5-5 to 5-7 show trends in the relative significance of the various expenditure functions of each level of government over the last five decades. As Table 5-5 shows, the more notable features at the federal level have been the decline in the relative importance of spending on protection of persons and property (primarily defence) from 35 percent of gross expenditure in 1954 to about 8 percent by 1995, and the increase in social services from about 22 percent to over 30 percent. The

TABLE 5-4: Consolidated Government Expenditure Functions, 1994-95
(Financial Management Statistics Basis)

Expenditure function	Total	Share spent by	
		Federal government	Provincial Territorial and local governments
	($ million)	(percentage of total)	
General services	18,237	41.1	58.9
Protection of persons and property	24,477	56.6	43.4
Transportation and communications	15,689	21.9	78.1
Health	47,100	2.7	97.3
Social services	85,783	57.7	42.3
Education	43,920	4.3	05.7
Environment	0,040	9.9	90.1
Foreign affairs and International assistance	4,934	100.0	0.0
Recreation and culture	7,215	18.2	81.8
Resource conservation and industrial development	14,199	43.9	56.1
Debt charges	71,325	59.2	40.8
Other		55.2	44.8
Total	357,568	39.7	60.3

Note: Intergovernment transactions are eliminated. Transfers from one level of government to another are excluded from the expenditure of the paying government but are included in the expenditure of the receiving government. The shares therefore reflect those transactions occurring between level of government and the general public.
Source: Statistics Canada, Public Sector Finance, 1995-1996, cat. 68-212-XPB.

costly programs in this category are Old Age Security and Employment Insurance, along with the transfers to provincial governments for welfare programs under the former Canada Assistance Plan. An expenditure that has grown dramatically has been public debt charges, more than tripling from 7.7 percent of federal spending in 1978 to almost 27 percent by 1995.

The most significant trend at the provincial level has been the increase in health care, social services, and education costs as a proportion of gross provincial expenditures (Table 5-6). The major increases took place in the late 1950s and early 1960s, when the provinces placed priority on these functions. In 1995, these three functions accounted for 64 percent of gross provincial expenditure. At the same time, expenditure on communications and transportation declined significantly, from almost 25 percent in 1954 to less than 5 percent in 1995. Another development has been the increase in the share of debt charges, from not quite 7 percent in the late 1970s to almost 15 percent by 1995.

TABLE 5-5: Shares of Federal Government Gross Expenditure[a] by Function for Selected Fiscal Years Ending March 31 (Financial Management Basis)

Expenditure function	1954[b]	1966	1978	1988	1995
		(percentage of total)			
General services	4.4	3.9	5.6	4.4	4.3
Protection of persons and property	35.3	19.0	10.4	9.5	8.2
Transportation and communications	3.2	6.8	6.4	2.7	1.8
Health	1.1	5.6	6.8	5.5	4.7
Social services	21.8	22.1	34.0	33.1	32.2
Education	0.4	2.9	4.2	3.1	2.9
Resource conservation and industrial development	3.9	6.1	7.7	6.3	4.6
General-purpose transfers to other levels of government	7.4	4.9	7.6	5.9	6.0
Debt charges	10.6	12.7	7.7	20.0	26.9
Other	11.9	16.0	9.6	9.5	8.4
Total	100.0	100.0	100.0	100.0	100.0
		($million)			
Total amount	4,663	8,756	49,965	136,264	177,703

[a] Includes conditional transfers to other levels of government.
[b] The figures for 1954 have been partially adjusted to the classifications of the revised series beginning 1966; although they are not strictly comparable with the revised series, the deviations are minor.

Source: Statistics Canada, *Financial Statistics of the Federal Government of Canada, 1953 and 1954*, *Federal Government Finance, 1969*, cat. 68-211; and *Public Sector Finance, 1995-1996*, cat. 68-212-XPB.

At the local level, education expenditures have been most prominent; although their significance tended to decline after the 1970s, they still accounted for close to 40 percent of gross expenditure in 1994 (Table 5-7). Communications and transportation functions have gradually declined in relative importance, as have expenditures for the protection of persons and property. At the same time, expenditures for recreation and culture, environmental improvements, and for health and social services have taken increasing shares of municipal budgets.

In general, total government expenditure as a percentage of GDP has continued to increase. During the last two decades, the most costly government functions at each level of government have been related to social services, particularly health care, welfare, and education, reflecting growing public demands for extended and improved services in these areas.

Demographic changes have played a major role in the trends in government spending. The baby boom of the 1940s and 1950s created a need for more educational facilities in the 1960s and 1970s. In recent decades, the

TABLE 5-6: Provincial Government[a] Gross Expenditure[b] by Function for Selected Fiscal Years Ending March 31 (Financial Management Basis[c])

Expenditure function	1954[c]	1966	1978	1988	1995
		(percentage of total)			
General services	3.6	3.3	6.6	5.2	4.1
Protection of persons and property	5.5	3.6	3.5	3.2	2.9
Transportation and communications	24.9	17.5	7.7	4.9	4.2
Health	17.5	23.4	24.3	25.4	25.8
Social services	8.6	10.0	14.6	17.0	19.7
Education	16.2	25.6	23.6	19.3	18.3
Resource conservation and industrial development	7.0	5.2	5.1	5.6	4.2
General transfers to local governments	2.0	3.1	2.6	1.6	1.2
Debt charges	11.4	4.4	6.5	12.3	14.9
Other	3.2	2.5	5.6	5.5	4.7
Total	100.0	100.0	100.0	100.0	100.0
		($million)			
Total amount	1,185	6,343	43,585	122,076	175,434

[a] Including governments of the Yukon and Northwest Territories.
[b] Includes all conditional transfers received from, and paid to, other levels of government.
[c] The figures for 1954 have been partially adjusted to the classifications of the revised series beginning 1966; although they are not strictly comparable with the revised series, the deviations are minor.

Source: Statistics Canada, *Financial Statistics of Provincial Governments, 1953,* cat. 68-207; *Provincial Government Finance, Revenue and Expenditure,* cat. 68-207; and *Public Sector Finance, 1995-1996,* cat. 68-212-XPB.

ageing of the population and the gain in life expectancy have produced a high growth rate for the elderly — the proportion of Canadians age sixty-five years and over increased from 7.6 percent in 1961 to almost 11 percent by the 1980s. This demographic trend has had a significant impact on the demand for health and social services and is expected to continue into the next century. It has also placed a strain on the Canada Pension Plan as a larger proportion of the population has begun to receive payments under the plan.

Changes in work and the work force have also influenced government spending. The increasing number of working couples and single-parent families has increased the need for day-care facilities. During the last few decades, rapidly changing technology has brought with it the need for a highly skilled and trained labour force and has thus increased demand for technical training facilities.

Expenditures of Public Enterprises

In addition to government activities administered by government departments, ministries, or

TABLE 5-7: Local Government Gross Expenditure[a] by Function for Selected Fiscal Years 1953-1994 (Financial Management Basis[b])

Expenditure function	1953	1965	1978	1994
	(percentage of total)			
General services	6.5	5.9	4.6	5.2
Protection of persons and property	10.6	9.9	7.5	8.0
Transportation and communications	17.8	17.2	11.6	9.2
Health and social services	8.0	5.1	7.9	9.1
Education	34.8	35.3	42.1	39.4
Recreation and culture	3.2	4.5	5.9	6.2
Environment	5.8	5.7	8.6	8.6
Debt charges	6.0	7.6	7.2	5.9
Other	6.8	8.8	4.6	8.5
Total	100.0	100.0	100.0	100.0
	($million)			
Total amount	1,091	3,943	23,125	71,986

[a] Includes all transfers from other levels of government.

[b] The 1953 and 1965 figures are part of a different time series from that of the 1978 and 1994 figures and are therefore not strictly comparable with the latter; however, the two series do indicate the general trends over the 1953-94 period.

Source: Statistics Canada, *Historical Review of Financial Statistics of Governments in Canada, 1952-1962*, cat. 68-503; *Municipal Government Finance, 1996*, cat. 68-204; and *Public Sector Finance, 1995-1996*, cat. 68-212-XPB.

agencies, which appear as expenditures in the government budget, a number of activities are undertaken through the corporate form. These government business enterprises are commonly called Crown corporations. The revenues and expenditures of the large commercial, industrial, and financial corporations appear separately in the government accounts. The federal budget does include as expenditures, investments in, and advances to, Crown corporations, and includes as revenues the returns on these investments in an item called non-budgetary transactions. The actual income and expenditures of these corporations, however, are not part of the federal government budget. Government budget expenditures, therefore, underestimate the extent of government operations.

Table 5-8 summarizes the income and expenditures of federal and provincial government business enterprises. Expenditures of federal Crown corporations totalled $23 billion in 1993-94, while the expenditures of provincial government enterprises exceeded $48 billion. The activities of Crown corporations range from regulatory duties performed by a small commission or board to large-scale commercial and financial operations under an elaborate corporate structure.[13] They either compete with similar operations in the private sector or monopolize activities that might otherwise be carried out in the private sector. Many of these corporations were established for the purpose of achieving government policy objectives. At the federal level, Air Can-

TABLE 5-8: Government Business Enterprise: Income and Expenditures ($ million)

Type of Business

	Transportation, Storage, and Communication	Manufacturing, Mining and Wholesale Trade	Finance, Insurance and Real Estate	Total
Federal Government 1993-94				
Income	11,812	8,384	7,154	27,350
Expenditure	11,953	7,292	3,775	23,020
Net Income	(141)	1,092	3,379	4,330
Provincial Government 1992-93				
Income				49,909
Expenditure				48,867
Net Income				1,042

Source: Statistics Canada, Public Sector Finance, 1995-1996, cat. 68-212-XP, pp.244-245; 262.

ada (formerly Trans Canada Airlines) and Canadian National Railway (both recently privatized) were used to provide transcontinental transportation services to help unify the country. The Canadian Broadcasting Corporation (CBC) has a mandate to express and promote the Canadian identity. The Canada Mortgage and Housing Corporation administers loans, grants, and subsidies to help improve housing for Canadians. Atomic Energy of Canada Ltd. was created in 1952 to develop domestic uses of atomic energy. In 1976, Petro Canada Ltd. was established as a major instrument of the federal government's National Energy Program with a mandate of actively engaging in oil and gas exploration, development, and marketing to ensure Canadians an adequate and continuous supply of oil and gas.

At the provincial level, Crown corporations are found in a large number of economic sectors including banking and finance, forest development and manufacturing, automobile insurance, hotels and tourism, housing, industrial development, liquor control and marketing, lotteries, power utilities, transportation, communications, and oil and gas production and distribution.

In addition to the Crown corporations that provide goods and services directly to the public, a number provide regulatory services and exert a major impact on markets in the private sector. These include the federal-level marketing and price stabilization boards, such as the Canadian Wheat Board, the Canadian Dairy Commission, the Agricultural Stabilization Board, and similar agencies at the provincial level.

Crown corporations of a commercial or industrial nature are expected to operate like firms in the private sector. Those that produce and sell goods and services, such as Canada Post Corporation at the federal level and the public utility corporations at the provincial and municipal level, are expected to be self-

TABLE 5-9: Federal Tax Expenditures 1992-93[a]
Estimates of Revenues Foregone

Tax Preference	Value $ million
Personal Income Tax	
Basic Personal Credit	17,130
Registered Pension Plans (deductions and non-taxation of investment income)	13,815
RRSPs (deductions and non-taxation of investment income)	7,815
Transfers of tax room to provinces	11,010
Preferential treatment of capital gains	8,312
Unemployment insurance premium deduction	3,740
Canada and Quebec Pension Plans preference	2,255
Child tax benefit	5,275
Corporation Income Tax[b]	
Low tax rates for small business and for manufacturing and processing	2,302
Loss carry-over	1,074
Investment tax credits	646
Goods and Services Tax	
Zero rated goods and services	2,905
Tax exempt goods and services	2,285
Tax credit	2,645
Tax rebates	1,880

[a] List contains only the more significant tax expenditures. The amounts are not aggregated because the methodology used by the Department of Finance does not permit a meaningful aggregation.
[b] Estimates are for the year 1991-92.

Source: Canada, Department of Finance, *Government of Canada Tax Expenditure, 1995*, cat. F1-27/1995E.

financing and even generate profits. Profitable Crown corporations may be required to return some of their income to the government as a shareholder. Deficits, on the other hand, may be financed by parliamentary appropriation. Many corporations rely heavily on government funding, in the form of appropriations or of loans, investments, and advances.

The reasons for providing certain services and conducting specific operations through a Crown corporation, rather than through a regular ministerial department, are varied. It is argued that the corporation is the most appropriate organizational form for undertaking government activities of a commercial nature because it allegedly combines public accountability with business efficiency. It provides greater flexibility for day-to-day operations as compared to regular government departments.

Tax Expenditures

The federal tax system contains a number of provisions that give preferential treatment to various groups and businesses in the form of tax exemptions, deductions, reduced rates, and tax credits. Through these tax preferences, the government provides assistance and incentives and, in the process, foregoes tax revenues. Since such tax forgiveness or postponement is viewed as an alternative to direct spending, it has come to be known as tax expenditure.[13] It is equivalent to the government's first collecting the sums involved by imposing tax and then making a direct expenditure of an equal amount.

Not all exemptions, deductions, or credits are classified as tax expenditures. In determining tax expenditures, the Department of Finance has attempted to define a "benchmark" or "normal" tax structure, and only the deviations from this structure are classified as tax expenditures. This definition leaves some arbitrariness and ambiguity regarding which tax provisions are tax expenditures. Included in the benchmark structure are deductions of costs incurred in earning income and deductions or credits to reduce or eliminate double taxation. These are considered as essential features of the tax structure and are not counted as tax expenditures.

Tax expenditures are also found in the corporation income tax and the Goods and Services Tax. Table 5-9 lists the most significant tax expenditures in each of the three taxes in terms of annual revenues foregone for 1992-93. The Department of Finance cautions, however, that the estimates of the revenues foregone cannot be meaningfully aggregated to determine the total cost of the tax expenditures for each tax or the group of taxes. This is because tax measures interact and taxpayers may change their behaviour in response to the elimination of a tax preference. In other words, the cost estimates of revenues foregone from a particular tax preference may be greater than the revenue increases that would have resulted if the preference was eliminated.[14]

Summary

The size of the public sector in Canada, measured as the government expenditure-to-GDP ratio, has steadily increased during this century to stand at 47 percent by the 1990s. Numerous factors have contributed to this growth, including the development of a social safety net of major health care and social welfare services, demographic changes and the ageing of the population, and increasing government involvement in programs designed to promote economic growth and stability. Expenditures on education, health care, and social services now account for approximately 50 percent of total government spending. A rapidly growing public debt, fuelled by large and continuous budgetary deficits, produced rapidly increasing debt charges so that by 1995 they accounted for 20 percent of government expenditures.

The increase in spending resulted in substantial increases in the tax burden on Canadians. Towards the end of this period questions began to be raised, fuelled by a growing public resentment against high taxes and a growing underground economy, as to whether Canada had perhaps reached a critical limit in the size of its public sector and tax burdens. As outlined in the next chapter, the last decade of the twentieth century has witnessed a trend towards the downsizing of government.

The government budgetary accounts on government spending tend to underestimate the total amount of government spending and the size of the public sector. These accounts usually do not include the expenditures of government enterprises or Crown corporations. They also do not include tax expenditures, which can be viewed as alternatives to direct expenditure for achieving government policy objectives.

NOTES

1   Some of these factors are discussed in R.A. Musgrave, *Fiscal Systems* (New Haven, Conn.: Yale University Press, 1969) ch.3; and in Thomas E. Borcherding, ed., *Budgets and Bureaucrats: The Source of Government Growth* (Durham, N.C.:

Duke University Press, 1977). A discussion of factors influencing government expenditure growth in Canada is presented in Richard M. Bird, *The Growth of Government Spending in Canada*, Tax Paper No. 51 (Toronto: Canadian Tax Foundation, 1970); and in Donald J. Savoie, *The Politics of Public Spending in Canada* (Toronto: University of Toronto Press, 1990).

2 A number of studies compare the efficiency and productivity of the public and private sectors for areas in which enterprises operate in both sectors and so offer opportunity for a meaningful comparison. For example, in the case of two Australian airlines, similar in every respect, the private one was found to be twice as efficient as the public one in terms of freight and mail, 22 percent more efficient in terms of passengers, and 13 percent more efficient in terms of revenue per employee. For more information on this study and others comparing the public and private sectors, see Borcherding, ed., *Budgets and Bureaucrats*, ch.4 and 6.

3 For example, see Borcherding, ed., *Budgets and Bureaucrats*, and W.N. Niskanen, *Bureaucracy and Representative Government* (Chicago: Aldine-Atherton Press, 1971). A survey of some collective choice and self-interest theories can be found in D.G. Hartle, *A Theory of the Expenditure Budgetary Process* (Toronto: University of Toronto Press, 1977), ch.1 and 2.

4 See Bernard P. Herber, *Modern Public Finance*, 5th ed. (Homewood, Ill.: Richard D. Irwin, 1983), ch.16; and Borcherding, ed., *Budgets and Bureaucrats.*

5 Musgrave, *Fiscal Systems*, ch.4.

6 See Musgrave; *Ibid.*; Bird, *The Growth of Government Spending in Canada*, and Herber, *Modern Public Finance.*

7 See Bird, *The Growth of Government Spending in Canada*, pp.107-17.

8 C. Clark, "Public Finance and Changes in the Value of Money," *Economic Journal* (December 1945). Clark argued that once the critical limit was ex-ceeded, the high taxes would result in disincentives to save, work, and invest and lead to inflation. The reduction in supply of goods and services and the inflation would put pressure on governments to reduce their spending and scale back taxes. While the theory as stated by Clark, and particularly his attempt to verify it, provoked considerable controversy and criticism, the concept of a limit to the size of government and the level of taxation may have some merit. See John C. Strick, "Critical Limits to Taxation," *Canadian Tax Journal*, 40, 6 (1992): 1315-1331.

9 The local authorities declared Elstow a "GST-free zone" and announced the municipal government would not charge the 7 percent tax on sewers, water, garbage collection, or licences and permits or the tax on equipment and other purchases. *The Globe and Mail*, September 21, 1990.

10 A detailed study of government expenditure in Canada before 1967 is contained in Bird, *The Growth of Government Spending in Canada*, R.M. Bird, *Financing Canadian Government: A Quantitative Overview* (Toronto: Canadian Tax Foundation, 1979); and J. Harvey Perry, *A Fiscal History of Canada — The Postwar Years*, Tax Paper No. 85 (Toronto: Canadian Tax Foundation, 1989).

11 An outline of earlier trends in government expenditure growth in the United States and other countries of the Organization for Economic Co-operation and Development is contained in G. Warren Nutter, *Growth of Government in the West* (Washington, D.C.: American Enterprise Institute, 1978).

12 An outline of Crown corporations in Canada is presented in Canadian Tax Foundation, *Finances of the Nation*, 1997 (Toronto: Canadian Tax Foundation, 1997), ch.17.

13 Canada, Department of Finance, *Government of Canada Tax Expenditures 1995*, cat. F1-27/1995 E.

14 *Ibid.*, pp.18-23.

CHAPTER 6

Alternative Program Delivery Systems

Government programs and services are provided to the public through a variety of delivery systems. They are provided directly by government through its utilization of resources, indirectly by government through the private sector, by the private sector through an arrangement with government, or via a public-private joint venture or partnership. This chapter reviews the traditional delivery systems, and then examines recent trends in the extensions of, and innovations in, delivery systems involving greater reliance on the private sector.

Traditional Delivery Systems

Government goods and services can be provided directly by government through public ownership and employment of resources. The vehicles for this purpose are government departments and agencies organized along functional lines, such as the Department of Agriculture, the Department of Defence, and Transport Canada. The delivery of programs and services is managed by government employees, utilizing supplies, materials, and other inputs purchased by the government as necessary to operate the program.

A form of government arms-length delivery system is commercialization, through the establishment and operation of Crown corporations (discussed in chapter 5). Crown corporations may range from small regulatory commissions to large commercial enterprises. While all are accountable to the government, the latter usually enjoy a large degree of autonomy, are expected to be self-financing, and are frequently in competition with private enterprise. Examples include Canada Post and Ontario Hydro, and, before being sold, Air Canada, Petro Canada, and the Canadian National Railroad.

Instead of providing goods and services with its own resources, governments may contract production to the private sector. In this case, the ownership and employment of resources remain with private enterprise. Contracting may take a variety of forms. Private enterprise may produce or construct facilities for government. Ownership of the facilities remains with the government which makes them available for public use as in the case of highways, recreational facilities, public housing, and other projects of a capital nature. Contracts may also be tendered for the maintenance of these facilities. In other instances, government may tender contracts with private companies to carry out public activities such as garbage collection and snow removal.

Government services may also be delivered through regulation. This consists of government-imposed rules and controls that require or prohibit specific actions in particular circumstances and consequently affect and influence economic, social, and moral behavior of individuals and business. Regulations derive from legislation and are administered by government regulatory agencies and commissions. For example, the Canadian Radio-Television and Telecommunications Commission has responsibility for licensing broadcast and cable television and regulates such aspects as program content and prices. The National Transportation Agency overseas transportation facilities and services that come under federal jurisdictions with the objective of achieving an efficient, effective, and safe transportation system.

Another method of delivering government-provided benefits to society is through tax expenditures (discussed in chapter 9). These are tax deductions, exemptions, and credits that reduce the amount of tax paid by individuals and business. Through these tax preferences the government provides benefits and incentives and, in the process, foregoes tax revenues. They are viewed as alternatives to direct government spending to achieve specific objectives. The personal income tax includes such tax expenditures as the basic personal credit, deductions for registered pension plans and retirement savings plans, the age and disability credits, and credits for education expenses.

In recent years, searching for ways of living within their means and still achieve their objectives, governments have sought to improve the efficiency and effectiveness by which programs and services are provided to the public. They have begun to explore the potential of extending particular delivery systems and to search for new and innovative methods of delivering services.

Alternative Means of Delivering Services

In 1993 the federal government embarked on a major program of restructuring its administrative system, spearheaded by the Treasury Board. Large, continuous budgetary deficits had been the trend since the 1970s, and it was questionable whether the level of government services could be sustained, even after the tax increases of the 1980s. In conjunction with a comprehensive review of its expenditure programs to identify areas where spending could be reduced, priorities determined, and resources reallocated, the government sought to determine the most appropriate means of providing programs and services to meet the needs of society. It sought to explore and develop alternative strategies for delivering services, strategies that would be cost effective and flexible and that could retain quality in programs and services.

Alternative delivery systems available to governments, which the federal government sought to extend or determine the feasibility of further application, included: privatizing programs and services that no longer served a public policy purpose, contracting services out to the private sector, negotiating partnering arrangements with other levels of government and the private and voluntary sectors, devolving programs and services to other governing authorities, commercializing services, and deregulation with greater reliance on voluntary codes.[1] These alternative delivery systems have been familiar to the public service and governments, and in varying degrees have been applied, but have not been pursued with the vigour witnessed in the past few years.

Privatization

Privatization, narrowly defined, consists of the transfer of government ownership of a Crown corporation or government facilities to the private sector.[2] The transfer may take the form of direct sale of a Crown corporation to a private sector company or to the public at large by selling shares in the corporation. Privatization is justified in cases where there is no continuing public policy reason for the government to retain responsibility for a facility or service.

During the 1980s, the Canadian government began to transfer ownership and control of some federal Crown corporations to the private sector. The divestiture trend was also evident in the provinces and in Western Europe and Great Britain. The main justification put forward was the desire to increase efficiency, competitiveness, and productivity.

Many government-owned corporations that engaged in commercial and industrial activities were either monopolies or operated in direct competition with companies in the private sector. Some had been established as instruments of government policy, designed to achieve specific objectives, and were deemed no longer required. Furthermore, certain corporations remained unprofitable, and government subsidization was a drain on government finances, contributing to the large deficits that were being incurred during the 1980s. Privatization at the federal level became a major element in the new Conservative government's agenda for economic renewal announced in 1985. In the words of the government:

Selling corporate interests will have a number of benefits. It will reduce the size of government in the economy and make room for private sector initiatives; it will improve market efficiency and the allocation of resources; it will improve firm efficiency through market discipline and by reducing political and bureaucratic impediments.[3]

The government announced plans to review its Crown corporations and their operations and to privatize those for which there was no convincing public policy reason for retaining in the public sector.

In 1986, the Office of Privatization and Regulatory Affairs was established to oversee the privatization process (along with a program of reforming and streamlining government regulatory activities). By 1989, the government had sold all or part of sixteen Crown corporations including Air Canada (1989), Canadair Ltd. (1986), de Havilland Aircraft of Canada Ltd. (1986), Canada Development Corporation (1987), Canadian Arsenals Ltd. (1986), Teleglobe Canada (1987), and Northern Transportation Ltd. (1985). The privatization movement continued into the 1990s. In 1992 the federal government sold its share of Telesat, and in 1995 sold two of its largest Crown corporations, Petro Canada and Canadian National Railroad. In 1997 Ottawa concluded the sale of its printing facilities, the Canada Communications Group, (formerly the Queen's Printer plus other printing facilities) to the highest bidder, St. Joseph Corporation, a private firm.

The provincial governments followed suit. During the 1980s, they privatized some thirty major government-owned companies, including relatively large commercial and industrial entities such as Québecair, Saskatchewan Oil and Gas, Pacific Western Airlines (Alberta), and various divisions of BC Hydro. During the 1990s, Manitoba sold the Manitoba Telephone System, while Alberta privatized Alberta Government Telephones and its liquor outlets. The corporations sold, like those at the federal level, were primarily those engaged in activities in competition with the private sector.

The privatization process generally took two forms: the sale of shares in the Crown corporation to the public or the direct sale of the corporation to a for-profit private company. An example of the former was the privatization of Air Canada, Petro Canada, and the CNR, where shares in the companies were issued and sold to the public. Using the latter process, Canadair was sold to Bombardier Inc., de Havilland to Boeing Commercial Airplane Co., and Teleglobe Canada to Memotec Data Inc.

An example of privatization to the private not-for-profit sector was the sale of Canada's civil aviation system, which provides civil air traffic control, flight information services, and a network of navigation aids. Facilities include air traffic control towers at airports, flight service stations, and a national radar and communications system. It was sold in 1996 to NAV CANADA, a private not-for-profit corporation, created to purchase and operate the system. NAV CANADA is incorporated with four members, one appointed by the federal government, two appointed by user groups (i.e., airlines), and one appointed by the unions representing air navigation system employees. Corporate governance is provided through a fifteen-member Board of

Directors nominated by the four-member corporation. The legislation governing this privatization process gave NAV CANADA a monopoly over civil air traffic control services in the country and the authority to recover its costs of purchase ($1.5 billion) and operation through user charges. These include terminal charges on users, charges on passenger tickets, and international overflight charges, and will replace the federal Air Transportation Tax on passenger tickets. In essence, the system is now owned, operated, and maintained by its principal user, the domestic air carrier industry, on a non-profit basis. The federal government's role is to regulate safety, review rates, and appoint a member to the corporation. While other countries have established separate entities similar to a Crown corporation to operate their systems, Canada is one of the few countries to transfer its system to the private sector.

In addition to sales, both the federal and provincial governments dissolved a number of Crown corporations that no longer provided important services and amalgamated others whose services overlapped.

While governments contended that privatization would lead to greater operational efficiency, improved services, and lower prices for consumers, there were also direct benefits to the government. Privatization of unprofitable corporations freed the government of their financial drains on the government budget. In addition, the sales produced large revenues for governments, and this at a time when they were incurring large budgetary deficits and were seeking new sources of revenue. For example, the sale of Air Canada netted the federal government about $700 million; the CNR sold for $2.3 billion of which $1.2 billion went into the federal treasury after payment of brokerage fees and the writedown of the railroad's debt; the sale of Petro Canada brought $1.9 billion; and the sale of the air navigation system and its facilities brought $1.5 billion. It was estimated that the cost of operating the system was about $800 million annually, of which $600 million was financed from ticket taxes and $200 million from the federal treasury.

A number of theoretical expectations are attached to the privatization of government enterprises and operations.[4] Among them, as the government pointed out in its 1985 policy statement initiating privatization, it brings market discipline to an operation and removes political and bureaucratic impediments. In the marketplace, the profit motive of a private firm provides an incentive to minimize costs of operation, provide services at affordable prices, and attract as many customers as possible. It is contended that a private firm has a greater incentive to develop new technology and innovate and is more responsive to the needs of consumers. Furthermore, a private firm is not restricted to government jurisdictional boundaries (i.e., as in a local government jurisdiction) and will attempt to attain optimal size, enjoying any economies of scale in the process. Privatization also offers the potential of competition and the consequent benefits of competition. All too frequently government Crown corporations have operated as monopolies (albeit regulated monopolies), where entry into the industry was barred by government legislation or regulation. This has been true of public utilities such as Ontario Hydro. There is considerable evidence that when protected regulated firms or industries have been deregulated and opened to competition, they have been forced to restructure and cut costs, particularly labour costs, and become more efficient.[5] It would appear, therefore, that while the transfer of government enterprises to the private sector may improve economic efficiency, the gains are likely to be the greatest if the transfer is accompanied by measures to establish or to increase competition.[6]

Contracting Out

Contracting out involves the transfer of the operation of a program or activity by formal contract to a for-profit private sector company for a specified period, but not transferring the responsibility for it. The service is provided by the private company with its resources and employees instead of by government with government-owned resources and public employees. The government, however, usually sets the conditions for the quantity and quality of the service. Selection of a provider, if it is through tender and competitive bidding, offers the advantage of providing the service at least cost to the taxpayer. The company which wins the contract is motivated to optimize performance and to respond to the preferences of the public by the periodic contract renewal process. There is widespread contracting out of services at the local government level. Examples of government services delivered by the private sector through government contract include garbage collection and snow removal, tourism and convention services, day care, elderly housing, and protection of persons and property. At the provincial level, the government of New Brunswick has contracted with a private security firm to build and operate a young offenders' centre.

Contracting for social services employing non-profit agencies and organizations is found at the provincial level. A wide array of children's services are provided through such non-profit agencies as the Children's Aid Society. Annual funding to the Society is provided in the form of government transfer payments.

One form of contracting out involves the long-term lease of government-owned facilities to private sector non-profit organizations. These organizations assume responsibility for operating, expanding, and modernizing the facilities, which are expected to be self-financing.

Canada's airports were at one time owned and operated by Transport Canada and were costing Ottawa hundreds of millions of dollars a year. Searching for an alternative to the existing system, the federal government rejected outright privatization and instead de-cided to create local airport authorities to operate the airports. Each authority would have its own board of directors representing the community, including business, labour, and airport users. These authorities would operate the air terminals on long-term leases from Ottawa, with the federal government exercising strict safety standards. The benefits of this arrangement include decentralization of decision making and reduced bottlenecks. It offered a new form of financing to modernize and expand airports, without imposing a burden on the taxpayer, and allowed airports to more quickly respond to changing public needs. As with some other forms of alternative delivery systems, these arrangements combine public service with a market orientation and independent revenue generation.

Partnership

A government may arrange a partnership with another level of government or with a party or company in the private sector. A public partnership is a relationship between two levels of government who agree to work cooperatively towards shared objectives. The agreement will specify the purpose and nature of the activity and the terms and conditions governing it, such as staffing, financing, and reporting. A number of such arrangements have been formed between the federal and provincial governments, including the Canadian Business Service Centres and the Canadian Tourism Commission. These types of ventures offer saving by reducing overhead costs and duplication of services.

Public-private partnerships are becoming an important form of alternative service delivery. One of the earlier partnerships between the federal government and the private sector which involved joint ownership was in the area of telecommunications. Telesat Canada was created in 1969 to operate and oversee Canada's communications satellite program. It was established as a joint public-private venture, 50 percent owned by the federal government and 50 percent owned by the major Canadian telephone companies (Stentor). In 1992 Ottawa sold its share to Alouette Tele-communications Inc., a company jointly owned by Stentor and Spar Aerospace.

Two recent examples where the private sector has participated in the development and operation of major government infrastructure projects are Confederation Bridge and Highway 407 Central.

Confederation Bridge, a thirteen-kilometre bridge across Northumberland Strait and linking Prince Edward Island with New Brunswick, was undertaken as a joint federal-provincial-private venture.[7] A private sector consortium contracted to design, build, operate, and maintain the bridge for a thirty-five-year period, following which ownership will be turned over to the Canadian government. Financing was a complex arrangement involving all three partners. Using a bond issue, a Crown agency of the New Brunswick government (Straight Crossing Finance Inc.) provided $630 million to cover the costs of construction. Funds from the bond issue were kept in trust and paid to the developer as construction proceeded. Ottawa agreed to make annual payments of $41.9 million (indexed for inflation) for a period of thirty-five years to Strait Crossing Finance which would be applied for bond interest and redemption. (This was roughly equal to the federal subsidy for the NB-PEI ferry service and essentially represents federal government guarantee of the bonds.) The bridge construction consortium collects the bridge tolls for the thirty-five-year term that it operates the facility. These tolls cover the costs of operation and maintenance plus a return to the consortium. Increases in tolls are regulated by the federal government. While the private consortium did not initially invest any funds to acquire a stake in the project, it did assume most of the risks of project construction, such as potential cost overruns, because the federal government's financial commitment was fixed at the $41.9 million annual payment.

The benefit to the government was that a fixed transportation link to PEI was provided at no greater cost than the ferry service subsidy. Furthermore, faced with a large budget deficit, the financial arrangements enabled Ottawa to undertake the project without borrowing and adding to its deficit.

The province of Ontario entered into a partnering arrangement with a private consortium of companies to build Highway 407 Central, a sixty-nine-kilometre, four-to-six-lane toll highway north of Toronto. Acting for the government was the Ontario Transportation Capital Corporation (OTCC), a provincial Crown agency. In 1994 the OTCC entered into an agreement with the consortium to design and build the highway for a fixed price of $930 million. The funding was provided by the government through direct provincial borrowing, to be fully repaid from the toll revenues collected. The construction consortium was also awarded the maintenance contract. In this arrangement, the government took most of the risk in assuming operating obligations for the project, while the private consortium assumed only the usual business risks associated with a fixed-price construction project.[8] The Office of the Provincial Auditor was critical of this arrangement and recommended that in future partnership agreements with the private sector, the government should strive for a better balance of risks and rewards.[9]

In early 1998 the Ontario government announced that it would permit local school boards to enter into public-private sector partnerships to deliver kindergarten and other early-childhood programs.

The Ontario Las Vegas-style casinos are operated as joint ventures. These casinos are owned by the Ontario Casino corporation, a Crown corporation, but are operated by private sector interests. Charity casinos in some provinces are licenced by government to charities, which hire private firms to operate them.

Commercialization

Commercialization is the adoption of more businesslike approaches to the delivery of services, while still allowing the government to continue to be involved in the delivery of a program or activity. The most common form is the establishment of an agency or enterprise which carries out its day-to-day activities at arms length from government as in the case of Crown corporations. It is expected that commercialization will achieve improved efficiency and reduced costs while at the same time protecting the public interest.

Both the federal and provincial governments have long relied upon Crown corporations to deliver services which have the characteristics of private services and can be priced and sold in the marketplace. These corporations were expected to operate like a business and be self-financing. Numerous examples of earlier established Crown corporations were found in the areas of transportation, hydro-electric power, and telecommunications at both the federal and provincial levels. Many of these enterprises were sold to private sector interests during the 1980s and 1990s, but the concept of commercialization as an alternative delivery system remains alive.

Some recent examples of commercialization at the federal level include Canada Post, the Canadian Food Inspection Agency, the announced plans to create a Parks Canada Agency, and a new organization to improve cost effectiveness and delivery of revenue services. Canada Post is expected by the government to produce a commercial rate of return.

Devolution

Devolution is the transfer of a program or service, or the transfer of funding for a program or service, to another governing authority. The reason for a transfer may be to eliminate duplication in the delivery of a service, or in recognition that another governing agency may be the more appropriate body to deliver the service.

Examples of devolution of federal responsibilities for services to other governing jurisdictions include transferring federal program delivery for Indians to Indian bands; transferring various responsibilities for northern affairs to the territorial governments of the north; and transferring responsibility for veterans' hospitals to the provinces.

At the provincial-local government level there has been a recent trend to realign the activities and services performed by each level of government. The Ontario government, for example, assumed greater responsibility for education costs while downloading one-half of the cost of social assistance on to local governments. The announced objectives of the realignment of responsibilities was improvement in the efficiency in the administration and delivery of the respective services.

Deregulation and Voluntary Codes

As part of the movement towards downsizing government and reducing its influence over economic activities, governments in the last two decades have followed a policy of deregulation. There was an attitude that economies were over-regulated and that inefficiencies were being created by government regulations that were proving to be excessively costly. These inefficiencies could be eliminated or reduced by substituting market elements for regulation. The assumption underlying this position was that the market is a more efficient allocator of resources and market competition a more efficient regulator of prices and output than are regulatory agencies. At the same time, deregulation would save government the expense of administering and policing regulations. Consequently, there have been movements within Canada and elsewhere to deregulate various traditionally regulated industries such as the airlines, trucking, and the telephone industry.

Along with deregulation, the federal and provincial governments began to explore alternatives to regulation in those areas where it was deemed that some rules of business conduct were desirable. An alternative to traditional regulatory practice was the use of voluntary codes of conduct. Voluntary codes are a form of private or self-regulation by an industry or a professional group whereby a set of rules, commitments, or standards is developed by the groups, designed to guide the behaviour of its members. In the case of an industry, each firm in the industry that was a signatory to the agreement would be obligated to adhere to the codes. Some procedure for monitoring firm behaviour would be required to assess compliance. The enforcement of standards by the industry, however, could be a problem since it does not have the legal authority of a government to impose fines and penalties. Governments could monitor the effectiveness of the codes and the threat of government regulation could serve as an incentive for signatories to comply to an agreed-upon set of voluntary codes. Publication of complaints against members who deviate from the codes and fear of adverse publicity could also serve to keep members in line.

An example of an organization developing codes of conduct is the Investment Funds Institute of Canada which desires to establish a code of sales practices with the encouragement of the Ontario Securities Commission. The cable television industry in Canada has developed a system of voluntary standards for customer service, marketing of cable services, and advertising, administered by the Cable Television Standards Council. The council was established in response to an offer by the government regulator, the Canadian Radio-television and Telecommunications Commission, to abandon some areas of regulation if the industry established acceptable standards of self-regulation and procedures for policing the standards. Other industries that have developed regulatory codes or standards include the tobacco industry, with its voluntary advertising and packaging code; the real estate industry, which has a comprehensive set of business standards governing all aspects of real estate trading; and the chemical industry, with its Responsible Care program dealing with the responsible management of chemicals and chemical products to protect the public and the environment.

In many instances, industry associations operate voluntary programs complementary to existing government regulation. They offer the potential for replacing government regulatory agencies if they can develop and demonstrate their capability for effective consumer and public protection.

Summary

While alternative delivery systems have been long known to governments, and have been used in the past, it is only in more recent times that governments in Canada have begun to extend their application and explore new and innovative methods of providing programs and services. The trend was sparked by the large government budget deficits of the 1980s and 1990s, forcing retrenchment in government spending and downsizing of the public sector.

Alternative delivery systems rely heavily, although not exclusively, on the private sector for providing programs and services formerly provided directly by government. They include the government transfer of enterprises and activities to the private sector and various forms of partnering of the public and private sectors for the provision of services. Among the alternative systems most frequently used are privatization, contracting out, devolution, commercialization, joint ventures, and replacement of regulation with voluntary codes. In recent years, some innovations and unique features have been witnessed in the application of alternative delivery systems.

The expectations from delivery systems utilizing the private sector include programs and services that respond more quickly to public needs, greater operational efficiency and improved services, more rapid developments in technology, and economies of scale and lower costs. At the same time, some of the alternative delivery systems may free the governments and the taxpayer of the financial burden of operating facilities, while the outright sale of enterprises to the private sector adds to government revenues.

NOTES

1 Canada, Treasury Board, *Framework for Alternative Program Delivery*, 1995, cat.BT 32-38/1995.

2 A broad definition of privatization would include all delivery systems involving the private sector.

3 Canada, Department of Finance, *Budget Papers*, May 23, 1985 (Ottawa), p.27.

4 For a discussion of various aspects of privatization, see The Fraser Institute, *Privatization: Tactics and Techniques*, Vancouver, 1987; and Lawrence Finley, *Public Sector Privatization: Alternative Approaches to Service Delivery* (New York: Quorum Books, 1989). A recent comprehensive study on the effects of privatization on a wide scale is presented in Rafael La Porta and Florencio Lopez-de-Silanes, *The Benefits of Privatization: Evidence from Mexico*, NBER Working Paper No.6215, Washington, 1998.

5 The airline industry and the telephone industry are frequently cited as examples.

6 R. Hemming and A.M. Mansoor, *Privatization and Public Enterprise*, International Monetary Fund Occasional Paper No.56, 1988.

7 The financial arrangements and other aspects of the Confederation Bridge project are examined in Canada, *Report of the Auditor General of Canada to the House of Commons*, October 1995, ch.15, cat. FA1-1995 12-15E.

8 The original plan for Highway 407 Central was for the private sector to assume full responsibility for financing, construction, operation, maintenance, and toll collection and turn the highway over to the government after a thirty-year period.

9 Office of the Provincial Auditor, *1996 Annual Report* (Toronto: Queen's Printer for Ontario, 1996), p.245.

CHAPTER 7

Budgeting and Financial Management

Decision making in government can be represented as a pyramid or hierarchy of responsibility. The higher the position of the decision-maker in this pyramid, the more general but more basic are the decisions made. At the upper levels, decisions must be made about the functions and policies of government, while the lower levels of administration usually implement policies.

In the Canadian government, the Cabinet is responsible for establishing priorities among the major economic and social functions of government and for determining policy in these areas. The Cabinet collectively establishes priorities in principle, defines broad objectives, and sets down the basic policies. It is the function of the individual ministries or departments to develop the objectives in detail, to determine alternative means by which the objectives may be achieved, to choose the most efficient or effective course of action, and to implement and administer the resulting programs. Decisions are therefore required at various stages of implementation and levels of administration.

This decision-making process is a lengthy and complex one in which the dividing line between politics and administration may be rather vague. The elected representatives or politicians are at the pinnacle of the decision-making pyramid and bear the ultimate responsibility for government policy and action, but their policies may be initiated or greatly influenced by lower-level administrators through the advice and information they provide.

Apart from major policy decision, many decisions on government activity are made during the formulation of the government budget. The budget document is a reflection of decisions made and, in this sense, the decision-making process and the budgetary process are synonymous.

The budget, simply defined, is a detailed statement of the government's expected revenues and planned expenditures. More specifically, it is the plan of operations prepared by the Cabinet for approval by the House of Commons, showing the government's objectives, programs and activities, and purchases for the coming fiscal year. It also shows revenues from various sources, expenditure and revenue trends, and fiscal targets. The budget serves the executive as a plan of action; it serves the legislature as a means of control over the executive; and it serves administrators in the internal management of their respective departments.

The Financial Structure of the Canadian Government

The financial structure of the federal government of Canada rests on a constitutional and statutory framework dating back to the Constitution Act, 1867 (formerly titled the British North America Act, 1867). This act gave constitutional foundation to the principles of public financing basic to responsible government; subsequent legislation established necessary financial administrative ma-

FIGURE 7-1: Financial Structure of the Federal Government

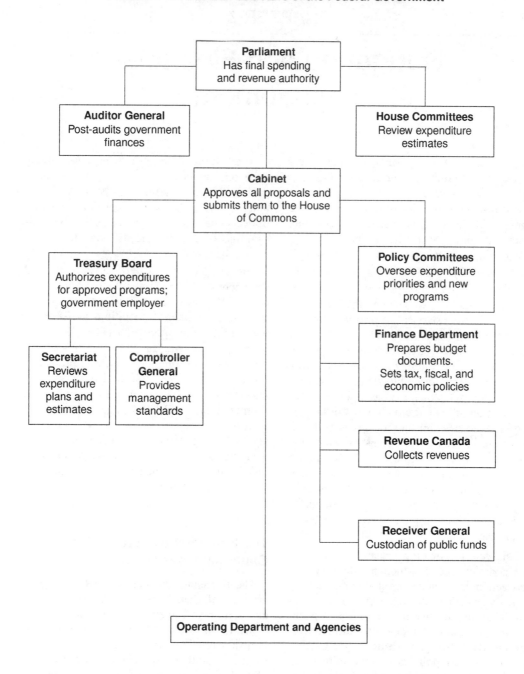

chinery and procedures. Many of the financial practices that were adopted had been developed in the pre-Confederation provinces and were simply carried forward in the new federal structure. Frequent revisions were required in both the financial structure and procedures over time to keep pace with changing conditions and the ever-increasing scale of government operations. Today, the basic statutory financial structure is governed by the Financial Administration Act, the Auditor General Act, and the Government Reorganization Act and is supplemented by arrangements established through Cabinet decisions. This structure is illustrated in Figure 7-1.

Parliament is supreme in the financial structure of the government, and ultimate control of the public purse rests with that body. It is responsible for examining and approving government expenditures and tax changes and for holding the executive to account for the use of public funds. All tax revenues must be placed in a central fund, the Consolidated Revenue Fund, and no money can be expended from this fund unless its appropriation is authorized by Parliament.

The Cabinet is responsible for preparing the budget and presenting it to Parliament. Much of this work is performed through a system of Cabinet policy committees and the Treasury Board. The policy committees formulate expenditure priorities, oversee the design of new programs, and reallocate resources from old programs to fund new programs.

The Treasury Board is a statutory committee of the Privy Council. Composed of the President of the Treasury Board, the Minister of Finance, and four other Cabinet ministers, it has legal responsibility for the authorization of expenditures and is generally responsible for allocating resources for approved policies and programs. More specifically, it is responsible for detailed review and analysis of departmental expenditure estimates prior to their submission to Parliament. The board

also assists the Cabinet policy committees in developing reallocation options. In addition, the board is responsible for personnel policy, for collective bargaining in the public service, and for promoting efficiency in government administration. Through the Office of Comptroller General, the board seeks to develop and maintain administrative and management systems and techniques to facilitate planning, financial control, and program evaluation.

The Minister of Finance and the Finance Department play a crucial role in the budgetary process. The minister is an active participant in the Cabinet committee system and is responsible for developing the budget strategy, preparing the budget documents, and presenting the government's budget to the House of Commons. The department provides information and advice on economic affairs and on the financial implications of alternative policies, forecasts economic conditions and anticipated revenues, and is responsible for determining tax policy and tax changes and the effects of these changes on revenues and on economic activity.

The Receiver General for Canada is the custodian of public funds. The Receiver General is responsible for the release of funds to operating departments, following appropriation by Parliament, and for the compilation and maintenance of the public accounts of Canada. Currently the Minister of Public Works and Government Services is named the Receiver General. Administration and interpretation of tax legislation is the responsibility of Revenue Canada, which also collects all tax proceeds for the government and deposits them in the Consolidated Revenue Fund.

An agency with a major function in the budgetary process is the Office of the Auditor General. The Auditor General is an agent of the House of Commons, responsible directly to the House and charged with auditing government expenditures and revenue collections. This agent's traditional role as the financial watchdog of Parliament has been to ensure that public funds are fully accounted

TABLE 7-1: The Budgetary Cycle
(The Expenditure Management System)

February	• Budget speech and tabling of Main Estimates.
March-June	• Departments prepare Business Plans and Reports on Plans and Priorities based on resources allocated in the budget. • Plans and Reports are reviewed by Treasury Board.
May-June	• House of Commons Standing Committees review Reports and Main Estimates.
June	• Cabinet and Cabinet policy committees identify expenditure priorities, which guide resource reallocation and policy options.
June-September	• Departments prepare Main Estimate. • Central agencies (Finance Department, Treasury Board, and Privy Council Office) develop options on budget strategies (i.e., fiscal targets, new spending, spending reductions). • Departments prepare and submit Performance Reports.
October-December	• Treasury Board reviews Estimates. • House Standing Committees consider Performance Reports. • Finance Department prepares and releases Budget Consultation Papers and begins consultation process with the House Standing Committee on Finance, the provinces and others to establish budget strategy. • Auditor General submits his report to the House of Commons. • Public Accounts of Canada (prepared by the Receiver General) is tabled in Parliament.
January-February	• Cabinet makes final decisions on budget strategy. • Finance Department finalizes budget documents. • Treasury Board finalizes Main Estimates. • House of Commons Public Accounts Committee reviews Public Accounts and Report of the Auditor General.
February	• Budget speech and tabling of Main Estimates.

Source: Canada, Treasury Board, *The Expenditure Management System of the Government of Canada* (Ottawa, 1995) cat. BT 22-27/1995; *Report of the Auditor General of Canada*, Chapter 5, "Reporting Performance in the Expenditure Management System," April 1997 (Ottawa: Public Works and Government Services, 1997), pp.5-10.

for and expended in accordance with the wishes of the legislature. In 1977, the Auditor General Act extended the auditor's function to making observations on the economy, efficiency, and effectiveness of government expenditures. (In regard to effectiveness, however, the Auditor General is restricted to assessing procedures established within departments to measure and report on the effectiveness of programs. This restriction prevents the auditor from evaluating policy or determining whether a particular policy or program is justified, thereby retaining the traditional political neutrality of the office and protecting it from becoming involved in partisan political debate.)

The budgetary process in which these agencies are key players combines traditional elements basic to the parliamentary system of government with historical practices and elements of theoretical budgetary systems. Changes over time have frequently consisted of incorporating into the process new developments in budget theory in attempts to promote efficiency in decision making and financial management and procedures reflecting the attitudes of the particular government in office. Agencies such as the Treasury Board and the Office of the Auditor General obtain their authority and responsibilities from statute. Certain basic budget practices, such as the preparation and submission of the Main Expenditure Estimates, the presentation of the budget speech, and preparation of the Public Accounts, are historical. But various other practices are subject to change, reflecting fiscal conditions faced by government and the attitude of the government and the Prime Minister, with more centralized authority in some periods, and new budget concepts. The budget system outlined below was in effect during the administration of Prime Minister Chretien's Liberal government and was called the Expenditure Management System. (Features of various budgetary systems and budget concepts or jargon and their interrelation are discussed in the appendix to this chapter). The focus of this chapter is on the statutory budget agencies and their functions and the well-entrenched traditional budget elements, with lesser attention on practices that have developed in response to particular fiscal conditions and that might change as government administrations change.[1]

The Budget Cycle

The Canadian government's fiscal year covers the period April 1 to March 31. The budget, however, is a rolling, multi-year expenditure plan, and the fiscal year is just one period in it. Budgeting in government, a series of annually repeated stages, involves determination of expenditure directions and priorities and of expenditure and revenue levels by the Cabinet and Cabinet committees; multi-year planning by departments of their expenditure programs; review and approval of these programs by Cabinet committees and the Treasury Board; preparation of detailed expenditure estimates for the fiscal year by departments and review by the Treasury Board; authorization and appropriation of expenditures by Parliament; determination of revenues, tax proposals, and their implications by the Finance Department; administration of spending and revenue collection; and finally an independent audit for the House of Commons by the Auditor General.

The various phases of the budgetary cycle are illustrated in Table 7-1. The presentation of the budget speech and supporting documents in late February, and tabling of the Estimates of expenditure on March 1 for the coming fiscal year commencing April 1, mark the beginning of the next budget cycle. Among the documents is the Budget Plan, outlining the government's fiscal and economic targets, its policy priorities and new expenditure initiatives for the coming fiscal year and one additional year, as well as documents on new policy initiatives. Cabinet policy committees oversee the design and implementation of the new initiatives and prepare new policy proposals for the next fiscal year. At the same time departments and agencies prepare their Business plans, which are strategic, three-year plans that set out goals, targets, and performance measures and show how departments are adjusting their operations to available resources and budget priorities. These plans are intended to be used as internal management tools as well as for control by central agencies. The Business Plan of a department is its main planning document.

As part of the estimates, departments submit Reports on Plans and Priorities, outlining the general direction a department plans to take during the estimates year and the next two fiscal years.[2] Trends in the expenditures of the department, planned reallocations of resources to higher priority programs, and changes in programs are highlighted. The Business Plans and the Reports are submitted to the Treasury Board secretariat for scrutiny to ensure adherence to the announced budget targets. The Business Plans are for internal use, but the Reports are tabled in the House of Commons and referred to the Standing Committees which review expenditures. The Reports on Plans and Priorities are also available to the general public.

After being tabled, the Main Estimates are submitted to the House of Commons Standing Committees for review. The committees draw on the Reports on Plans and Priorities as the starting point for their reviews of the Estimates which they conclude by the end of June.

In late spring the Cabinet assesses the results of the last budget and identifies priorities and reallocations of resources drawing on the advice of the policy committees. The strategy determined by the Cabinet guides the preparation of the budget for the coming fiscal year.

During the summer, departments and agencies prepare the Main Estimates of expenditure for the coming fiscal year. It is also during this period that the Department of Finance, the Privy Council Office, and the Treasury Board work together to begin to develop and analyze budget strategies (fiscal targets respecting deficit or surplus, new spending, spending reductions, revenues and taxes, the expected performance of the economy), which will form the basis of the Minister of Finance's consultation late in the year with the provinces and others. These consultation strategies are then reviewed by the Cabinet.

Departments are also required to prepare, during the summer and early fall, Performance Reports. These reports cover a department's operations up to the previous March 31 (the end of the fiscal year) and are intended to provide information on results actually achieved in its various lines of activity.[3] These reports are tabled in the House of Commons in the fall and are referred to the appropriate Standing Committees, which review them and report their conclusions to the House. In this way, the views of the committees are made known to the government as it carries out its fall budget consultations. The objective of this practice was to enhance the role of the Standing Committees, giving them an opportunity to influence spending plans and priorities in the next and subsequent fiscal years.

During the last quarter of the year, the Treasury Board reviews the Estimates. At the same time, the Minister of Finance prepares consultation documents based on earlier discussions, which provide information on the economy, expenditure targets, and fiscal policies. The Minister releases the budget consultation papers to his provincial counterparts and to the House of Commons Standing Committee on Finance and begins consultation with these parties along with the general public and others. The Finance Minister then determines the budget strategy, drawing on the inputs of the provinces, the recommendations of the Standing Committee on Finance and the Cabinet policy committees, and the expenditure reductions and reallocations proposed by the Treasury Board from its review of the Estimates.

In early winter the Cabinet reviews and finalizes the budget strategy, including fiscal targets, new spending initiatives, reallocations, and reductions. The Finance Department finalizes the budget documents and the Treasury Board finalizes the Main Estimates, incorporating late budget changes if possible.

The Minister of Finance delivers the budget speech and the President of the Treasury Board tables the Estimates, following which the cycle begins again with the Treasury Board requesting departments to begin preparing their Business Plans and Reports on Plans and Priorities.

As the above budgetary cycle illustrates, the budgetary process is an ongoing process involving expenditure program planning and review, priority determination, new expenditure initiatives, expenditure reductions, reallocation of resources among programs, establishment of expenditure targets and the budget balance (surplus or deficit), and tax policy.

Once the budget preparation cycle is complete it remains for Parliament to authorize and appropriate spending as set out in the budget, for Revenue Canada to collect tax and other revenues, and for the Auditor General to conduct a post-expenditure audit. These features of the financial management system, along with other key budget phases and functions of central financial agencies, are discussed in greater detail below.

Features of the Budgetary System

Budget Documents

Budget Plan. The Budget Plan is a document tabled by the Minister of Finance when he presents his budget speech, along with several other documents. It is the product of medium-to long-term planning and contains the budget strategy including fiscal targets, policy priorities, spending initiatives, and resource reallocations. It presents information and data on expenditure and revenue trends and the outlook for program spending, tax revenues, the budget balance, economic growth, employment, inflation, interest rates and other aspects of the economy for the coming fiscal year and one year thereafter.

The Budget Plan highlights government priorities and new spending initiatives in the priority areas. For example, in the February 1998 Budget Plan, the government placed priority on expanding access to knowledge and skills needed for better job opportunities and on assistance to low-income families with children. Consequently, new spending initiatives focussed on financial assistance to post-secondary students by establishing a Canada Millennium Scholarship Fund and offering further tax concessions to students. For families with children, the Canada Child Tax Benefit program was enriched and deductions for child care expenses were increased.

In essence, the Budget Plan is the culmination of the deliberations of the key players in the budget preparation process including the Cabinet and Cabinet policy committees, the Department of Finance and Treasury Board, departments and agencies, and the consultation process initiated by the Minister of Finance.

The Estimates. The estimates of expenditure of the various government departments and agencies communicate to Parliament the nature and level of the government's expenditures and provide information to support its request for authority to spend public funds. The Estimates are tabled in the House of Commons by the President of the Treasury Board on March 1. They consist of three parts, each providing successively more information on government expenditure plans.

Part I, titled *The Government Expenditure Plan and Highlights by Ministry*, provides an overview of federal spending and describes the relationship of the Estimates to the expenditure plan as set out in the budget.

Part II is simply entitled *Estimates*, and traditionally is known as the "Blue Book." It forms the basis of parliamentary authorization of spending through the Appropriations Act. It lists the resources that departments and agencies, presented in alphabetical order, require in the upcoming fiscal year for their operations.

Part III consists of individual department and agency reports. Each department prepares a spring planning document called the Report on Plans and Priorities and a fall report on performance called the Performance Report. As outlined earlier, the Report on Plans and Priorities highlight trends in departmental spending, changes in activities, and planned reallocations of resources to higher priority programs. The Reports are intended to assist the House Standing Committees in fulfilling their function of examining future-year expenditure trends and priorities. The Performance Reports cover operations up to the end of the previous fiscal year. They are expected to explain the programs of the department, discuss the strategies used to meet objectives, explain what exactly is to be accomplished over the three-year planning period and at what cost, and describe what has been accomplished within the context of previously stated expectations. These Reports are examined by the House Standing Committees, which use the information as input during the fall budget consultations.

The format of the Estimates has been revised under the revamped Expenditure Management System. The former activity structure, in which the main program of a department was broken down into activities, is being replaced by a business and service line structure. The new structure follows a department's main roles with each business line reflecting a role. The expenditures of each business line is then detailed by service lines and where appropriate by capital projects and by transfer payments. This structure is illustrated in Table 7-2 for Transport Canada.

The business lines of Transport Canada reflect its four main roles; namely policy, safety and security, programs and divesture, and departmental administration. Each business line or role is then described by the services provided by the department in each role. These include aviation, marine, railway, and road safety as well as other services. Capital projects in each service are also shown. The expenditures as classified by business line, service line, and capital projects are shown for the coming fiscal year (NY), plus the next two years.

The expenditures of the department are also classified by spending authority or Appropriation Vote numbers. There are three standard categories of authorities; namely, operating expenditures, capital expenditures, and grants and contributions, plus supplementary categories (which may differ among departments). Each category is assigned an appropriation or vote number, which forms the basis for the annual parliament vote of supply — that is, the approval of expenditures and appropriation of funds. Certain other expenditures that have been authorized by separate statute do not require annual parliamentary approval through the Appropriation Act. These expenditures are identified as statutory or "S" in the Estimates and changes to them require an amendment to the statute that authorized them. Expenditures classified by spending authority are shown in the Estimates for the current fiscal year and the coming fiscal year. The appropriation vote numbers serve parliamentary controls — once the expenditure is authorized and the appropriation made, funds cannot be transferred from operations under one vote number to operations under another without the approval of Parliament.

Another form of presentation of the department's expenditures is by the standard objects classification. There are thirteen of these objects, such as wages and salaries, materials and supplies, professional and special services, repair and maintenance, and rentals. These objects identify inputs, that is, expenditures in terms of personnel, goods, and services purchased and necessary for the operations of the department.

Departmental plans and expenditures are presented in this format in the Main Estimates, in the departmental Report on Plans

**TABLE 7-2: Expenditure Estimates Format
Transport Canada 1997-98 (NY)**

Transport Canada Estimates
Planned Expenditure by Business Line　　　　NY　NY + 1　NY + 2
        Policy
        Safety and Security
        Programc and Divocturc
        Departmental Administration

Safety and Security
  Expenditure by Service line
    Service Lines
      Aviation safety
      Marine safety
      Railway safety
      Transport dangerous goods
Capital Projects
  Safety and Security
    Aviation oafoty
      Automated weather observation system
Standard Objects　　　　　　　　　　　　CY　NY　　NY + 1　NY + 2
  Salaries and wages
  Materials and supplies
Department Spending Authorities　　　　　　　　　　　CY　　NY + 1
Vote
  1 Operating expenditures
  5 Capital expenditures
  10 Grants and contributions

Source: Canada, Treasury Board, *Transport Canada, 1997-98 Estimates, A Report on Plans and Priorities*, (Ottawa: 1997).

and Priorities, and in the departmental Performance Reports. In addition to data, the Report on Plans and Priorities contains considerable narrative on the goals and plans of the department and information on business and service line operations. Similarly the Performance Report describes the results achieved in each of the various business and service lines.

The Role of the Treasury Board

The Treasury Board occupies a unique position in the budgetary system of Canada.[4] Created in 1867 by an order-in-council as a committee of the Queen's Privy Council of Canada, it was given a statutory basis by the Department of Finance Act, 1869, which empowered it to act "on all matters relating to Finance, Revenue, Expenditure or Public Accounts, which may be referred to it by Council."[5] At that time, it consisted of the Minister of Finance as chairman and three other members of the Privy Council and was served by a staff organization or secretariat within the Department of Finance.

An 1885 amendment to the Department of Finance Act increased board membership from four to six. In 1967, a new Cabinet portfolio of President of the Treasury Board was created, and the secretariat was transferred out of the Finance Department to form a separate department. The board currently consists of the president, the Minister of Finance as an ex officio member, and four other Cabinet ministers.

The Treasury Board has been described as "an inner Cabinet on financial and administrative policy."[6] Its role did not develop in a planned or systematic fashion, however, but evolved slowly, moulded by the exigencies of the times, until the board emerged as the central financial control agency in the government's administrative structure and the managerial arm of the executive. Its traditional function has centred on allocating among competing uses the limited resources at the government's disposal and on using them efficiently. In essence, the board performs a function in government similar to that of the price mechanism found in the market economy, and this function stems from its key position and role in the budget system. In addition, the Treasury Board is responsible for establishing the government's personnel policy and representing the government in collective bargaining. The Treasury Board has two administrative arms: the Treasury Board Secretariat and the Office of the Comptroller General.

The Treasury Board secretariat conducts comprehensive examinations of the departments' proposed expenditures, as contained in the multi-year plans and the main Estimates. This review concentrates on whether programs and activities are consistent with previously approved strategies and policies; whether expenditures for programs are within approved resource levels; and whether cost estimates are realistic and reflect the most efficient use of resources. During this review process, the performance and efficiency of operations within departments are also examined. If the secretariat judges that estimates are inflated or inadequate justification has been provided, it is likely to recommend a reduction in estimated expenditures.

Following a review of the secretariat's recommendations, the Treasury Board submits the approved Estimates to the Cabinet for ratification. The ratified Estimates are forwarded to the departments and agencies, which adjust their operational plans for any changes made during the review process.

After final approval by the Cabinet, the expenditure Estimates are presented to and tabled in Parliament on March 1.

The Treasury Board is concerned with efficiency in government administration as part of its function of financial supervision. In 1978, this function was strengthened with the creation of the Office of Comptroller General within the board secretariat. The Comptroller General, a deputy minister, was made responsible to the President of the Treasury Board for the promotion of improved financial management techniques and reporting systems in government, including adequate accounting procedures, improved cash management, and procedures for program evaluation.

More specifically, the Comptroller General's responsibility includes the development of government-wide policies on financial and operational administration, internal audit and related planning, and reporting control systems. Considerable emphasis has been placed on the need for program and activity evaluation within departments, and the Comptroller General provides guidelines for this purpose. The Comptroller General's office is also responsible for monitoring the departmental actions in response to the Auditor General and Public Accounts Committee reports.

Review and Appropriation by Parliament

Parliament is constitutionally vested with the ultimate responsibility for the control of public funds; section 53 of the Constitution Act provides that all financial bills, revenue, and appropriation must originate in the House of Commons. This requirement is further clarified in the Financial Administration Act, which stipulates that no payments may be made out of the Consolidated Revenue Fund without the authority of Parliament. Yet only the executive collectively can introduce money bills into the House; in this respect, it is Cabinet that is responsible for the direction and use of government funds.

The three parts of the expenditure Estimates are tabled by the President of the Treasury Board in the House of Commons, which immediately refers them to standing committees for a detailed examination. Various House standing committees, each generally consisting of ten to fifteen elected members from all parties, specialize in particular major functions of government. Thus, the Standing Committee on Agriculture reviews the estimates of Agriculture Canada, and the Standing Committee on Transport and Communications examines the estimates of the Department of Transport. The work of scrutinizing the government's Estimates is done in these committees, which are empowered to call the minister and the officials of the department concerned to give evidence on its plans, operations, and expenditures. They can recommend changes in the Estimates but do not have the power to effect changes.

The standing committees are given three months (March, April, and May) to complete their examination of the Estimates. Then they must report to the House. On the last day of May, committees which have not formally approved their Estimates are deemed to have reported them unchanged. Upon receipt of the Estimates the House conducts a general debate on government policy and departmental operations. That debate occurs during the twenty-five days allotted to "business of supply" which are allocated as follows: thirteen days before the end of June, five days in the fall, and seven days before the end of the fiscal year. The days need not be consecutive. The minister of each department is responsible for explaining departmental policies and objectives and answering questions. Collectively, the Cabinet is responsible for the general budget of expenditure, but individually each minister is responsible for the administration of his or her department and the implementation of its programs.

The approval of the expenditures is followed by the introduction of the appropriations bill, which is subject to three short, formal readings in the House and passed. After being considered by the Senate, it is signed by the Governor General and becomes an act of Parliament.

The three-part expenditure Estimates document contains the major estimates of government expenditure, but they are by no means the only ones submitted to Parliament. Several sets of supplementary Estimates are usually presented during the course of the fiscal year. Since each department must prepare its estimate of expenditure for the following year at the beginning of the current fiscal year, the Main Estimates are frequently incomplete. Departments discover that original Estimates did not provide for some needed items and requests on other items were insufficient. (This is certain to be the case if a change in government policy calls for increased activity and services and consequently increased expenditure.) The supplementary Estimates must be submitted to the Treasury Board, and follow the review routine discussed earlier. It is through supplementary Estimates that a certain degree of flexibility is maintained in the expenditure side of the budget.

Since the Main Estimates are not approved by Parliament until some time after the beginning of the fiscal year on April 1 and since appropriations for the preceding fiscal year lapse on March 31, provision must be made to carry on the functions of government until the main appropriations bill is enacted. This is accomplished by interim bills, which grant a fraction of each of the tabled Estimates to meet expenses in the new fiscal year until the main bill is passed. An interim supply act is complete in itself and remains operative even if Parliament refuses to appropriate the Main

Estimates of one or more of the departments concerned.

As already noted, the Constitution requires that any expenditure of public money from the Consolidated Revenue Fund be made only on the authority of Parliament. The federal government adheres to their provision with one exception: the use of Governor General's warrants for meeting unforeseen and emergency expenditures. The Consolidated Revenue and Audit Act, 1878, authorized the use of Governor General's warrants, and this provision was re-enacted in the Financial Administration Act. The government has this authority only when Parliament is not in session or is adjourned sine die, and such warrants must be presented to the House of Commons within fifteen days after the commencement of the next session. The Financial Administration Act stipulates that amounts granted by warrants must be included in, not additional to, the next appropriation act. Expenditures covered by warrants are, therefore, subjected to a post facto approval by Parliament.

Over the years there has been considerable debate on the effectiveness of the House of Commons in its authority over government spending. It has been contended that the House of Commons' review of the Estimates amounts to simply rubber stamping what the government has already decided. Prior to 1968 the Main Estimates were examined by the House in Committee of the Whole. Reform in 1968 referred the Estimates automatically to the appropriate standing committees. In 1993 the House of Commons Liaison Committee on Committee Effectiveness concluded that "the practical effect of this reform has been to reduce the impact of parliamentary debate on government expenditure to the point where it is virtually non-existent."[7] The Liaison Committee found that the Standing Committees saw "little point in committing precious time to reviewing estimates that will not be modified as long as the Government has a majority."[8] The 1968 rule changes

"made it virtually impossible for Members to carry out effectively their responsibility for scrutinizing government expenditures."[9] The Liaison Committee recommended that members of the House be provided with an opportunity to offer their views on expenditures before all decisions on the Estimates had been made. As a result the House rules were modified in 1994 to enhance the role of Parliament in the budget process. The new rules authorized the Standing Committees to receive the Reports of Plans and Priorities of departments outlining their expenditure goals, plans, and spending priorities. These Plans provide a context for the committees' traditional role of reviewing and reporting on spending proposals in Estimates for the current fiscal year.

The House Standing Committees also receive the departmental Performance Reports, submitted in the fall of each year, which cover departmental operations up to the end of the previous fiscal year. As explained earlier, the committees use the information from the spring and fall departmental reports to prepare submissions which contribute to the budget consultation process. Another development designed to strengthen Parliament's involvement in the expenditure preparation process was the submission of the budget consultation papers, prepared by the Minister of Finance, to the House Standing Committee on Finance. These papers form the basis for hearings that the Standing Committee holds during the late fall to consider and report on the budget proposals. The Cabinet and the Minister of Finance are expected to take into account the reports of the Standing Committees in developing the upcoming budget.

Administration of Spending

Following the appropriation of funds by Parliament, each department is required to submit to the Treasury Board a division of each appropriation into allotments, generally based on the expenditure classification detailed in Part II of the Estimates. The release of funds from the Consolidated Revenue Fund and the consequent spending is made in accordance with this allotment division. Only on Treasury Board approval may funds be transferred from one allotment to another; doing so is generally a routine board operation. Under no circumstances, however, may funds be transferred between appropriations without parliamentary approval.

The Minister of Public Works and Government Services is designated as the Receiver General for Canada, responsible for the Consolidated Revenue Fund and for releasing funds to departments on request. The funds are released following a pre-audit by the deputy minister of each department, certifying that the amounts requested are in accordance with the appropriations and allotments authorized.

Another responsibility of this Ministry is the preparation of the Public Accounts of Canada. Released at the end of the calendar year, they include a report on the financial transactions of the fiscal year, statements of revenue and expenditures, and statements of the government's assets and liabilities, together with financial reports of Crown corporations.

Revenue Determination and the Budget Speech

The determination of expected government revenues is closely related to forecasts of economic conditions. Responsibility for these forecasts rests with the Department of Finance, working in close liaison with other government departments and agencies such as Statistics Canada and the Bank of Canada. From the information obtained, the Finance Department estimates the yield of various revenue sources in the coming fiscal year and determines the effects upon revenues of possible tax changes. These estimates are included in the budget plan.

The budget speech, presented by the Minister of Finance to the House of Commons, brings together estimated expenditures and revenues and introduces proposals for changes in taxation. Historically, there was no set date for the budget speech. In recent years, attempts have been made to establish an early calendar-year date (February); it has not been uncommon, however, for the minister to present two budgets within a fiscal year as changing economic conditions force changes in economic and taxation policies.

Most budget speeches follow a standard pattern in form and presentation. They begin with a general review of the country's economic and financial conditions and government economic policy during the previous year. An outline of proposed government policies follows. Finally comes an outline of the government's fiscal position, including proposals for tax changes and the effect they are expected to have on the budget and the economy. Estimates of revenues are compared with the expenditure estimates, and the size of the surplus or deficit is predicted.

Following the presentation of the budget speech, the House holds a debate, which is limited to six days (not necessarily consecutive). It provides an opportunity for the members to discuss government policy in financial and economic matters, such as unemployment, economic growth, and taxation.

The budget speech document is frequently accompanied by supplementary budget papers. There are generally papers explaining budget proposals in greater detail and a notice of ways and means motion containing the proposed amendments to existing tax legislation. Major government policy initiatives may also be presented as papers accompanying the budget speech.

Traditionally, proposals for tax changes are made only during the presentation of the budget speech. There have been notable exceptions, however, with tax changes introduced by the Minister of Finance, not in a budget, but in an economic statement to the House. No matter how introduced, proposed tax changes are presented to the House as tax bills, which are required to go through the usual three readings before passage. Tax changes consisting of amendments to existing legislation can, however, be made effective immediately upon the introduction of the resolutions in Parliament during the budget speech if the government so desires.

Responsibility for the administration of tax legislation — that is, control and management of all internal taxes and levies — rests with Revenue Canada. The department has two components — taxation, and customs and excise — each of which is administered as an independent department. All revenue collected is deposited in the central Consolidated Revenue Fund.

Budget Secrecy

Traditionally, the budget speech has been prepared under a cloak of secrecy, and any leaks prior to its presentation were viewed as extremely serious, leading to demands for the resignation of the Finance Minister. For example, Minister of Finance Marc Lalonde was severely criticized by the opposition parties in the House of Commons when part of a page of his April 1983 budget was photographed during a pre-budget meeting with the news media.

This concept of secrecy originated at a time when the main concern of the budget was taxes and tariffs; the government wanted to keep changes secret until they were announced in order to prevent anyone from financially profiting from advance knowledge. By the 1980s, however, the budget had become a complex document dealing with a large variety of economic and social issues on which consultation between government and elements of the private and public sectors was considered desirable. The need for a more open approach was officially addressed in a 1982 green paper, *The Budget Process — A Paper on Budget Secrecy and Proposals for Broader Consultation*. The paper contained recommendations for more openness and consultation, including the establishment of

task forces to analyze proposed budget measures and the presentation of pre-budget position papers for public discussion.

In his February 1984 budget the Minister of Finance reported that most of the green paper proposals had been implemented and that his budget had been "characterized by a dramatic increase in the use of task forces, advisory committees, discussion papers, draft legislation, and technical explanatory notes"[10] to provide better understanding and debate over budget proposals. The Minister reported that consultations on a variety of tax and economic issues had been held before and after his previous budget and had continued through the preparation of the budget at hand; organizations representing labour, business, farm groups, and others had participated and he reported that such meetings were accepted as an integral part of the budget process. The minister emphasized, however, that precautions would continue to be taken to ensure that no one could profit from advance knowledge of proposed tax and tariff measures.

This position on budget secrecy was repeated in 1985 in a white paper entitled *The Canadian Budgetary Process: Proposals for Improvement*. It stated:

> The government believes that the fundamental rationale for budget secrecy now, as always, is to prevent the possibility of profit from advance knowledge about matters to be announced in a budget .... [but] ... this commitment to budget secrecy should not be incompatible with government intentions to involve the public more meaningfully in the budgetary process.[11]

Consultations with outside parties were continued, with efforts to obtain public input without compromising the principle of secrecy that the traditionalists and successive governments continued to emphasize.

The government suffered a major embarrassment in 1989 when the 1989/90 budget came into the hands of the news media one day prior to its planned presentation in the House of Commons. The incident could serve as the plot for an espionage movie. On the eve of the budget day, the Global Television office in Toronto received an anonymous call from someone who claimed to have a copy of the budget and wished to make it available to the network at no charge. A rendezvous between the caller and Doug Small, Global's Ottawa bureau chief, was arranged. Two cars met momentarily in the parking lot of a west-end Ottawa gasoline station, a parcel was exchanged, and the mysterious messenger drove off. Inside the parcel was a copy of the summary "budget in brief." Small read the document on the network's 7:00 p.m. news telecast.

A panicky and highly embarrassed government decided that it must present the budget immediately. Since the House of Commons had adjourned for the day, Finance Minister Wilson called a late-evening press conference; at it, he presented the highlights of his budget, although by this time the entire country was already aware of the contents. In the days following, the opposition parties clamoured for Wilson's resignation over the budget leak. The Finance Minister refused, arguing that the leak was a breach of trust. Prime Minister Brian Mulroney went further, declaring over national television that the document had been stolen and a crime committed. The Royal Canadian Mounted Police immediately launched an investigation and then, amid allegations from some of its own members of political interference, charged Small and two other people with possession of stolen goods. After weeks of court hearings, the judge dismissed the case, calling the prosecution an abuse of the judicial process. No theft had occurred. The document in question was one of a pile of misprinted copies that had been dumped into a trash container at the government printing plant and had been retrieved by a recycling-firm worker. It remained for Small to put the whole bizarre episode into perspective: asked if he would leak a federal budget again, he replied, "Darn tootin."[12]

This incident clearly demonstrated the difficulties of maintaining budgetary secrecy, given the many opportunities for leaks as the budget is prepared, printed, distributed, and finally presented. It also further undermined a practice that many have argued is outdated and unnecessary. An examination of the federal budgets for the last several years shows very few measures that could have produced significant financial gains from advance knowledge. Consultations during the preparation of the budget have now become a standard practice, as outlined earlier, with the release and discussions on the budget consultation papers initiated each fall by the Minister of Finance. The Standing Committee on Finance is also a forum for interested parties to be heard, and its hearings and subsequent report are an important reference in preparing the budget. The only budget items that are still kept under wraps are tax changes which might affect financial markets and from which parties could profit if they were aware of the proposals in advance.

Many of the proposals in the February 1998 budget, for example, were being hinted at or made openly public by government officials before the date of the budget presentation. The Millennium Scholarship Fund for post-secondary students had been announced along with other measures to assist students, the Minister of Finance and other government members had suggested the need for tax relief for low-income groups, and had also indicated that the budget would be balanced.[13]

Office of the Auditor General

The final stage of the budgetary cycle is the audit of financial transactions. Following the collection and disbursement of public funds, the Auditor General conducts a post-audit of the financial transactions and reports the findings to the House of Commons. Although appointed by the Governor in Council, the Auditor General is independent of the executive and answers only to the House. The Auditor General Act requires that the Auditor General examine government accounts and report instances of misuse or mismanagement of public funds, fraud, over-expenditure of appropriations, expenditures not authorized by Parliament, and other irregularities; make observations on the economy and efficiency of departmental operations; and assess procedures within departments for measuring the effectiveness of their expenditure programs. Through this post-audit, the House receives a full accounting for the manner in which approved budgetary plans are administered.

The Auditor General's annual report is normally tabled in the House of Commons simultaneously with the public accounts to which it relates. These two documents are then referred to the Public Accounts Committee for review. In examining the accounts, that committee may call the Auditor General to give evidence and public officials to explain and justify the operations of their departments and account for inefficiencies or mismanagement.

The office of the Auditor General, created in 1877, is one of the oldest agencies in the federal government. Although the Auditor General is officially appointed by the Governor in Council, the office is an agency of the House of Commons and responsible directly to it.

Until 1977, the Office of the Auditor General operated under the provisions of the Financial Administration Act. The Auditor was responsible for examining the government accounts to ensure that they were properly kept, that all public money was fully accounted for, and that public funds were expended in accordance with parliamentary appropriations.

In 1977, the functions of the office were expanded with passage of the Auditor General Act. Two significant changes were the extension of the traditional role of the Auditor to include a value-for-money evaluation and the introduction of a cyclical approach to comprehensive auditing for Parliament.

The legislation sets value for money as the criterion for the Auditor General's examination of government expenditure accounts. This kind of audit focuses on the adequacy of financial management and control systems departments employ to gauge the economy, efficiency, and effectiveness of their programs and activities. The objective is an assessment of government progress in these three areas.

Economy refers to the terms and conditions under which personnel and material resources are acquired; an economical operation is one that acquires appropriate quality and quantity at minimum cost. Efficiency relates to inputs and outputs; an efficient operation is one that produces the maximum output for any set of resource inputs. Effectiveness concerns the extent to which a program achieves its stated objectives. In the value-for-money audit, however, the Auditor General does not question the appropriateness of departmental program and activity goals or the values underlying them; thus the Auditor does not really measure effectiveness. Rather, the mandate is to determine if departments have established satisfactory procedures for measuring and reporting the effectiveness of programs. This restriction protects the Auditor General from political issues and partisan political debate.

The cyclical, comprehensive audit approach represents a considerable change from the traditional transactions audit, which focussed on improprieties in the management of public funds. Parliamentary review of such findings tended to be time-consuming and controversial and did not facilitate or contribute to members' understanding of the strengths and weaknesses of the financial administrative system or the management of public funds. The cyclical, comprehensive audit requires the Auditor General to do a detailed examination of each major department or agency at least once every four years. The objective is to provide Parliament with information that will facilitate members' understanding of the general effectiveness of departmental operations and financial control systems. (The four-year period was selected because it coincides with the average life of Parliament.)

These changes in the audit functions have, to a degree, made the office of the Auditor General an agency of change and improvement in government financial administration. In addition to disclosing deficiencies in the management of public funds, the Auditor General provides concrete, written recommendations for improvements in administration, achievement of economies, increased efficiency, and enhanced program results. Although the Auditor General cannot impose any suggestions for improvements on the government, the office can exert considerable influence by working closely with the Comptroller General and the Public Accounts Committee.

Features of Provincial and Local Government Budgeting

Provinces

Many of the budgetary and financial practices found at the provincial level of government parallel those existing in the federal government. Departments are required to prepare estimates of expenditures for each fiscal year and submit them to Cabinet for approval, which in turn must present them to the legislature for authorization. A number of provinces have established Cabinet committees and treasury boards or central financial screening agencies, similar to the federal Treasury Board. Provincial offices of auditor general or comptroller general exist to perform pre-audits and post-audits. Most provinces have established requirements for the government and individual ministries to report performance information to the legislative assemblies. In general, public accounts are prepared and tabled in the provincial legislatures, which have established public accounts committees to review the accounts, together with audit reports.

Provincial governments have experimented with a variety of budgeting systems: planning-programming-budgeting, management by objectives, management by results, and program-based management information. (Outlined in the appendix to this chapter).

Local Government Jurisdictions

The administrative jurisdictions established by provinces for purposes of governing generally consist of cities, towns, townships, villages, and municipalities. (The term "municipality" frequently refers to a rural jurisdiction.) All of these various jurisdictions are grouped under the term "local government," although they range from small villages to huge cities.

Local governments are the creations of the provincial government and have only those powers granted them by it. With hundreds of such governments, the provinces must impose control to maintain a degree of uniformity and order in financial management. Consequently, provincial governments prescribe some basic local government budget features and procedures.

Budgeting at this level varies depending on the organization of the local government. It generally consists of an elected council, committees of the council, a treasurer, and various departments and boards. Each year the departments and boards submit expenditure estimates to the treasurer or commissioner of finance, who submits them to council. These estimates are reviewed by the council or its finance committee and are revised as the council sees fit, although its authority to alter the estimates of some boards is limited. Where there is a board of control or a city manager, the estimates are first reviewed by these offices before submission to council. As in the case of their higher counterparts, these governments are required to have their accounts audited at the end of the fiscal year.

In general, local governments distinguish between current and capital budgets for the purpose of finance. Long-term borrowing is mainly restricted for capital budgets and is also subject to provincial approval. Local governments may also engage in short-term borrowing to finance current expenditures, but as a rule it is reserved to provide financing pending receipt of taxes; borrowing for this purpose is frequently done by promissory note.

The current budgets of local governments generally follow the widely accepted format of classification of expenditures by function or department and agency, by program and activity, and by items of expenditures. Like their higher-level counterparts, these jurisdictions have attempted various versions of budget systems: program and performance budgeting, zero-base budgeting, and management by objectives. In essence, however, most local government follow incremental budgeting for current operations. Expenditures are presented for the current fiscal year along with estimates for the new year and corresponding changes from one year to the next.

Capital budgets are usually prepared over a multi-year (often five-year) period and are updated annually, representing a long-term plan for capital works. Capital projects are given priorities. Also outlined are methods of finance, which may take the form of provincial government grants and loans, revenues from current taxes and reserves, or proceeds from debentures sold in the capital market. The provincial governments exercise control over the capital budgets of local governments, their borrowing, and the debts incurred. Requirements and methods vary among the provinces, but the objectives are similar. In Ontario, for example, control is exercised by the Ontario Municipal Board. Its approval is required for any local government expenditure to be financed by borrowing. Limitations are placed on the terms of repayment for debentures and on the total debt outstanding. As a general rule, the debt outstanding is not permitted to exceed 25 percent of taxable assessment.

The structure of local government has been subject to change in recent years. In many provinces there has been a trend towards larger geographical jurisdictions with the establishment of regional districts and regional governments and mega cities. These larger jurisdictions offer a local authority a wider revenue base but at the same time require more extensive budgetary planning to service these jurisdictions.

Summary

The financial structure and the functions of key central budgetary agencies of the federal government are governed by statute and some of the practices date to the time of Confederation. The budget is prepared under the direction of the Cabinet for final appropriation of expenditures and approval of revenue measures by Parliament. Central agencies which have key roles in the budgetary process are the Department of Finance, which is responsible for the fiscal framework, budget strategy, tax measures, and the preparation of budget documents; the Treasury Board, which reviews departmental expenditure plans and estimates and helps determine resource allocation; and the Office of the Auditor General, which conducts a post-audit of expenditures and a value-for-money evaluation of departmental operations.

The budgetary process is an ongoing one of annually repeated phases in a budgetary cycle beginning with the budget speech and the tabling of the Main Estimates. Departments prepare their expenditure plans and priorities which are reviewed by Cabinet policy committees, the Cabinet, and Treasury Board. Preparation and review of the Main Estimates follows. After the examination and appropriation of the expenditure Estimates by the House of Commons, the departments proceed to implement their programs and activities. A record of the government's financial transactions are maintained by the Receiver General for Canada and published in the Public Accounts of Canada.

Budget strategy, including expenditure targets, new spending initiatives, expenditure reductions, and the balance on the budget is the product of the budget consultation process involving the Cabinet, Cabinet policy committees, Treasury Board, the House Standing Committee on Finance, the Department of Finance, and interested outside parties. This consultation process has reduced although not eliminated the historical secrecy surrounding the contents of the budget.

Provincial budget practices parallel those of the federal government, and the essential elements of responsible financial planning and control are also found at the local government level.

NOTES

[1] Information on the budgetary process of the federal government can be found in Canada, Treasury Board, *The Role of the Treasury Board and the Office of the Comptroller General* (Ottawa: 1992), cat. BT22-24/1992; Treasury Board, *The Expenditure Management System of the Government of Canada* (Ottawa: 1995) cat. BT22-37/1995; and *Report of the Auditor General of Canada*, chapter 5, "Report-

ing Performance in the Expenditure Management System" (Ottawa: 1997), cat. FAI-1997/1-SE.

[2] See, for example, Canada, Treasury Board, *Transport Canada, 1997-98 Estimates, A Report on Plans and Priorities* (Ottawa: 1997).

[3] See, for example, Canada, *Treasury Board, Transport Canada, Performance Report, For the period ending March 31, 1997* (Ottawa: 1997), cat. BT31-4/14-1997.

[4] For a detailed examination of the development of the role of the Treasury Board, see J.C. Strick and W.L. White, *Policy, Politics and the Treasury Board in Canadian Government* (Toronto: Science Research Associates, 1970).

[5] Norman Ward, *The Public Purse* (Toronto: University of Toronto Press, 1964), p.212.

[6] *Statutes of Canada*, 1869, ch.4.

[7] Canada, House of Commons, *Report of the Liaison Committee on Committee Effectiveness*, 1993, p.7.

[8] *Ibid.*, p.9.

[9] *Ibid.*, p.10.

[10] Canada, Department of Finance, *Budget Papers*, February 15, 1984, p.33.

[11] Canada Department of Finance, *The Canadian Budgetary Process: Proposals for Improvement*, May, 1985, p.27.

[12] *Ottawa Citizen*, July 17, 1990, p.1.

[13] A summary of the budget contents that had been made public or had been indicated by the government was reported in the news media. See *The Globe and Mail*, February 24, 1998.

FINANCIAL MANAGEMENT SYSTEMS IN GOVERNMENT

As noted throughout chapter 7, a number of management systems have been developed over the years to promote efficiency in resource allocation, to improve operational performance, and to improve other aspects of financial management in government. Different systems have been in vogue at different times as earlier ones fell from favour and were replaced with new concepts or as old concepts were rediscovered and new labels attached to them. Basically, these systems are not mutually exclusive but in varying degrees are complementary. They differ primarily in their orientation and the emphasis each places on a particular aspect of the financial management process. For example, program budgeting emphasizes planning in government and the identification of program outputs; performance budgeting focuses on the measurement of performance or efficiency in government operations; management by objectives stresses the organizing of work to achieve specified objectives in a defined period of time; systems analysis consists of a variety of techniques for analyzing alternative uses of resources; zero-base budgeting emphasizes the review of programs and the establishment of priorities among program expenditure levels (packages); and the planning-programming-budgeting system (PPBS) emphasizes planning, the establishment of clearly defined objectives, the presentation of expenditures on the basis of programs and activities, the relation of resource inputs to output, and quantitative techniques for evaluating programs and alternatives and for measuring performance.

The Canadian government formally adopted PPBS in 1966. Attempts to improve some of its practical limitations led to further changes, including the introduction of the concept of expenditure envelopes in 1980. With these changes, the system became known as the Policy and Expenditure Management System (PEMS). Changes were made in this system with the introduction of a new Cabinet committee system in 1989. Further changes were introduced during the early admini-

stration of Prime Minister Jean Chretien's Liberal government that revised the Expenditure Management System. This appendix provides a chronology of the changes in financial administration practices in the federal government and the objectives they were designed to achieve.

Background

Until after the middle of this century, the estimates of Canadian government spending were prepared annually on the basis of the objects of expenditure. The major limitations of this process were the almost complete lack of formalized planning within departments, the absence of clearly enunciated objectives to which expenditures could be related, and the deficiency in quantitative justification of expenditure proposals. As result, expenditure review and control functions, such as those exercised by the Treasury Board, proved to be extremely difficult. Attention was focussed on inputs, rather than on outputs. Furthermore, there was a tendency to concentrate on the proposed increments to continuing programs, rather than on periodic examinations of entire programs. Without quantitative information and criteria, the expenditure review and priority-determining procedures developed into exercises in judgement with considerable arbitrariness in expenditure changes and reductions. The budgetary process produced a budget document that was a poor reflection of decisions made and did not permit the House of Commons to conduct meaningful scrutiny of proposed policy and consequent operational activity, resulting in a weakening of that body's traditional function as guardian of the public purse. Parliament did not focus on the real issues or objectives but concentrated on the incremental changes in expenditure items, which were trivial relative to total government spending.

Recognizing the need to modernize and improve its financial management system, the federal government undertook an extensive review of the system through the Royal Commission on Government Organization (the Glassco Commission).[1] In its 1962 report, the commission proposed sweeping changes in the budgetary process. Among its recommendations were planning departmental operations and identifying objectives; developing and applying objective criteria for evaluating alternates and reviewing performance; changing the form of the estimates and the allotment control system; and delegating increased authority to departments in the management of their financial operations.

Although the majority of the commission's financial recommendations were approved in principle by the government, its report was not taken as a rigid blueprint for change. Its importance stemmed from its philosophy; it served as a catalyst for change and the modernization of government financial administration. In the developments that followed, new techniques and possibilities were explored and adopted for improved effectiveness in budgeting, and these developments led to the formal acceptance and introduction of PPBS in 1966.[2]

Strengths and Shortcomings of PPBS

Some of the features of the PPBS approach in Canada included long-range planning and program submission, the classification of expenditures in the form of programs and activities, and the identification and explanation of program objectives. In addition, emphasis was placed on the development of quantitative techniques for evaluating programs and measuring performance. These features of PPBS were of primary concern to the Treasury Board and senior department managers to supplement judgement in decision making and permit a more objective evaluation of programs and operational performance.

Generally, the direction and intent of PPBS was to facilitate decision making and efficiency in management at all levels of government. It was designed to provide department administrators, individual ministers, the Treasury Board, Cabinet, and the House of Commons with a more orderly array of information as well as with more meaningful information. The manner in which information is presented by administrators may have a significant influence on the decisions made. Ideas for policy and advice on ministerial proposals come from the administrators, and both groups benefit from a more orderly system. Collectively

and individually, ministers can more effectively discharge their decision-making responsibilities on objectives and priorities if they possess relevant facts. The system also had the potential to assist Parliament in its traditional function of financial control, the effectiveness of which had occasionally been openly debated.

Although PPBS was widely acclaimed in theory, difficulties were encountered in its practical operation. The problems stemmed largely from the inappropriateness of an analysis-based system in a political, decision-making environment characterized by pressure groups, compromises, and political expediency. Other difficulties also reduced the effectiveness of the system. Successive reports of the Auditor General in the 1970s[3] pointed to a number of shortcomings in the operation of the federal government's PPBS and financial management in general: poor quality of data in the expenditure proposals; the Treasury Board's lack of intensive evaluation of continuing department programs; the departments' and board's lack of program analysts trained to apply analytical techniques; and deficient financial control within departments. One of the Auditor General's recommendations to improve financial management and control was the creation of the Office of Comptroller General.

The federal government's immediate response to the Auditor General's recommendations was to appoint the Royal Commission of Enquiry on the Financial Organization and Accountability in the Government of Canada (the Lambert Commission) in November 1976 to examine the structure, systems, and procedures whereby financial management and control were exercised and administrators held accountable for their administration.

The 1979 Lambert Commission report[4] concluded that financial planning and control in the federal government were clearly inadequate. Many of the commission's recommendations for improvement were accepted by the government and formed the basis of a reformed system, which was outlined in the December 1979 budget in a white paper entitled *The New Expenditure Management System*.[5] Most notable among the features of this system were the "envelope" or resource-sector concept, long-term forecasting of both revenues and expenditures, and comprehensive auditing.

The Policy and Expenditure Management System (PEMS)

The policy and expenditure management system was introduced in 1980 with the envelope concept, Cabinet policy committees, the establishment of expenditure limits for envelopes, and value-for-money assessments. Many other features of PEMS were carry overs from the earlier PPBS, including long-term planning, the program-activity format of budget estimates, the identification of program objectives, the development and use of analytical techniques for evaluating programs and performance, and an emphasis on program outputs.

The envelope concept was a primary feature of PEMS, designed to facilitate planning and Cabinet control of policy and expenditure. Within the federal government, ten policy sectors and corresponding resource envelopes were identified. The policy sectors consisted of major functions of government and groups of closely related function identified by departments, agencies, or programs. The envelopes defined the resources allocated to each policy sector and contained the estimated cost of existing and projected programs. It was the responsibility of Cabinet's Priorities and Planning Committee to determine an overall expenditure limit and government priorities among envelopes. If P & P identified an envelope as having priority, it would be allocated additional funds or "new policy" reserves. Once the expenditure limits were placed on the envelopes, it was the responsibility of the Cabinet policy committees to determine priorities within their respective envelopes and how any new policy reserves would be used.

Envelope priorities were established before detailed expenditure programs were developed, so proposed programs had to be in accordance with these priorities and within the fiscal constraints. Having expenditure limits on envelopes implied that choices had to be made among new program initiatives and among new and existing programs. The system was to provide opportunities to reduce or eliminate existing programs in order to free resources for new programs. Furthermore, expenditure limits over a multi-year period required that future costs of proposed and ongoing programs be considered in current decisions.

The grouping of related functions and programs into envelopes was intended to provide the Cabinet committee members with an opportunity to view the relationships among programs and program objectives and to facilitate comparison of the costs of programs and trends in these costs. The requirement that funds for new initiatives be generated from savings in existing programs was expected to provide each policy committee with an incentive to devote attention to systematic review and evaluation of programs within its envelope.

The PEMS decentralized budgetary decision making. Before the system was put in place, the P & P Committee would issue guidelines on expenditure priorities, which would be conveyed to the departments through the Treasury Board. The responsibility for interpreting the guidelines and ensuring that departments followed them, for effecting cost reductions, and for exercising general expenditure restraint fell on the Treasury Board, particularly on its secretariat. In contrast, the PEMS committee system assigned greater responsibility for these duties to the Cabinet policy committees and a much larger number of Cabinet ministers.

In part, PEMS had been introduced to correct some practical shortcomings in the PPB system, particularly in the expenditure planning and control phases of the budgetary process. There appears to be little evidence that PEMS achieved its objectives, however. Its introduction coincided with large increases in federal spending and heralded the beginning of the era of high government deficits. This should not, however, be attributed to the system per se. A budgeting system operates in a political environment and is subject to the whims of its users. Expenditure and deficit reduction in government, in the final analysis, can be achieved only if there is the political will to do so.

It could be argued that the decentralized system of decision making featured in PEMS involved too many Cabinet ministers and was, therefore, subjected to excessive pressures. Each policy committee member in essence wore two hats: one as a member of a committee directed to examine and control new policy and program proposals, and another as a member of an operating department who desired to obtain funding for expanding operations or new programs. The two were frequently in conflict.

Centralized Expenditure Management System

The Cabinet committee system introduced in 1989 centralized expenditure control in a newly created Expenditure Review Committee and in the Priorities and Planning Committee. It has been contended that the creation of the centralized system was driven primarily by financial crisis — the inability of the government to control the deficit. The system was geared to expenditure control in which the ERC targeted certain departments and programs for varying degrees of constraint or reduction. In effect, a department's spending authority was reduced, and it was then left to the department to determine the programs and personnel that had to be axed. All Cabinet committees — with the exception of Treasury Board, which is a statutory committee of the Privy Council and fulfills statutory duties — were placed under the Cabinet P & P Committee. The policy committees that were responsible for policy and spending priorities in their respective areas were stripped of financial responsibilities. Cash reserves, previously directed to policy sectors and allocated among priorities within the sectors as determined by these committees, were placed under the exclusive control of the ERC. In addition, all issues directed to P & P were first screened by an Operations Committee. The objective was to ensure that no new policy or expenditure proposal was submitted to P & P unless it was first examined and approved by the ERC. Thus, control was at the top with the Prime Minister, as chairperson of P & P and of the ERC, and the Deputy Prime Minister, as the chairperson of the Operations Committee. The effectiveness of this system in controlling expenditures, like that of the previous systems, depended, however, on political will and remained subject to the particular whims of the Prime Minister and a select group of Cabinet ministers. That the political will to control expenditures and the deficit was absent is reflected in the fact that program spending increased from $103.8 billion in 1989-90 to $122.6 billion by 1992-93 and the deficit rose from $29 billion to $41 billion over this period.

Revised Expenditure Management System

The newly elected Liberal government began in 1994 to revamp the Expenditure Management System to help the government meet its fiscal target of reducing expenditures and eventually bringing the budget into balance. In announcing changes to the system the government contended that it would improve strategic planning, would focus on critical reviews of existing programs to identify ineffi-

cient, low priority or obsolete programs, and would emphasize reallocation of resources from low to higher priority programs.[6] The central policy reserve was abolished so that new initiatives within departments had to be funded through reallocations from other programs. A Program Review process was initiated which required all departments to closely scrutinize their programs and activities to identify which activities the government could continue to support and which could be scaled back within a much reduced budget. Departments were required to prepare Business Plans and Reports on Plans and Priorities, which showed how they were managing programs with reduced resources. In addition, performance reporting was strengthened with the requirement that departments prepare full Performance Reports showing accomplishments up to the end of the previous fiscal year.

In essence, most of the earlier budgetary practices were carried over under the revised Expenditure Management System, with attempts to strengthen the planning and review process and the presentation of performance results. There were changes in terminology or budget jargon but without significant change in the substance of the practice described by the terminology. For example, the Budget Plan replaced the Fiscal Plan; the Business Plan and Report on Plans and Priorities replaced the Strategic Overview and the Operational Plan. Strategic Overviews and Operational Plans had been multi-year plans setting out a department's objectives, alternative strategies, proposed changes in programs and activities, performance measures, and trends. Business Plans and the Report on Plans and Priorities essentially provide similar information in a somewhat different manner. The focus is now on lines of business and services as opposed to lines of activities, and this is reflected in the change in the structure of the Estimates. Consider Transport Canada as an example. The previous system identified the department's program by activities which were: Policy and Co-ordination, Marine, Aviation, Airports, Surface, and Departmental Administration. This activity structure reflected the organizational structure of the department which featured a Marine Branch, an Aviation Branch, and so on. The new business line structure is designed to reflect the roles of the department. The lines of business, which replaced the activity lines, are: Policy, Safety and Security, Programs and Divesture, and

Departmental Administration. The expenditures in each business line are then classified by service lines. For example, Safety and Security is broken down into services such as Marine Safety and Aviation Safety, which focus on what the department is doing in the marine and aviation areas. In the earlier structure, these operations were presented as activities. Consequently, the new structure offers a different way of presenting and describing the departments operations, intended to provide clearer descriptions of mandate, mission, and operations.

One of the more meaningful changes in the budgetary process was the separation of Part III of the Estimates into a spring Report on Plans and Priorities and a fall Performance Report. The objective was to separate information on future plans from information on past performance, and was expected to draw more attention to the performance achieved by programs. In addition, the separation provides performance information on previous fiscal years several months earlier than before and does so in time to be used as input in the fall budget consultation process.

The revamped Expenditure Management System, as outlined earlier, also attempted to involve Parliament more actively in the budget process so that it could shed its label as a rubber stamp for budget expenditures. There is an attempt to provide shorter, more readable documents focusing on key strategies. The Auditor General, in his 1997 report, noted that in his consultations with Parliamentarians they expressed the view that the separation of planning and performance information was helpful and that the documents were more focussed and clearly organized than the previous Estimates Part III.[7]

Program Evaluation and Performance Measurement

Program evaluation has become an increasingly important element of government management systems. The nature of the federal government's program review and evaluation process has evolved from a focus primarily on inputs to an analysis of how resources are used, the objectives of programs, and the effectiveness of programs in achieving these objectives. There is an ever-increasing emphasis on outputs and the need for expanding and improving the information base on which budgetary decisions are made.

Program evaluation involves the formal assessment of programs and their results. The focus is on such basic elements as program rationale, impacts and effects, objectives achievement, alternatives, and cost effectiveness. Consideration of program rationale raises questions about the relevance of the objectives of the program and whether the program makes sense. The examination of impacts and effects and the analysis of objectives achievements concentrate on the results of the program and on whether the program achieved what was expected. In addition, analysts and policymakers examine alternatives to consider whether there are better, more cost-effective ways of achieving the results.

Benefit-cost analysis, one method of evaluating programs and projects, involves identifying, quantifying, and comparing benefits and costs in money terms. On the basis of criteria such as benefit-cost ratios or net benefits, priorities can be established among programs and uneconomical programs can be identified. Benefit-cost analysis has numerous limitations as a decision-making aid, however, and its practical usefulness is restricted primarily to "lumpy" capital projects for which benefits and costs can be realistically quantified. It is of little value in determining priorities between two functions of government or between two activities with large-scale but intangible benefits and costs. In such cases, judgements are made by the decision-maker responsible, with the political process as the ultimate judge of the value of the program.

Once the decision is made to implement a program and it becomes operational, there is a need for performance measurement to provide its administrators with information to monitor how well it is operating. These administrators do not possess indicators found in the business world, such as profits and returns on investment, and must develop other indicators. Government departments and agencies compile many kinds of information about performance, such as information on the economy with which resources are acquired, the efficiency with which they are transformed into goods and services, the quality and volume of outputs, productive and idle time, client demand for services, and the effectiveness of government operations in terms of their contributions to achieving the objectives of programs.

Economy and efficiency indicators are generally concerned with information relating resource inputs to outputs or results achieved, while effectiveness indicators relate results achieved to results planned. The former indicators often express the results-to-resources relationship in terms of output per unit of labour input and costs per output. Efficiency generally concerns the minimization of costs while maintaining an adequate level and quality of service. Effectiveness indicators depend on the nature of the program. Consider, for example, an occupational training program designed to increase the employability of unemployed and low-income workers. The training itself is the resources-related output, and the efficiency indicator would be the cost per workers trained. The effectiveness of the program, however, would be measured by the percentage of retrained workers who find training-related employment.[8] The fall Performance Reports submitted by departments are expected to include performance measures and data where feasible. Consider for example the Performance Report of Transport Canada for 1997. The section on the Rail Safety service included a description of activities, trends on the accident rate per million train-miles and the fatalities and injuries at railway crossings, data on the number of freight and passenger cars inspected, and data and trends on the miles of track inspections and crossings inspections.[9]

Program evaluation techniques and performance measures are widely applied in federal departments and agencies, yet it is unlikely that anyone in the public service believes that all relevant factors and variables can be quantified or all activities evaluated in apolitical terms. There are few areas of decision making, however, that would not benefit, in varying degrees, from the attempt to introduce improved methods of analysis — whether they take the form of a more orderly array of data on resource requirements, physical outputs, or objectives, or whether they emphasize comparative measurements of costs and benefits of competing programs or of alternative methods of achieving a stated objective.

NOTES

[1] The Royal Commission on Government Organization was appointed in September 1960, under the chairmanship of J. Grant Glassco, to "inquire into and report upon the organization and methods of operation of the departments and agencies of the Government of Canada and to recommend changes therein which they [the Commissioners] consider would best promote efficiency, economy, and improved service in the dispatch of public business." Canada, *The Royal Commission on Government Organization* (Ottawa: Queen's Printers, 1962), vol. 1.

[2] For a brief description of the development of PPBS in the federal government, see J.C. Strick, "Recent Developments in Canadian Financial Administration," *Public Administration,* no. 48 (Spring 1970).

[3] Canada, *Supplement to the Annual Report of the Auditor General to the House of Commons for the Fiscal Year Ended March 31, 1975* (Ottawa, 1975); and *Report of the Auditor General to the House of Commons for the Fiscal Year Ended March 31, 1976* (Ottawa, 1976).

[4] Canada, *Royal Commission on Financial Management and Accountability,* Final Report (Ottawa, March 1979)

[5] Canada, Department of Finance, *The New Expenditure Management System* (Ottawa: 1979).

[6] Canada, Treasury Board, *The Expenditure Management System of the Government of Canada* (Ottawa: 1995), cat BT-22-37/1995.

[7] Canada, *Report of the Auditor General of Canada to the House of Commons,* chapter 5 "Reporting Performance in the Expenditure Management System" (Ottawa: 1997).

[8] For some of the initiatives of the Office of Comptroller General to improve management and analysis in government, see Canada, Treasury Board, *Cash Management in the Government of Canada* (Ottawa, 1988); *Enterprising Management* (Ottawa, 1989); and *Management Update* (monthly).

[9] Canada, Treasury Board, *Transport Canada, Performance Report for the Period Ending March 31, 1997* (Ottawa: 1997).

PART THREE

FINANCING THE PUBLIC SECTOR

CHAPTER 8

Introduction to Taxation

The primary source of government revenue is taxation. It is usually supplemented with revenues from user charges, fees and permits, and other sources. This chapter focuses on taxation and the possible effects of some taxes on the economy.[1] It also outlines the development of taxation in Canada. Other sources of revenue are discussed in chapter 11.

Tax Bases

The kinds of taxes found in a typical tax structure include taxes based on income, on consumption, on wealth and transfers of wealth, and on business activity.

Income-Based Taxes

Two important revenue sources for Canada are taxes on income; the personal income tax and the corporation income tax. In addition, wages earned and paid are often subject to payroll taxes.

Personal Income Tax. An income tax requires a definition of the tax base. For the personal income tax, the most widely accepted theoretical definition of income is often called the Haig-Simons definition, so named after the two economists who developed it. Income is defined as the value of an individual's increase in net wealth plus his or her consumption in a specified period of time, normally one year. This measure is a comprehensive one that includes both money income and income received in the form of goods and services. (As noted in the next chapter, the Canadian Income Tax Act uses a variation of the Haig-Simons concept in its definition of income.)

Total or gross personal income is not, however, usually considered a measure of capacity to pay taxes. An individual may incur unavoidable personal expenses, such as medical costs. He or she may also have costs associated with earning income, including interest paid on funds borrowed for investment purposes. In addition, a certain minimum amount of income is required for purchase of food, clothing, and shelter necessary for subsistence. Consequently, specified amounts of income are normally exempt from taxation, and deductions are permitted for non discretionary expenditures. Taxable income then consists of gross income minus these exemptions and deductions.

An alternative method for taking into account non-discretionary costs and permitting a minimum allowance to reflect lack of tax-paying capacity is to provide tax credits for these items. Total tax is first calculated on gross income and then amounts are subtracted from the total tax to arrive at the tax payable.

Corporation Income Tax. A corporation is taxed on net income, which is defined as the total income it has earned less all expenses incurred in earning that income. There are two alternative treatments of corporate income for tax purposes. The most common method treats the corporation as a separate tax-paying entity and grants shareholders a tax credit on their dividends for the amount of tax paid by the corporation. The second method taxes corporation income through its shareholders. Net income is allocated to shareholders in proportion to the number of shares held, and this income is then subjected to the personal income tax. Both methods permit the integration of personal income and income earned by shareholders through the corporation. Integration avoids double taxation of corporation income — that is, once by a corporation income tax and again by the personal income tax on dividends received.

Payroll Taxes. Payroll taxes are levies on wages and salaries. Separate from income taxes, they may be payable by workers on wages earned and/or by the employer on wages paid. Revenues are usually earmarked for specific purposes, such as the Canada Pension Plan and the Employment Insurance fund at the federal level, and premiums to finance health services by provincial governments in some provinces.

Consumption-Based Taxes

Taxes based on consumer spending include the spending tax, general sales taxes, and specific taxes called excises.

The Spending Tax. A direct approach to the taxation of consumption is the spending tax. It is applied to the amount of an individual's total income spent on consumption, which can be calculated, in effect, as gross income minus savings for a given period — say, one year. Deductions and exemptions may be permitted and various rates applied, as for a personal income tax. This type of tax rewards savings because an individual can reduce the tax burden by increasing the proportion of total income saved.

Sales Taxes. A general sales tax may be applied to transactions at various stages of the production and distribution process. It may be a multi-stage or a single-stage levy. Taxes of the former type include the turnover tax and the value-added tax: those of the latter type include the manufacturers' sales tax, the wholesale tax, and the retail sales tax.

A general sales tax is a widely used consumption-based tax that is an important source of government revenue in many countries. It is a broadly based tax, applied as a percentage of the sale price of all goods and services except those specifically exempted. For the most part, a sales levy taxes consumption indirectly. The tax is usually imposed on the seller, who collects and remits the amount but is expected to pass the tax forward to consumers through an increase in the selling price.

A turnover tax is imposed at a constant rate on sale value at every transaction in the production and distribution process. For instance, the tax is imposed on raw materials, on semi-finished goods, and on the finished product. A widely used variation is the value-added tax, which is applied in almost fifty countries. Like the turnover tax, a value-added tax is imposed on transactions at all the various stages of production, but it is levied only on the value that has been added at each stage. In the administration of a value-added tax, credits are usually given to sellers for the tax they have paid on purchases or inputs; this approach avoids tax pyramiding (tax paid on tax) and multiple taxation (taxation of the same product more than once). Given the tax rate, the total amount remitted to the government by the vendors at all the different stages of taxation equals the amount of tax paid by the consumer on the selling price of the finished product. The Goods and Services Tax (GST) introduced by the Canadian government in January 1991 (described in the next chapter) is essentially a value-added tax.

A manufacturers' sales tax is imposed on producers, often of final and near-final goods. The base prices to which the tax is applied are those charged for finished goods and services. Double taxation can be avoided by exempting inputs, such as raw materials and semi-finished products, or by giving a credit for any tax paid by one manufacturer to another on the purchases of inputs. A tax on the manufacturer's selling price is called a hidden tax. It becomes built into the prices of goods purchased by consumers, who frequently are unaware of the tax or the amount they are paying. A manufacturers' sales tax was part of the Canadian tax structure from 1921 to 1990 but was replaced by the GST in January 1991.

A wholesale sales tax is basically similar to the manufacturers' sales tax, except that it is levied on the prices the wholesaler charges the retailer and is remitted by the wholesaler.

Retail sales taxes are imposed at the retail level on goods and services sold to the consumer. The retailer collects the tax and remits it to the government. This is the nature of the general sales tax levied by all provinces in Canada except Alberta, which does not impose a sales tax.

An excise is a tax on specified goods or services or a selected group of them. The tax may be expressed as a percentage of the selling price (an *ad valorem* tax) or as dollars or cents on weight, volume, or number (a unit tax). Traditionally, excise taxes have been imposed on two groups of goods. One group consists of goods deemed to generate external diseconomies in consumption, such as alcohol and tobacco products. To the extent that the excise tax is reflected in higher selling prices of the goods, the tax is viewed as a means of curtailing their consumption and thereby reducing external costs. These excises are known as sumptuary taxes, designed to limit purchases of the goods taxed. The second group of goods taxed are considered luxury items. They include such consumer goods as cosmetics, jewellery, wine, and tobacco. (As applied in Canada, the luxury tax at one time also included radios and television sets, automobiles, and clocks and watches.) In addition to these two groups of goods, excise taxes are also imposed on items such as motor fuel, air conditioners in automobiles, and air travel.

Taxes on Wealth and Transfers of Wealth

In contrast to personal and corporation income taxes, which are based on income flows, wealth taxes are based on stocks of personal and real property. Wealth taxes include the net wealth tax and real property taxes. Taxes on transfers of wealth include death and gift taxes.

Net Wealth Tax. A tax on net wealth consists of an annual levy on the value of all a person's assets (land, vehicles, stocks and bonds, savings, jewellery, and so on) minus any claims against these assets.

Property Tax. A real property tax is a levy on land and accompanying buildings. The property tax is much used in Canada, where it is imposed primarily by municipalities (as discussed in chapter 10).

This tax is levied on the property and is not related to the income or ability to pay of the owner or to the equity he or she may have in it. The usual justification for this tax is that local governments use revenues from the tax to service the property and thus tend to increase its value. Services such as law enforcement protect property, while streets and sidewalks make the property accessible.

A tax may also be imposed on transactions in property such as the land transfer tax. This is a tax on the value of real estate property, paid by the buyer, and imposed by several provinces.

Death Taxes. A death tax is one imposed on wealth at the time of death. When it is applied to the wealth of the deceased before it is distributed to heirs, it is known as an estate tax. When it is levied on the heirs of the estate in proportion to the amounts each receives, it is called an inheritance tax or succession duty. Before 1972 the Canadian federal government imposed an estate tax. The provinces, on the other hand, applied succession duties. All the provinces have now discontinued this tax, but inheritance taxes are still levied by many state governments in the United States.

Death taxes are controversial. The reason for their imposition can generally be traced to objectives of income redistribution. There may be a desire to limit intergenerational accumulations of wealth. It may also be argued that death taxes tap income that may have escaped the personal income tax. On the other hand, to the extent that the accumulated wealth had earlier been taxed as income under the personal income tax, death taxes may be viewed as double taxation.

Gift Taxes. It is common for a death tax to be accompanied by a gift tax, which is a levy imposed on the donor of a gift. The purpose is to prevent avoidance of estate taxes. Without a gift tax, all death taxes could be avoided by transferring wealth before death.

Business Taxes

In addition to the corporation income tax, a wide variety of levies may be applied to business establishments and business activities. They include commercial concentration taxes, which are based on square metres of floor space; taxes on storage capacity; taxes on an establishment's rental value; and taxes on paid-up capital of a company. These taxes usually contribute only a very small proportion of total government revenues and are mostly imposed by the lower levels of government.

Lump Sum Tax

A lump sum tax is a fixed amount levied on an individual, to be paid each year, and is independent of that individual's annual income, consumption, or wealth. Imposed in Great Britain in the 1980s, it was called a "community charge" to finance local government services and fell equally on taxpayers. Before it was declared unconstitutional in 1964, it was used by a number of states in the United States. Called a poll tax, it was required to be paid by individuals as a condition of being permitted to vote in political elections.

Principles of Taxation

Some of the early literature on taxation focussed on attempts to develop principles on which a tax or tax system could be structured. Such criteria were viewed as desirable to avoid or reduce arbitrariness in taxation. Over time, most people have come to accept three principles as embodying the primary features that a tax or a tax system should possess: (1) equity in the distribution of the burden of taxation; (2) economic efficiency; and (3) administrative feasibility.[2] These principles sometimes conflict; in such cases, unless a government places priority on a particular principle, compromises are required.

Equity

The principle of tax equity is related to society's goal of an equitable distribution of income. In fact, taxes, combined with transfers, are employed for purposes of income redistribution. Accordingly, the distribution of the burden of a tax should adhere to the standards of equity or fairness adopted by society for income distribution. The generally accepted rule of equity in taxation is equal treatment of equals. Horizontal equity requires those in similar circumstances to pay equal taxes. Vertical equity requires those who are better off to pay more taxes.

The benefit approach to taxation uses the benefits from government expenditures as the base for taxation. According to the equal treatment of equals rule, people should pay taxes in proportion to benefits received. Difficulties arise, however, in applying this approach. First, there is the difficulty of measuring and allocating benefits from government activities. Second, the distribution of the tax burden in proportion to benefits received could result in a situation in which — to take an extreme example — a millionaire and a pauper, each receiving the same benefits, would be required to pay the same amount in tax dollars. This distribution is unlikely to conform to the standards of equity established by society for income distribution, since it is generally accepted that extremes in income disparities should be avoided.

In contrast is the ability-to-pay approach in the application of the equal treatment of equals rule. Individuals who have equal ability to pay taxes should pay equal taxes, while those with greater ability pay more taxes. The most widely adopted measure of ability is income, but a combination of income and wealth is used in some cases. Horizontal equity is attained by requiring two individuals to pay equal amount of tax if they have the same amount of income after adjustments for factors that may affect their well-being, such as number of dependents and medical expenses. Vertical equity requires individuals with larger incomes to pay more taxes. An issue that arises here is the determination of how much more higher-income groups should be required to pay.

Taxes may be progressive, proportional, or regressive with respect to income. These concepts are generally defined in terms of the average tax rate — that is, the proportion of income that is paid in taxes as income increases. In a proportional tax, the average tax rate is constant; in a progressive tax, it rises as income increases; and in a regressive tax, it falls as incomes rise.

The same concepts can be used to describe marginal tax rates, which are the tax rates that are applied to increments of income as income rises. Marginal tax rates should not be confused with average tax rates. Marginal tax rates are progressive when the rates on additional amounts of income increase as income rises. An example of a progressive marginal tax rate structure is: a 10 percent rate on the first $1,000 of taxable income, a 15 percent rate on the next $1,000, and a 20 percent rate on the third $1,000. Marginal tax rates are regressive when they fall as income rises.

Given efficient tax collection, progressive marginal tax rates produce progression in the average tax rate.

It has been extensively argued that vertical equity in taxation requires progressive taxation. Of the numerous theoretical attempts to justify progression, most are based on the assumption of the diminishing marginal utility of income. In this concept, as income increases, the utility or welfare gain from additional dollars of income falls. Therefore, taxing away additional dollars results in a smaller sacrifice or loss of welfare to a high-income individual than to a low-income person. These theories remain controversial, however, and the case for progressive taxation, including the degree of progression, is inconclusive.[3] Nevertheless, governments commonly apply progressive marginal tax rates in the personal income tax.

Many other taxes in a country's system may not have progressive rates, however. Sales taxes, for example, are considered regressive with respect to income; although the statutory tax rate may be a constant percentage of price, the dollar value of the tax paid on an item constitutes a higher percentage of the income of a low-income purchaser than of a high-income purchaser.[4] The degree of regressiveness of the sales tax can be reduced by exempting from it items that usually make up a large proportion of the budgets of low-income families (that is, food and clothing) or by a system of sales tax credits that produce tax refunds to low-income families as compensation for sales tax paid. Similar tax refunds can be applied to property taxes to help ease their burden on low-income families.

Economic Efficiency

In raising revenues, taxes transfer control over real resources from the private sector to the public sector. According to the tax principle of economic efficiency, a tax should raise the revenues required in a way that does not distort the efficient allocation of resources. In other words, in an economy characterized by an efficient allocation of resources shaped by market forces, a tax should be neutral in its effect on this allocation. A tax is considered economically neutral and efficient if it does not alter choices or decisions in production, consumption, savings, and investment. To the extent that market imperfections and externalities contribute to an inefficient allocation of resources, however, taxes may be applied in a non-neutral manner to help the economy achieve an optimal allocation of resources. Tax incentives may be used to achieve certain economic goals, and tax penalties to discourage particular courses of action.

Raising or lowering the personal income tax affects the level of disposable income that people have available for consumption and can thus affect total consumption and production. But in the process, the tax is unlikely to cause changes in the relative prices of consumer goods or, therefore, in consumption patterns. The personal income tax is consequently considered to be neutral in consumption. It may, however, affect the supply of labour by altering workers' labour/leisure decisions. Similarly, a general sales tax, although it is passed on to consumers and causes an increase in prices, is unlikely to change relative prices and encourage consumers to make substitutions in consumption. But since such a tax penalizes current consumption, it may alter savings/consumption decisions. Excise taxes on selected goods may produce direct non-neutral effects. Assume two commodities, X and Y, that are substitutes in consumption. A tax on X but not on Y may cause the price of X to rise relative to that of Y and bring about substitution of Y for X. Excise taxes may, however, be imposed precisely for their non-neutral effects. As already noted, goods whose consumption is deemed to generate external costs, such as alcohol and tobacco, may be taxed to curtail consumption and reduce the amount of externalities produced. Similarly, a tax on the commodities produced by a firm that pollutes

the environment may serve to increase prices and reduce production and associated pollution. In such cases, taxes have a positive non-neutral impact on the allocation of resources, serving to move the economy to a more efficient allocation.

A large body of literature in public sector economics has been devoted to analyzing the effects taxes may have on incentives, labour/leisure decisions, savings/consumption decisions, investment decisions, and decisions in production. These possible effects are influenced by the degree of shifting and the incidence of various taxes, issues that are discussed later in this chapter.

Administrative Feasibility

A tax should not be so complex that it cannot be understood by the taxpayer, yet it should be sufficiently comprehensive so that the potential for tax avoidance is minimized. Simplicity is required for ease of administration. Also, a tax should be inexpensive to administer relative to the revenues it generates, and sufficiently flexible to be changed easily in response to changing economic conditions.

Tax legislation should clearly define the tax base and specify exemptions and deductions if tax avoidance is to be minimized. The equity concept of equal treatment of equals is undermined if, given two individuals with equal taxable income, one finds loopholes in the legislation that enable reduction of his or her tax burden. A major difficulty facing government, however, is how to devise tax rules comprehensive enough to block all possible loopholes while keeping the legislation readily understandable and the tax forms simple. Furthermore, taxpayers should be able to comprehend the rules and understand the tax implications of any course of action they may take.

Tax administration involves both the government bureaucracy and the taxpayer. Individuals, as well as businesses, large and small, are required to keep income and expense records for tax purposes. If the tax is complex, record keeping can be time-consuming and expensive. Tax complexity may even force ordinary individual taxpayers to seek professional assistance to interpret tax rules and to complete their tax returns.

Fiscal policy requires, in part, tax flexibility to meet changing economic conditions that may bring inflation, recession, or unemployment. A long delay in implementing tax policy changes to combat, for example, the beginning of an economic slowdown could reduce the effectiveness of such a policy.

Tax Incidence, Tax Shifting, and Economic Effects

Tax incidence refers to the distribution of the burden of a tax; in essence, it is the final resting place of the tax burden. A tax may be imposed on and remitted by one entity, but if the burden of the tax can be shifted — passed on — to another entity, then the tax incidence is on the latter. Taxes may be shifted forward to consumers in the form of increased prices or backwards to factors of production. The incidence of taxes and the degree of shifting are significant for analyzing the economic effects of taxes.

Personal Income Tax. It is generally acknowledged that the personal income tax is not a tax conducive to direct shifting of the burden. For income that consists of wages and salaries, the person on whom the tax is levied will pay it and bear the burden.

As noted earlier, the personal income tax is considered neutral in its effects on consumer choices and consumer patterns of spending. It may, however, affect both choices between work and leisure and investment decisions. The labour/leisure decision may be subject to an income and a substitution effect from the income tax. The income effect is positive, causing people to work more in an attempt to maintain their pre-tax incomes and standards of living. At the same time, the tax reduces

the cost of leisure, prompting individuals to substitute leisure for work. Theoretically, the net result of the positive income and negative substitution effects is indeterminate. Empirical studies show various results.[5] In various surveys of professional and non-professional groups in the labour force, some workers report income effects, others report substitution effects, and still others report no effects on work decisions. Econometric studies indicate some loss of efficiency in the labour market caused by the disincentive effects of taxes.

The effect on investment decisions results from including investment income, such as interest, dividends, and capital gains, in the personal income tax base. Such taxation reduces the amount of funds available for investment. A reduction in private investment could, in the long run, reduce economic growth and production unless balanced by an increase in public investment. The tax may also adversely affect incentives to take risks and invest, although the disincentive effect on risk taking may be offset by permitting the deduction of losses from income for tax purposes. As with work/leisure decisions, there is no conclusive evidence on the net effect of the income tax on investment decisions. Some investors may be inclined to take more risk and attempt to increase their potential yield to offset their taxes on investment returns, while others may opt for safer though lower-yielding investments.

Corporation Income Tax. The corporation income tax offers a number of potential economic effects, including effects on prices, output, and production efficiency. The results depend on the assumptions of tax shifting and incidence. According to the theory of the firm, profits are maximized at the output at which marginal costs equal marginal revenue. A tax on monopoly profits does not disturb the profit-maximizing conditions; therefore, the firm pays the tax with no adjustments in production or prices. In practice, however, corporations may be motivated by factors other than profit maximization, particularly in the short run, and the imposition of a tax on profits may cause adjustments in corporate behaviour.

Assuming that corporations do not shift the income tax, it reduces corporate profits and the funds the firm has available for investment and expansion of production capacity. The incentive to expand capacity and increase potential profits may also be reduced if a significant portion of those profits will be absorbed by tax. In addition, the firm's incentive to maintain efficiency in production to maximize profits may be lessened if those profits are subjected to tax.

Assume that a firm does not operate at a profit-maximizing position but desires instead to earn a certain satisfactory level of profit or rate of return on capital while pursuing other objectives, such as increasing its sales and market share. When the corporation income tax is imposed, the firm may adjust its output and raise its prices in order to increase profits by an amount sufficient to pay the tax and retain its acceptable level of profits.[6]

A firm may also attempt to shift the tax backwards to factors of production. One way of doing so is to not pass to factors the full benefits of increased productivity. Instead, the firm may use part of the cost savings to increase its pre-tax profits, pay the tax, and hold after-tax profits at the original profit level.

Some empirical studies have focussed on corporation pre-tax and after-tax rates of return on capital, and indicate that, despite a major increase in corporation income tax rates over the past several decades, corporate after-tax rates of return on capital have, on the average, either increased or remained constant. These studies conclude that in the long run corporations have managed to shift the corporation income tax fully. Some evidence indicates that, over time, output from each unit of investment has generated larger profits before taxes, and it is out of the gains from this increased productivity that higher taxes

appear to have been paid.[7] Others have argued that labour bears part of the burden of the corporation income tax through the effects of the tax on capital.[8] In general, the various methodologies of attempting to determine corporate income tax shifting, and the conflicting results, leaves the issue of shifting and incidence unresolved.

Various features, other than the tax rate, are frequently built into the corporation income tax structure for the purpose of attaining certain economic effects or fiscal objectives. The expenses incurred by a firm on capital equipment are deducted from gross income over time by a schedule of depreciation rates or capital cost allowances. In attempts to encourage investment in capital equipment, governments have used a policy of accelerated depreciation, which permits more rapid write-offs than normally allowed. Another device for stimulating business investment is the investment tax credit, which is a deduction from tax payable of a certain percentage of the amount of investment the firm made during a tax year. This policy serves to increase the amount of after-tax profits, leaving the firm more funds to invest.

Sales and Excise Taxes. In general, sales and excise taxes are imposed on the seller with the expectation that they will be shifted to the consumer in the form of higher prices. In certain cases, such as the retail sales tax in the Canadian provinces, the tax is imposed directly on the consumer at the time of purchase of the taxed items.

The degree of forward shifting and, consequently, the effect of sales taxes on the prices and output of the taxed commodities depend on their price elasticity of supply and demand. A unit sales tax on the seller is generally treated as a cost of production and causes the seller's supply curve to move to a higher position. In a competitive market, a new, higher price is established by the interaction of supply and demand. In general, the greater the price elasticity of demand, the smaller will be the increase in price and the larger will be the reduction in quantity. Given that the price elasticity is greater in a competitive market than in a monopolistic market, it follows that the degree of tax shifting will be lower in the former than in the latter. A sales tax that is not completely shifted forward will be absorbed in part by the seller through reduced profits or by factors of production out of productivity gains.

It was mentioned earlier that excise taxes are frequently imposed on goods with external diseconomies in order to curb their consumption and reduce the amount of diseconomies generated. The effectiveness of a tax for this purpose depends on the price elasticity of demand for the product. If the demand is highly inelastic, the tax will produce an increase in price by practically the full amount of the tax but will not be very successful in curbing consumption. It is difficult to determine empirically the degree of shifting of the sales tax because other, difficult to isolate factors may also be contributing to the price changes observed for the taxed goods. Nevertheless, the general conclusion of empirical analysts has been that, in most cases, the prices of commodities rise by roughly the amount of a sales tax imposed on them and fall by the amount of tax when it is eliminated. In other words, there appears to be full shifting of the sales tax.[9]

Historical Development of Taxation in Canada

The tax structure of a country is usually a product not of systematic creation but of evolution, shaped over time by variety of forces. This is certainly true of Canada, as is evident from Table 8-1. Taxes or levies of one form or another can be traced to early colonial days. The pre-Confederation provinces of Canada were administering a number of taxes and charges, and these formed the basic tax structure of the new Canadian nation and provided the framework for future development.

The development of taxation following Confederation was influenced by a number of factors.[10] The division of taxing powers contained in the Constitution Act, 1867, probably played the strongest role in shaping the future direction of taxation at the federal and provincial levels of government. The act limited the provinces to direct taxes while granting unlimited taxing powers to the federal government. In 1867, direct taxation was unpopular and uncommon, and most of the revenue of the former provinces of Canada was derived from two indirect taxes — excise taxes and customs duties — which were assumed by the federal government. The provinces were left with the property tax and a variety of direct charges, licences, fees, and fines.

A second influence on the development of taxation in Canada was the government's effort to promote economic development of the country. In 1879, the federal government introduced the National Policy, a program designed to stimulate industrial development, transportation facilities, and westward expansion and settlement. The policy featured high tariffs to encourage and protect infant industry and to produce, along with higher excises, larger revenues to finance the construction of a transcontinental railway and other facilities. Economic development was, therefore, the major force behind federal taxation in the late nineteenth century. It also influenced provincial taxation, for, as the economy and population grew, increased demands were placed on the provinces for services and activities falling under their areas of jurisdiction. They responded by finding a number of new sources of revenue and extending existing sources.

Many of the tax sources that were tapped by both levels of government in their search for revenues were based on American precedents. For example, succession duties were in wide use by U.S. state governments before being adopted by Ontario in 1892. Similarly, personal and corporation income taxes and

TABLE 8-1: Major Tax Events in Canada

	Event
Before 1916	Federal taxes: customs duties, excise taxes; Provincial and Municipal taxes: real and personal taxes, property taxes, succession duties, taxes on corporations, personal income taxes
1916	Federal corporation income tax
1917	Federal personal income tax
1920	Federal manufacturers' sales tax
1921	Monopoly sale of liquor by provinces
1922	Gasoline tax by provinces
1936	Retail sales tax by provinces
1941	Rental by federal government of personal income tax, corporation income tax, and succession duty fields from the provincial government
1949	Major reconstruction of federal personal income tax; dividend tax credit introduced
1962	Return of rented tax fields to provinces; provision of tax abatements by federal government
1972	Reform of the federal personal and corporation income tax following some recommendations of the 1966 report of the Royal Commission on Taxation. Capital gains tax introduced; tax base expanded; federal death and gift taxes repealed
1974	Federal indexation of tax brackets and personal exemptions
1988	Reform of the personal and corporation income taxes: personal marginal tax rates reduced to 3 rates of 17, 26, 29 percent; exemptions and deductions replaced by tax credits; corporation income tax rates reduced from 36 to 28 percent
1989	Canada-US Free Trade Agreement providing for gradual elimination of customs duties on imported goods produced in Canada and the U.S.
1991	Goods and Services Tax (GST) of 7 percent, replacing 13.5 percent manufacturers' sales tax
1997	Harmonization of the federal GST with provincial sales tax in New Brunswick, Nova Scotia, and Prince Edward Island

various excises imposed by the federal government were in existence for a considerable period in the United States before being imposed in Canada.

The American influence on Canadian tax structure and rates has continued to the present. The Canadian and U.S. economies have traditionally been closely related and became even more so following the Canada-U.S. Free Trade Agreement that came into effect on January 1, 1989. Taxation can affect trade and investment between the two countries. For example, tax burdens on corporations and investment gains that are significantly higher in Canada than in the United States have the potential for adverse effects on the competitiveness of Canadian industry, on exports, and on foreign investment in this country. The same can be said of sharp differences in the taxation systems of any trade partners. With the increasing trend towards global trading patterns and multinational corporations, there is pressure for international tax harmonization. Introducing a tax reform package in 1987, Minister of Finance Michael Wilson emphasized that it is "important that our tax system not place Canadians at a competitive disadvantage in domestic or international markets" and that Canada must "recognize the competitive reality of tax systems in other countries."[11]

Finally, taxation in Canada, as in most countries, has been influenced by international events such as wars and major economic disturbances. Historical trends show significant increases in tax levels during the two World Wars and the Korean War, with the imposition of new taxes and increases in the rates of existing ones during these periods. After these emergencies were over, taxes were usually lowered, but precedents for taxes in new fields and for higher rates had been established, and it was only a matter of time before they rose to their previous levels. The federal government entered the direct tax field for the first time during World War I, imposing personal and corporation income taxes. Seeking additional revenue, it also extended its excise tax structure to include a variety of new goods and imposed a general sales tax at the manufacturers' level. Taxes were lowered during the 1920s, but they were again increased during the Depression as both the federal government and the provinces sought to bolster sagging revenues. During World War II, federal taxes reached new levels. They were reduced following the war, only to be increased later to finance the Korean War, defence commitments, and expanding government activities in new areas of social service.

By the 1960s, the Canadian tax structure was well entrenched, with a host of different levies at all levels of government. At the federal level, the personal and corporation income taxes were supplemented by the manufacturers' sales tax, excise taxes, excise duties, customs duties, estate and gift taxes, and revenues from contributory welfare programs. Provinces were also tapping personal and corporate incomes and imposed sales taxes, succession duties, and a variety of charges. The property tax remained the primary tax source at the municipal level of government.

The federal tax system has experienced two recent attempts at major restructuring — in 1972 and 1987 — as well as some other important developments. The changes that came into effect in 1972 implemented the most comprehensive tax reform in Canada since the income tax had been introduced in 1917. It was the climax to a tax reform movement begun ten years earlier with the appointment of a royal commission on taxation. There had been no major study of the Canadian tax system since the Rowell-Sirois Commission's investigation in the late 1930s. Many inequities existed in the tax system, and little was known of the effects of the tax structure on the economy.

The Royal Commission on Taxation did not propose patchwork changes in the existing tax system but instead offered an entirely new structure based on premises and principles established by the commission.[12] Numerous novel concepts and features were contained in the recommended system, which many termed a radical departure from the tax structure of the time. The focus of the commission's investigation and report was personal and corporation income taxation. Among the significant features of the proposed system were a comprehensive tax base, the taxation of capital gains, the concept of the family as the tax-paying unit, changes in personal and business deductions and exemptions, changes in tax rates that would shift more of the burden from lower-income to higher-income groups, integration of personal and corporate income, income averaging, elimination of the dual rate of corporation income tax and of special concessions to the extractive industries, and the closing of numerous tax loopholes.

Although the system proposed by the commission was not accepted in its entirety, legislation in 1972 did make some notable changes in income taxation.[13] The most significant in the personal income tax included increases in personal exemptions and exemptions for the elderly, an increase in deductions for pension plans and registered retirement savings plans, changes in the dividend tax credit, and the extension of income averaging. Also introduced were deductions for employment expenses, moving expenses, and child-care expenses. The tax base was broadened by bringing into it previously exempt income including capital gains, unemployment insurance benefits, training allowances, and research grants and fellowships. The introduction of the tax on capital gains resulted in the abolition of the estate and gift tax.

Nineteen seventy-four saw another significant development in federal taxation: the introduction of indexation, whereby the marginal tax brackets and certain exemptions were to be adjusted annually by an inflation factor. The 1970s also witnessed moves by both federal and provincial governments to tap more and more heavily the natural resource industries of oil and gas for revenue.

Major changes in features of personal, corporation, and sales taxation were again proposed by the federal government in June 1987.[14] The changes in personal and corporation taxes became effective in January 1, 1988, while replacement of the manufacturers' sales tax with a form of value-added tax was set for some unspecified future date. (The manufacturers' sales tax was eventually replaced by the more comprehensive Goods and Services Tax (GST) effective January 1, 1991.)

Several objectives were specified in the tax reform of 1987. First and foremost was an attempt to make the tax system more equitable. Higher-income individuals and profitable businesses would be required to carry a larger share of the tax burden. This goal was to be achieved by expanding the tax base through the elimination (or reduction) of some of the selective preferences by the higher-income groups and profitable corporations, by increasing the sales tax credit for lower- and middle-income families, and by converting

personal exemptions and some deductions into tax credits. (Exemptions are subtracted from income; credits are subtracted from tax payable. Tax credits provide the same absolute dollar reduction in tax regardless of income level, whereas exemption and deductions provide greater benefit to taxpayers in the higher tax brackets.) More effective rules would reduce artificial tax avoidance to ensure that individuals in similar economic circumstances were taxed more equitably. In essence, the government was emphasizing taxation according to the familiar ability-to-pay principle and the concepts of horizontal and vertical equity.

The second objective of tax reform was to make the tax system more compatible with economic growth, job creation, and industry competitiveness. Marginal tax rates for both individuals and corporations were reduced as a means of encouraging investment, rewarding success, and increasing productivity. In 1987, the federal personal income tax had a total of ten tax brackets with marginal rates progressing from 6 percent on the first $1,318 of taxable income to 34 percent on income in excess of $63,347. Tax reform reduced the number of tax brackets to three, with marginal rates of 17 percent on the first $27,500 of taxable income, 26 percent on the next $27,500, and 29 percent on the remainder. The corporation income tax rate for general business was reduced from 36 to 28 percent, and the small business rate from 15 to 12 percent.

A third objective was to simplify the tax system, making it easier for taxpayers to understand and comply with the system. It was expected that a simpler structure of tax rates and fewer special preferences would facilitate such understanding. One of the casualties of simplification was income averaging for tax purposes. A system of forward averaging had been in effect, permitting a taxpayer to spread across several years an unusually large amount of income received in any one tax year (such as a lump-sum payment) and consequently avoid the higher marginal tax rates that would normally have applied to the increased income. As a consequence of the lowering of tax rates and moving to only three tax brackets, the forwarding averaging system was eliminated after 1987.

The government also sought closer consistency and integration of the tax system with the objectives of other government programs. For example, numerous social programs and transfer payments had been designed to redistribute income and to assist the needy. Reducing the income tax burden on low-income groups by converting tax exemptions and deductions to tax credits was viewed as complementary to these other programs and their objective of income redistribution.

A final objective of the 1987 tax reform was to make the tax system a more reliable source of government revenue by removing special preferences and curbing opportunities for tax avoidance. Special preferences erode the tax base and create inequities among taxpayers. For example, in 1984, the many tax preferences in the system reduced taxable personal income to only 60 percent of assessed income. In that year, the Minister of Finance claimed, 52 percent of taxpayers with incomes in the $75,000 to $100,000 range paid an average federal tax rate of 20 to 25 percent, while 21 percent of the same group paid a rate of less than 15 percent, and 4 percent of taxpayers with incomes in excess of $100,000 paid no tax at all.[15] Similar inequities had developed in the corporate sector because of special allowances and credits and growing tax avoidance.

In announcing the 1987 proposals, the government, as in previous cases of tax reform, attempted to assure Canadian taxpayers that it was not instituting tax increases in the guise of tax reform. Indeed, with reference to the reform of the personal income tax, the Minister of Finance estimated that the changes would reduce income taxes for more than 80 percent of taxpaying households and that about 850,000 individuals would no longer pay federal income tax.

Summary

Taxes are the major source of government finance. They are imposed on a variety of bases and include income-based taxes, consumption-based taxes, taxes on wealth and the transfer of wealth, taxes on business and on individuals.

The theory of taxation identifies three basic principles or criteria that a tax or tax structure should possess. The principle of equity requires that the distribution of the burden of taxation among members of society should be fair. Economic efficiency stipulates that taxes should be neutral and not distort the efficient allocation of resources in the economy. The third criterion is administrative feasibility, which calls for efficiency in the collection of taxes.

An analysis of the effects of taxes on the economy includes the determination of the degree of tax shifting and tax incidence. Taxes may be imposed on one entity, only to be shifted onto another. There is little opportunity to shift the personal income tax. Both economic theory and empirical evidence, however, indicate varying degrees of shifting of other taxes such as the sales and the corporation income tax.

The tax structure in Canada is a product of historical development. Various factors contributed to shape this structure. Major changes were also introduced periodically through deliberate tax reform, until currently taxation in Canada is imposed on a very comprehensive base and includes most of the taxes that can be found in the tax basket.

NOTES

1 A detailed discussion and analysis of taxation, including kinds of taxes, principles, economic effects, and other theoretical and practical aspects, can be found in most standard textbooks on public sector

economics. See, for example, David N. Hyman and John C. Strick, *Public Finance In Canada: A Contemporary Application of Theory and Policy* (Toronto: Harcourt, Brace and Co., 1995).

2 The three principles discussed in this chapter embody most of the desirable features of a tax that are frequently mentioned in public finance literature.

3 See W. J. Blum and H. Kalven, *The Uneasy Case for Progressive Taxation* (Chicago: University of Chicago Press, 1978).

4 Evidence of the regressive nature of provincial retail sales taxes in Canada is presented in Francois Vaillancourt and Marie-France Poulaert, "The Incidence of Provincial Sales Taxes in Canada, 1978, and 1982," *Canadian Tax Journal* 33 (May/June 1985).

5 Canada, *Studies of the Royal Commission on Taxation*, No. 4, *The Effects of Income Taxation on Work Choices* (Ottawa: Queen's Printer, 1967); Jerry A. Hausman, "Labor Supply" in Henry J. Aaron and Joseph J. Pechman, eds., *How Taxes Affect Economic Behavior* (Washington, D.C.: The Brookings Institution, 1981); Robert K. Triest, "The Effects of Income Taxation on Labor Supply in the United States," *Journal of Human Resources*, 25, 3 (Summer 1990): 491-516.

6 This type of behaviour of the firm is described in the Baumol model of sales-maximization and is illustrated in many textbooks on public sector theory. See W. Baumol, *Economic Theory and Operational Analysis*, 3rd ed. (Englewood Cliffs, N.J.: Prentice-Hall, 1973).

7 Canada, *Studies of the Royal Commission on Taxation*, No. 18, *The Shifting of the Corporation Income Tax in the Short Run* (Ottawa: Queen's Printer, 1967).

8 Martin Feldstein, "The Incidence of a Capital Income Tax in a Growing Economy With Variable Savings Rates," *Review of Economic Studies*, 41 (October, 1974): 505-513; J.G. Ballentine, "The Incidence of a Corporation Income Tax in a Growing Economy," *Journal of Political Economy*, 86 (October, 1978): 863-876.

9 O. Brownlee and G.L. Perry, "The Effects of the 1965 Federal Excise Tax Reductions on Prices," *National Tax Journal*, XX, no. 3, 1967.

10 For a detailed history of taxation in Canada, see such standard works as A.E. Buck, *Financing Canadian Government* (Chicago: Public Administration Service, 1949); J. Harvey Perry, *Taxes, Tariffs, and Subsidies* (Toronto: University of Toronto Press, 1955), vol. 1 and 2; J. Harvey Perry, *Taxation in Canada* (Toronto: University of Toronto Press, 1961); A. Milton Moore, J. Harvey Perry, and Donald I. Beach, *The Financing of Canadian Federation* (Toronto: Canadian Tax Foundation, 1966), ch.1; and Irwin W. Gillespie, *Tax, Borrow and Spend: Financing Federal Spending in Canada, 1867-1990* (Ottawa: Carleton University Press, 1991).

11 Canada, Department of Finance, *The White Paper: Tax Reform 1987* (Ottawa, June 18, 1987), p.4.

12 Canada, *Report of the Royal Commission on Taxation* (Ottawa: Queen's Printer, 1966).

13 Canada, *Summary of 1972 Tax Reform Legislation* (Ottawa: Queen's Printer, 1971).

14 Canada, Department of Finance, *The White Paper: Tax Reform 1987* (Ottawa, June 18, 1987); *Tax Reform 1987: Income Tax Reform* (Ottawa, June 18, 1987); and *Tax Reform 1987: Sales Tax Reform* (Ottawa: June 18, 1987); *Canada, Goods and Services Tax: An Overview* (Ottawa, August 1989); and Department of Finance, *Goods and Services Tax Technical Paper* (Ottawa, August 1989).

15 Canada, *The White Paper*, p.8.

CHAPTER 9

The Federal Tax Structure

The Canadian federal tax system includes a variety of taxes, including the personal income tax, the corporation income tax, consumption-based taxes (the general sales tax, excise taxes, excise duties, and customs duties), and payroll taxes. This chapter presents an outline of the revenues generated by these taxes, along with a non-technical examination of the basic features of these taxes.[1]

Tax Revenue Features

Canadian tax and other revenue sources are shared by the federal and the provincial/local governments, as shown in Table 9-1. The federal government is dominant in the income tax field and has sole jurisdiction over custom import duties. Consumption-based taxes (sales and excises) are shared almost equally by the federal and provincial governments. The provincial and local governments control property taxes.

Table 9-2 shows the proportion of gross domestic product absorbed by federal government revenues. From 1950 to 1980, this proportion fluctuated between 16 and 18 percent, with the lowest figures occurring during the mid-1960s and the later 1970s. From 1980, however, there was a gradual increase from about 16 percent of GDP to over 19 percent by 1995.

The changing significance of each federal tax in terms of revenue yield is shown in Table 9-3. The most notable trends since the 1960s were the relative increase in the share of personal income tax and the decline in the corporation income tax and excise taxes and duties. The latter change reflected decreasing

tax rates on corporations and on commodities and a reduction in the scope of excise taxes over the period shown.

The personal income tax remains the most important source of revenue for the federal government, accounting for almost 45 percent of total revenue for 1996-97. It increased from about 32 percent of total federal budgetary revenue in 1962. This large increase occurred despite the transfer of personal income tax points to the provinces under the 1978 federal/provincial fiscal agreement. It reflects changes in the tax, which expanded the personal income tax base, increased tax rates, and imposed surtaxes.

Commodity- or consumption-based taxes, such as sales taxes, excises, and customs duties, are the second highest revenue-producers at about 21 percent. Employment Insurance premiums have increased significantly from about 4 percent of revenues in 1962 to over 14 percent by 1997.

Non-tax revenue consists primarily of returns on investments and sales of goods and services and has fluctuated between 6 and 7 percent of budgetary revenues.

Personal Income Tax

The various items constituting income, deductions, exemptions, and credits in the federal personal income tax structure are outlined in Table 9-4. These items are explained, along with certain qualifications that may not be evident from the table, in the following pages.

TABLE 9-1: Shares of Tax Revenue for All Canadian Governments, 1994-95

| | Percentage of total collected by | |
Source	Federal government	Provincial, territorial, and local governments
Personal income tax	60.5	39.5
Corporation income tax	64.1	35.9
General sales tax	49.9	50.1
Other consumption taxes	56.7	43.3
Natural resources	1.3	98.7
Health and social insurance	64.3	35.7
Property and related taxes	0.0	100.0
Custom duties	100.0	
Total taxes	48.7	51.3

Source: Statistics Canada, *Public Sector Finance, 1995-1996*, cat. 68-212-XPB, pp.113,167.

TABLE 9-2: Total Federal Revenues as Percentage of Gross Domestic Product for Selected Years 1950-1996 (National Accounts Basis)

	% of GDP
1950	15.8
1960	16.5
1970	17.4
1980	16.3
1990	19.0
1995	19.1
1996	19.3

Source: Canada, Department of Finance, *Economic Reference Tables*, August 1996, cat. F1-26/1996E; *Fiscal Reference Tables*, October 1997, cat. F1-26/1997E.

Income

The Income Tax Act defines income for tax purposes as all gains from offices held, employment, business, property, and other sources. Income includes both money gains and certain real gains and therefore represents increases in wealth during a year on a source-by-source basis.

Money gains consist of wages, salaries, gratuities, rents, dividends, interest, Employment Insurance benefits, fellowships, bursaries and scholarships in excess of $500, research grants, training allowances, amounts contributed on an employee's behalf to a public medical care plan, pensions, capital gains, annuities, alimony or spousal support received, gifts from an employer, tuition fees

TABLE 9-3: Historical Summary of the Federal Government Budgetary Revenue

Source	Revenues for fiscal year ending March 31			
	1962	1975	1985	1997
	(percentage of total revenue)			
Taxes				
Personal income	31.7	40.0	41.2	44.9
Corporation income	20.1	16.5	13.2	12.1
Other income tax	3.0	1.5	1.6	2.0
Sales and excises	34.1	29.1	25.6	20.7
Employment insurance premiums	4.3	5.4	10.6	14.1
Total tax revenue	93.3	92.5	92.2	93.7
Non-tax Revenue				
Return on investments[a]	4.8	6.2	6.0	3.0
Other	2.0	1.3	1.8	3.3
Total non-tax revenue	6.7	7.5	7.8	6.3
Total	100.0	100.0	100.0	100.0
	($ billion)			
Total Amount	6.4	29.3	71.1	140.9

[a] Income derived from loans and advances to government enterprises and other governments and from investments in government enterprises.

Source: Department of Finance, *Fiscal Reference Tables*, October 1997, cat. F1-26/1997E, pp.11, 13.

paid on a taxpayer's behalf, living and expense allowances, and foreign income received. Real gains consist of income in kind — that is, in the form of goods and services rather than cash. Examples include the value of board and lodging freely provided and the use value of a company-supplied automobile. Similarly, if an employer sells assets to an employee at a bargain price, the difference between the price charged and the fair market value is a taxable gain to the employee. The same calculation must be applied to stock options whereby an employer purchases shares of the employer corporation at a price that is less than their market value. Real income in the form of imputed gains from consumer durables is, however, excluded from the measurement of income. Durables, such as owner-occupied homes, yield a stream of services valued as the rent that could have been received if the home had been rented out. The benefit received is imputed income and adds to the wealth of the individual, but because of practical difficulties of measuring such income, it is excluded from the concept of income for tax purposes. Income is viewed as economic gain in the form of measurable flows of wealth.

The base to which the personal income tax applies consists of total income, as defined above, received during a calendar year. To arrive at net income, the taxpayer makes vari-

**TABLE 9-4: Federal Personal Income Tax: Calculation of
Taxable Income and Tax**

Income

Income from employment

Pension income
    Old Age Security
    Canada Pension Plan
    Other pensions

Income from other sources
    Employment insurance benefits
    Taxable amount of dividends from Canadian corporations
    Interest and other investment income
    Rental income
    Taxable capital gains
    Spousal support
    Registered retirement savings plan income
    Other income (specify)

Self-Employment Income (net)
    Business income
    Professional income
    Commissions
    Farming and fishing income

	Total income	1

Deductions from total income

Annual union and professional dues

Child-care expenses

Spousal support paid

Moving expenses

Registered pension plan contribution

Registered retirement savings plan contributions

Carrying charges

Capital gains deduction

Other deductions

	Total deductions	2
	Taxable income (1-2)	3

	Federal income tax on taxable income	4

TABLE 9-4 — *Continued*

Non-refundable tax credits

Basic personal amount

Age amount

Married amount

Canada or Quebec Pension Plan contributions

Employment insurance premiums

Pension income amount (maximum $1000)

Disability amount

Tuition fees (self)

Education amount (self)

Tuition fees and education amount transferred from child

Amounts transferred from spouse

Medical expenses less 3 percent of net income

Total amount	5
17 percent of total amount	6

Charitable donations and gifts to Canada or province
17 percent of first $200
29 percent of balance

Total	7
Total Non-refundable tax credits (line 6 + line 7)	8

Other tax credits

Federal sales tax credit (refundable)

Federal political contribution tax credit

Federal dividend tax credit

Foreign tax credit

Total other tax credits	9
Total tax credits (line 8 + line 9)	10
Net federal tax payable (line 4 - line 10)	11

ous subtractions from total income. These consist of business and personal expenses incurred in earning the income or non-discretionary expenditures that reduce tax-paying ability. From net income, certain other deductions, such as the capital gains deduction and business and property losses, are made to arrive at taxable income. The tax is calculated on that amount. Then various tax credits are subtracted. They are adjustments for tax-paying ability, non-discretionary expenditures, and taxes already paid on the taxable income.

Business Income and Deductions

A business is an activity involving the production, purchase, or sale of goods and/or services. It may consist of manufacturing, commercial trade, or the practice of a profession. In arriving at taxable income, the taxpayer must deduct expenses incurred in the process of obtaining income from the business, including wages and salaries paid, cost of materials, interest on borrowed money used in the business, contributions to an employee's pension fund, expenditures on scientific research, expenses in connection with attending conventions (limited to two per year), advertising costs, donations, automobile expenses, and foreign taxes paid. Deductions for capital expenditures are made by way of capital cost allowances (depreciation) as specified in the Income Tax Act.

There are two methods of accounting used in determining income from a business: the cash method and the accrual method. Farmers and fishermen may use the cash method, but most other businesses are required to use the accrual method. In the cash method, amounts are included in income in the year in which they are actually received and expenses are deducted in the year paid. Under the accrual method, amounts are included as income in the year they are earned, and expenses are deducted in the year incurred, whether or not they have been paid.

A business may choose a fiscal year other than the calendar year. If it does so, income and expenses are calculated for that fiscal period, and it is considered the taxation year.

Personal Deductions

In addition to any business expenses a taxpayer may have, there are other deductible outlays, justified on the grounds that they are non-discretionary and reduce tax-paying ability or on economic grounds.

Retirement Plans. The Canadian government assists and encourages people to save for retirement by permitting deductions for contributions to a Retirement Pension Plan (RPP) and to a Registered Retirement Savings Plan (RRSP). Pension reform in 1990 provided generous deductions for such plans. Beginning in 1991, a taxpayer could contribute 18 percent of the previous year's earned income, up to a limit of $11,500. This limit was scheduled to rise by $1,000 each year to $15,500 in 1995, but was frozen in 1993 at $13,500. If an individual belongs to a registered employer-sponsored pension plan, the annual RRSP contribution limit is reduced by a pension adjustment, a measure calculated by the employer based on the value of the benefits that have accrued in the employer-sponsored plan.

Employment-Related Expenses. Certain expenses incurred by an employee are deductible from income. A taxpayer may deduct expenses incurred while working away from home, such as board and lodging, provided the employer does not reimburse for them. (This applies only if employees must leave their ordinary residences and live and work at distant sites where they cannot reasonably be expected to establish a home for their families.) Similarly, moving expenses incurred by taxpayers who change jobs (whether for a change in employers or a transfer) are deductible provided that the new residence is at least 40 kilometres closer to a new job location. Students who have been in full-time attendance at a university or other post-secondary education institution in Canada can deduct expenses incurred in moving within Canada to take a job, including summer employment. A student who moves to attend a university or postsecondary institution full-time within Canada or outside of Canada may deduct moving expenses against scholarships, research grants, and other awards if the move results in a new residence at least 40 kilometres closer to the educational institution.

Annual membership dues in a trade union or in an association required to maintain professional status, such as those paid by a lawyer, engineer, or accountant, are deductible.

An employee who is required to travel as part of his employment and does not receive an allowance for travelling expenses may deduct travel expenses. Commission salespersons who pay their own expenses may deduct all expenses incurred in earning their commissions. Employees who maintain offices in their homes and meet certain requirements may deduct a proportion of the expense of operating and maintaining the home, such as those incurred for electricity, fuel, and minor repairs. Similarly, taxpayers who maintain an office in their place of residence for the purpose of conducting a business may deduct a portion of the household expenses if they meet specified conditions, but the amount deducted cannot exceed the income from the business.

Child-Care Expenses. If a family has both parents working or only one parent and he or she is working, deductions for child-care expenses, such as the costs of babysitting and nursery day-care are allowed up to $7,000 per child for children less than seven years of age and up to $4,000 per child for those between the ages of seven and sixteen. For a two-parent family, the deduction is available to the parent with the lower income and may not exceed two-thirds of that person's earned income. Expenses must be supported with receipts and must be incurred to enable the claimant to be employed or to conduct a business.

Spousal Support. Spousal support paid on a periodic basis under a written agreement or court order is deductible from income by the payer and included in the income of the recipient. Child support payments, however, provided for under a court order made after 1997, are not deductible by the payer and are not taxable to the recipient.

Investment-Related Deductions. Certain expenses related to the income earned from investments are deductible from total income. These include interest paid on funds borrowed to purchase bonds, stocks, and other investments; safety deposit box charges paid to banks or others for safe custody of investments; and investment counselling fees and portfolio management fees paid to a bank, a trust, or an investment dealer or counsellor.

Tax Credits

Tax credits are deductions from the tax payable. They are employed to reduce the tax burden on members of lower income groups, to achieve equity, to achieve economic objectives and, in certain instances, to avoid or reduce double taxation.

Before the tax reform put in place in 1988, the primary tax credits found in the federal personal income tax structure were the dividend tax credit, child credits, and credits for the federal sales tax and foreign taxes paid. One of the main features of the reform was the conversion of the personal exemptions and certain other deductions into tax credits. The exemptions and deductions that were converted into credits were the basic personal exemption, the married exemption, the exemption for the aged, and deductions of pension income, tuition fees and other education expenditures, Employment Insurance premiums, medical expenses, disability allowances, contributions to the Canada (or Quebec) Pension Plan, and charitable donations.

The rationale behind the conversion of these exemptions and deductions into credits was in keeping with the central objective of tax reform: to make the personal income tax more equitable by eliminating loopholes and by shifting a greater proportion of the tax burden to higher-income groups. Deductions from taxable income benefit high-income earners more than low-income earners because the former are subject to higher marginal tax rates and therefore enjoy a greater tax reduction from a deduction. For example, under the previous system, each $1,000 of exemption was worth $60 of federal tax saving to a taxpayer in the lowest tax bracket but $340 to a taxpayer in the highest tax bracket. Tax credits, however, provide the same dollar reduction of tax to all taxpayers, regardless of their level of income. Lower-income and middle-income families with large personal exemptions were expected to benefit significantly from the conversion.

Since the 1988 tax year, personal exemptions have been replaced by "personal amounts." Various other former deductions are now also referred to as "amounts." These amounts are added together and converted into tax credits by multiplying the aggregate by 17 percent, the lowest personal tax rate. (Special rates are applied to charitable donations and gifts to government, as illustrated in Table 5-1.) Under the tax rate structure, that rate is applied to the first $29,590 of taxable income. Consequently, a 17 percent tax credit provides benefits equivalent to a deduction for taxpayers with taxable income of or less than $29,590 and limits the tax benefits for those at higher income levels and higher marginal tax rates.

Tax credits may be refundable or non-refundable. If the total of refundable credits exceeds the total tax payable, the difference is refundable — returned to the taxpayer. With non-refundable tax credits, however, if the credits are more than the federal income tax, the difference is not refunded. The only refundable federal tax credit is the federal sales tax credit, which existed in the pre-reform tax system. All of the tax credits introduced by the reform of 1988 are non-refundable.

Non-Refundable Tax Credits

This section describes the tax credits that are conversions of former exemption and deduction amounts and that came into effect with tax reform in January 1988. The credit is 17 percent of the amounts shown, unless otherwise specified.

Personal Credits. Invariably, a tax structure exempts from taxation a certain amount of income determined as essential for existence and, therefore, unrepresentative of tax-paying ability. The amount is usually arbitrarily determined but takes into consideration such factors as marital status, support of dependants, age, and physical or mental disability. The Canadian tax system provides these exemptions in the form of non-refundable credits of 17 percent of personal "amount." Each taxpayer is entitled to a basic personal amount. In addition, there is a married amount, amounts for dependent children, an age amount for taxpayers aged sixty-five years or over, and a disability amount for the taxpayer or dependants.

The basic personal amount for the 1997 taxation year was $6,456, so the basic personal tax credit was 17 percent of this amount or $1,098. Like other personal amounts, it is increased annually through tax indexation, [2] which, since 1986, has been limited to the annual increase in the consumer price index in excess of 3 percent.

The married amount for 1997 was $5,918 if the taxpayer's spouse had a yearly net income of less than $538. If that income was more than $538 but less than $5,918, then the taxpayer could claim a married amount of $5,918 less the spouse's net income. If the spouse's net income exceeded $5,918, the spouse was required to file a separate return.

A taxpayer can claim an amount for his or his spouse's dependent child or grandchild if that child is mentally or physically infirm and over 18 years of age. The maximum amount that can be claimed was $2,353 in 1997.

A special age amount, maximum $3,482 or credit of $592 in 1997, may be claimed by taxpayers sixty-five years of age and over. This amount could also be claimed by taxpayers who suffered physical or mental disabilities, such as the blind or the bedridden. It is reduced by 15 percent of net income in excess of $25,921.

In each of these cases, the tax credit is 17 percent of the specified amount.

Private Pension Income Credit. A taxpayer may claim a tax credit of 17 percent of the first $1,000 of certain types of pension income. This amount is restricted to income from private pension plans, annuity payments from Registered Retirement Savings Plans, and other annuity payments. Income from the Canada (or Quebec) Pension Plan, Old Age Security benefits, and lump-sum payments from registered retirement or savings plans are excluded. A taxpayer, however, can claim contributions to the Canada (or Quebec) Pension Plan; the maximum in 1997 was $893, which converted into a tax credit of $152.

Education Expense Credits. A student may claim, as a tax credit, 17 percent of tuition fees paid (but not amounts for books or other expenses) if the fees exceeded $100 and were paid to an educational institution in Canada or to a degree-granting institution outside Canada where the student attended a degree course full time for at least thirteen consecutive weeks. Only the student may claim tuition fees, even if someone else paid them. Tuition must be claimed on a calendar-year basis; for example, only fees paid for courses taken from January 1 to December 31, 1997, could be claimed on the student's return 1997.

In addition, there is an education claim of $150 for each month during the tax year that a student was in full-time attendance at a designated educational institution. Such institutions include universities and colleges in Canada, universities outside Canada if the student was enrolled in a degree course of at least thirteen consecutive weeks, and some schools that have job retraining or education courses.

If a student does not need to claim tuition fees and the education amount to reduce federal tax to zero, the unused part, to a maximum of $5,000, may be transferred to his or her parent or grandparent (but not to more than one person). In other words, the amount transferable is $5,000 less the amount used by the student.

The credit is 17 percent of the amount, transferred or not.

Medical Credits. A taxpayer may claim as an "amount" all medical expenses in excess of $1,614 or 3 percent of net income, whichever is less. Expenses paid on a taxpayer's behalf by a government or private medical plan are not deductible. If a medical plan pays only a portion of the total medical expense and the taxpayer is required to pay the remainder, the difference may be claimed as a medical expense.

The term "medical expense" includes payments to a medical practitioner, a dentist, a hospital, or a nursing home and payments for eyeglasses, crutches, and the like and for prescription medicines and drugs, whether paid within or outside of Canada. Premiums a taxpayer pays to a private medical plan may be claimed, but not payments to a government plan. Premiums paid by a taxpayer's employer on his or her behalf under a government hospitalization or medical plan are reported as taxable benefits, but premiums paid by an employer under a private health services plan are not taxable benefits.

Once the medical amount is calculated (by subtracting $1,614 of 3 percent of net income from the allowable expenses), the credit is figured at the rate of 17 percent.

Amounts Transferred from Spouse. If an individual has certain amounts available that need not be claimed to reduce his or her federal income tax to zero, they may be transferred to the spouse's return. The amounts that may be transferred are the age amount, the pension income amount, the disability amount, and the tuition fees and education amounts. The spouse's unused amounts are converted to tax credits at the rate of 17 percent.

Charitable Donations Credit. Claims are permitted for contributions to registered charitable institutions up to a maximum of 75 percent of net income. Institutions that qualify as registered charities include organizations such as the Canadian Red Cross, the Canadian Cancer Society, United Appeal, hospitals, churches, educational institutions (including specified foreign universities), and United Nations agencies. The donations may include cash or property. If the gift is property, the taxpayer is deemed to receive proceeds equal to its value, so he or she may be liable for tax if a capital gain is involved.

Any unused or unclaimed donations may be carried forward five years. Official receipts are required for all donations claimed. The amount of the tax credit for charitable donations depends on their total. If they add up to $200 or less, the tax credit is 17 percent of the donations. If the total is larger, the tax credit is 17 percent of the first $200 and 29 percent of the excess amount.

The rationale for permitting deductions for charitable donations appears to be that charities perform important social functions similar to those performed by government and supplement numerous government services.

Gifts to Canada and Provinces. The full amount of gifts to the government of Canada or a province is eligible for a tax credit. The credit is calculated as 17 percent of the first $200 of total gifts and 29 percent of the remainder. Unlike the claim for charitable contributions, which is limited to 20 percent of net income, the claim for donations to government is unlimited.

Federal Political Contribution Tax Credit. Credit may be claimed for contributions to a registered federal political party or to a candidate for election to Parliament. The allowable credit is 75 percent of the first $100 of the contribution, 50 percent of the next $450, and 33.3 percent of the amount in excess of $550. The maximum credit that may be claimed in a tax year is $500, which is reached when $1,150 has been contributed. Any amount that is not required to reduce federal tax payable to zero cannot be carried forward.

Dividend Tax Credit. Dividends received by shareholders on equity shares have already been subject to corporation tax as income of corporations. The federal government permits a taxpayer to deduct from federal tax 13.3 percent of the taxable amount of dividends received from taxable Canadian corporations. The tax on dividends is computed by grossing-up the dividend received by 25 percent, calculating the tax payable at the taxpayer's marginal rate, and subtracting from the amount 13.3 percent of the grossed-up dividend. The method of computing the taxable dividend and the dividend tax credit is as follows:

Dividend received	$400
Gross-up: $400 x 25%	*100*
Taxable dividend	$500
Tax (assume 17% rate)	
$500 x 17%	85
Dividend tax credit: $500 x 13.3%	*67*
Tax payable	$18

Foreign Tax Credit. The federal government grants a tax credit for taxes paid to a foreign government on income from that country. The foreign tax credit deduction is, however, the lesser of the foreign taxes paid or the amount of the Canadian tax payable on the income received from the foreign country.

Refundable Tax Credit

The refundable tax credit in Canada's federal personal income tax is the sales tax credit. In this case, if the credit reduces tax payable to an amount less than zero, the taxpayer is entitled to a refund from the government.

Federal Sales Tax Credit. The sales tax credit was introduced as a credit for the federal manufacturers' sales tax. When the manufacturers' sales tax was replaced by the Goods and Services Tax (GST) in 1991, the credit was increased. The credit is independent of actual sales taxes paid by the taxpayer. It is available for all persons nineteen years of age or over.

For 1997, the credit for the GST amounted to $199 for the taxpayer, plus $199 for a spouse and $105 for each dependent child under the age of nineteen. It was reduced by 5 percent of the total net income of the two spouses in excess of $25,921. For single individuals there is a supplementary credit of 2 percent of income in excess of $6,456 to a maximum of $105. The GST credit is paid in advance every three months.

Taxation of Non-Residents

Persons not resident in Canada but receiving income from either employment or a business in the country are subject to income tax at regular rates on income from Canadian sources. Non-residents are required to file a Canadian tax return, but certain restrictions apply to the deductions and credits that may be claimed. Following the "90 percent rule," if at least 90 percent of a non-resident's income for the year is included in the taxable income he or she earned in Canada, all the deductions and credits may be claimed. Non-residents are taxed on capital gains from property held in Canada, but they were not eligible for the lifetime capital gains tax exemption that residents enjoyed when that provision was in effect.

Investment income and certain types of other income earned by non-residents is subject to a withholding tax at the source of the income. The general non-resident withholding tax rate is 25 percent of the gross amount, with no deductions permitted. The rate is reduced to 15 percent for residents of countries with which Canada has a tax agreement or treaty. The non-resident receiving the payment is not required to file a Canadian tax return as the tax is remitted to the Canadian government by the payor. Income earned by non-residents that is subject to the withholding tax includes interest, dividends, certain pensions and retirement allowances, rents, royalties, estate or trust income, and alimony payments.

Tax Rates

The federal personal income tax uses a different rate for each of three tax brackets. For 1997, they were:

Taxable Income	Tax
0 to $29,590	17%
$29,591 to $59,180	26%
$59,181 and over	29%

The rates are fixed but the tax brackets are indexed annually (that is, they are increased by the amount of increase in the consumer price index in excess of 3 percent, as described in the next subsection).

Provincial personal income tax rates, except in Quebec, are expressed as a percentage of federal basic tax and vary from province to province. In 1997, they ranged from 45.5 percent in Alberta to 69 percent in Newfoundland, averaging about 55 percent. Applying this average, the combined federal and provincial rate was approximately 26 percent on taxable income less than $29,590 and approximately 46 percent on income in excess of $59,180.

Rate Structure Changes. The rate structure of the federal personal income tax has been revised a number of times over the years. The trend has been towards fewer tax brackets and reduction in the progressiveness of the marginal tax rate structure.

Before the major tax reform introduced in 1972, there were thirteen brackets; marginal rates progressed from 12 percent on the first dollars of taxable income to 60 percent on taxable income of $400,000 and over. The combined federal and provincial rates ranged from 15 to 82 percent. The tax reform of 1972 gradually reduced the lowest federal tax rate to 6 percent and set the maximum rate at 47 percent on taxable income of $60,000. The maximum combined federal and provincial tax rate was 61 percent. Subsequent tax revisions, together with changes in federal/provincial fiscal arrangements, had, by 1987, reduced the number of tax brackets to ten, with a maximum federal rate of 34 percent on income in excess of $63,347.

Surtaxes. The tax rates shown in the previous subsection do not include the federal surtax. A surtax is an additional tax expressed as a percentage of tax payable. The federal government has frequently used a surtax as a temporary tax increase, either to pursue some fiscal policy or to obtain additional revenues to help cover budgetary deficits in particular years.

The federal surtax for 1998 was 3 percent of the basic federal tax plus 5 percent on the amount by which the basic federal tax exceeded $12,500. The surtax does not apply to taxpayers earning below $50,000, and is reduced for those earning between $50,000 and $65,000. The surtax is calculated as a percentage of the basic federal tax, which is the tax payable before deductions of the foreign tax credit, the federal sales tax credit, or the political contribution tax credit. Since most provincial taxes are calculated as a percentage of the basic federal tax, the federal surtax does not affect the provinces' personal income tax revenues.

Indexation

In 1974, the federal government introduced a system of indexing two of the elements of the personal income tax (personal exemptions and the tax brackets) by an inflation factor based on annual increases in the consumer price index. The rationale for indexing was to avoid letting inflationary gains in money income increase the tax/income ratio for taxpayers. In other words, if an individual's money income increased by 10 percent in any one year but the inflation rate was also 10 percent, that individual's real income in terms of purchasing power would remain constant. Therefore the tax/income ratio should remain constant. But since the income tax base is defined in nominal terms, any increase in money income is subject to the tax and may push the taxpayer into a higher marginal tax bracket. In that case, the person ends up paying a higher tax rate simply because of inflation. Such "bracket creep" is one significant way that inflation increases individual tax burdens and indexation is designed to reduce this bracket creep.

Between 1974 and 1982, the tax index — calculated as the full amount of the increase in the consumer price index for the twelve-month period ending September 30 of the previous year — ranged from a low of 6.6 percent to a high of 12.2 percent. For 1983 and 1984, as part of the government's inflation-control program, ceilings were placed on the income tax index at 6 and 5 percent respectively. In 1985, indexation based on the full consumer price index increase was resumed, only to be changed again in 1986. For 1986 and subsequent taxation years, the indexing factor has been limited to the annual increase in the consumer price index in excess of 3 percent. Between 1974 and 1987, the compound effect of indexing increased the dollar amount of tax brackets and personal exemptions by 163 percent.

Tax reform in 1988 introduced changes in tax brackets and the amounts of certain personal exemptions, and indexing is now based on these amounts. Currently, the items indexed are the tax brackets, the basic personal amount, the married amount, the age amount, the disability amount, the amount for dependent children 18 years of age and over who are physically or mentally infirm, and the base amount for the recapture tax or social benefits repayments. Between 1992 and 1997, the inflation rate was less than 3 percent; therefore the tax brackets and amounts subject to indexation have remained unchanged.

Social Benefits Repayment

Effective in the 1989 tax year, the government introduced a special recapture or "clawback" tax on Old Age Security (OAS) and family allowance payments, a tax technically called "social benefits repayment." The termination of the family allowance program left only OAS payments subject to recapture. This tax applied to recipients of OAS who had income in excess of a base amount. That amount was $50,000 for 1989, and it has been indexed in subsequent years by the amount that the consumer price index exceeds 3 percent. In 1994 the base amount was $53,215.

The tax was calculated by subtracting the base amount of $53,215 from net income, multiplying the result by 15 percent, and adding the lesser of this amount or the OAS payment to net federal tax. Assume, for example, that a taxpayer received an OAS payment of $4,600 and had a net income of $70,000. The recapture tax was calculated as $16,785 multiplied by 15 percent, which would equal $2,513. With a base amount of $53,215 an OAS payment of $4,600 was completely recaptured at an income level of $83,881. The social benefits repayment is deducted from total income and added to net federal tax payable. Beginning in 1996, the government began to withhold an amount equivalent to the recapture tax from monthly OAS payments if the taxpayer had an OAS repayment for the previous year.

The social benefits repayment provision was introduced as a means of gearing family allowance and OAS payments to need. The federal government had earlier proposed ending the universality of these two programs and subjecting claimants to a means test. In other words, payments from these two programs would have been made dependent on income levels, and in effect they would no longer have been available to upper-income groups. Strong public opposition to terminating the principle of universality in social assistance programs, however, caused the government to retreat from its plans, and, as an alternative, it introduced the recapture tax.

Capital Gains Tax

A capital gain is the income or profit realized when assets (such as stocks and bonds) are sold at higher prices than were originally paid.

Although capital gains taxation has long existed in many countries, Canada refrained from imposing such as a tax before 1972. It was a deliberate economic policy to stimulate growth and development in the country. The Royal Commission on Taxation contended in its 1966 report, however, that the lack of a capital gains tax produced gross inequities in taxation. It further argued that the evidence of adverse economic effects from such a tax was inconclusive. Given that equity was its overriding principle, the commission strongly recommended a capital gains tax as part of the new tax system it proposed.[3]

The government imposed a capital gains tax effective January 1, 1972. The general rule was that half of a capital gain was included in income for tax purposes, while half of capital losses was deducted from gains. Certain types of gains, such as those realized on the sale of principal residence and farms were given special treatment, and there was an exemption of $1,000 on personal property and items such as works of art and jewellery.

In 1985, the basic structure of the capital gains tax was changed. A lifetime exemption of $500,000 in capital gains was introduced, to be phased in over a six-year period. Further changes in 1988 maintained the lifetime exemption for capital gains realized on the disposition of farm property and small business corporation shares but reduced it to $100,000 for other types of capital properties. In 1994 the lifetime exemption was eliminated for all capital gains. Three-quarters of capital gains are taxed at personal income tax rates. The deductible portion of capital losses is three-quarters of losses. Capital losses are deductible only from realized capital gains. They may be carried back against capital gains of the three preceding years and carried forward indefinitely against future gains.

Current exemptions from the capital gains tax include gains realized on a principal residence, gains on the sale of personal-use property if the proceeds of disposition are less than $1,000, and windfall gains such as lottery winnings for which chance is the determining factor.

The federal gift and estate tax was abolished effective January 1, 1972, with the institution of the capital gains tax, which covers gifts and estates. Gains on estates are subject to tax upon the death of a taxpayer. Bequests between husband and wife are exempt from the tax. A wife who inherits an asset from her husband, for example, is deemed to have acquired it at her husband's original cost, and the capital gains tax is payable when she sells the asset or transfers it by gift or bequest. A gift of an asset is considered a sale at fair market value, and the donor includes in income the difference between the cost and that value.

The capital gains tax also applied to taxpayers entering or leaving Canada. A departing taxpayer is given two options: the tax can be paid on the accrued gains on assets upon departure, or the payment can be deferred until the assets are sold. In the latter case, security must, of course, be given at the time of departure to cover the tax on the accrued gain, and when the assets are sold, the taxpayer must file a tax return as a Canadian resident.

When a taxpayer enters Canada, any assets are valued at their fair market value as of the date of arrival. Tax must be paid only on gains realized while the taxpayer is in Canada. Gains that non-residents realize on assets held in Canada are treated in the same manner as those of Canadian residents.

Special rules apply for calculating capital gains and losses on assets purchased before 1972 when the capital gains tax went into effect. Furthermore, a method known as "crystalization" is applied for those taxpayers who had not taken full advantage of the lifetime exemption prior to its elimination. For those taxpayers, the base value of their assets for tax purposes would be value of the asset on February 22, 1994, the day the lifetime exemption was lifted.

Alternative Minimum Tax (AMT)

Beginning in the 1986 tax year, the federal government implemented an alternative minimum tax (AMT), a tax directed to those high-income individuals who would otherwise pay little or no tax in a particular year because of tax shelters, loss carry-overs, or the like. The tax is payable if it is greater than the tax that would be payable if calculated in the ordinary manner. In other words, an individual's income tax is calculated using the various standard deductions and tax credits applicable, together with any other deductions, such as loss carry-overs and capital gains exemptions, that may apply. The AMT is then calculated, and it applies if it is found to be greater than the tax calculated in the normal manner.

The basic exemption for the AMT is $40,000 of adjusted taxable income. The rate is 17 percent of adjusted taxable income in excess of $40,000. The adjusted taxable income in this case equals gross income minus most normal deductions but not deductions for such items as contributions to registered retirement plans or deductions that are viewed as tax shelters. The latter include capital cost allowances on buildings and certified films, and depletion and exploration allowances relating to resource investments. These can be deducted only from income generated by such investments and cannot be used to generate a loss. Furthermore, certain personal amount credits are not allowed. The combined federal and provincial rate for the AMT is approximately 26 percent averaged among the provinces.

Major variations in tax liability from one period to another may, of course, result from timing differences in the receipt of income, for which taxpayers should not be penalized. A tax shelter in one year may simply defer taxes if it produces taxable income in future years. It would be double taxation to impose income tax on income when it is placed in the tax shelter and then again when it is taken out. For this reason, the amount by which the AMT exceeds the tax liability calculated in the normal manner can be carried forward as a tax credit for up to seven years and can be deducted from ordinary tax payable in excess of AMT payable.

Administration

The personal income tax is paid on income received during the calendar year. A withholding system applies to wages and salaries, with the tax deducted at the source by the employer. Each taxpayer with income in excess of the basic personal exemptions (for a single or a married person, as appropriate) is required to file an income tax return by April 30 of the following year. The employer furnishes the taxpayer with two copies of a T-4 income statement showing total earnings and amounts withheld as tax and pension contributions.

If income tax is deducted from less than three-quarters of an individual's total income for the year (because of self-employment or other reasons), he or she is required to pay quarterly instalments of the estimated tax on the amount not subject to withholding. For most taxpayers, these instalment payments are due on or before March 15, June 15, September 15, and December 15. Farmers and fishermen are required to pay two-thirds of their estimated tax by December 31 and the balance by April 30 of the following year.

In completing the annual tax return, the taxpayer calculates his or her taxes and makes any adjustment required through additional payment or, in the event of an overpayment, a request for a refund. The completed tax return is sent to Revenue Canada, where it is processed. Calculations are checked for accuracy, T-4 statements are compared, and the information is put into a computer. Each taxpayer then receives a notice of assessment indicating whether the return is in order or the department has made adjustments. The taxpayer has the right to appeal if he or she disagrees with the department's assessment. Even if the case is under appeal, however, unpaid taxes bear interest after April 30.

The penalty for late filing of a tax return is 5 percent of the unpaid balance of tax plus 1 percent of the unpaid balance for each full month that the return was late. A taxpayer who files a return late more than once during a four-year period may be subject to larger penalties. Failure to file a return subjects a taxpayer to a fine of $1,000 to $25,000 and as much as twelve months' imprisonment. A taxpayer who fails to make or is deficient in required instalment payments is charged interest on the amount owing; he or she is also liable for a penalty equal to 50 percent of the amount by which the instalment interest exceeds $1,000. Penalties for deliberate evasion of tax or for false returns are fines of 50 to 200 percent of the tax sought to be avoided, and imprisonment for as much as five years.

Corporate Income Tax

The reform of the corporation income tax introduced in 1988 produced significant changes, which were phased in between 1988 and 1991. The changes were designed to reduce corporate tax rates in order to encourage industrial investment and expansion, to keep Canadian industry internationally competitive, to broaden the tax base by about 20 percent by reducing or eliminating certain tax preferences, and to curb artificial tax avoidance. It was estimated that these changes would increase federal corporate tax revenue by $5 billion dollars over five years.

The corporation income tax as it applied to the 1997 tax year is outlined in the following subsections, with some comments on the changes introduced by tax reform.

Corporate Income Tax Base

The corporation is treated as a separate tax-paying entity in Canada. The only integration between the corporation income tax and the personal income tax is the partial credit permitted individuals on their personal income tax for dividends received from a corporation.

The base for the corporation income tax consists of the firm's gross income from all sources, including three-quarters of capital gains, minus expenses incurred in earning the income. These expenses include wages and salaries paid; cost of materials, light, heat, and so on; interest on borrowed funds used in the business; and the cost of capital equipment. The cost of capital equipment is deducted over time in accordance with a system of set depreciation or capital cost allowances, reflecting the fact that such equipment is used in the production process over a number of years.

Depreciation (Capital Cost) Allowances

Depreciation represents the decline in value of an asset through usage or the passage of time. The federal government has established a schedule that corporations must follow in calculating depreciation costs for tax purposes. The schedule identifies 41 asset classes, each of which is assigned an annual depreciation charge, ranging from 4 percent on such durable property as roads and bridges to 100 percent on such quickly used-up assets as tools and dies. For most of the asset classes, the diminishing-balances method of depreciation is applied, by which a given percentage is deducted each year on the balance value of the asset. Ten classes employ the straight-line method whereby a given percentage of the cost of the asset is deducted each year.

The federal government has, on occasion, introduced policies of double or accelerated depreciation, temporarily increasing the allowance permitted on certain assets in an attempt to stimulate investment in plant and equipment or encourage industry to modernize. Similarly, policies of deferred depreciation have been employed in past periods of inflation to discourage excessive investment.

Tax reform reduced the capital cost allowance for a number of classes of assets, some by as much as 40 percent of the earlier rate. In addition, a special allowance for resource industries, known as the depletion allowance, was phased out.

Corporate Income Tax Rates

The federal government employs a basic rate on taxable corporate income with reduced rates for manufacturing businesses and for small, Canadian-controlled, private corporations (CCPCs). For 1997, the general corporation tax was 28 percent of corporate net income or profits. This rate was reduced to 21 percent for manufacturing corporations and to 12 percent for the first $200,000 of income of CCPCs, manufacturing or non-manufacturing. In addition, a surtax of 4 percent is imposed on the federal corporate income tax payable.

Over the years, the federal government has used special provisions and tax rates in the corporation income tax as part of its fiscal policy to stimulate investment, employment, and regional development. One such provision, as already noted, has been acceleration or deceleration of the capital cost allowance for particular assets or classes of assets.

Another such tool is the investment tax credit, which is the deduction from tax payable of a certain percentage of a specified investment. The current investment tax credits are primarily for selective investments of a regional or research-related nature. They include a 10 percent general investment credit for the Atlantic region, and rates ranging from 20 to 35 percent of the costs of research and development.

Special provisions in the tax legislation apply to the extractive resource sector — that is, the oil, gas, and mining industries. Royalties are levied on oil and natural gas produced on federally owned lands in the north and in the offshore areas of the east and west coasts. These royalties escalate from 1 to 5 percent of gross revenue of companies until the initial investment is recovered by the company. The rate then increases to 30 percent of gross revenue. Royalties escalating from 3 to 12 percent with the value of production are imposed on mineral production in the Yukon and the Northwest Territories.

Payment of Corporate Income Tax

Corporations are taxed on a fiscal year basis rather than a calendar year. They are required to pay their income taxes in monthly instalments. Payments must be remitted by the last day of each month and are considered to have been on time only if actually received by the due date. To ensure prompt payment, late or deficient instalments are subject to interest charges. The charge for a calendar quarter is the average rate of interest on 90-day federal Treasury bills sold during the first month of the preceding quarter, plus two percentage points. The same interest rate applies to refunds to corporations for overpayments of tax.

Other Business Taxes

In addition to the tax on business, the federal government also imposes taxes on business capital and on payrolls. (The payroll tax is discussed at the end of the chapter).

Capital Taxes

In 1989 a tax was imposed on the capital of large corporations, called the large corporation tax. It applied to about 3,600 of Canada's largest corporations and was expected to generate approximately $1 billion in revenue in its first year of application.

The large corporation tax rate of 0.225 percent is applied to a capital base consisting of the shareholders' equity, surpluses, reserves, loans and advances to the corporation, and specified indebtedness represented by goods, debentures, mortgages, and other securities of the corporation. The tax is levied only on that part of a corporation's capital employed in Canada, and non-resident corporations that have permanent establishments in this country compute capital employed here on the basis of their Canadian assets. All corporations are permitted a $10 million basic capital deduction from taxable capital employed in Canada. This deduction has the effect of limiting the tax to larger corporations. The tax is applied to both non-financial corporations and financial institutions, including insurance companies; for deposit-taking institutions, however, deposits and similar liabilities are not included in financial capital.

A special capital tax is imposed on financial institutions at a rate of 1 percent of paid-up capital between $200 and $300 million, rising to 1.5 percent on capital over $300 million.

Consumption-Based Taxes

Before 1991, the federal government levied three consumption-based taxes: the manufacturers' sales tax, excise taxes, and excise duties. Effective January 1, 1991, the manufacturers' sales tax was replaced with the Goods and Services Tax (GST). The GST has been highly controversial. Therefore its imposition and workings are examined in particular detail in this section. Excise taxes and excise duties are also described.

Terminating the Manufacturers' Sales Tax

The replacement of the manufacturers' sales tax with the GST was a time-consuming process in a climate of considerable controversy and debate. The manufacturers' sales tax had been introduced by the federal government in 1920 and appeared adequate at the time, given the relatively uncomplicated nature of production and distribution and the fairly clear dividing lines between production and distribution. But as the economy became more complex, with increasing degrees of vertical integration among manufacturers, wholesalers, and retailers, the inadequacies of the manufacturers' sales tax became increasingly apparent. Numerous studies, such as those by the Royal Commission on Taxation in 1966 and the Federal Sales Tax Review Committee in 1983, detailed its faults and recommended major reform. Yet the tax continued as a major component in the federal government's revenue structure with nothing but piecemeal changes to attempt to correct its most glaring deficiencies.

The manufacturers' sales tax was a general sales tax levied at the manufacturers' level on all goods manufactured in or imported to Canada. Two groups of goods were exempt. In order to avoid double taxation, the first such group was various producer goods, including materials and partly finished goods used in further production, production machinery and equipment, and fuel and power used in the production process. (Building materials were, however, subject to the tax.) In an attempt to reduce the degree of regressiveness of the tax, the second group of exempt goods included certain consumer goods that constitute a significant portion of the purchases of lower-income families, including most foods, clothing and footwear, prescription drugs, and household fuel and power. Also the tax did not fall on most services.

The general tax rate fluctuated between 9 and 12 percent during most of the 1970s and 1980s; in 1989, it was increased to 13.5 percent. Certain items were subject to a different rate, such as construction materials and equipment, taxed most recently at 9 percent, and alcoholic beverages and tobacco products, at 19 percent. The tax was applied on the manufacturers' selling price exclusive of all other excise taxes but inclusive of excise duties and customs tariffs.

Problems with the Tax. The government pointed to numerous structural failings of the manufacturers' sales tax: notably, that it damaged competitiveness, favoured imports, was discriminatory, and was excessively complex and therefore subject to avoidance. The tax harmed the competitiveness of Canadian industry in that it included many goods used as inputs in the production process, which led to a degree of double taxation and to higher prices for the final products. It favoured imports over domestic goods because it was levied on the price of the former exclusive of the costs of marketing and distribution, whereas these costs were usually included in domestic manufacturers' selling prices. The importer consequently paid less tax and could price more competitively than a Canadian producer. It was estimated that the tax as a percentage of the retail price was about one-third higher on domestic goods than on competing imports.

The base of the tax was very narrow, applying to only about one-third of the goods and services Canadians purchased. It therefore discriminated against certain sectors of the economy and the consumers of the goods subject to the tax.

Finally, the tax was viewed as excessively complex and costly for government to administer and caused major compliance difficulties. The distinction between taxed and non-taxed items was difficult to define and resulted in major disputes and court challenges. In an attempt to increase fairness and equity in the application of the tax, the government had provided more than 22,000 special provisions and administrative interpretations to the governing legislation. The Auditor General of Canada contended that administrative complexities and poor monitoring of the approximate 75,000 companies that paid the sales tax probably cost the government billions of dollars in unpaid tax. This was in addition to an estimated $300 million of revenue lost by other measures that manufacturing companies took to avoid the tax, such as setting up separate marketing and distribution subsidiaries so as to exclude advertising and other marketing costs from the price on which the tax was applied.[4]

Opposition to the Change. The Conservative government's views on the merits of replacing the manufacturers' sales tax with the GST were not shared by the political parties then in opposition, the provincial governments, various sectors of the economy, or many taxpayers. The provinces complained that the GST encroached on the retail sales tax field, a major source of revenue to them. Consumer groups and labour unions argued that the imposition of the GST would increase consumer prices and fuel a wage/price spiral and a new round of inflation. They refused to accept the government's contention that the new tax would add no more than 1.25 percentage points to the consumer price index in 1991 and have almost no impact in subsequent years. The residential construction industry and prospective homeowners argued that the GST would add substantial increases to the prices of new homes and make new housing unaffordable to many Canadian families. Many small businesses and the professional services sectors expressed opposition to the administrative burden being thrust upon them and irritation at becoming tax collectors for Revenue Canada.

It was further argued that the GST, like any general sales tax, was regressive and inequitable. It would impose a greater burden on the poor than on the wealthy in the sense that lower-income groups would pay relatively more of their income in tax than would higher-income groups. In addition, it was contended that the GST represented a major tax increase on all Canadians. In presenting the details of his proposal in August 1989, the Minister of Finance produced data showing that, at the then-proposed rate of 9 percent, the GST would generate $5.5 billion more in revenue in 1991 than the manufacturers' sales tax would have yielded, but this increase would be offset by higher sales tax credits and other tax reductions.[5]

The original GST legislation contained various provisions that addressed some of these concerns — there were, for example, tax-free and tax-exempt items, housing rebates, and tax credits for lower-income families. Other potential problems were dealt with by changes after the proposal was first tabled, and the proposed rate was reduced from 9 to 7 percent. Nevertheless, opposition to the tax remained widespread and strong, with some of the more vocal opposition groups calling for a tax revolt (that is, for taxpayers to refuse to pay federal taxes).

Few disputed the fact that the manufacturers' sales tax had major deficiencies and that past attempts to eliminate them had proved inadequate. The GST is viewed as technically superior because it is comprehensive in coverage and is imposed at the retail level, thereby avoiding the distortions caused by the manufacturers' sales tax. The GST is also very similar to the general sales taxes imposed by some forty-eight other countries. The emotional outrage expressed in various quarters of the country, as evident in public statements and the media, was characteristic of opposition to a major tax increase. People saw themselves paying tax on many more purchases, and collecting the tax — which would fall to many individuals and firms — was viewed as an inconvenience and a burden. Many also feared the GST as a potential major tax grab by the federal government. Ottawa attempted to assure the public that the government's overall fiscal position would be essentially unaffected by the impact of sales tax reform, with additional revenues applied to increasing the sales tax credit and to offsetting increases in the costs of indexed social programs. Critics, however, feared that the government would move quickly to exploit the large revenue-generating potential of the GST to reduce its huge annual budgetary deficits, with consequent increasing tax burdens on consumers.

The outpouring of opposition proved futile. The Conservative government mustered majorities in both houses of Parliament, and after much emotional debate there, the GST legislation became effective on January 1, 1991.

Goods and Services Tax (GST)

Unlike the manufacturers' sales tax, which is a single-stage levy on manufacturers' selling prices, the GST is characterized by a multi-stage collection process. It is a tax on all sales or supply of goods and services that are not specifically excluded. A system of input tax credits removes the tax from productive inputs and ensures that it falls on final consumption. The tax rate is 7 percent of selling prices, exclusive of any provincial retail sales taxes.

In the GST system, a purchaser is required to pay the 7 percent tax to the seller of the good or service. The seller is required to remit to the government the difference between any tax paid on inputs (input tax credit) and

the tax received on sales. Consider the following example as illustrated in Table 9-5. Assume that producer A sells an input to producer B for $100 on which A collects the GST of $7. Producer B uses the input to produce a semi-finished product, which she sells for $300 to producer C. The tax paid by C on the $300 sale is $21, and B remits to the government $14, the difference in the amount of tax she paid and the amount she collected from C. If producer C finishes the product and sells it to the consumer for $800 (excluding tax), the consumer pays the GST of $56. C claims an input tax credit of $21 paid to B, and he therefore remits $35 to the government. The total amount of tax to the government is $56, which is paid by the consumer but has been collected by the three sellers, A, B, and C. The tax charged at each stage of production has been fully refunded at the next stage.

The total amount paid by the consumer is identical to the amount of tax that she would have paid under a 7 percent retail sales tax applied on the final sale. It is argued, however, that the multi-stage GST is superior to the retail sales tax because the latter may not completely avoid the taxation of productive inputs, which could lead to double taxation, higher production costs, and higher prices.

The GST applies to all business transactions throughout the production, distribution, and retailing chain, unless they are specifically excluded from the tax. Small businesses and individual traders with sales transactions of less than $30,000 annually are given the option of whether they wish to join or not join the GST system, a choice provided in recognition of the fact that very small suppliers may have limited resources to administer the tax. Those who choose to opt out of the system neither collect tax on sales nor claim input tax credits on their purchases. This arrangement can be suitable for small suppliers who sell directly to consumers, but those selling mainly to business may find it advantageous to join the GST as doing so permits the

TABLE 9-5: Goods and Services Tax

	Sale by producer A to producer B	Sale by producer B to producer C	Sale by producer C to consumer
Sale value	$100.00	$300.00	$800.00
GST	7.00	21.00	56.00
GST credit		7.00	21.00
GST remitted	7.00	14.00	35.00

Total GST remitted = $56.00 = Amount paid by the consumer

customers, as well as the supplier, to claim input tax credits.

Tax-Free and Tax-Exempt Commodities. The goods and services not subject to the tax comprise two groups: tax-free and tax-exempt sales. For tax-free sales, sometimes referred to as zero-rated sales, vendors do not collect the GST, but they are still able to claim input tax credits for any tax they have paid on purchases for production. This provision removes all tax from these goods and services. For tax-exempt sales, retail vendors also do not collect the GST, but they are not permitted credits on inputs purchased.

For the most part, the non-taxed items are basic consumer goods and services on which low-income groups spend a large proportion of their budgets, and their exclusion for the tax was designed to reduce the regressiveness of the GST. Tax-free items comprise basic groceries, agricultural and fish products, prescription drugs, and medical devices such as wheelchairs, contact lenses, eyeglasses, and so on, as well as exports. The list of tax-free groceries does not include soft drinks, candies, snack foods, or restaurant meals. Tax-exempt items include health and dental care, educational services, day-care services, legal aid services, residential rents, and financial services such as loans, deposits, and life and property insurance. Other exemptions include the sale of used residential homes, sales by

charities, gambling and lottery winnings, sales of used goods by private individuals, trade union and mandatory professional fees, and meals and lodging provided by non-profit organizations.

Tourists to Canada who purchase taxable items to take home may apply for a full rebate of the GST.

Housing and Real Property. Resale of old homes are exempt from the tax. Special provisions in the GST apply to new housing. The previous manufacturers' sales tax had excluded direct taxation of new homes, but it was applied at varying rates to building materials, such as lumber, bricks, windows, wallpaper, and so on; it was estimated that these taxes added up to the equivalent of about a 4 percent effective tax rate on new homes. The GST rate of 7 percent applies to the retail price of newly constructed residential dwellings (including the value of the land component). To relieve the tax burden on new homes, however, the government provides a rebate on the purchase of new dwellings, including single-detached and semi-detached houses, row houses, and condominium apartments. To qualify for the rebate, the purchaser must be a Canadian resident, and the dwelling must be the purchaser's principal residence.

The size of the rebate varies with the price of the unit. Houses priced at $350,000 or less qualify for a rebate which reduces the tax to

4.5 percent. The amount of the rebate is reduced for houses priced at more than $350,000 and is removed completely for those priced in excess of $450,000.

Special provisions also apply to other real properties. In general, the GST applies to any sale or rental of real property (land and buildings) unless it is specifically exempt. For example, the sale of farmland to a farmer-operator is exempt, but other sales or leases of farmland, such as a sale to a developer, are subject to the tax.

Public Sector Activities. Most public sector commercial activities, like private sector commercial activities, are subject to the GST. In recognition of the special role of the government, however, certain non-commercial public sector activities are exempt. Regulatory activities including drivers' licences, patent fees, and construction permits, are not taxable. Most municipal-provided services financed by a direct levy, such as water supply, are also exempt. But other utilities such as telecommunications, hydro-electric power, and natural gas are taxed, as well as the services supplied by Canada Post and most other Crown corporations. Municipalities, universities, schools, and hospitals are given rebates on their purchases. The rebates reduce the tax on local government purchases to 3 percent. Schools pay a tax of 2.2 percent while the rebate for hospitals reduce their tax to 1.2 percent. The rebate on university purchases lowers their tax to 2.3 percent, except for books for which the entire tax is rebated.

Imports and Exports. The GST applies to imports. It is payable on the duty and excise paid value of goods imported into Canada and collected at the same time as customs tariffs. Importers who have paid the tax can receive an input tax credit when they resell goods to consumers or others. The GST, however, does not apply to imports of the tax-free items already listed.

Goods made in Canada and exported are classified as tax-free items, and exporters are allowed to claim any input tax credits that may apply. This exemption from sales tax, of course, makes Canada's exports more competitive in the international market.

Sales Tax Credit. Incorporated into the GST legislation is a sales tax credit for the personal income tax that is more generous to Canadians than that provided for the manufacturers' sales tax. The GST credit is a refundable credit calculated on the basis of information from income tax returns. The amount of the credit depends on family size and income. For 1997, the GST credit for a family with income of less than $25,921 was set at $199 per adult and $105 per each dependent child under the age of 18 years. A supplementary credit of 2 percent of net income over $6,456, to a maximum of $105, is provided for single adults. For households with net income of more than the threshold amount, the credit is reduced by $5 for every $100 of net income in excess of $25,921. The credit is based on the past year's income and family status and is paid quarterly in equal instalments. Both the credit amounts and the threshold are indexed annually by any increase in the consumer price index in excess of 3 percent.

Administration

A purchaser of a good or service is liable for payment of the GST on the day on which payment for the item is made or on the day on which the payment becomes due, whichever is earlier. The timing of payment generally corresponds to the time in which the sellers normally record the sales in their accounts.

Sellers are required to remit the tax to the government on a monthly, quarterly, or yearly basis, depending on volume of sales. Vendors with annual revenue from taxable and non-taxable items in excess of $6 million are required to file a GST return and remit the tax monthly. Vendors with sales less than $6 million remit quarterly. Those with annual revenue of $500,000 or less have the option of filing returns annually but remitting instalments quarterly. Tax returns must be filed within one month of the end of a vendor's registered reporting period. Penalties and interest are charged on late returns and on unpaid tax.

Aid for Small Business. The government financially assisted small businesses with the costs of complying with the GST. Those with annual revenue of less than $2 million were eligible for a one-time administration payment of up to $1,000. Small businesses with annual sales of less than $30,000 are exempt from collecting and paying the tax.

The government also developed simplified GST accounting methods for small businesses: the quick method and two streamlined methods. The quick method is available to businesses with annual sales of $200,000 or less. Under this method, the vendor collects the 7 percent GST on sales (except for groceries) but does not claim specific tax credits. Instead, the amount of tax the vendor remits is calculated by multiplying total receipts (sales plus GST collected) by a specific rate. There are two quick method rates, 2.5 percent and 5 percent. The 2.5 percent rate applies to retailers and wholesalers who purchase goods to resell (i.e., convenience stores, book stores, boutiques.) The 5 percent rate is used by small businesses providing services (i.e., auto repair shops, dry cleaners, caterers, taxi drivers). This shortcut in GST calculation eliminates the need to keep track of separate input tax credits on expenses. The tax credits that normally would be claimed are accounted for by the discounted percentages applied to receipts.

The two streamlined accounting methods are available to retail merchants selling a combination of zero-rates basic groceries and other taxable goods with total sales less than $2 million. Although somewhat more complicated than the quick method, they eliminate the need to keep track of every GST transaction at the cash register. One method enables the vendor to calculate the amount of tax to be remitted by applying its own standard markup on purchases of goods for resale that are taxable. In the other method, the amount remitted is calculated by applying a prescribed markup on purchases for resale of zero-rated items. The first method is particularly useful if the vendor sells primarily basic groceries and only a few goods taxed at 7 percent; the second is most useful to vendors that primarily sell taxable items.

Harmonization with Provincial Retail Sales Taxes

During the federal election campaign of 1993 the Liberal party under Jean Chretien promised to eliminate and replace the unpopular GST. Following its election, the Liberal government requested the House of Commons Standing Committee to conduct an extensive review of sales tax reform options. The committee considered a wide range of alternatives and rejected all of them. The recommendation of the committee was not the abolition of the GST, but to seek an arrangement with the provinces to harmonize the GST with the provincial retail sales taxes.[6]

When the federal government had first introduced the GST in 1991 it desired to obtain the co-operation of the provinces to blend the GST with provincial retail sales taxes into one national sales tax, with revenue shared by the two levels of government. Quebec agreed to harmonize its retail sales tax with the GST shortly after its introduction. The remaining provinces were not receptive to the idea, but Ottawa continued to attempt to negotiate a harmonization arrangement with them. In 1996 the three provinces of Newfoundland, Nova Scotia and New Brunswick signed an agreement with Ottawa by which the GST and the provincial sales tax would be replaced, effective April 1997, with a single combined value-added tax, called the Harmonized Sales Tax (HST).[7] The HST is levied at a single rate of 15 percent on the same base of goods and services as the GST. Seven percentage points represents the federal component and eight percentage points the provincial component. The tax is administered and collected by the federal government through Revenue Canada, which proposed to make every effort to offer employment to provincial tax administrative staff. It was estimated, however, that the reduced overlap and duplication of administration resulting from harmonization would save the governments about $10 million annually.

The provincial component of 8 percent of the HST represented a reduction in the sales taxes of the three provinces, and consequently a reduction in revenues despite the extended tax base of the HST compared to the previous provincial taxes. To offset the lost revenue, Ottawa agreed to a compensation payment to the three provinces amounting to almost $1 billion over a four-year period.

As part of the sales tax harmonization process the federal government proposed to incorporate the new tax rate into the shelf prices of the taxed items. The tax would then become a hidden tax rather than an open one. Retailers in the Atlantic provinces vigorously objected to this proposal, citing problems such as costs of implementing tax-inclusive pricing, confusion for consumers over differences that they would observe in nationally advertised prices and local prices, and additional costs to national suppliers in establishing suggested retail prices for items. Pressure from retailers forced the federal government to retract its tax-inclusive pricing proposal until such time as all provinces with a retail sales tax agreed to harmonization with the GST.

The remaining provinces refused to join the three Atlantic provinces to harmonize their sales taxes with the federal GST. Alberta, of course, did not impose a sales tax and was therefore not interested. Among the objections voiced by the other provinces was the contention that a HST of 15 percent, employing the GST base, would represent an increase in sales taxation on their residents. The provinces furthermore feared that a HST administered by Ottawa would result in less control for them in the area of sales taxation, since they would no longer decide what was taxable in their jurisdictions.

Assessing the GST

While it is generally acknowledged that the GST is an improvement over the previous manufacturers' sales tax (MST), it has not been without its own limitations and problems. It has improved Canada's competitive position because it applies equally to imports and domestic goods, and it excludes exports. In other areas such as administration, however, it has been troublesome and costly. For example, it has been reported that administering the GST required 6,800 federal employees compared to 1,800 employees for the MST, and costs of administration soared from $85 million for the MST to $400 million for the GST. While about 75,000 corporations paid the MST, the GST pulled in almost two million companies and individuals as tax collectors. The reported cost to small companies to collect the GST was over 17 cents for each dollar of tax remitted.[8] For large companies, the cost was reported to be about 4 cents for each dollar of tax remitted, which is about equal to the cost of collecting the MST.

The MST produced more than 22,000 special arrangements and interpretations and posed problems for defining taxed and non-taxed goods. The GST did not appear to be an improvement in this area as retailers are required to keep track of a complicated list of exemptions.

The GST proved to be a highly unpopular tax compared to the MST. Most consumers were unaware that they were paying a federal sales tax when the MST was in effect because it was hidden and built into the retail price. In contrast, the GST is very obvious and this factor, combined with the broader scope of the GST, contributed to consumers' dislike of the tax. There is considerable evidence to show that tax evasion increased after 1991 as the GST produced a larger underground economy in Canada (discussed later in this chapter).

Excise Taxes

In addition to the general goods and services sales tax, the Canadian commodity tax structure has a number of specific taxes that take the form of unit and *ad valorem* taxes. Unit taxes are applied to a commodity on the basis of weight, volume, or amount. *Ad valorem* taxes are expressed as a percentage of the selling price.

These excise taxes have traditionally been applied to goods labelled as luxuries and to items deemed to have social costs. Recently, they have also been used as a conservation measure, such as the tax on automobile air conditioners and on automobiles with large engines.

The following excise taxes were in effect during 1997.[9]

Cigarettes	$0.1388 per 5 cigarettes
Manufactured tobacco	$10.65 per kg
Cigars	50%
Jewellery, watches, etc.	10%
Wines	
1.2 % or less alcohol	$0.0205
1.2 % to 7% alcohol	$0.2459
Other	$0.5122
Gasoline	$0.85 per l
Diesel and aviation fuel	$.04 per l
Air conditioners in cars, trucks, etc.	$100 per unit

Excise Duties

Various features distinguish excise duties from excise taxes. Excise duties are unit levies, apply to domestic goods only, are limited to liquor and tobacco products, and are imposed under the Excise Act (excise taxes are imposed under the Excise Tax Act). Furthermore, excise duties are more closely related to the supervision of production, which explains the difference in the timing of payment. They are paid at various stages of production, while excise taxes are paid at the end of the month following the sale. For example, excise duties on beer are paid at the fermenting stage, about six weeks before the beer is bottled and shipped. The excise tax on tobacco products is paid with the purchase of the excise stamp, which must be placed on the product prior to its sale. In both cases, the producer bears the burden during the period between tax imposition and sale.

The most significant excise duties and their rates as they applied in 1997 were:[10]

Distilled spirits (absolute alcohol)	$11.061
Beer (not more than 2.5% alcohol)	$13.991
Beer (regular)	$27.981
Cigarettes	$27.47 per 1000
Cigars	$14.781 per 1000
Manufactured tobacco	$18.33 per kg
Raw leaf tobacco	$1.57 per kg

Cigarettes, cigars, and manufactured tobacco are subject to both the excise tax and excise duty.

Excise duties do not apply to imported goods. Instead, a customs duty is imposed on imports; the amount is equivalent to the excise duty on the domestic products.

Customs Tariffs

The customs tariff has traditionally been imposed on a wide range of goods imported into Canada and consists of both *ad valorem* and unit levies. In the early days following Confederation, the customs tariff not only protected Canada's infant industries and fostered economic development but was also the major source of federal revenue. The General Agreement on Tariffs and Trade (GATT), introduced at the end of World War II, served to reduce general tariffs worldwide, including the Canadian tariff structure. The large number of countries who participate in GATT meet periodically to renegotiate tariffs, and the result has been falling tariff barriers around the world. Consequently, tariffs have become a relatively decreasing source of revenue over the years. In 1989 Canada and the United States concluded the Canada-U.S. Free Trade Agreement, eliminating tariffs between the two countries. This agreement was extended in 1994 to include Mexico (the North American Free Trade Agreement or NAFTA). Given that a high proportion of Canada's foreign trade is in North America, the gradual elimination of tariffs under NAFTA will greatly reduce the revenues generated by tariffs.

Payroll Taxes

Payroll taxes are levies on wages and salaries that may be imposed on the employee, on the amount paid out by the employer, or both. They are generally used to finance social security programs.

The federal government uses payroll taxes to finance the Employment Insurance program and the Canadian Pension Plan. The Employment Insurance program is financed entirely by premiums paid by employees and employers. These premiums have been frequently adjusted to cover the estimated costs of the program. Prior to 1990, the federal government made special contributions to the Employment Insurance account to finance extended benefits and to cover benefits paid to fishers, but these contributions have been eliminated. In 1997, employee contributions amounted to $2.90 per $100 of weekly insurable earnings to a maximum contribution of $1,131. Employer contributions equalled 1.4 times the amount of the employee contribution or $4.06 per $100 of weekly insurable earnings.

The Canada Pension Plan is financed by equal contributions from employer and employee. In 1997, their combined contributions were 5.85 percent of pensionable earnings, scheduled to rise to 9.9 percent by the year 2003.

Other Revenue Sources

In addition to taxes on individuals, business, and consumption, the federal government obtains revenues from the sale of goods and services, permits and licences, returns on investments, and through borrowing. The sale of government goods and services and borrowing are viewed as alternatives to taxation as a means of financing government and are discussed in later chapters. This section will briefly cover revenues from permits and licences and returns on investments.

Ottawa receives about $550 million annually from licences and permits. These include: radio and other communications licences; park and campground permits; timber and other forest permits; and permits, leases and rentals of Crown lands for mineral exploration and production and with respect to natural resources in the Yukon and Northwest Territories over which the federal government has jurisdiction.

The federal government earns approximately $5 billion annually as returns on its investments. These returns include interest on loans and advances to other governments and to Crown corporations. They also include profits earned by Crown corporations which are remitted to Ottawa. Over 60 percent or $3.5 billion of the total is accounted for as returns on loans and investments in federal Crown corporations, primarily the Bank of Canada, the Central Mortgage and Housing Corporation, and the Farm Credit Corporation. Revenues realized as returns on investments are classified as non-budgetary transactions in the governments financial accounts and are not reflected in the annual budgetary surplus or deficit.

The Underground Economy and Tax Evasion

High taxes, increasing taxes, or unpopular taxes may lead to more tax evasion and may spawn an underground economy, where payments for goods and services are made in cash or barter and are not reported to government. With no records or receipts for transactions, an individual may evade both income and sales taxes, leading to government revenue losses. Considerable evidence was produced following the introduction of the GST in 1991 that this highly unpopular tax, combined with the numerous other tax increases in the 1980s, contributed significantly to the underground economy in Canada.

Estimates of the size of Canada's underground economy have ranged from about 3 percent of GDP to over 20 percent. Statistics Canada has estimated its size at approximately 2.7 percent of GDP, while the Department of Finance placed its estimate at 4.5 percent of GDP. At 5 percent of GDP, an underground economy would cost Ottawa about $5 billion in lost revenues annually. A committee of the Ontario legislature, however, placed the underground economy at between 9.5 to 16.5 percent of Canada's GDP, valued at a staggering $70 billion to $120 billion annually.[11]

Some studies have focussed on the increase in the underground economy caused by the GST. One study estimated the contribution of the GST to the underground economy in 1992 at $5.7 billion, which would have cost the federal government $2.3 billion in lost revenues.[12] The Department of Finance estimated the GST may have added 10 percent per year to the underground economy between the years 1990 and 1993. Given a GDP of approximately $670 billion in 1990, an underground economy equal to 4.5 percent of GDP would amount to $30 billion and a 10 percent increase would equal $3 billion.

In addition to these aggregate estimates, there were other indicators of a growing un-derground economy in the early 1990s. It was reported that about one-third of jewellery sales was paid under the table; that 55 percent of all home renovations in Canada in 1992 were done underground compared to 30 percent prior to the GST; that 17 percent of new home sales and 41 percent of house renovations in Ontario went unreported; that many trades persons took on outside jobs for cash at much lower rates than their union rates; that many businesses not only sold their goods for cash but also purchased inventory for cash so that there would be no record of the transaction; and that many retailers recorded sales as tax free items when they were actually taxable.[13]

Another example of how high taxes can lead to a black market to avoid taxes occurred in 1994 in the cigarette market. Rapidly rising federal and provincial excises on cigarettes had pushed the price of a carton of 200 cigarettes to $48.50 in Quebec and Ontario, of which 75 percent consisted of taxes. These high prices resulted in massive smuggling of cigarettes from the United States, which sold on the black market for about one-half the legal price. It was estimated that this black market was costing the federal and the Ontario governments nearly $1 billion in lost tax revenue annually. Unable to halt the smuggling activity through law enforcement, the provincial and federal governments decided to combat it through reduced excise taxes, which dropped the price of cigarettes to approximately the price prevailing on the black market.[14]

That high taxes and unpopular taxes could contribute to turning a country into a nation of tax cheaters was evident from surveys and polls conducted after the GST was introduced. A 1995 national public opinion poll conducted for *The Financial Post* produced the following responses: two out of five persons surveyed admitted to paying cash for goods or services to avoid the GST; 20 percent admitted to having hidden income in order to evade the income tax; 72 percent reported they would pay cash to avoid taxes if given the opportunity; 34 percent said they would buy smuggled cigarettes or alcohol; and 77 percent of those polled said they had become more determined to avoid taxes after the GST was introduced. While high taxes were cited as a primary reason to cheat, other motivating factors cited included government waste, corrupt politicians, the welfare system, overpaid bureaucrats, and an overall disdain for Canada's large and expensive governments.[15]

A survey for the accounting firm KPMG Peat Marwick Thorne in 1994 produced similar results, with 49 percent of those polled saying they would pay cash to avoid the GST if the opportunity arose. Of the people polled, 86 percent agreed that governments tended to squander taxpayers' money, while 75 percent agreed that if taxes were lower, fewer people would try to avoid them.[16]

Summary

The federal tax structure has developed and expanded over time, with old taxes revised and new taxes added. The personal income tax is by far the most important revenue source, followed by the sales tax and excises, Employment Insurance premiums, and the corporation income tax. Non-tax revenue, such as the sale of goods and services, accounts for less than 8 percent of total federal revenue.

A very broad personal income tax base is employed. Various deductions are allowed to arrive at taxable income, and once the tax is calculated, tax credits are applied to further reduce tax liability. The number of tax brackets has declined over time, along with the marginal tax rates.

The most important tax imposed on consumption by the federal government is the GST, introduced in 1991. It has proved to be a controversial and unpopular tax. Excise taxes and excise duties on selective, or groups of, goods and services, along with tariffs, complete the taxation of consumption.

Two important payroll taxes are included in the federal tax structure. These are Employment Insurance and Canada Pension Plan premiums. The latter is scheduled to practically double over the next few years.

The unpopularity of the GST, combined with increasing rates of other taxes and the public's conception of government corruption and waste, appears to have contributed to increased tax evasion and to a growing underground economy.

NOTES

1   The main sources of information on the federal tax system are Revenue Canada's series of tax information guides and pamphlets and the tax acts contained in Statutes of Canada. Details on the most recent changes in federal taxation are presented in the Department of Finance's budget papers, supplementary information, and notices of ways and means motions on recent budgets. For up-to-date coverage of tax changes, along with data on tax revenues, the reader can also consult the Canadian Tax Foundation's annual publication, *Finances of the Nation.*

2   The personal exemption was established in 1973 at $1,600 for a single person and $3,000 for a married couple. Effective January 1, 1974, the federal government introduced a system of indexing the personal income tax by an annual inflation factor based on the consumer price index.

3   Canada, *Report of the Royal Commission on Taxation,* vol. 3, ch.15 (Ottawa: Queen's Printer, 1966).

4   Canada, House of Commons, Finance Committee, February 8, 1990.

5   Canada, Department of Finance, *Goods and Services Tax: An Overview* (Ottawa, August 1989), p.32.

6   Canada, Department of Finance, *Towards Replacing the Goods and Services Tax* (Ottawa, 1996).

7   Canada, Department of Finance, *Harmonized Sales Tax,* Technical Paper (Ottawa, 1996).

8   Plamondon & Associates, *GST Compliance Costs for Small Business in Canada,* A Study for the Department of Finance Tax Policy, 1993.

9   Revenue Canada, Customs and Excise Branch, Excise Bulletins (Ottawa).

10 *Ibid.*

11 *The Globe and Mail,* February 3, 1994.

12 Peter S. Spiro, "Evidence of a Post-GST Increase in the Underground Economy," *Canadian Tax Journal* 41, 2 (1993): 247-258.

13 *The Globe and Mail,* November 15, 1995.

14 *Ibid.,* February 9, 1994, A1, A3.

15 *The Financial Post,* June 3, 1995, p.19.

16 *The Globe and Mail,* March 4, 1994, B3.

CHAPTER 10

Provincial and Local Government Finance

The provincial, territorial, and local governments rely heavily on taxation to finance their activities but, similar to the federal government, they also tap other sources of revenue such as permits, fees, fines, returns on investments, and the sale of goods and services and lotteries.[1] This chapter focuses on taxation. Other principal means of financing are covered in chapter 11.

Provincial Taxation

The Constitution Act, 1867, outlined the powers of the provinces for raising revenue and limited them to direct taxation. No mention is made in the act of lower levels of government, such as local or municipal governments. Since they are the creation of the provincial governments, the only powers local governments have are those delegated to them by the province.

Taxation at the provincial level is not uniform across Canada. In addition to the personal and corporation income taxes, which all provinces impose, there are a variety of levies, often including a retail sales tax, gasoline tax, taxes on liquor and tobacco, and taxes on specific services such as communications.

The provinces' revenue from the various taxes they impose and from other sources is illustrated in Table 10-1 for all provinces combined. Tax revenue accounted for more than 60 percent of total provincial revenue in 1994-95 compared to 53 percent in 1977. The personal income tax has been the most significant source of revenue accounting for

more than 25 percent of revenue in 1994-95. The trend of increasing importance for the personal income tax was accompanied by a decline in the share of revenue from transfers; this change resulted mostly from the federal/provincial fiscal agreements, which gave the provinces increased tax room in the personal income taxes as a partial substitute for specific transfers, particularly for provincial health programs and post-secondary education.

The second most important tax has been the general sales tax, contributing over 13 percent of provincial revenue. Two notable trends since 1967 have been the decline in the significance of the corporation income tax and of the tax on motor fuel. Revenue from natural resources increased relative to other sources in the 1970s, reflecting higher oil and gas prices and a prosperous energy sector in some western provinces, particularly Alberta, but then declined in later years.

The relative importance of the various revenue sources varies considerably from province to province. Table 10-2 shows the significance of revenue sources for each province for the year 1996-97. In Newfoundland and New Brunswick, revenue from the general sales tax exceeded revenue from the personal income tax. Shares of personal income tax revenue ranged from a low of 16 percent of total revenue in Newfoundland to a high of 33 percent in Quebec, while those of corporation income tax revenue ranged from a low of 1.4 percent of total Newfoundland revenue to a high of 7.8 percent in Ontario. The retail

TABLE 10-1: Historical Summary of Provincial and Territorial Government Revenues

Source	Revenues for the fiscal year ending March 31			
	1968	1977	1990	1995
	(percentage of total)			
Taxes				
Personal income	17.1	19.1	24.4	25.4
Corporation income	7.0	5.7	5.0	4.1
General sales	14.7	11.9	13.3	13.2
Motor fuel	9.2	4.1	3.4	3.9
Health and social insurance levies	2.6	5.7	7.5	6.5
Other	5.1	7.0	6.0	8.5
Total tax revenue	55.7	53.5	59.6	61.6
Non-tax revenue				
Natural resources	5.9	7.9	4.0	4.7
Licences, permits, etc.	5.0	2.3	2.4	2.5
Sales of goods and services	1.8	2.4	1.9	2.1
Return on investment	6.7	9.0	9.1	9.1
Other	0.2	1.0	3.9	.8
Total non-tax revenue	19.6	22.6	21.3	19.2
Total own-source revenue	75.3	76.1	80.9	84.8
Transfers				
Specific purpose	15.7	15.5	12.1	12.4
General purpose	9.1	8.4	7.0	6.8
Total	24.8	23.9	19.1	19.2
Total	100.0	100.0	100.0	100.0
	($million)			
Total amount	8,571	38,467	135,549	159,634

Source: Statistics Canada, Provincial Government Finance, *Revenue and Expenditures*, cat. 68-207; Public Sector Finance *1995-1996*, cat. 68-212-XPB.

sales tax brought more than 15 percent of total revenue in all provinces except Alberta, which does not impose a general sales tax.

Revenue from taxation produced less than 50 percent of the total revenues of the Atlantic and Prairie provinces and the territories. The Atlantic provinces rely heavily on transfers from the federal government as does Manitoba (discussed in a later chapter), while Alberta derives large revenues from natural resources.

Some features of the various taxes imposed by the provinces are presented in the following sections.

Personal Income Tax

Each of the provinces and the two territories imposes a personal income tax. Except in Quebec, the tax is collected on behalf of the provincial or territorial government by the federal government, the tax rate is expressed as a percentage of the basic federal tax, and consequently the tax base used is the same as that defined by the federal government. Quebec collects its own income tax with its own set of rates.

In 1997, the rates imposed by the various provinces as a percentage of the basic federal tax (as calculated in the federal income tax return) were:

Alberta[a]	44.0%
British Columbia	50.5
Manitoba	52.0
New Brunswick[a]	61.5
Newfoundland	69.0
Northwest Territories	45.0
Nova Scotia[a]	57.5
Ontario[a]	45.0
Prince Edward Island	59.5
Saskatchewan[a]	48.0
Yukon	50.0

[a]1998 rates

Over the years the provinces have resorted to additional income taxes by imposing surtaxes on the basic provincial income tax payable and by levying additional taxes on taxable income. In 1997 the Alberta income tax included a surtax of 8 percent on basic Alberta income tax in excess of $3,500 plus a flat rate of 0.5 percent of taxable income. Saskatchewan applied a flat rate tax of 2 percent of net income plus a surtax of 15 percent of the basic provincial tax payable in excess of $4,000 and a debt reduction tax of 10 percent of the basic and flat tax. Manitoba imposed a flat tax of 2 percent of net income plus a surtax of 2 percent taxable income over $30,000. Ontario applied a surtax of 20 percent of basic Ontario tax between $4,500 and

$6,000, plus 46 percent on tax above $6,000. Prince Edward Island levied a surtax of 10 percent on provincial tax in excess of $52,000.

A number of provinces give low-income taxpayers tax relief in the form of tax credits or tax reductions. Many also offer tax relief on various investments as an incentive to promote investment and economic development in the province, as well as tax credits for political contributions.

The features of Quebec's personal income tax parallel fairly closely most of those found in the federal tax. These include the definition of income for tax purposes and the various reductions used to arrive at taxable income and tax payable. Personal "amounts" converted into tax credits have replaced personal exemptions and deductions, and many of these amounts are indexed. These include a personal amount of $5,900 for a single taxpayer; an equal married amount; a $2,600 amount for the first child and $2,100 for each subsequent child; a $2,200 age amount; a $2,200 physical or mental impairment amount; and a $3,300 tuition/education amount for dependent children in post-secondary studies. The tax credit equals 20 percent of these amounts. A family with children could receive an additional refundable tax credit for a portion of child-care expenses. A refundable sales tax credit of $104 per adult and $31 for each dependent child, plus a property tax credit equal to 40 percent of property taxes are also part of the tax structure. The tax rate structure for 1997 began at 16 percent on taxable income of $7000 or less, 19 percent on income between $7,000 and $14,000, 21 percent on income between $14,000 and $23,000, 23 percent on income between $23,000 and $50,000, and 24 percent on income of $50,000 and over. A surtax is imposed equal to 5 percent of tax between $5,000 and $10,000, and 10 percent on tax above $10,000.

TABLE 10-2: Revenue Sources by Province, 1996-97

(percentage of total)

Source	Nfld.	P.E.I.	N.S.	N.B.	Que.	Ont.	Man.	Sask.	Alta.	B.C.	Terr.	Total
Taxes												
Personal Income	16.1	15.8	18.1	16.5	33.1	31.2	20.0	18.8	20.9	21.2	5.8	26.8
Corporate Income	1.4	2.0	2.2	2.4	3.5	7.8	2.6	3.4	6.1	5.8	1.9	5.3
Sales and excises	20.1	21.7	21.1	19.4	16.4	23.5	16.2	20.0	5.6	17.7	2.8	18.2
Property and related taxes	.2	4.7	.3	5.0	3.0	2.4	4.5	3.5	7.6	10.0	.5	4.3
Health and Social Ins.	2.9	1.9	3.0	2.1	12.6	5.2	2.1	1.8	7.1	7.5	2.4	7.1
Other	2.4	1.0	.7	.7	.8	5.9	4.5	1.7	1.1	.8	.1	2.7
Total Taxes	43.1	47.1	45.4	46.1	69.4	76.0	49.9	49.2	48.4	63.0	13.5	64.4
Non-Tax Revenues												
Natural resources	1.3	.1	.2	1.3	.4	.7	1.6	9.3	20.7	11.2	.3	4.5
Licenses, permits	2.5	1.6	1.6	1.9	3.5	2.8	1.2	1.9	1.4	1.8	.5	2.5
Return on investments	8.9	11.7	12.2	14.5	6.8	6.7	16.4	19.1	18.1	13.6	3.8	10.2
Other	2.8	4.1	3.3	3.5	4.1	2.3	6.3	4.7	2.9	2.6	4.9	3.3
Total non-tax	15.5	17.5	17.3	21.2	14.8	12.5	25.5	35.0	43.1	29.2	9.5	20.5
Total own source revenue	58.6	64.6	62.7	67.3	84.2	88.5	75.4	84.2	91.5	92.2	23.0	84.9
Federal transfers	41.4	35.5	37.3	32.7	15.7	11.5	24.6	15.8	8.5	7.8	76.9	15.3
Total	100.0	100.0	100.0	100.0	100.0	100.0	100.0	100.0	100.0	100.0	100.0	100.0
Total general revenue *($million)*	3,617	836	4,966	4,931	42,937	53,237	6,926	6,300	15,860	25,315	1,698	166,622

Source: Tax Foundation, *Finances of the Nation 1997* (Toronto: Canadian Tax Foundation, 1997), p. A9.

Corporation Taxes

All the provinces impose a corporation income tax on taxable income earned within their boundaries. Some supplement this tax with other levies on corporations.

Corporation Income Tax. Seven provinces — namely, Newfoundland, Prince Edward Island, New Brunswick, Nova Scotia, Manitoba, Saskatchewan, and British Columbia — and the two territories are party to an agreement with the federal government whereby Ottawa collects their corporation income taxes, as it does their personal income taxes. These governments accept the federal government's corporation tax structure as the base for corporate taxation, including its definition of income and the various deductions applied in arriving at taxable income. The provincial general tax rates are expressed as a percentage of corporate taxable income, ranging from a low of 14 percent in Newfoundland to a high of 17 percent in New Brunswick. All provinces offer lower rates for manufacturing and processing companies.

Most of these jurisdictions follow the federal system of applying lower rates to small businesses. The small business rate ranges from a low of 5 percent in some provinces to a high of 9.5 percent in Ontario. Periodically, the provinces may apply special provisions, such as tax holidays for new enterprises or investment tax credits.

Ontario, Quebec, and Alberta collect their own corporation income taxes. Although doing so involves administration costs, a province that administers its own tax does have increased flexibility in taxation. It can establish its own tax base, with its own concept of income for tax purposes and its own exemptions and deductions. Ontario applies a three-tier tax rate structure (based on the federal government's classifications of business); the rate on small businesses is 9.5 percent, the rate for manufacturing and processing firms is 13.5 percent, and the general rate on all other corporate income is 15.5 percent. Credits are given for research and development expenditures and for job training.

Alberta also employs a three-tier rate structure based on the federal structure. The rates for small business, manufacturing and other corporations are 6, 14.5, and 15.5 percent respectively. The principal tax credits offered cover royalties paid by oil and gas corporations.

Capital Tax. Ontario, Quebec, Manitoba, Nova Scotia, New Brunswick, Saskatchewan and British Columbia impose a tax rate on a corporation's paid-up capital, defined as the value of issued stock, debt, and reserve funds. Tax rates differ among various types of businesses. The general rate of tax ranges from 0.1 percent to 0.6 percent of paid-up capital. All provinces impose a tax on the paid-up capital of banks, trusts, and loan companies ranging from approximately 1.0 to 3.0 percent. The rate may vary with the financial institution taxed.

Consumption Taxes

Consumption or commodity taxes, as already noted, are generally considered to be indirect taxes imposed on one entity but expected to be passed on to another. The Constitution Act, 1867, prohibits the provinces from imposing indirect taxes. A province may, however, administer consumption or commodity taxes in a manner that qualifies them as direct taxes, which are permissible under the constitution. The provinces contend that most such taxes are consumer-purchase taxes levied on the purchaser with the seller acting as a paid collecting agent for the province. The courts have upheld this contention, thereby enabling the provinces to impose a number of sales and excise taxes, ranging from a general retail sales tax to taxes on specific items such as tobacco, fuel, and utilities. In terms of revenue, the retail sales tax is clearly the most important consumption tax imposed by the provinces.

Retail Sales Tax. All provinces except Alberta impose a retail sales tax, with most rates at either 7 or 8 percent. The tax is paid by purchasers when they buy a commodity, and the seller receives a small percentage of the revenue collected as a collection fee. The seller is required to forward the tax receipts to the government each month.

Interprovincial variation in retail sales tax exemptions and rates defies neat summary. Several categories of items, including food, clothing (in some provinces), and prescription drugs are exempted in an attempt to reduce the regressiveness of the tax. Double taxation is reduced through exempting goods used in further production, such as production equipment and materials. Some provinces provide exemptions on certain items purchased by municipalities and on building materials for the construction of schools, hospitals, and other public buildings.

When the federal government first outlined its plans for replacing its manufacturers' sales tax with the Goods and Services Tax (GST), Ottawa invited the provinces to co-operate and together establish a federal-provincial national sales tax, which would reduce administrative complexities and costs. Businesses and consumers were expected to benefit from the administrative efficiencies of substituting a single tax for a two-tiered system of federal and provincial taxes that required a duplication of bureaucracy. The provinces refused, opposing a federal GST as an encroachment on the retail sales tax field. Some provinces were also reluctant to expand the base of their retail sales tax to correspond to the broader base of the GST, which harmonization of the sales tax with the GST would require.

Shortly thereafter, however, Quebec announced its intention of merging its sales tax with the GST, which was completed in 1994, followed by Newfoundland, Nova Scotia, and New Brunswick in 1997. The provincial taxes would be reduced but extended to the wider range of goods and services covered by the GST. Consumers would pay one consumption tax at a single rate. In Quebec the rate was set at 14.5 percent, collected by the province, which remitted 7 percent to Ottawa. The new blended tax in the three Atlantic provinces was called the Harmonized Sales Tax (HST), with a rate established at 15 percent, collected by Ottawa, which remitted 8 percent to the provinces. Newfoundland had been imposing a retail sales tax at the rate of 12 percent, and the tax in Nova Scotia and New Brunswick was 11 percent. Despite the expanded base of the harmonized tax, the lower rate resulted in lower revenues for these provinces. To offset this loss of revenue, the federal government agreed to pay almost $1 billion as adjustment assistance to the three provinces over a four-year period.

Separate Consumption Taxes. In addition to the general retail sales tax, the provinces levy separate sales taxes on a number of goods and services. All provinces impose taxes on tobacco products. Gasoline is taxed in all provinces at a rate ranging from 9 to 16 cents per litre. Diesel fuel is generally taxed at lower rates. Fuel used for commercial and industrial purposes, in farming and fishing, and by some municipal services is either exempt or taxed at very low rates. Several provinces impose special taxes on utilities, while others apply their retail sales tax to these services. Other services taxed include the price of admission to amusements and entertainments, and pari-mutuel betting at race tracks. The sale of liquor is a monopoly in all provinces (except Alberta which has privatized liquor sales), with the province imposing a markup (or tax) on the manufacturers' price.

Health-Care Premiums and Payroll Taxes

Alberta and British Columbia levy premiums to help finance health-care programs; other provinces finance them solely from tax revenue. In British Columbia, the annual premium in 1996 was $432 for a single subscriber to the provincial health plan, $768 for a family of two, and $864 for a family of three or more. In Alberta the rates were $408 for a single individual and $816 for a family.

Ontario, Quebec, Manitoba, and Newfoundland rely on payroll taxes for financing some part of their health services. The Employer Health Levy (EHL) in Ontario is applied to the total amount of gross wages, salaries, and other remuneration paid by an employer. The rate varies with the level of remuneration, beginning at 0.98 percent on gross remuneration of less than $200,000 and increasing to 1.95 percent on remuneration in excess of $400,000. Quebec imposes a tax on employer payrolls at a rate of 4.26 percent to finance its health services. In addition, Quebec imposes a combined employee-employer levy on payrolls at a rate of 4.1 percent of specified pensionable earnings to finance the Quebec Pension Plan. Newfoundland levies a tax of 2 percent on the payrolls of corporations with annual employee earnings totalling more than $100,000. The tax includes federal corporations but excludes companies engaged in fishing, forestry, and agriculture. Manitoba imposes a 2.25 percent tax on the payrolls of companies with remuneration in excess of $1,500,000. Payrolls of less than $750,000 are exempt, while those between $750,000 and $1,500,000 are taxed at 4.5 percent.

Other Taxes

All provinces levy a tax on insurance premiums, including those for life, sickness, and fire and accident insurance. Rates generally range from 2 percent to 8 percent, with some provinces including premiums in their retail sales tax base.

All the provinces impose a number of miscellaneous taxes. Ontario and Quebec levy taxes on the transfer of securities and bonds. New Brunswick, Ontario, Manitoba, and British Columbia levy land-transfer taxes on real estate transactions. Manitoba's tax is graduated, beginning at 0.5 percent and increasing to 1.5 percent on value of property in excess

of $150,000. In New Brunswick, the rate is 0.25 percent. The British Columbia property-purchase tax equals 1 percent on the first $200,000 of value and 2 percent on any excess. In Ontario, the land-transfer tax is 1.5 percent on the value of property exceeding $250,000, and 2 percent on the value of residential property exceeding $400,000. Non-residents are required to pay a 20 percent tax on transfers of agricultural and recreational property.

A number of provinces impose taxes on public utilities to meet the cost of the boards and commissions that regulate them. In Prince Edward Island and New Brunswick, the provincial governments, as well as the local governments, impose taxes on real property. For the most part, property taxes in Canada are reserved for the local governments, with the province imposing them only in unorganized or unincorporated areas.

Provincial Non-Tax Revenue

Some of the main forms of government non-tax finance are discussed in detail in other chapters. The following is a brief outline of sources of provincial non-tax revenue. As shown in Table 10-1, non-tax revenue, excluding transfers from the federal government, accounts for about 20 percent of total provincial government revenue. The sources of this revenue include charges on natural resource industries, liquor profits, profits from provincial government enterprises, charges for incorporation and company registration fees, fines, penalties, and a variety of licences, such as those for motor vehicles, hunting, and fishing. Federal transfers, which are another form of non-tax revenue, make up almost 15 percent of total provincial revenue on average, while ranging from over 40 percent of the revenue of the government of Newfoundland to 10 percent of the revenue of Alberta and British Columbia. Transfers from the federal government to the provinces are discussed in later chapters. Provincial governments may also raise revenue by borrowing, which is covered in chapter 12.

Natural Resources. Charges for natural resources take the form of levies on profits, land, and assessed value of minerals, returns from rental and leases of land, and royalties on production. The most important are levies on mining and logging and on oil and natural gas.

Revenues from natural resources increased in the 1970s but declined in recent years to constitute only 4 to 5 percent of total provincial revenue by the 1990s. These revenues, however, still account for 20 percent of the total revenues of Alberta and about 10 percent of those of Saskatchewan and British Columbia.

Provincial Enterprises. In all provinces, bottled liquor is sold through government liquor stores. (Alberta has privatized its liquor outlets.) Beer and wine, on the other hand, are sold through both government stores and privately licenced outlets, such as brewery retail stores and, in Quebec, even grocery stores. The direct profits from sales in government-owned stores provide considerably more revenue than the sales of licences and permits to brewers, distillers, and sellers.

Provincial government enterprises other than liquor stores are found primarily in the areas of transportation, communications, electric power, and more recently, gaming. Although the gross expenditures and revenues of these enterprises may be substantial, only those revenues actually remitted to the government are considered revenues in the budget accounts, while only losses underwritten by the government are considered expenditures. The revenues remitted, plus interest and receipts from other investments, are recorded in the accounts as "return on investment." For example, in 1994 the income of provincial and territorial government enterprises totalled over $51 billion. Their net

profit amounted to $7 billion, of which some portion would be remitted as a return to investment for inclusion in provincial government budgetary revenues.

Federal Government Transfers. Transfers from the federal government account for about 15 percent of provincial government revenues. These include transfers for specific purposes, such as health and post-secondary education, and general grants. The latter consist primarily of equalization payments to the provinces with a poorer tax base, whose per capita revenue from their own tax systems falls below that of provinces with a richer tax base. Federal transfers to the provinces and territories are covered in detail in chapter 14 on intergovernmental transfers.

Local Government Revenues

Local government consists of the various local governing authorities established by the provincial governments and vested with specific responsibilities and powers. They include the governments of municipalities (cities, towns, and villages), which are called municipal governments; school boards, which are responsible for administering education; and special boards and commissions established to administer particular functions. All of these authorities are considered part of local government in the data presented. The power of local governments to impose taxes is governed by provincial legislation. The only tax of significance that they levy is the property tax. As shown in Table 10-3, property and related taxes account for about 70 percent of local governments' own-source revenues and more than one-third of their total revenues. The other major source of revenue for local governments is the provincial government. Transfers from other levels of government, primarily the provincial government, account for over 45 percent of total local government revenues. Table 10-3 illustrates that there was a significant drop in

TABLE 10-3: Historical Summary of Local Government[a] Gross General Revenue

Source	1967	1976	1994
		(percentage of total)	
Taxes			
Real Property	41.5	32.8	31.9
Other Property and related taxes	8.4	5.7	6.3
Total tax revenues	49.9	38.5	38.2
Non-tax revenue			
Licenses and permits	1.2	0.5	.6
Sales of goods and services	4.8	6.7	11.6
Other	4.0	6.2	4.4
Total non-tax revenue	10.0	13.4	16.6
Total own-source revenue	59.9	51.9	54.8
Transfers from other levels of government	40.1	48.1	45.2
Total	100.0	100.0	100.0
		($ million)	
Gross general revenue	5,340	17,055	70,458

[a] Includes Yukon and Northwest Territories.

Source: Statistics Canada, Local Government Finance, cat. 68-204; Public Sector Finance, 1995-1996, cat. 68-212-XPB.

the importance of the property tax as a source of revenue from the mid-1960s to the mid-1970s, but relatively little change since then.

Property Tax. The base for the local government property tax is real property — land and buildings — in all provinces, with the addition of machinery and equipment in some. Most provinces exempt church-, school-, and government-owned property, as well as the property of charitable organizations. The federal and provincial governments provide transfers in lieu of the taxes local authorities forgo on government property, and some provinces also provide transfers in lieu of local taxation of schools and hospitals.

The property tax is applied to the assessed value of the property and bears no relation-ship to the owner's ability to pay. The authority governing property assessment and taxation varies to some degree from province to province. In Ontario, for example, assessment is the province's responsibility, governed by the Assessment Act and administered by the Ministry of Municipal Affairs. In other provinces, the responsibility is divided between the provincial government and the local governments, with large city governments generally authorized to undertake the assessment function.

Local tax rates have been commonly expressed as mill rates. The first step in the imposition of the property tax is to determine the assessed value of the property. Meanwhile, the local authority determines the amount of revenue it requires from property taxes. Then the latter amount is divided by the total assessed value of taxable property. The figure obtain is multiplied by 1,000. The result, which is known as the mill rate, is the tax rate expressed as mills per dollar of assessed value. One mill is equal to one-tenth of one cent. Thus for example, if property is assessed at $10,000 and the tax rate is 50 mills, the tax amounts to $0.05 per dollar of assessed value for a total tax of $10,000 (.05) = $500.

Most municipal governments distinguish between residential and commercial property and impose a slightly higher mill rate on commercial property. More than one authority may be involved in determining the mill rate. For instance, city council may determine one rate for general government purposes, and an additional rate may be set for education, determined by the budget presented by the school board.

Taxpayers receive a notice of assessment, which they have the right to appeal if they believe too high a value has been placed on their property. They also receive a statement of tax owing. Some municipalities have adopted an instalment system by which a taxpayer may pay the tax in several parts over the year instead of in one lump-sum payment. Failure to pay the tax results in the imposition of a lien against the property; if it is not paid within a certain period of time, the property can be possessed by the government and sold at public auction.

Practices in assessment vary, but attempts are made to base it on the market value of property. (Some provinces use the term "real value" or "actual value.") The market value is generally interpreted as the price that the property could command if sold by a willing seller to a willing buyer. Since property values change over time, with some appreciating and others depreciating, and with increases from owner improvements, maintaining the equivalence between assessed and market values requires periodic reassessment of all property. Most provinces specify the time period for revaluing property. The most common practice is to reassess every three to five years, although Quebec requires revision of assessed values annually while Saskatchewan requires reassessment in rural municipalities every twelve years.

A major criticism of the property tax is its alleged regressiveness. The traditional view is that the property tax is one of the most regressive of all taxes. More recently, however, this view has been challenged by a number of economists using a different empirical approach in their study of the incidence of the property tax. The traditional approach uses income as the base for determining tax incidence and shows that lower-income families pay a larger proportion of their total income in property taxes than do wealthier families. The new approach uses capital as the base for determining incidence and views the property tax as a tax on capital income. Since capital and capital income are highly concentrated in the hands of the relatively wealthy, this approach shows that it is they who bear most of the burden of the property tax. The two approaches are based on different assumptions that are difficult to verify empirically; therefore, the question of property tax incidence remains controversial among academics.[2]

A number of provinces have attempted to alleviate the burden of the property tax on lower-income families through schemes involving tax rebates and tax credits. In addition, some provinces have tried to prevent property taxes from escalating by assuming a greater responsibility for municipal functions, either directly or indirectly, through larger grants to municipal governments.

Business Taxes. Municipal governments across Canada impose a wide variety of levies on businesses. These business taxes may take the form of a percentage of assessed value or may use as a base the business establishment's rental value, storage capacity, or square metres of floor space. The most commonly used tax employs the assessed value of a property, with the tax expressed as a percentage of the assessed value. These business taxes are usually levied on the occupant of the property rather than on the owner.

Other Taxes and Charges. Provinces authorize local governments to impose user charges for certain services, such as fire protection and garbage collection, and the use of recreational facilities, such as arenas. Charges may also be imposed for area improvements, such as streets, street lighting, and sewers. In some Ontario municipalities, the charge for fire protection is a fixed fee added to the charge for utilities (hydro and water).

Some municipal governments also employ special assessments and fees for local improvements such as sidewalks, sewers, and street lighting. These assessments are made on the properties adjacent to or in the area of the improvement — the benefitting properties — with the costs assigned on the basis of frontage size.

Revenues from these miscellaneous taxes and charges for services have followed a gradual rising trend, increasing from 10 percent in 1967 to more than 16 percent by 1994. Various issues concerning the application of government user fees are discussed in the next chapter.

Provincial Transfers. One of the most important sources of revenue for the local governments is transfers from provincial governments. These transfers constitute about 40 percent of their total revenue. In addition, municipalities also receive transfers from the federal government and from government enterprises, although the amounts are relatively minor.

Like all transfers, provincial transfers to local authorities may or may not be for a designated purpose. Specific-purpose transfers far outweigh general-purpose transfers as a share of total municipal revenue.

The form of general transfers also varies among provinces. The transfers may be tied to revenues collected locally, take the form of

per capital grants, be related to property assessment, or consist of grants in lieu of local taxes on provincial government property.

Federal governments general-purpose transfers to local governments consist primarily of grants in lieu of taxes on federal government property. Specific-purpose transfers are primarily for capital and community improvement projects, such as public works, sanitation, urban renewal and housing. Provincial transfers to local governments are discussed in greater detail in chapter 14.

Borrowing. Another source of local government revenues is borrowing. The borrowing powers of those governments are, however, limited by provincial legislation. These limitations vary. In some provinces, a municipality may borrow only on approval of the provincial government, which must also approve the use of the funds, the type of debenture issued, and the rate of interest offered. Other provisions limit municipal borrowing to a specific percentage of total taxes collected or limit the total outstanding debt to a proportion of taxable assessment. In some cases, long-term borrowing is restricted to capital projects, upon the approval of the province.

Some provinces guarantee payment of the principal and interest of municipal debentures. The province may also purchase debentures from the local governments or establish loan funds from which they may borrow for specific purposes.

Summary

The tax structures of the provincial governments are similar to that of the federal government. The provinces rely heavily on the taxation of income and consumption. Over the years the personal income tax has grown in significance as a source of revenue, while the revenues from the corporation income tax have fallen, and revenue from the sales tax has remained fairly constant.

Provinces with a weak tax base, such as the Atlantic provinces, rely heavily on transfers from the federal government. Resource-rich provinces, such as Alberta and British Columbia, are able to supplement tax revenue with revenues from natural resources such as oil, gas, and forestry.

The primary tax source of the local governments is the property tax. Their remaining revenue comes from the sale of goods and services, licences and fees, and transfers from the provincial governments.

NOTES

[1] The primary sources of information for this chapter are: Statistics Canada, *Provincial Government Finance: Revenue and Expenditure*, cat. 68-207, annual; Statistics Canada, Local *Government Finance*, cat. 68-204, annual; Statistics Canada, *Public Sector Finance*, 1995-1996, cat. 68-212-XPB; and Canadian Tax Foundation, *Finances of the Nation* 1997 (Toronto: Canadian Tax Foundation, 1997).

[2] For a discussion of property tax incidence and the approaches to analyzing it, see Harry M. Kitchen, "Property Taxation as a Tax on Wealth: Some New Evidence," *Canadian Tax Journal*, 35 (July/August 1987).

CHAPTER 11

Non-Tax Sources of Revenue

While taxation is the major form of financing government services in Canada, it is supplemented by a variety of non-tax sources of revenue.[1] These non-tax sources include the sale of goods and services, revenues from natural resources, profits from government enterprises, returns from various investments, and revenues from licences, fees, and fines. Table 11-1 shows the revenues from five groups of non-tax sources as classified by Statistics Canada. In 1994-95, these non-tax revenue sources accounted for over 30 percent of local government own-source revenues, about 24 percent of provincial and territorial government own-source revenue, but only about 8 percent of federal revenues.

This chapter examines briefly each of the categories of non-tax revenue presented in Table 11-1, then focuses on two controversial forms of finance used by government but which are not necessarily restricted to the above classifications. The two forms of finance analyzed in some detail are user charges and gaming.

Miscellaneous Revenue Sources

Revenue from Natural Resources

Natural resource revenue comes from the use and development of the country's natural resources base. They include royalties on petroleum and mineral production; revenues from the lease and rental of government lands; revenue from forest harvesting, such as pulp production and logging; revenue from hunting and fishing licences; and from permits and charges for the use of government parks. It is primarily the provincial governments which receive this source of revenue. The amount of revenue differs between provinces, with the petroleum-rich provinces of Alberta and Saskatchewan benefiting the most along with forest-rich British Columbia.

Sale of Goods and Services

Certain goods and services provided by government have the characteristics of private goods and services and may be priced and sold directly to the public. These include tolls on roads and bridges, airport and dock fees, tuition at post-secondary school institutions, sale of government publications, charges for recreational facilities, and charges for certain health facilities and services. Prices for the use of government goods and services, along with licences and permits, are generally referred to as user charges.

Licences and Permits

Certain activities require a government licence or permit before they can be undertaken. These activities include the ownership and use of motor vehicles, the sale and consumption of alcoholic beverages, the operation of business enterprises, the construction of buildings and other structures, owning pets, and getting married. In some cases, the licence has to be annually renewed. Levies for the right to pursue these activities usually take the form of flat fees.

TABLE 11-1: Non-Tax Revenue Sources, 1994-95
(Percentage of Own-Source Revenue)

| Source | Federal | Level of Government | |
		Provincial and Territorial	Local
Natural Resources	.1	5.9	–
Sale of Goods and Services	.4	3.1	1.0
Licenses and Permits	2.5	2.6	21.1
Return on Investments	3.7	11.3	4.3
Other Revenue from Own Sources	1.1	.9	3.8
Total Non-Tax Revenue	7.7	23.7	30.3
Total Non-Tax Revenue ($ million)	10,500	30,633	11,683

Source: Canada, Statistics Canada, Public Sector Finance, 1995-1996, Cat. 68-212-XPB.

Return on Investments

This class of non-tax revenue includes profits remitted by government enterprises or Crown corporations and interest on loans to these enterprises, to governments, and to others. At the provincial level, the sale of liquor is controlled by government monopoly and the net revenue of these enterprises is treated as a return on investment. At the local level of government, many government-established business enterprises are treated as part of local government. These include local public utilities that provide hydro-electric power, water supply, natural gas, urban transit, and public housing.

Many of the above-mentioned non-tax revenue sources involve direct charges to consumers or users in the form of prices for goods and services provided, or licences and permits providing authorization to undertake an activity. User charges are a controversial form of financing government activities and require special attention and analysis.

User Charges

User charges may be defined in the narrow or the broad sense.[2] The narrow approach de-fines user charges as prices applied to goods and services sold directly to the consumer, and the amount that an individual pays depends on the amount consumed. They could include charges applied for local water supply, hydro-electric power, public parks and recreational facilities, certain health services, toll roads and bridges, transit, parking, libraries, tuition fees, air transportation, waste disposal at landfill sites, ambulance services, and day care. These prices paid for government goods and services have the same basis as prices paid for private sector goods and services. The broad definition would include all of the above plus fees for permits and licences which are levied to recover the costs of particular government services. In most cases the service is mandatory, such as automobile registration, building permits, marriage licences, pet licences, hunting and fishing licences, and drivers' licences, for individuals who wish to engage in the activity to which it pertains. The fees paid give an individual the right to engage in the activity, but unlike user charges in the narrow sense, are unrelated to any quantity or volume of consumption. The user charge concept employed in this chapter is the broad definition outlined above.

Not included in the definition of user charges are levies which are sometimes referred to as benefit taxes. For example, the excise tax imposed on gasoline is frequently justified on the basis of the benefit principle of taxation. Whether or not the tax revenue collected is earmarked for the construction and maintenance of roads, the tax may be viewed as an indirect levy on those who drive vehicles and who therefore receive the benefit of the transportation facilities provided.

Justification for User Charges

It is contended that user charges, in addition to financing goods and services, promote economic efficiency in the use of resources and the consumption of goods and services. They provide a degree of discipline in government spending by bringing market-type forces to bear on both demand and supply. Goods and services are purchased in the same manner as private goods — that is, in accordance with consumers' desire and ability to pay for them. Assuming that the fees charged cover costs of production, user charges also focus attention on costs and tend to promote efficiency. The alternative to the discipline provided by user charges is political or bureaucratic judgement, with the resulting possibilities that too much or too little may be supplied relative to public preferences and that there is no indicator to gauge the efficiency of production.

User charges also discourage wasteful use of government services, which may be the case when they are provided free of direct charge and financed by taxation. Freely provided services are prone to overuse and misuse. Users will tend to carry consumption to the point where marginal benefits equal zero. Market equilibrium for goods and services, on the other hand, is attained at the point where demand equals supply, or marginal benefits from consumption equal marginal costs of production. Without the discipline of the market, consumer use may be carried to

the output level where marginal costs exceed marginal benefits, resulting in a net loss of welfare to society. It is sometimes argued that even nominal charges, for example, covering visits to a physician for health care, would cause people to use the service more conservatively and not abuse it as may be the case if the service is provided free of charge.

User charges may also be applied as a means of regulating or rationing the use of a facility to avoid congestion. In periods of high or peak demand, charges could be increased (as in the case of a traffic bridge or a transit system) to absorb excess demand and reduce the delays and costs associated with congestion.

User charges are favoured by those who subscribe to the benefit principle of government finance. According to this principle, beneficiaries of government services should bear the burden of the cost of the services and pay in proportion to the amount consumed.

Opposition to User Charges

The main argument against user charges to finance government goods and services is that they represent an inequitable distribution of the cost burden of the goods and services among members of society. The resulting distribution is regressive. Both low-income and high-income users will pay the same price for a service, but the amount paid by the low-income user represents a higher proportion of income than the amount paid by the high-income user. The regressive nature of user charges is contrary to the generally accepted principles of ability-to-pay and progression applied in the personal income tax.

In addition, low-income groups who cannot afford to pay the user fee will be excluded from the benefits of the services, which might include essential health services and education. This would also be viewed as inequitable.

The application of direct charges based on the operation of demand and supply in the marketplace could result in an insufficient quantity of the service provided if the service has external economies. (This was demonstrated in the appendix to chapter 2). It is generally acknowledged that external economies exist in health services and education, two important social services. The application of market prices would produce prices which are too high to ensure a socially optimum level of output. In other words, an inadequate quantity of the service would be provided.

Increased Application of User Charges

User charges have long been applied by public utilities such as water supply, hydro and natural gas as a means of financing the services as well as conserving and regulating use. Similarly, charges in the form of fees for permits and licences are standard for motor vehicle registration and use, building construction, operation of a business enterprise, and hunting and fishing. Also fairly common are fees charged for use of parks, arenas, and other recreational facilities. In recent years, however, particularly during the 1980s and 1990s when governments were operating large budget deficits and were seeking additional revenues, many argued that greater reliance should be placed on user charges for financing government. Indeed, in the last decade, governments have extended their application of user fees.

Areas frequently mentioned where user fees could be imposed or applied more extensively include education, recreational facilities, garbage and refuse collection, disposal at landfill sites, transportation facilities, various health care services, inspection services, and other services where costs might be recovered by the application of fees.

In his 1990 budget, the Treasurer of Ontario introduced proposals for extending user fees in the long-term care of the elderly. Elderly people living in nursing homes or homes for the aged would be required to pay a greater share of the cost of room and board;

those with low incomes would be exempt from the higher fees. Elderly people who remained in their own homes but required services such as housekeeping and meal preparation would be charged on a sliding scale according to income. The additional fees, it was estimated, would yield $100 million by the middle of the decade.[3] As the 1990s progressed and Ontario's deficits continued, fees continued to increase. The government cut transfer payments to post-secondary school educational institutions and empowered them to raise tuition fees from 15 to 20 percent. Seniors and welfare recipients were required to pay a new $2 user fee for each prescription under the province's drug plan. Reduced grants in support of cultural institutions such as museums and art galleries meant increases in admission fees. And reductions in transfers to local governments resulted in increases in user fees for many local government-provided facilities and services.

Similarly, user fees were expanded and increased in other provinces. For example, Alberta, faced with an annual deficit of approximately 20 percent of its budget, reportedly increased some eighty user fees during 1994 and 1995,[4] including kindergarten, day-care, and university fees, and introduced fees for a number of non-essential medical services.

The federal government also sought increased revenues from user charges. In 1989, the former Conservative government approved a new policy for extending application of user charges as part of its deficit-reduction program and in the belief that "users and other beneficiaries of government services should pay their fair share, rather than have these services funded, in general, by all taxpayers."[5] As an incentive to encourage departmental managers to recover costs of services through charges, the government provided that part of the proceeds could be invested in improvements of the services generating the revenues. The government forecast that the extended application of user fees would bring an additional $120 million in revenue by 1992-93.

This policy was continued with the election in 1993 of the Liberal government. In its budget of 1995 the government rationalized that "it is appropriate that certain programs be financed at least partly through increased cost recovery and user fees, especially those that confer a private benefit."[6] With reference to efficiency Ottawa contended that user fees bestowed market discipline and "forced a more cost-conscious and client-oriented government."[7]

New or increased fees were announced for food and meat inspection, drug approvals , fisheries inspections, fishing licences, and marine services. The Department of Citizenship and Immigration increased the fees for citizenship and imposed a fee of $975 per immigrant to cover administrative and application processing costs. Customized services by Environment Canada were to be provided on a fee-for-services basis. The government estimated that the user fee policy announced in 1995 would generate about $600 million annually.

User charges have been common at the local level of government for a variety of services. But as the provincial governments began to restrict transfer payments and download some services to the local governments in the 1990s, these lower-level governments looked to generate more revenues from innovative application of user charges. Some local authorities began to bill insurance companies for costs incurred when local fire fighters respond to car accidents. New fee structures were imposed on recreational facilities such as ice arenas to eliminate the practice of the entire community subsidizing the cost of the arena. Fees were imposed for fire inspections required for real estate transactions, and charges levied for the cost of environmental cleanups in accidental oil spills. Indeed many activities and services performed free or at little charge by local authorities in the past

and that local residents had come to accept as such, were now being subject to full-cost user charges.

In their increased reliance on user charges, the governments did not appear to be deterred by the traditional argument that such fees were regressive and therefore inequitable. Indeed, user charges tend to be no more regressive than many of the taxes found in the tax structure, such as sales and excise tax, the property tax, and Employment Insurance and Canada Pension Plan premiums. In some of these levies, the degree of regressiveness is reduced through exemptions and tax rebates for low-income families. Similar accommodation, one could argue, could be made for user fees if the government was concerned over their regressive nature.

Gaming

Gaming is a concept applied to describe games of chance or gambling. Government involvement in gaming as a source of revenue is a relatively recent development, but it has grown rapidly and is becoming an increasingly important source of revenue at the provincial level in Canada. The most significant forms of gaming used by the provinces are lotteries, casinos, and video lottery terminals (VLTs). Together they generate about 4 percent of provincial government own-source revenue or roughly $5 billion annually. The involvement of government in each of these areas of gambling, along with associated problems and issues, are analyzed in the following sections.

Lotteries

A lottery involves the purchase of a ticket with a chance to win a prize. Lotteries vary in terms of ticket prices, the amount of the prize, and the odds of winning. They may range from monthly or weekly draws with high ticket prices and huge pay-offs, to low-priced "scratch-and-win" tickets with relatively small pay-offs.

Lotteries were common in the United States during the late nineteenth century, but a series of scandals and other problems caused the federal and state governments to impose a ban on lotteries until 1964. In the 1960s, several state governments began to experiment with lotteries, with revenues earmarked for specific purposes. As the state lotteries became more imaginative, with larger and larger pay-offs, they gained in popularity, and other state governments climbed on the bandwagon and also legalized state-run lotteries for revenue purposes.

The development of provincial lotteries has been interesting. The Canadian criminal code prohibits organizations other than governments and licenced charities from operating lotteries. During the 1970s, the federal government entered the field with a national lottery, but it withdrew in 1980 in favour of provincial operation of lotteries. In return, Ottawa received from the provinces for several years an annual payment of $24 million, which represented its share of the profits. In 1985, Ottawa and the provinces signed an agreement that the provinces would pay the federal government $100 million over three years in return for amendment of the criminal code to remove the federal government as a potential participant in lottery and gaming activities.

The provinces were quick to exploit this new revenue source and established a variety of provincial and regional lotteries. Provincial lotteries are operated and administered by provincially owned lottery corporations, including the Atlantic Lottery Corporation, Loto Québec, the Ontario Lottery Corporation, the Western Lottery Foundation, and the BC Lottery Corporation. Regional and national lotteries are operated by the Interprovincial Lottery Corporation; revenues are allocated to the participating provinces in proportion to the sales in each. The most prominent of the provincial lotteries include Lotto 6/49, the Provincial, Super Loto, Lotario, Loto-Québec, Western Canada Lottery, and the sports lottery Pro Line.

Lottery profits represent approximately 30 to 35 percent of lottery sales. These profits may be placed in a province's general revenue fund or earmarked for specific purposes. Earmarked profits have been directed to areas such as sports and recreational activities, cultural activities, hospital construction, medical research, and senior citizens' housing. In Ontario, for example, lottery profits are paid into the province's Consolidated Revenue Fund and are distributed by the government to a wide variety of programs and projects; lottery profits from interprovincial games go to health care and environmentally related health research, hospital buildings and equipment, and the support of social-service organizations such as the United Way, the Ontario Lung Association, and the Arthritis Society.[8] Manitoba established its lottery funding system to include "funding umbrellas" — organizations designated by the provincial government to distribute lottery revenue to non-profit community groups. In addition, three provincial government departments, all of them involved in culture, tourism, recreation, and health, receive lottery revenue.

Government use of lotteries as a revenue source has sparked considerable controversy. Lotteries are attacked on the grounds that they are a form of very regressive taxation and are inequitable. Numerous studies have shown that expenditures for lottery tickets absorb a much higher percentage of the incomes of low-income groups than high-income groups, with the lowest-income group spending a share of its income two to five times greater than that of the highest-income group.[9] A 1995 study by Statistics Canada showed that lottery players with incomes of less than $20,000 spent 1.2 percent of their incomes on lottery tickets, while those with incomes in excess of $60,000 spent only .3

percent of their income on lottery ticket purchases.

Proponents of lotteries counter that lotteries are games of chance similar to various other legalized forms, including betting on horse racing and bingo. Even if lotteries are viewed as a tax, they contend, the tax is a voluntary one since no one is obligated to participate in a lottery. As a voluntary activity, the purchase of lottery tickets should not be considered a regressive tax, even though it may cause hardships in the sense that gambling does.

Critics of lotteries also oppose them on social and moral grounds. Private gambling, it is argued, is severely restricted and closely regulated by government because of perceived potential for adverse social and moral repercussions and for criminal elements to creep into the system. In operating and actively promoting lotteries through extensive media advertising, charge the critics, government is condoning and encouraging gambling. It has been reported that in 1996 lottery corporations across Canada spent about $43 million on advertising and lottery promotion encouraging Canadian to gamble.[10] Furthermore, it is inconsistent that such activity is made permissible for governments yet is essentially barred in the private sector.

Casinos

Casinos are gambling establishments featuring various games of chance with cards, dice, and slot machines. In Canada the first Las Vegas-style casino was introduced in 1989 in Winnipeg by the Manitoba government. Other provinces soon followed so that, by 1997, there were sixteen large-scale casinos operating in the country, along with a number of smaller charity casinos.

There are a variety of models governing the ownership and operation of casinos in the provinces. In the casino model used in Manitoba, the casinos are owned and operated by the provincial government and their employees are provincial public servants. The opera-

tor of the casinos is the Manitoba Lotteries Foundation, a provincial Crown corporation. In the charity casino model, the casinos are licenced by government to charities, which hire private firms to operate them. Profits are shared by the charities, the operator, and the government. This was the model favoured by Alberta and British Columbia for their early casinos. Beginning in 1993, Ontario had permitted roving charity casinos, held in rented banquet halls and moving from one location to another, but in 1997 determined to replace them with permanent charity casinos.

A third model is used by the government of Ontario for its Las Vegas-style casinos in Windsor and Niagara Falls. These casinos are owned by the Ontario Casino Corporation, a Crown company which licences the casinos to professional operators with interests in the large casinos in Las Vegas and elsewhere. Windsor casinos are operated by Windsor Casino Limited, which is equally owned by Caesar's World Inc. and Hilton Hotels Corp. Casino Rama is a three-way partnership between the province of Ontario, the Chippewas First Nation band, and a private sector operator — Carnival Hotels and Casinos.

The formula for sharing casino revenue may vary. A standard practice is for government to impose a "win tax" on casino winnings, which consists of casino gross revenues minus paid out winnings. Operating costs are deducted from the remaining revenues to arrive at profits which are shared by the casino operators and the government. In the case of the Windsor casinos, the Ontario government levies a 20 percent win tax, the operators receive an operators fee calculated as 2.75 percent of gross revenues plus 5 percent of net revenues. In the case of Casino Rama, the Chippewas band receives an annual fee of $4.5 million, adjusted for inflation.[11]

For 1997, the revenues of the Ontario Casino Corporation totalled 1.1 billion. Of this amount, $50 million was paid out in operators' fees and $201 million to the Ontario government as a win tax. After paying other expenses, the Corporation distributed $364 million of the net revenues to the province. The government's share of revenues consequently was approximately 51 percent.[12]

Some provinces have permitted small, roving casinos. In Ontario these casinos netted the charities in the provinces about $10 million per year. In 1997 the Ontario government proposed to replace these roving casinos with forty-four larger charity casinos, permanently located. Licences were issued to seven multinational companies to operate these casinos. The province's share of the profits was estimated at $1 billion, with charities receiving about $180 billion, and the operators paid a management fee. In November 1997, during the local government elections, these casinos were rejected by about fifty communities in Ontario, but the provincial government ruled that local municipal governments were to make the first decision, even though voters had rejected the casino.

As in the case of lotteries, the government promotion and involvement in casino gambling has been controversial and has sparked a lively public debate. The controversies focus on economic, social, and moral issues.

Economic Issues. One of the main economic arguments in support of casinos is the employment they generate in the community where they are located. Not only are workers employed directly by a casino, but additional jobs are created in associated industries such as transportation, accommodations, and suppliers. A study of Casino Windsor in 1995 reported the creation of 7,200 person-years of employment. The two temporary casinos, Casino Windsor and Northern Belle (the river boat), employed 3,700 workers between them, and it was estimated that the permanent casino, which opened in 1998, would employ approximately 5,000 workers.

While casinos are labour intensive and provide major employment, a recent study by Statistics Canada showed that certain aspects of casino jobs fell below the average for Canada. Only 69 percent of casino jobs were full time compared to 81 percent in non-gambling jobs. Earnings also tended to be lower in the casino industry. Full time workers in non-casino employment earned an average of $33,000 per year and part-time workers earned $9,300. Comparative earnings in the casino industry were $29,000 and $8,000.[13]

It has been argued that the economic benefits of a casino to a community is not how much money it brings in, but where the money comes from. It has been estimated that a casino must draw at least 50 percent of its customers from outside the local area in order to generate new wealth for the community. Otherwise the impact of the casino is to simply redistribute income within the local economy; income that would have been spent in other local retail outlets such as restaurants, movie theatres, and so on. To the extent that consumer expenditures are diverted from other local retail shops to the casino, casinos have a negative impact on these retailers.

Only the casinos in Windsor and Niagara Falls meet the 50 percent criterion. Given the proximity of the Windsor casinos to the United States, it is estimated that the Windsor casinos draw 82 percent of their patrons and about 90 percent of their gross revenues from south of the border. In contrast, 75 percent of those who visit the Winnipeg casinos are local, while about 95 percent of the customers at Casino de Montreal are local.[14]

The origin of casino patrons also has a relationship to the revenues casinos generate for provincial governments. While casinos form a very lucrative source of revenues, the total revenues they generate should not be viewed as new revenues. Local casino customers may well have spent the income they wager in casinos on other goods and services which are subject to provincial sales and excise taxes. Therefore, in viewing a casino as a source of new revenue, governments should take into account the amounts that would have been collected in taxes elsewhere had consumer spending not been diverted to the casino.[15]

While casinos have proved to be good sources of supplementary revenue to the provincial governments, their long-run economic value to a local community tend to be less certain. First, the provincial governments have been less than generous in sharing casino revenues with the local government jurisdictions where they are located. For example, the Harris government in Ontario indicated that the City of Windsor would receive about 10 percent of casino revenues, but this has not materialized.

Second, the value to the local community in terms of spin-off benefits to other business establishments is questionable. Other than hotels providing accommodations for out-of-town gamblers, there appears to be little benefit to restaurants, entertainment enterprises, and local shops. Evidence indicates that patrons of casinos come to gamble and then leave. Other than Las Vegas and Reno, Nevada, which are unique, communities which have elected to permit casinos have not fared very well. A prime example is Atlantic City, New Jersey. Beginning in 1978, numerous casinos were constructed along a stretch of oceanfront. Heralded as the Las Vegas of the East, Atlantic City experienced an initial boom in job creation, construction, and an influx of visitors. But there has been little long-run gain to the city, and indeed evidence points to a negative net impact. During the twenty years following the establishment of the first casino, Atlantic City experienced a reduction in population and non-casino jobs, an increasing number of business bankruptcies and shop closures, and a continuation of a high incidence of poverty and crime. The indications are that casinos, when located in the business sector of a city, tend to siphon off the vitality of other businesses.[16]

Social Issues. A controversial issue surrounding casinos is their impact on the social fabric of the country. It is contended that they are associated with increased criminal activity and organized crime, and produce addiction or compulsive gamblers. Evidence on the casino-crime relationship is inconclusive. There is no solid empirical evidence of an increase in the crime rate in communities in Canada which host casinos.[17]

It is recognized that people can and do become addicted to gambling, but the extent to which casinos contribute to this problem is unclear. Some studies in the United States estimate that up to 5 percent of the population in states with casinos are addictive gamblers. In Ontario, a government commissioned study in 1995 reported that 1 percent of adults were compulsive gamblers, and that up to 10 percent have gambling-related problems. In addition to criminal activity, gambling addiction can lead to such social, family, and personal problems as family discord, family breakup, bankruptcy, unpaid bills, unproductive workers, and increased demands for welfare and other social services. There have also been documented cases of suicide related to gambling.[18] Communities whose casinos rely more heavily on local patronage, of course, will experience a higher incidence of the social costs of gambling than do those casinos who draw a high percentage of their patrons from outside the local community.

Governments have been accused of establishing, promoting, and expanding casinos without conducting sufficient research on their economic and social consequences. Indeed many communities in Canada are beginning to take the initiative in opposing the establishment of casinos in their areas because of the perceived undesirable impact. Voters and local governments in many towns and cities across Canada have indicated, through referendums and resolutions, that they do not want casinos in their communities. In the Ontario local elections in November, 1997, in response to a ballot question on the establishment of casinos, over fifty communities rejected the establishment of a casino in their area. Toronto rejected the proposal of a Las Vegas-style casino by a vote of 2 to 1, as did London, Peterborough, and other major cities. In Windsor, while 77 percent of the voters agreed that Windsor Casino had been positive for that city's economy, 53 percent of the voters opposed the establishment of a second Las Vegas-style casino.

Video Lottery Terminals (VLTs)

VLTs are video gambling machines very similar to the slot machines found in casinos except that, instead of direct pay-outs, the machine prints up a credit slip which is exchanged for cash. In addition to casinos, they are placed at racetracks, bars, restaurants, hotel lobbies, and other similar establishments. They represent the latest development in the government's expansion of gaming as an income source, and are also the most controversial.

Their wide dispersion in popular establishments such as restaurants and bars provide easy access to gambling and are particularly tempting to young people, whom studies show tend to have a higher incidence of gambling addiction compared to the general population. In the provinces which have adopted VLTs, the machines are generally placed in smaller cities and towns where, it is contended, they siphon off money which might otherwise be spent in other establishments on goods and services. Furthermore, local governments have complained that very little of the revenue generated by VLTs is returned to the local government and community by the provincial government. These negative results have prompted a backlash in many small communities against VLTs. Referendums in numerous communities have favoured withdrawing VLTs from the communities where they have been placed. In 1997 the government of British Columbia, after lengthy deliberation, expanded licenced charity casinos but, faced with growing opposition to the introduction of VLTs, decided to prohibit them in the province. The public's strong disapproval and rejection of VLTs may be viewed as an indication that governments, in their extension of gaming as a source of revenue, may have, with the introduction of VLTs, stepped over the line of society's tolerance of gambling.

Summary

Governments have access to a large number of non-tax revenue sources. These sources account for only about 8 percent of federal revenues but range from about one-quarter to one-third of provincial and local government own-source revenue.

The main sources of non-tax revenues are the sale of goods and services, natural resources, government enterprises, and investments, along with licences, fees, and fines. Two sources of non-tax revenue which have expanded rapidly in recent years, and are among the most controversial, are user fees and gaming.

The greatest potential for the employment of user fees is at the provincial and local levels of government. Both of these governments, faced with the need for more revenues and reluctant to raise taxes, have extended the scope of their application of user charges in areas such as education, health care, child care, recreation, and sanitation services. While they raise revenue to finance these services, a strong argument against user fees is their regressive nature.

Beginning with lotteries in the 1970s, gaming at the provincial level has expanded to include innovative scratch-and-win lottery tickets, sports lotteries, casinos, and video lottery terminals (VLTs). Casinos and VLTs especially have become more and more controversial as they have spread, with many communities voting to reject the establishment of casinos and VLTs. The provincial governments, however, find gaming a lucrative source of revenue.

NOTES

1 A summary of government non-tax revenue is presented in Canadian Tax Foundation, *Finances of the Nation, 1997* (Toronto: Canadian Tax Foundation, 1998), ch.7.

2 For an analysis of user chargers and their applications, see Richard M. Bird and Thomas Tsiopoulos, "User Charges for Public Services: Potentials and Problems," *Canadian Tax Journal*, 1992, vol. 45, no.1.

3 Treasurer of Ontario, *1990 Ontario Budget* (Toronto: Ministry of Treasury and Economics, 1990).

4 Institute of Public Administration of Canada, *Public Sector Management*, 1995, vol. 6, no. 3, p.11.

5 Canada, Treasury Board, *Information: Federal Expenditure Reductions and Management Improvements* (Ottawa, December 15, 1989), p.7.

6 Canada, Department of Finance, *Budget Plan*, February 27, 1995, p.40.

7 *Ibid.*

8 Ontario Lottery Corporation, *Annual Report*, various years.

9 See, for example, Francois Vaillancourt and Julie Gagnan, "Canadian Lotteries as Taxes: Revenues and Incidence," *Canadian Tax Journal*, March/April 1988, vol. 36.

10 *The Globe and Mail*, February 21, 1998, D.2.

11 Ontario Casino Corporation, *Annual Report*, 1996-1997.

12 *Ibid.*

13 Statistics Canada, *Perspectives on Labour and Income*, 1996.

14 Lennart E. Henrikson, "Hardly a Quick Fix: Casino Gambling in Canada," *Canadian Public Policy*, 1996, vol. XXII, p.117.

15 *Ibid.*

16 *Ibid.*, pp.117-118.

17 *Ibid.*, pp.118-119.

18 *The Globe and Mail*, February 21, 1998, D.1, D.2.

CHAPTER 12

Debt Finance

Debt finance is the process of borrowing by government to finance its expenditures when the expenditures exceed revenues and budgetary deficits are incurred. At the federal level, budgetary deficits were recorded continuously from 1975 through 1997. The provincial governments also resorted to debt financing during the 1980s and into the 1990s. As will be explained in following chapters, budgetary deficits were made acceptable in Keynesian economics under certain conditions. The seemingly endless string of deficits in Canada, however, was not in accordance with Keynesian policy. They were not brought under control until the mid-1990s in most provinces and the later 1990s by the federal government, and their accumulation produced a huge public or government debt.

This chapter examines various aspects of debt finance, including the process of borrowing and source of borrowed funds, the effects of borrowing and the existence of a public debt, features and trends of the public debt in Canada, and the struggles of governments in Canada to bring debt financing under control.

Borrowing

Borrowing is a supplement to taxation as a means of raising revenue to finance government operations. But rather than being compulsory, like taxation, borrowing is a voluntary transfer of funds from the public to government. In the process, the government sells securities and pays interest for the use of the borrowed funds.

Governments can borrow from a number of sources, including individuals, the chartered banks, financial institutions other than banks, and the central bank (only the federal government can borrow from the central bank). The economic effects of borrowing vary with the source, as will be described later.

Before the development and acceptance of Keynesian economics and discretionary fiscal policy, borrowing was generally reserved for emergencies or abnormal situations; for example, much of the federal government's debt in 1946 was the result of having borrowed to finance World War II. With the emergence of Keynesian policy and the consequent acceptance of deficit financing to stimulate the economy, governments have tended to rely more heavily on borrowing as a means of finance. But borrowing was not reserved for covering government deficits in periods of unemployment and economic decline. During the 1970s and 1980s, the federal and many provincial governments began to employ borrowing to finance general expenditure when revenue fell short and they were reluctant to raise taxes sufficiently to cover expenditures.

At the municipal level of government, borrowing is commonly used to finance large capital or non-recurring expenditures, which, if financed by taxation, could result in a heavy tax burden during the period the expenditures are made. Borrowing permits the government to spread the burden over a number of years, an approach particularly appropriate for major capital projects, such as the construction of highways, schools and hospitals, sewage plants, and hydro-electric plants, that yield benefits to society over many years or decades.

There are no constitutional limits to federal and provincial borrowing powers, and they may borrow from both within and outside the country. Traditionally, the provinces have been less reluctant than the federal government to borrow by floating bond issues in other countries, and as a result, a greater proportion of their debt is held externally. With recent huge deficits and consequent heavy financial requirements, however, the federal government has come to rely increasingly on foreign sources of borrowed funds. The main places outside Canada where both federal and provincial bonds are sold are the United States, the United Kingdom, Western Europe, and Japan.

Features of Securities

The two basic types of securities commonly used to obtain financing are debt securities and ownership securities. Debt securities are generally called bonds, debentures, or notes; their purchasers do in fact lend their money to the issuer. Ownership securities take the form of stocks, shares, or equities: the purchasers of these securities become part owners of the entity issuing the security. Governments issue debt securities, although some government-owned (Crown) corporations issue ownership securities (in which case, they become jointly owned by the government and the private sector investors). The holder of a debt security is paid a stipulated amount of interest on specified dates during its term, usually annually.

The backing or security behind government bonds and other debt issues is the government's authority to impose taxes on the country's citizens, residents, and businesses. In addition, the federal government possesses the power to print money, which it could use to meet interest payments and to redeem maturing securities.

Governments can issue a number of different types of debt securities. Two primary features differentiating them are their term and their marketability. Term is the security's lifespan; it may be short term (generally less than three years), medium term (three to ten years) or long term (more than ten and as much as or more than twenty-five years). At the end of its term, the security is said to mature and is redeemed. That is, on the maturity date, the issuer repays the full principle or amount borrowed, which is known as the face or par value of the security.

Securities that are marketable are bought and sold (before maturity) in the bond or money market. Their prices fluctuate as interest rates fluctuate. The prices of outstanding — "old" — bonds move in the direction opposite to the movement of interest rate levels in the economy. As interest rate levels rise, say from 8 to 10 percent, the holders of old bonds who wish to sell them are forced to offer them on the bond market at a discount from their face since potential investors are unwilling to purchase old 8 percent bonds when newly issued securities are now yielding 10 percent. The price of the old 8 percent bond will therefore fall to the level at which the yield — return to the investor — is 10 percent.

Non-marketable securities are not transferable by the holder so they do not trade in the money market. The only non-marketable bond issued by Canadian governments is the Canadian Savings Bond (CSB). A unique feature of CSBs is that although they have a specific maturity date, they can be redeemed at full face value at any time before maturity.

Securities may also have callable and extendable features. A callable bond is one that may be redeemed — called in — by the issuer before its maturity date. This feature is not commonly used by government because it tends to diminish the attractiveness of a bond. An extendable bond has a specified maturity date, but the purchaser has the option of continuing to hold it for a specific number of additional years. Some medium-term bonds issued by the federal government can be exchanged on maturity date for new bonds bearing the same interest rate.

Federal Securities

The Canadian government issues several types of securities, including Treasury Bills, fixed coupon marketable bonds, Canada Savings Bonds, as well as Canada bills and notes payable in foreign currencies.[1] To raise funds in the Canadian domestic market, the government relies primarily on the first three debt instruments. These borrowing transactions, domestic and foreign, comprise Canada's unmatured debt. The amounts as of March 31, 1997 are shown in Table 12-1.

Rates of interest on government securities vary depending on their specific features and the current interest rates in the market. Traditionally, interest rates on long-term securities have been higher than those on short-term securities as an incentive for lenders to part with liquidity for the longer period. This was not the case during the early and late 1980s, however, when short-term interest rates, reflecting economic conditions and expectations, temporarily surged ahead of long-term interest rates.

Treasury Bills. A Treasury bill is a short-term certificate of indebtedness issued by the government of Canada to pay a sum of money on a given date. The most common terms are 91, 182, and 364 days, and bills for all three terms are issued weekly. Treasury bills are sold at a discount of their face value; the difference between the price paid and their face value is the yield expressed as an interest rate per annum. For example, suppose a 91-day Treasury bill of $100 is bought at a price of $96.750; then $100 is paid at the end of 91 days (Treasury bill prices are quoted from a $100 maturity value to three decimal points). The $3.250 earned over those 91 days is equivalent to about 13.4 percent yield on an annual basis.

Treasury bills are offered in denominations ranging from $1,000 to $1 million. The Bank of Canada acts as the federal government's fiscal agent. It auctions new Treasury bills each Tuesday for delivery on Thursday to a group of chartered banks and securities dealers (the primary distributors) through a competitive process of sealed tenders. The size of the weekly offering of bills depends on the amount of funds the government requires to finance its operations and for redeeming maturing bills. Successful bidders are determined in descending order with the tenders of the highest bidders (lowest discount rate) filled first. The Bank of Canada places a reserve bid to prevent the sale of bills at less than a minimum price, and there is generally a very small spread between high and low bidders.

The primary distributors of Treasury bills resell them in secondary markets, which are dominated by large institutional buyers. In this active secondary market — the money market — Treasury bills are redeemed at face value to the holder by the Bank of Canada.

When Canada first issued Treasury bills in 1934, they were held primarily by financial institutions and their total amount was relatively small. They have become much better known and more widely held over the past decade and now account for over one-third of the federal government's total market debt. During the period when large government deficits persisted and the public debt increased correspondingly, large transactions of Treasury bills were recorded.

Fixed Term Marketable Bonds. Government of Canada marketable bonds are interest-bearing certificates that are bought and sold in the open market and have fixed dates of maturity. They may be expressed in Canadian or in a foreign currency. The Bank of Canada, acting as the government's distributing agent, sells the bonds to a group of primary distributors (chartered banks and investment dealers). The sales are made via bid-price auction. The primary distributors resell the bonds to the public through an active secondary market. The term on these government bonds ranges from one to twenty-five years. Interest is payable in either coupon or registered form. In the former case, the bonds have attached coupons, one for each date on which interest is due and the coupon can be cashed. A registered bond shows the owner's name, and interest payments are sent directly to that person by the Bank of Canada on the date specified on the bond. At maturity, the bonds are redeemed by the Bank at their face value. Fixed coupon Government of Canada marketable bonds represent the largest component of the federal government's marketable debt (at almost 53 percent in 1995-96).

Canada Savings Bonds. Canada Savings Bonds (CSBs) have long been one of the most familiar and popular securities issued by the Canadian government. Starting as the Victory Bonds of World War II, they were continued after the war as Canada Savings Bonds.

The CSBs which are issued in denominations from $100 to $10,000 are non-marketable, interest-bearing certificates issued only to Canadian residents only once each year (in early November). Available through chartered banks or by payroll deductions, CSBs are very popular with the small investor because they offer an attractive yield and are highly liquid — they are redeemable on demand by the holder with accrued interest calculated to the end of the previous month.

Canada Savings Bonds are usually issued with a maturity date of seven years or more and are not subject to call before maturity. During periods of rising interest rates, the government has often increased the rates on outstanding CSBs or offered cash bonuses payable at maturity, both actions being inducements for individuals to hold the bonds to maturity and thereby reduce the degree of refunding required. For example, the November 1981 issue offered 19.5 percent for a one-year period, and the rate on all outstanding CSBs was increased for the year to the same level. Similarly, in early 1990, with interest rates rising and people dumping CSBs for

higher-yielding investments, the federal government increased the rate on all those outstanding from 10.5 to 11.5 percent for a period of six months. In recent years, the government has offered "step up" rates on new issues with a specified rate for the first year and designated increases in each successive year for a five-year period (i.e., 4 percent in year 1, 4.5 percent in year 2, rising to 7 percent by year 5).

Over the years, as Treasury Bills and other investment instruments such as mutual funds have become better known to investors and savers, CSBs have become less popular and have lost ground to them.

Other Securities. Governments also borrow from special funds which they administer. The federal government borrows from the accumulation in the Public Employees Superannuation fund by issuing to the fund special non-marketable bonds. They are non-negotiable and non-transferable. The provincial governments have borrowed from the surplus in the Canada Pension Plan.

Foreign Currency Securities. The Canadian government also borrows from other countries. Most foreign borrowing is from the United States, Switzerland, Germany, and Japan. The instruments used are Canada Bills and Canada Notes, which in recent years were denominated exclusively in U.S. dollars and amount to about 4 percent of outstanding market debt. These borrowings are for the purpose of raising foreign exchange to be used to promote stability and order of the Canadian dollar on the foreign exchange market.

Provincial and Municipal Securities

The provincial governments issue debt securities similar to those issued by the federal government; Treasury bills are auctioned through competitive tender to fiscal agents consisting of banks and investment dealers. New issues of marketable bonds are also sold to fiscal agents, who in turn distribute them to other investors. Both types of securities are actively traded in the secondary market. Some provinces, such as Ontario, have started to issue provincial savings bonds similar in nature to the Canada savings bonds.

Municipal borrowing is governed by provincial regulations. In most cases, specific borrowing must be authorized by the province. The exception is short-term or interim borrowing to meet current expenditures; in this case, however, limitations are placed on the amount that may be borrowed. Municipal debentures are issued through arrangement with the province or, for large cities, through a fiscal agent.

Public Debt in Canada

Public debt results from government borrowing and the accumulation of deficits. Features of the public debt at all three levels of Canadian governments are illustrated in the tables in this chapter. Before discussing these tables, however, it is useful to define some of the terms found in them.[2]

Gross debt represents the total liabilities of the government; it includes unmatured debt and other liabilities. Unmatured debt represents the government's financial obligations resulting from bonds, Treasury bills, and other certificates that mature or are redeemable in the future. Unmatured debt is net of the government's holding of its own debt. "Other" liabilities include accounts, such as pension accounts, accounts payable, insurance and trust accounts, and loan guarantees. Government liabilities are partly offset by various assets, such as cash, investments, sinking funds, securities held in trust, and loans to other levels of government, Crown corporations, and international governments and agencies. These items are called net recorded assets (notice that they do not include real assets, such as buildings). Subtracting these net recorded assets from gross debt produces net debt.

Features of Public Debt

Tables 12-1 and 12-2 illustrate the liabilities of the federal and provincial and municipal governments. Liabilities include unmatured debt, specific-purpose accounts (for example, government employees's pension plans), and various advances and payables. The provincial data shown in Table 12-2 does not include the guaranteed debt of the provinces, which consists primarily of guarantees as to principal and interest of loans and securities of government enterprises and amounted to over $90 billion in 1996.

Table 12-3 shows the distribution of debt for the federal government. Roughly 30 percent of the federal debt is held by the Bank of Canada and the chartered banks, with over 25 percent held by life insurance and pension funds.

One of the significant features of the distribution of the federal and provincial debt is the proportion held externally, which has long been considerable and is increasing. In the 1970s, less than 5 percent of the federal debt was held externally. By 1997 over 20 percent of gross federal debt was held by non-residents. At the provincial level, in 1980 less than 20 percent of provincial government bonds was held externally. By 1995 this proportion had increased to approximately 40 percent. Having large amounts of external borrowing and reliance on foreign exchange affects the foreign exchange rate and Canada's balance of payments. An externally held debt also imposes a burden on the country when interest is paid to foreigners and when the debt is redeemed (discussed later in the chapter).

Debt Management

In addition to issuing securities to finance the current deficit, governments continually engage in refinancing or refunding debt by redeeming maturing securities. To obtain the funds to do so, they issue new securities. For

TABLE 12-1: Composition of Federal Government Debt, 1996-97

	($ billion)
Unmatured debt	
Held by residents	357.2
Held by non-residents	119.7
Total	476.9
Public sector pensions	114.2
Canada Pension Plan	3.7
Interest and matured debt	10.4
Other accounts and liabilities	35.6
Total gross public debt	640.7
Less: Net recorded assets	57.5
Net public debt	583.2

Source: Canada, Department of Finance, Fiscal Reference Tables, October 1997 (Ottawa), p.23.

TABLE 12-2: Provincial and Local Government and Hospitals Composition of Liabilities

	($ billion)
Bonds	
Provincial	265.7
Municipal	38.9
Loans and short-term paper	34.4
Other	55.6
Total Liabilities	394.6

Source: Canada, Department of Finance, Fiscal Reference Tables, October 1997 (Ottawa), p.50.

example, in 1995-96 the outstanding stock of Treasury bills increased by only $1.6 billion to $166 billion. But the total gross issuance of Treasury bills in that year amounted to $390 billion, reflecting the short term to maturity and frequent turn-over of these securities. The principal objective of debt management is to raise the funds required at minimum cost over the long run. This involves judgements about the types of debt securities to issue, their terms and maturities, and the level of cash balances to retain. The refunding of a high volume at any one time could strain the money market, pushing up interest rates and thus increasing the cost of refunding; such sharp rises in interest rates could also produce adverse effects on the economy. Furthermore, major refunding at a time when interest rates are high increases the cost of servicing the debt.

**TABLE 12-3: Distribution of Domestic Holdings of
Government of Canada Securities
(Treasury Bills, Bonds and Canada Savings Bonds), 1995**

Holder	Percentage of Total
Life insurance and pension funds	25.7
Chartered banks	22.5
Public and other financial institutions[a]	17.0
Persons and unincorporated businesses	14.4
Bank of Canada	6.9
All levels of government[b]	6.7
Non-financial corporations	3.6
Quasi-banks[c]	3.2
	100.0

[a] Includes investment dealers, mutual funds, and federal and provincial financial institutions.
[b] Includes holdings of the Canada Pension Plan and the Québec Pension Plan.
[c] Includes credit unions, trust and mortgage companies.

Source: Canada, Department of Finance, Debt Operations Report, November 1996 (Ottawa), p.16.

In the view of the Department of Finance, one of the most important elements of debt management is the appropriate mix of fixed and floating rates for the debt.[3] The federal government's fixed-rate securities are its marketable bonds that have fixed coupons; most are medium or long term. Its floating-rate securities are Treasury bills and CSBs. In the long run, savings in interest charges can be realized by maintaining a substantial proportion of outstanding debt in floating-rate form because generally it is cheaper to borrow short term than long term. In a period of high interest rates, borrowing short term allows for opportunities for savings once interest rates decline, whereas issuing long term locks in the high rates. Savings can be achieved by issuing short-term securities even when short-term rates are higher than long-term rates, since such a situation is likely to be temporary. Issuing fixed-rate securities offers savings, however, if rising interest rates are anticipated and expected to last for some time.

During the 1980s and into the 1990s approximately 50 percent of the federal debt was of the floating-rate form (CSBs and Treasury bills) and therefore had to be refunded or refinanced every year. The government claimed that by maintaining a large proportion of its debt in short-term floating instruments, particularly Treasury bills, it benefited from the trend to lower short-term rates. This benefit was particularly evident during the period 1981 to 1987, when the trend in interest rates was downward (the bank rate declined from 17.9 percent to 8.4 percent).

In addition to holding a large part of the debt in floating form, the government also changed the maturity structure of its marketable bonds during the 1981-87 period. As interest rates went down, the proportion of marketable bonds with maturities of three years or less declined from 36 percent of the total in 1981 to about 18 percent in 1987, while bonds with maturities of three to ten years increased from approximately 22 to 46 percent of the total, and long-term bonds decreased from 42 percent to 36 percent of the total. In essence, the government's debt management strategy with respect to marketable bonds during 1981 to 1987, when interest rates were falling but long-term rates exceeded short- and medium-term rates, was to lock an increasing proportion of its marketable bond debt into medium-term maturities, thereby avoiding both the higher long-term rates and the potential costs of unexpected increases in short-term rates. As interest rates started to rise in 1988, the government began to switch more of its maturing long-term marketable bonds into maturities of three years or less.

One of the problems with a large proportion of floating-rate debt is that it exposes the government to interest rates. In 1992 the federal government embarked on a debt strategy to increase the fixed-rate portion of its debt to a target level of 65 percent.[4] The objective was to protect the government against significant increases in debt interest costs arising from interest shocks. The government's strategy of issuing a higher proportion of longer-term debt after 1992 proved fruitful as interest rates continued to decline to a near post-war low by 1997. The government was able to lock in long-term debt at relatively low interest rates.

Issues and Concerns of Borrowing and Debt

Large scale, continuous borrowing and the accumulation of a large public debt raise a number of potential problems and issues for the economy and society as outlined in the following.[5]

Crowding-Out. To the extent that individuals, chartered banks, and financial institutions switch funds into government securities from alternative investment opportunities in the capital market, government borrowing may crowd out private borrowing. In other words, the competition for available loanable funds may contribute to an increase in interest rates, making capital more expensive for the private sector and possibly retarding private investment, business expansion, and operations. Whether crowding-out does indeed occur has been a topic of considerable debate, partly fuelled by the enormous budget deficits of the federal governments of Canada and the United States in the 1980s. Much depends on the overall supply of and demand for loanable funds. Some analysts have argued that crowding-out did not occur in the early 1980s and again in the 1990s despite the deficits because the recession during these periods was not conducive to investment and expansion by private industry, and consequently the demand for borrowed funds by the private sector was relatively small. In addition, the savings rate in Canada was exceptionally high, providing an adequate supply of funds. There has been concern, however, that in an expanding and prosperous economy, such huge government budget deficits could lead to crowding-out and consequent upward pressure on interest rates. During the latter part of the 1980s, and again after 1994, when the economy did prosper and large government deficits continued, some of the pressure in Canadian capital markets from public borrowing was eased by greater government reliance on foreign sources for funding. Only about 2.6 percent of the outstanding federal debt was held by foreigners in 1975, but this proportion had increased to almost 20 percent by 1988 and increased further to 21 percent by the mid-1990s. In addition, the provincial governments also relied relatively heavily on foreign markets as sources of borrowed funds. While foreign borrowing may ease the pressure on domestic interest rates, costs appear later as large principal and interest payments to foreigners represent a transfer of resources out of the country.

Inflation. Large-scale borrowing from the Bank of Canada can produce inflationary pressures through expansion of the money supply. When the government sells securities to the Bank, the amounts borrowed are credited to the government's account and drawn upon to finance its expenditures. The chain reaction through the banking deposit process creates an increase in the money supply and increased consumer and business spending; to the extent that excess aggregate demand is created, there is upward pressures on prices which is inflation.

Transfer of Burden. Economists have a long-standing and lively debate about whether borrowing to finance current expenditure programs shifts the burden of paying for these programs to future generations when the debt is repaid. Two opposing views have been put forward.

The traditional theory considers burden in real terms (the use of resources) and holds that the real burden of current borrowing can rarely be shifted. It falls on the present generation in the form of reduced consumption when current resources are transferred from the private to the public sector and are used by government as it spends the borrowed funds. Only if the present generation reduces its rate of savings can the burden be shifted to future generations. Reduced savings lower investment. The result is that future generations have a smaller quantity of productive capital to inherit and consequently a smaller amount of production of goods and services — and therefore less income and consumption for the future. Before concluding that the future generations of society will experience such a burden, however, one must consider the application of the borrowed funds. Losses from reduced investment and capital accumulation in the private sector may be balanced by potential gains from public investment. The government's present use of borrowed funds for public use and public investment may provide benefits that extend to future generations.

The alternative view interprets the concept of burden mainly in financial terms, rather than real terms. These analysts maintain that the present generation bears no burden when purchasing government securities since they are bought voluntarily. Buyers exchange savings or postpone consumption for government securities and do not consider that they are making a sacrifice. There is no reduction in their assets, only a change in their asset mix. The sacrifice (or burden) rests with future generations, who suffer reduced consumption when they pay the higher taxes needed to finance the debt or to redeem the debt.

Although proponents of both views recognize that there is a burden involved in financing government by borrowing, they disagree about the time that the burden is realized. The traditional view, despite detractors, remains widely held in public finance theory.

The real burden of borrowing may also be shifted forward to future generations by borrowing abroad. In this case, borrowing does not cause any reduction in current domestic consumption. Future consumption suffers, however, when taxes are imposed to service and redeem the external debt.

Financial Mismanagement. Some view a growing public debt as a sign of poor financial management on the part of the government; that borrowing and increasing the public debt in a period of economic prosperity is inappropriate and unsound fiscal policy. It is contrary to the Keynesian formula of balancing the budget over the course of the business cycle and reflects a lack of fiscal discipline by government. In this regard, the Canadian government received failing grades for its huge deficits and the massive growth of the public debt during most of the 1980s.

Income Redistribution. To the extent that the debt is held by wealthy individuals and large corporations and financial institutions, it can be argued that the tax and transfer process involved in financing deficits and debt charges leads to a redistribution of income to the wealthy. This is contrary to the accepted

**TABLE 12-4: Federal Government Debt Charges
for Selected Years as at March 31**

Year	Gross Public Debt Charges ($million)	Debt Charges as % of Federal Expenditures
1965	1,050	12.3
1975	3,238	10.3
1980	8,494	16.0
1985	22,393	22.8
1990	38,789	27.2
1995	42,046	26.2
1996	46,905	29.5
1997	44,973	30.0

Source: Canada, Department of Finance, *Fiscal Reference Tables*, October 1997 (Ottawa), p.15.

standards of equity and other government programs designed to raise the income levels of low-income groups and reduce the gap between the poor and the rich. Table 12-3 shows that most of the federal debt is indeed held by corporations, banks and financial institutions.

The effect on income distribution, however, depends not only on the distribution of debt holdings, but also on the tax structure. A progressive tax structure would serve to lessen the adverse impact on income distribution of servicing the debt. In Canada, the late 1980s witnessed a reduction in the number of tax brackets in the personal income tax and a reduction in marginal rates of tax. At the same time the government switched from the manufacturer's sales tax to the more comprehensive goods and services. Both developments likely combined to reduce the degree of progression of the federal tax structure and aggravated the adverse effect of the debt on income distribution. This effect, however, may be reduced by the extent that debt holders who receive the interest payments are in turn taxed on these payments.

Budget Reallocation. A growing debt requires increasing interest payments which re-

duce the proportion of the budget allocated to social and economic programs, or result in increased taxes. Between 1955 and 1975, federal debt charges remained relatively constant at 10 to 12 percent of federal budgetary expenditures. As shown in Table 12-4, by 1996 public debt charges had risen to $47 billion or 30 percent of budgetary expenditures, which contributed to the continuing deficits, increased taxes as seen earlier, and reduced amounts available for other programs. By the 1990s, 35 cents of every dollar collected in federal taxes went to pay the interest on the public debt, and that money represented funds that would otherwise have been available for tax reduction and/or to address urgent social and economic needs such as health care and education, environmental protection, and research and development.

Strains on the Economy. It is frequently alleged that a large public debt undermines domestic and foreign confidence in the economy with consequent adverse effects on investment and expansion of productive capacity; that it places heavy strains on the economy in the form of interest charges; and that it may even produce national bankruptcy in the sense of the government's being unable to meet its interest and security redemption obligations. The issue of strain on the economy must be viewed in terms of the size of the debt and of the proportion of it held externally. There is general agreement that the significance of the public debt is not its absolute amount but its size in relation to GDP. The larger a country's GDP — its productive capacity — the greater its ability to carry debt. If this debt is held internally — that is, by Canadian residents — payments of interest on the debt from tax proceeds simply involve a transfer from the taxed party to the parties holding the debt and involve no loss of resources to society. It is then said of the debt, we owe it to ourselves.

The consensus among economists is that the existence of a public debt normally poses little threat of national bankruptcy or major adverse effects on the economy if it is declining relative to GDP and the government enjoys a sound credit position domestically and abroad. A government in such a position should have little difficulty in meeting its obligations. A problem may arise, however, if the size of the debt begins to rise relative to GDP. The debt/GDP ratio could conceivably become so large as to require relatively high levels of taxation to finance the debt charges, providing disincentives for investment and retarding economic growth. In Canada, the federal net public debt declined after World War II from 106.6 percent of GDP in 1947 to less than 20 percent in the 1970s. Fuelled by continuous deficits the debt began to increase until the net federal debt reached approximately 72 percent of GDP in 1996 (Table 12-5).

The debt, growing faster than the economy and consequently faster than the nation's ability to pay, caused growing alarm among Canadians. To business and financial communities especially, the public debt seemed to be growing out of control, portending dire financial and economic consequences. Similar problems may arise at the provincial and municipal government levels.

An individual province or municipal government, given its limited revenue sources and inability to print currency, could be faced with default if it exceeds its ability to service or manage debt. Although Canadian provincial and municipal governments have so far been able to manage their debts without major difficulty, some U.S. city governments were on the verge of defaulting on their public debt interest payments in the early 1980s.

In general, the Canadian provinces have been better able to control the size of their budgetary deficits and debts than has the federal government. They are not, however, free from problems. Historically, the Atlantic provinces have usually had a higher debt/GDP ratio than the other provinces, but during the late 1980s, the ratios in Manitoba and Saskatchewan surpassed those in all provinces except Newfoundland. The trend since 1966 for most provinces and for all provinces combined has generally been upward, but the increase in total provincial debt as a percentage of aggregate GDP since 1975 has been much smaller than the corresponding increase in the federal debt. Some of the largest relative increases in the debt/GDP ratio have occurred in the west, particularly in Alberta and British Columbia, two provinces that were virtually debt-free in 1966.

External Burden. Various problems may arise if a substantial proportion of a large public debt is held externally. Large principal and interest payments to foreigners represent a transfer of real resources out of the country and are, therefore, a drain on the economy. Furthermore, the value of the domestic currency may decline as foreign investors convert it into their own currency; the decline causes import prices to rise, which may fuel inflation. Moreover, there is always the danger that domestic economic or political problems may cause foreign debtholders to lose confidence in the government and begin dumping its securities, forcing it either to offer higher interest rates as an incentive to foreign investors, or to increase taxes to meet its redemption obligations. Both options have potentially serious effects for the national economy.

Traditionally, the Canadian government avoided large foreign debt; until the late 1970s, less than 5 percent of the federal debt was held by non-residents. But the financial requirements resulting from the continuing large deficits of the last decade forced the federal government, as well as provincial governments, to rely more heavily on foreign markets for funds. By 1988 almost 20 percent of the federal debt was held by non-residents while 29 percent of provincial securities was held externally. This trend continued into the 1990s. By 1995, over 25 percent of federal market debt was held externally. Approximately one-third of foreign-held federal debt rests with United States investors.

The Federal Debt Treadmill

Table 12-5 illustrates the growth of debt of the federal government as a percentage of gross domestic product. Much of the federal government's debt before 1960 consisted of the debt that had been incurred to finance Canada's involvement in World War II. In 1947, the net public debt measured 106.6 percent of GDP, but as the economy grew in subsequent years and budget deficits, when incurred, were relatively small, the size of the debt relative to GDP continued to decline until it reached a post-war low of 19 percent in 1975. Beginning in that year, the federal government began to accumulate a string of consecutive budgetary deficits that not only increased the dollar amount of the debt but also increased the debt-to-GDP ratio until it stood at 71 percent by 1997.

The federal government began its long run of consecutive deficits in 1970. By 1980-81 the deficit had risen to $14.6 billion on the public accounts basis (Table 12-6) and continued to rise to reach $32.9 billion in 1983-84, or 34 percent of budgetary expenditures.

The large increase in the deficit during the early 1980s was due partly to rapid increases in government spending and the expenditure-revenue structure (structural deficit) and partly due to the recession which damaged revenue growth and caused an increase in such payments as Employment Insurance (cyclical deficit).[6]

High interest rates, which reached double digits, contributed to the increase in government spending as the ballooning public debt was refinanced.

The newly elected Conservative government in 1984 made a commitment to bring the deficit under control and presented a budgetary plan to eliminate the deficit over a five-year period. Indeed, this period ushered in a series of five-year plans to eliminate the deficit, announced by the Minister of Finance in his annual budget speeches. The government, however, only managed to reduce the deficit to $27.8 billion by 1988, despite numerous tax increases. Following 1988, fuelled by program expenditure increases and rising interest rates, the deficit began to increase once again. By 1993-94 it stood at an all-time high of $42 billion on a public accounts basis and to $35 billion in the national accounts.

Deficit reduction was hampered by the drain of financing the deficits themselves. Each year that a deficit was incurred meant a substantial increase in the revenue required just to cover interest charges. For example, an average interest rate of 10.5 percent on the $30 billion budgetary deficit in 1984 added $3.2 billion to the government's revenue requirements for that fiscal year alone.

In addition, the compounding effect of interest on the public debt contributed to a debt spiral. Each year deficit-financed interest payments were added to the public debt, so in each subsequent year, interest was paid on the accumulated interest (compound interest). Money invested at a compound rate of 10 percent approximately doubles in seven years and grows to almost eight times its original size in twenty-one years. The same holds true

TABLE 12-5: Trends in Federal Public Debt, 1927-1997
($ million, and percentage of GDP)

Fiscal Year	Gross Public Debt	Net Public Debt	Net Debt Percentage of GDP[a]
1926-27	2,726	2,348	45.6
1936-37	3,452	3,084	66.6
1946-47	16,849	12,669	106.6
1956-57	16,491	11,446	34.8
1966-67	28,399	17,707	27.5
1976-77	69,270	41,517	21.0
1986-87	308,945	273,323	54.1
1996-97	640,657	583,186	71.8

[a] GDP for the corresponding calendar year.

Source: Canada, Department of Finance, *The Budget*, February 20, 1990 (Ottawa), p.148; and *Fiscal Reference Papers*. October, 1997 (Ottawa), p.23.

of money owed. For example, Minister of Finance Michael Wilson estimated the net public debt for 1989-90 to be about $350 billion, an increase of about $150 billion over a five-year period. Of this increase, the minister estimated that more than 80 percent consisted of the compounding of interest on the $200 billion debt of 1984-85. As these statistics illustrate, the public debt is self-perpetuating; it feeds on itself. In the words of Finance Minister Wilson, the government was on a "treadmill of borrowing money to pay interest on the past debt ... [and this] ... helps to explain why the deficit is still at $30 billion in spite of the reduction in spending and increased tax revenues over the past five years."[7]

As long as the interest rate exceeds the growth rate of GDP and public debt charges are financed wholly by deficits, the public debt will grow not only in dollar terms but also as a percentage of GDP. The situation is aggravated during a period of rising interest rates. It was estimated that approximately 60 percent of the government's total outstanding debt (primarily Treasury bills and Canada Savings Bonds) has to be refinanced or re-priced each year. If a year is characterized by rising interest rates, revenue requirements are raised further because part of the public debt issued earlier at lower interest rates matures and has to be refinanced at the new, higher rates. For example, with unmatured debt at about the $300 billion level, refinancing 60 percent of it with a 1 percent increase in interest rates would require an additional $1.8 billion.

The government, however, benefited from falling interest rates between 1984 and 1987 when the three-month Treasury bill rate fell from 11.1 percent to 8.2 percent and the rate on ten-year Canada bonds decreased from 12.7 percent to 9.9 percent. It was only in 1988 that interest rates began to rise again.

It wasn't until the fiscal year 1994-95 that the government began to bring debt finance under control. The newly elected Liberal government made a firm commitment to reduce and eventually eliminate the deficit. It instituted a program of retaining the high taxes imposed in earlier years to maintain revenues and making large reductions in program spending from $120 billion in 1993-94 to $104 billion by 1996-97. This included a reduction in transfers to the provinces from $27 billion to $22.5 billion by the fiscal year 1996-97. Falling interest rates contributed in the government's struggle to bring the deficit under control. The three-month Treasury bill rate fell from 12.8 percent in 1990 to 4.3 percent by 1996, while the Canada ten-year bond rate fell from 10.8 percent to 7.5 percent. Refinancing maturing debt at these falling interest rates served to moderate the increase in debt charges as the debt increased. Indeed, debt charges were reduced from $47 billion in 1995-96 to 41.5 billion by 1997-98. These developments, combined with a strong economy which produced increases in revenues of about $10 billion per year, reduced the budgetary deficit to $28.6 billion in 1995-96 and to $8.9 billion in 1996-97. In the Fall of 1998, the government announced a budget surplus of $3.5 billion for 1997-98 and forecast surpluses for the next two years. It was the first federal budgetary surplus on a public accounts basis since 1969-70.

Provincial Deficits, Debt, and Struggle for Control

Throughout most of the 1980-94 period, every province was experiencing budgetary deficits. Even the three resource-rich western provinces of British Colombia, Alberta, and Saskatchewan, which had earlier enjoyed large surpluses, thanks to high oil and gas prices and royalties, ran deficits throughout most of the 1980 decade. As the economy recovered from the 1980-83 recession and continued to grow, there was a movement towards deficit reduction through policies aimed at restraining government spending and maintaining or increasing taxes. By 1990, most provinces had succeeded in reducing their reliance on deficit finance. The recession from 1990 to 1993 dampened revenue growth, and had the effect of reducing budg-

etary revenues. The budgetary deficits in all provinces increased, fuelled by large increases in government spending as was the case in Ontario and Quebec. In Ontario, government spending under the newly elected New Democratic government of Bob Rae increased from $45.9 billion in 1990-91 to $54.9 billion by 1993-94 and the budget balance changed from a surplus of $90 billion in 1989-90 to a deficit of over $11 billion. Between 1990 and 1992, the deficit in every province rose substantially as shown in Table 12-6.

The period following the recession witnessed a major effort on the part of all provincial governments to bring their budgets into balance. In most provinces this was achieved through a growing economy that brought revenue growth, combined with retrenchment in government program spending and falling interest rates, which reduced provincial debt charges. By 1995-96, the provinces of Newfoundland, Prince Edward Island, New Brunswick, Manitoba, Saskatchewan, and Alberta recorded budgetary surpluses, and the remaining provinces had substantially reduced the size of their deficits. At the end of fiscal 1996-97, only Ontario, Quebec, and the territories were in a budgetary deficit position.

During their struggle to bring their budgets into balance, some provinces enacted balanced-budget legislation or expenditure limitations of one form or another to prevent future budget deficits. Manitoba, Alberta, Saskatchewan, New Brunswick, and Nova Scotia took the lead in this direction. In 1995 Manitoba enacted legislation which requires all future governments to balance both current and capital budget accounts. To give this measure substance, a fine is imposed on the premier and his Cabinet if the government runs a deficit. The fine is a 20 percent salary deduction for the first year of a deficit and 40 percent if there is a deficit in the next year. Exceptions to the balanced-budget requirement are allowed only in the event of war,

TABLE 12-6: Federal and Provincial Budget Balances 1980-1996
(Public Accounts Basis)

($ million)

Fiscal Year Ending	Federal	B.C.	Alta.	Sask.	Man.	Ont.	Que.	N.B.	N.S.	P.E.I.	Nfld.	Yukon & Territories
1981	-14,556	-257	+1,404	+233	-90	-1,297	-3,482	-150	-142	-14	-87	+4
1984	-32,877	-1,012	+129	-232	-429	-3,153	-2,164	-345	-316	+4	-326	+40
1988	-27,794	-48	-1,365	-542	-300	-2,489	-2,393	-439	-227	-16	-197	-32
1990	-28,930	+456	-2,116	-378	-142	+90	-1,760	-154	-267	-8	-175	-7
1992	-34,357	-2,532	-2,629	-842	-334	-10,930	-4,301	-516	-406	-50	-276	-42
1994	-42,012	-910	-1,384	-272	-430	-11,202	-4,921	-290	-547	-71	-205	-16
1996	-28,617	-347	+1,132	+18	+157	-8,800	-3,950	+51	-201	+4	+9	+12
1997[a]	-8,897	+432	+322	+318	+73	-5,406	-4,131	+130	+24	+9	+37	-48

[a] Estimates.

Source: Canada, Department of Finance, *Fiscal Reference Tables*, October 1997, cat. F1-2E/1997E and Canadian Tax Foundation, *Finances of the Nation, 1997* (Toronto), A.9.

natural disasters (such as a flood or crop failures) or a drop of more than 5 percent in government revenue. In addition, the legislation requires referendums for tax increases. The province also introduced a thirty-year plan to retire its $7 billion debt in annual installments.

Of course, balanced-budget legislation, as with all legislation, can be overturned by future governments. For example, in 1992 when the New Democrat party swept into power in British Columbia, it repealed that province's Taxpayer Protection Act, which had required balancing the budget over a five-year cycle and had frozen tax rates. Moreover, statutory limits do not necessarily remove the possibility of fiscal deception, as deficits can be hidden with the help of creative accounting and vague definitions.

A problem with a balanced-budget requirement is that it reduces budget flexibility and the ability of the government to actively pursue fiscal policy to counter the swings of the business cycle (see chapter 16). But it may be necessary to sacrifice budget flexibility to achieve fiscal responsibility and accountability. Balanced-budget legislation is ultimately a vote of no-confidence in politicians. The continuous deficits and huge accumulation of public debt in the last two decades serve as a good indicator that politicians and governments cannot always be trusted to budget responsibly when they are given free rein in the financial affairs of the country. Too often they tend to neglect the established principles of fiscal policy theory of balancing the budget over the course of the business cycle.

Debt Retirement

The issue of debt retirement or reduction has stirred considerable debate recently as the federal government and the provinces reached a position of balancing their budgets and producing surpluses. Many provinces have made commitments to use budget generated surpluses to pay down their debts. In 1997 the federal government indicated that it would apply one-half of future budget surpluses to restoring previous spending cuts and new program initiatives, with the remainder allocated to debt reduction and tax cuts.

Public opinion polls showed that people were divided on the application of budget surpluses, but did show wide support for applying them to reduce the debt. Asked what governments should do with budgetary surpluses in an October 1997 Angus Reid poll, 47 percent of the respondents favoured public debt reduction, 37 percent favoured tax reduction, and only 13 percent opted for spending more on government programs.

With federal net public debt of almost $600 billion in 1998, Canada had a debt-to-GDP ratio of over 70 percent, the second highest of the G-7 countries. This was still below the level reached at the end of World War II when the federal debt ($17 billion) peaked at 106 percent of GDP. A small portion of that debt was retired in the immediate post-war period and this combined with rapid economic growth brought the debt down to 35 percent of GDP by 1957. Continued increases in GDP, despite some increase in the debt due to deficit financing, further reduced the level to 21 percent of GDP by 1970. As these development show, assuming no significant deficits in the future, the debt-to-GDP ratio will decline with the growth of the economy to a more manageable level in future years.

Many contend, however, that the government should use expected surpluses in the next few years to make a concerted effort to reduce the absolute level of the debt to lift the burden of debt from future generations. Applying current tax revenue for debt reduction would put some of the burden of debt reduction on the current generation, which has benefited from the deficits of the last two decades. Federal government borrowing to finance programs during that period bestowed benefits of lower taxes on citizens and higher current consumption.

TABLE 12-7: International Comparison of Government Net Debt[a]
in Selected Years 1980-1996 for G-7 Countries

	Canada	U.S.	Japan	U.K.	Germany	France	Italy	G-7 Average
			(Percentage of GDP)					
1980	13.0	21.6	16.4	36.2	9.3	-3.3	53.0	20.5
1985	34.7	32.2	25.9	30.6	19.2	10.8	80.0	31.6
1990	43.1	38.5	10.6	18.8	20.7	16.3	84.4	32.1
1996	70.3	49.2	14.3	44.2	48.1	39.3	111.7	47.2

[a] Total government net debt (all levels of government) national income and expenditure accounts basis.

Source: Canada, Department of Finance, *Fiscal Reference Tables*, October 1997 (Ottawa), p.57.

Without current debt reduction, future generations are saddled with the financial burden of these benefits enjoyed by the current generation. They will be required to pay the debt charges and to pay off the debt, and will consequently suffer reduced consumption. Some of this burden could be lifted from the shoulders of future generations by maintaining the current tax levels on the current generation and using the budget surpluses to pay down the debt. In other words, the current generation will be paying for the benefits it enjoyed through government borrowing rather than passing the burden to future generations.

In its 1998-99 budget, however, the federal government announced expenditure initiatives totalling $10.9 billion up to the year 2000-01 and tax reduction measures amounting to $7.2 billion for the same period, a cumulative total of $18.1 billion. For each year, $3 billion was set aside in a contingency reserve, which if not required for unforeseen emergencies, would be applied to repay the debt to the sum of $9 billion.[8] It was apparent that Prime Minister Chretien's Liberal government was placing priority on expenditure increases and tax reduction rather than debt repayment.

Comparison with Other Countries

Canada was not alone in struggling with large budgetary deficits and a growing public debt. The United States too had difficulty. During the 1980s and into the 1990s, the United States, like Canada, was plagued by a string of consecutive deficits. Concern over these deficits led the U.S. Congress, in 1985, to legislate the Balanced Budget and Emergency Deficit Control Act, which specified annual deficit reductions until a balanced budget was achieved. The deficit targets, however were not achieved and were revised with a target date of 1993 for a balanced budget. But as deficits continued, Congress in 1990 passed the Budget Enforcement Act, specifying a balanced budget sometime after

1995. In 1995 a proposed constitutional amendment to require a balanced federal budget (many U.S. state constitutions had been amended requiring balanced budgets) passed the House of Representatives but failed to gain the support of the Senate.

Table 12-7 shows the trend in the net government debt relative to GDP for the G-7 countries since 1980. Only Italy has a higher debt-to-GDP ratio than Canada. Whereas the ratio actually fell in Japan, increased slightly in the United Kingdom, and more than doubled in the United States, it increased more than five-fold in Canada. Germany and France experienced similar large increases in their debt-to GDP ratios.

Summary

Debt finance involves borrowing by government to finance part of its expenditure. The federal and provincial governments began to rely increasingly on debt finance during much of the 1980s and into the 1990s. It was only in the mid- and later part of the 1990s that most provinces and the federal government were able to bring their budgets into balance.

Government borrowing and the existence of a large public debt may have significant repercussions for the economy and society. These include crowding-out private borrowing and inflation. The distribution of income may be negatively affected; high debt charges crowd out government spending on other goods and services; and the burden of the debt may be transferred from current to future generations. An increasing portion of the debt has become concentrated in foreign hands, placing a drain on the economy and increasing the vulnerability of the Canadian currency and economy.

It has been a major struggle for both the federal and provincial governments to bring their budgets into balance and reduce or eliminate their reliance on debt finance. Some of the provinces have enacted balanced-budget legislation to prevent future reliance on debt finance.

NOTES

1 The various debt instruments are described in Canada, Department of Finance, *Debt Management Report*, 1997, pp.19-27.

2 These terms are presented as defined by the Department of Finance and Statistics Canada.

3 Canada, Department of Finance, *Debt Operations Report*, November, 1996, p.15.

4 *Ibid.*

5 A general discussion and analysis of various aspects of borrowing and the public debt are contained in most standard textbooks in public sector economics. See, for example, David N. Hyman and John C. Strick, *Public Finance in Canada: A Contemporary Application of Theory and Policy* (Toronto: Harcourt Brace & Co., Canada, 1995), ch.12.

6 Structural and cyclical deficits are discussed in chapter 16.

7 Canada, Department of Finance, *The Budget*, February 20, 1990, p.9.

8 Canada, Department of Finance, *The Budget Plan, 1998*, cat. F1-23/1998 1E.

PART FOUR

INTERGOVERNMENTAL FISCAL RELATIONS

CHAPTER 13

Historical Development

Canada has a federal system of government in which powers are constitutionally divided between the federal government and provincial governments, and each is sovereign within its respective sphere of jurisdiction. This division of powers was established by the Constitution Act, 1867, at Confederation. Over time, however, changing economic and social conditions and the interpretations of the division-of-powers provisions of the act have produced a number of problems in intergovernment relations and difficulties for both levels of government.[1]

First, there is the issue of achieving a balance between expenditure responsibilities and revenue sources at the different levels of government. The federal government was given unlimited taxing powers and the provinces restricted to direct taxation, but the most expensive functions turned out to be those under the jurisdiction of the provinces. The provinces have complained of the difficulty of raising sufficient revenues to meet their large and ever-increasing expenditures. A lack of balance of expenditures and revenues between two levels of government is known as vertical fiscal imbalance.

Second, differences arise in the provinces' relative fiscal capacities, a situation known as horizontal fiscal imbalance. Because the provinces differ in economic potential and economic development, some have a good tax base while others have poor revenue sources. Ontario, for example, has a good industrial base with relatively high per capita income. It therefore has a greater capacity to obtain tax revenue to provide a wide range and high standards of services for its citizens than does a province such as Newfoundland with its relatively low per capita income. Even if Newfoundland resorts to higher levels of taxation, it has difficulty obtaining sufficient revenues to provide the same level of services as Ontario.

A third problem stems from the joint occupancy of tax fields. To a considerable degree, both levels of government levy the same taxes (income, sales), a situation that results in overlapping administration and the possibility of excessively high tax rates.

Fourth, conflicts occasionally arise from shared jurisdiction over certain responsibilities of government, such as natural resources or communications. Each level of government may have its own view regarding the direction of policy or development in the area and the extent of its jurisdiction. Examples include the disagreement between Ottawa and Newfoundland over offshore mineral rights and between Ottawa and Alberta over oil and gas pricing policies.

Finally, difficulties may arise in the implementation of fiscal policy. Unless there is close co-operation between the two levels of government, provincial expenditure and tax policies can counter federal measures introduced to achieve fiscal policy goals. For example, the federal government may reduce its income tax as part of a policy to stimulate the economy; the provinces could then conceivably take advantage of the tax room created, viewing this as an opportunity to increase their relative share of the income tax field.

Such problems have been common in Canada's history as a nation, and attempts to alleviate or solve them have been varied and numerous. The three chapters in this section examine some of the basic issues and developments in federal-provincial relations in Canada. This chapter focuses on developments that led to the tax agreements between the federal government and the provincial governments and on the main features of those agreements.

Historical Development of Fiscal Relations

Constitution Act, 1867

The Constitution Act, 1867, which created the Canadian nation (as the British North America Act), provided a federal system of government. Desiring a strong central government, the founders of Confederation assigned the federal government the most costly functions of the time, together with the most important revenue sources. The provinces were given what were then lesser powers, specifically enumerated in the act to include responsibility for education, hospitals, property and civil rights, licensing of business, administration of justice within the province, and matters of a local nature. At the same time, the provinces were assigned the less significant revenue sources then in existence, and each was limited to direct taxation within its own borders. Direct taxes, such as the personal income tax, were unpopular in the mid-nineteenth century and were not considered to have much potential as sources of revenue.

The residual powers of government — those not specifically assigned to the provinces — were granted to the federal government in the all-embracing section 91 of the act, which stipulates that the federal government is to "make Laws for the Peace, Order and Good Government of Canada in relation to all matters not coming within the Classes of Subjects by this Act assigned exclusively to the Legislatures of the Province."

To clarify federal responsibility, section 91 enumerates thirty-two specific federal powers. Included in this list is the power to raise revenue "by any mode of taxation." The most important sources of revenue in 1867 were customs and excise duties, which were classified as indirect taxes and assumed by the federal government. The provinces were left with the property tax and revenues from charges and licences. Since these revenue sources were somewhat meagre — they had accounted for only one-fifth of total revenues of the provinces of Canada in 1866 — the federal government agreed to supplement them by giving the provinces annual payments, which were specified in the act. They consisted of per capita subsidies and flat annual grants in support of government. In addition, special annual grants were arranged for Nova Scotia and New Brunswick for a ten-year interim period to give them time to develop their own taxes.[2] Grants and subsidies accounted for approximately 80 percent of the total revenues of these two provinces in the early post-Confederation period.

The arrangements just described achieved a reasonable balance between revenue needs and expenditure responsibilities in 1867. The federal government had been assigned the most costly functions and had been given the main revenue sources. The less costly functions assigned to the provinces were not expected to become financially significant, and provincial revenue needs were considered to be well below federal needs.

Any semblance of balance achieved in 1867 was shattered shortly thereafter, however, and continued to erode over time. As Canada developed following Confederation, the demands on both levels of government increased.[3] In 1879, the federal government introduced the National Policy as part of its plan for the economic development of the country. High tariffs were imposed to promote industrialization, immigration was encouraged, and transportation facilities — above all, the Canadian Pacific Railway — were constructed. The tariffs and higher excises on liquor and tobacco brought increased revenues to the federal government to finance its policy.

At the same time, despite increased federal subsidies, the provinces were finding it difficult to meet their increasing obligations in the developing economy. They began to look for and tap new sources of tax revenue. The first personal income tax was introduced by the province of British Columbia in 1876; it was followed by Prince Edward Island in 1894. In 1884, Quebec levied a flat-rate tax on corporations. The first succession duties were levied by Ontario in 1892, and by 1896, all provinces had imposed such a tax.[4] As the provinces developed and expanded their tax structures, federal subsidies became increasingly less significant relative to total provincial revenues.

World War I marked the beginning of direct taxation by the federal government, with substantial consequences for future federal-provincial fiscal relations. Ottawa introduced a tax on corporate profits in 1916 and followed it with a personal income tax in 1917. At the same time, in an attempt to obtain increased revenues to finance the war effort, the federal government extended its participation in indirect taxes. Existing tariffs and excises were increased, and excise taxes were imposed on a large number of other items, such as luxuries, railway tickets, telegrams, and drugs. In 1920, a general sales tax at the manufacturers' level was introduced.[5]

Despite the imposition of direct taxes, the relative importance of indirect taxes to the federal government was maintained. More than 93 percent of total federal revenue was obtained from indirect taxes in 1913, and the share had dropped only to 90 percent in 1921.[6]

The Post-War Period and the Depression

The 1920s were a decade of relative prosperity for Canada. A rapidly growing economy and the spread of urbanization during the period brought a need for transportation facilities, public utilities, education, and welfare services. Many of these new and increased demands on the public sector came within provincial jurisdiction, producing a trend opposite to that expected by the founders of Confederation. The functions assigned to the provinces were becoming more socially important and more financially burdensome, yet the provincial taxing powers were limited, both constitutionally and by the practical reality of the federal intrusion into direct taxation. In seeking new sources of revenue, the provinces imposed taxes on gasoline, assumed monopoly control over the sale of liquor, and sold automobile licences. By the end of the decade, provincial tax revenues had doubled and federal subsidies had declined to only 8 percent of total provincial revenue.[7] In contrast, federal tax revenue declined during the period.

The 1920s fostered two significant developments in federal-provincial fiscal relations: specific-purposes transfers, also known as conditional grants,[8] emerged as an increasingly important means of federal financial assistance to the provinces; and the federal government entered the field of social services.

Specific-purpose transfers had first appeared in Canada at the turn of the century in the area of agriculture. They proliferated following World War I when projects in transportation, vocational training, and health were undertaken jointly by the federal and provincial governments. The federal government contributed up to half of the cost of the projects but established conditions that the provinces were required to meet if they were to qualify for the federal payment. In 1927, Ottawa, in co-operation with the provinces, introduced an old age pension plan with the federal government paying half of the cost. This was the federal government's first major experiment in the field of social services, and it proved the most expensive of the early specific-purpose transfer programs.

Although the transfers eased the problem of the provinces' shortage of revenues and provided a means by which the federal government could assist all provinces in providing essential services, the problem of unequal fiscal capacity remained. From the beginning of Confederation, the Atlantic provinces had faced a poor tax base and the inability to provide the standard of services found in other provinces. Since 1867, the federal government had attempted to alleviate this problem by using special subsidies and grants to these provinces. The situation became critical in the 1920s, however, and in 1926, the federal government appointed a royal commission to investigate the problem. The commission recommended increased general-purpose — unconditional — transfers to the Atlantic provinces.[9]

Through taxation and federal subsidies, the provinces generally managed reasonably well in obtaining revenue before 1930. The Depression, however, brought major difficulties. Rapidly declining employment and incomes reduced revenues substantially, while demands increased for expenditures in areas such as social services and unemployment relief. These were areas of provincial jurisdiction, and to assist the provinces, the federal government relied heavily on specific-purpose transfers, which increased from $2.4 million in 1927 to $72.9 million in 1937, mostly for aid to farmers and the unemployed. Specific-purpose transfers were supplemented by special grants to the Atlantic and Prairie provinces, the two regions suffering the most severely from the Depression. In 1934, the White Royal Commission was appointed to study the problems in these two regions; it recommended special assistance in the form of increased transfers to the two regions.[10]

Both the federal and provincial governments attempted to prevent revenues from declining during the Depression by increasing taxes. The federal government increased its sales tax from 1 to 8 percent, doubled the personal income tax rate, and imposed new import duties. The provinces increased the gasoline tax by 50 percent and raised succession duties and flat-rate taxes on corporations. By 1940, all the provinces were taxing personal and corporate incomes, and Saskatchewan and Quebec had introduced a retail sales tax.[11] There was little or no co-operation between the federal and provincial governments in taxation as both governments scrambled for revenues, producing a chaotic tax jungle of joint occupancy, high tax rates, duplication of administrative machinery, and regressiveness in taxation that contributed to the severity of the Depression by undermining business confidence and incentives. Moreover, the lack of co-operation made if difficult to implement effective anti-Depression fiscal policy late in the 1930s when other countries were beginning to adopt the Keynesian remedy.

The Royal Commission on Dominion-Provincial Relations

The Depression clearly highlighted the problems that can arise in a federal system when the two levels of government compete for revenues from a shrinking pool to meet increasing social and economic demands and when regions have major disparities in fiscal capacities. In 1937, the crisis gave rise to the appointment of the Royal Commission on Dominion-Provincial Relations, known as the Rowell-Sirois Commission after its chairmen. Its general purpose was to reassess the entire Canadian federal structure. More specifically, it was charged with investigating the distribution of powers between the federal and provincial governments, the increasing responsibilities of the provinces, their capacity for meeting these responsibilities, and the overlap and duplication of services and taxes at the federal and provincial levels of government. After an exhaustive investigation, the commission reported its findings and presented its recommendations in May 1940. Among its major recommendations were:

- The federal government should assume the sole responsibility for imposing personal and corporation income taxes and succession duties. This would bring simplicity and efficiency to the tax structure and avoid overlapping taxation.

- The federal government should assume responsibility for the unemployed. This would ensure a national standard of service and greater efficiency in administration.

- The federal government should assume provincial debts to permit the provinces to make a new start. They had incurred considerable debts during the Depression and the interest charges were absorbing a significant portion of their revenues.

- Canada should introduce a system of national adjustment grants — general grants to the poorer provinces based on the amount necessary to permit them to provide levels of services equal to the national average. Such a system would enable the poor provinces to provide adequate services without having to resort to heavy taxation and, being unconditional, the grants would not interfere with provincial autonomy.

- The federal government should introduce a program of emergency grants to provinces suffering from adverse economic conditions. It was recommended that grants be paid immediately to Saskatchewan, which was suffering from severe drought and crop failures.[12]

A federal-provincial conference was called in January 1941 to discuss the recommendations of the commission. The recommendations were rejected. The provinces in general felt that the proposals for the transfer of powers to the federal government involved a greater degree of centralization of power than they were prepared to accept. There was also conflict among provinces, with Ontario, Alberta, and British Columbia refusing to shoulder the burden of adjustment grants to the poorer provinces.

By this time Canada had become involved in World War II, and it was recognized that the hostilities would place a heavy financial burden on the federal government. Although the provinces rejected the Rowell-Sirois proposals, they indicated that in the national interest they would be prepared to co-operate with the federal government in financial matters for the period of the war. The result was a series of federal-provincial fiscal agreements, which have been renegotiated every five years since the war.[13]

Federal-Provincial Fiscal Arrangements: 1941-2002

Tax Rental Agreements: 1941-1957

The financial burden of World War II prompted the federal government to seek exclusive rights over the major tax sources. It proposed to "rent" the personal and corporation taxing powers of the provincial governments for the duration of the war, and the provinces agreed. In 1941, the first tax rental agreement was negotiated. It ended in 1947 and was followed by a series of five-year tax rental agreements, which continued until 1962. For a summary of these federal-provincial arrangements, see Table 13-1.

Under the terms of the early agreements, the provinces withdrew from the personal and corporation income tax fields in return for annual rental payments. They were offered a variety of formulas and bases for calculating the rental payments, including revenues collected in earlier years from the vacated tax fields and per capita payments. For example, one option offered in 1947 was $12.75 per capita, based on the 1942 population of the provinces, plus 50 percent of the revenue received by the province from personal and corporation income taxes in the 1940-41 fiscal year.

TABLE 13-1: Summary of Federal-Provincial Tax Agreements

Major provisions

1941	First tax rental agreements: provinces rent to the federal government their personal and corporate tax fields plus succession duties.
1957	Equalization payments to provinces are formally adopted. Equalization base consists of personal and corporation income taxes and succession duties.
1962	Federal government returns the three rented tax fields to the provinces and provides tax room through abatements of the federal tax.
1965	Opting-out arrangements: federal government offers provinces increased tax points in lieu of conditional grants for shared-cost programs. Only Quebec chose this option.
1967	Conditional grants for post-secondary education are replaced by additional tax abatements points. Equalization base is increased to 16 provincial revenue sources.
1977	Established programs financing (EPF) adopted. Conditional grants for hospital insurance, medicare, and post-secondary education are replaced with 13.5 points of personal income tax and one point of corporation income tax, plus cash payments.
1982	Equalization base increased to 33 provincial and municipal revenue sources.
1990	Canada Assistance Plan (CAP) payments to non-equalization-receiving provinces (British Columbia, Alberta, and Ontario) restricted to an annual increase of 5 percent.
1995	Federal transfers under EPF and CAP merged into a single, block transfer of cash payments and tax points called the Canada Health and Social Transfer (CHST).
1997	Provinces of Nova Scotia, New Brunswick and Newfoundland and the federal government harmonize the provincial retail sales tax with the GST to form the Harmonized Sales Tax.

Considerable emphasis was placed on the temporary nature of these arrangements, with Ottawa assuring the provinces that it was not attempting to take away their taxing powers permanently.

In 1947, special arrangements were offered to provinces not wishing to enter the agreements. The federal government provided room for them to levy their own taxes by withdrawing from the personal and corporation income tax by 5 percent of the federal tax and by 50 percent of succession duties.

Ontario and Quebec refused to sign the agreement. Instead, they imposed a 7 percent tax on corporate income and continued to levy succession duties. Ontario also enacted a tax on personal income equal to 5 percent of the federal tax; it did not put it into effect, however, because it lacked administrative machinery, and Ottawa refused to collect the tax for the province.[14]

All provinces signed the 1952 agreement except Quebec, which imposed a 7 percent corporation income tax and received a 7 percent abatement from Ottawa. In 1954, Quebec introduced a tax on personal income equal to 15 percent of the federal tax, to which Ottawa responded with a 10 percent abatement.

As the 1952 agreement neared an end, the federal and provincial governments met to discuss the possibility of establishing a more permanent taxation arrangement between the two levels of government. The provinces were experiencing rapidly escalating expenditures in the 1950s, and although most were prepared to continue to rent their tax fields, they demanded substantially increased compensation. The concept of tax-sharing emerged from the discussions and formed the basis of the 1957 agreement.

Tax-Sharing Agreement: 1957-1962

In essence, the tax-sharing agreement of 1957 was a continuation of the tax rentals. The provinces agreed to refrain from imposing personal and corporation income taxes and succession duties and in return received the following compensation:

- *Rental Payments.* The rental payments consisted of a share of the three standard taxes:
  - 10 percent of the personal income tax collected in the province (excluding the old age security tax);
  - 9 percent of corporation profits;
  - 50 percent of federal succession duties (later to become the estate tax), based on a three-year average.
- *Equalization payment.* The federal government agreed to pay to qualifying provinces, in the form of an unconditional transfer, an amount that would bring the level of per capita yield from the three standard taxes in each province up to the average yield in the two wealthiest provinces, Ontario and British Columbia. Thus, the 1957 agreement marked the beginning of explicit equalization payments,

which, in 1982, were entrenched in the Constitution Act.
- *Stabilization.* The federal government guaranteed that the amount of annual payment received by each province would not fall below previous payments.

For provinces wishing to impose their own taxes, the federal government offered abatements equivalent to the rental payment. Quebec chose this route, while Ontario agreed only to rent its personal income tax. The equalization and stabilization features of the agreement, however, applied to these two provinces.

The 1957 arrangements maintained the simplified feature of the earlier tax rental agreements in that only one level of government levied the taxes. In addition, certain basic principles could be readily discerned in these arrangements.

The rental payments were calculated on the basis of shares that took into account relative fiscal capacity. Equalization grants were designed to assist the poorer provinces in providing levels of service comparable to those of the richer provinces. All provinces except Ontario qualified for equalization payments. Prince Edward Island's equalization grants were approximately triple the amount it received in tax rental.[15] The stabilization guarantee permitted provinces to make long-term plans without the fear of declining revenues.

The arrangements also respected provincial autonomy in taxation. A province was free to impose its own taxes without being placed at a financial disadvantage relative to other provinces. Aside from acting out the principle of provincial autonomy, however, a province had little to gain from not renting its taxing powers. In fact, renting was politically attractive for provinces since it allowed them to enjoy the revenues from unpopular taxes yet not be responsible for imposing them.

Even though the provinces entered the agreement, they were not completely satisfied with its financial terms and continued to press for larger payments. After a new Conservative government was formed in 1957, a federal-provincial conference was called to consider the provinces' demands. The result was an increase in the provincial share of the personal income tax, from 10 to 13 percent. In addition, to further alleviate the problem of unequal fiscal capacities and regional disparities, Ottawa offered the four Atlantic provinces special grants, labelled Atlantic Adjustment Grants, totalling $25 million annually. In 1959, Newfoundland was given a further grant, amounting to $8 million annually for a five-year period. Another adjustment in the arrangements was made in 1960 as a special concession to Quebec; the corporation income tax abatement was increased to 10 percent for a province not wishing to accept federal specific-purpose transfers in support of universities.

During this period, specific-purpose transfers were increased substantially with the introduction of a public health plan under the Hospital Insurance and Diagnostic Services Act. For this major shared-cost program, the federal government contributed to each province 25 percent of the national average per capita cost of the program plus 25 percent of the actual per capita cost of services within the provinces.

Tax rentals and tax-sharing expired with the end of the 1957-62 arrangements. In a series of conferences beginning in 1960, the provinces voiced their dissatisfaction with the share of revenue they were receiving and demanded substantial increases. The federal government, however, was having second thoughts about tax rental and tax-sharing. Provincial demands could be met only through increased federal taxes. Since tax increases are never popular with the electorate, Ottawa was beginning to look at the tax-sharing system with more and more political disfavour. The federal view was that if the provinces required revenue, they should take the political responsibility for increasing taxes. Consequently, Ottawa proposed to return the taxing powers to the provinces,

claiming federal recognition of provincial autonomy and provincial need in the sense that provinces could impose their own taxes at rates necessary to meet their needs. (Actually, this idea was not novel; the provinces had had a similar option open to them in 1957, although only Quebec had exercised it.)

The provinces were generally not pleased with the federal proposal. It did not represent any financial improvement for them; furthermore, they would be forced to assume partial responsibility for personal and corporation income taxes. Nevertheless, the federal government stood firm, and in 1962 a new five-year arrangement was adopted on federal terms.

The arrangements were extended along similar lines every five years thereafter. In the following section, the essence of each five-year tax agreement is outlined along with developments that occurred while it was in force.

Tax Agreements: 1962-1967

Tax Arrangements. Beginning in 1962, the provinces were to resume their personal and corporation taxing powers with the federal government granting abatements to make room for the provincial taxes. Ottawa agreed to abate its "basic" personal income tax payable by 16 percent in 1962 and by one additional percentage point each year thereafter until the abatement reached 20 percent of basic personal income tax in 1966. This abatement schedule was increased in 1964 to 21 percent for 1965 and 22 percent for 1966 and then was increased again in 1965 to 24 percent for 1966. The corporation income tax abatement was fixed at 9 percent of corporation taxable income. In addition, Ottawa agreed to return 50 percent of the federal estate tax collections within a province to that province if it refrained from imposing succession duties. Provinces that levied their own succession duties were granted a 50 percent tax credit. In 1964, the provincial return and tax credit was increased to 75 percent.

To avoid unnecessary administrative duplication, the federal government offered to collect the taxes for any province, provided it adopted the personal and corporate income tax bases defined in the Federal Income Tax Act. This provision would restrict the provinces' taxing powers in that participants would have to accept Ottawa's definition of income and its exemptions, deductions, and credits. This tax collection arrangement would, however, not only spare the provinces the expense of collecting the taxes involved but also reduce the compliance costs of taxpayers who would need to file only one tax return. All the provinces except Quebec signed the collection agreement, although Ontario agreed to permit the federal government to collect only the personal income tax. Quebec, refusing to accept any direction from Ottawa, preferred to levy and collect its own taxes.

In determining their tax rates for 1962, seven provinces set their personal income tax rates at the same level as the federal abatement of 16 percent. Manitoba and Saskatchewan adopted a rate of 22 percent and in subsequent years were followed by other provinces. In 1962, Manitoba and Saskatchewan also adopted a corporation income tax rate higher than the federal abatement. They levied a tax of 10 percent, while Ontario imposed a tax of 11 percent and Quebec 12 percent.[16]

Equalization. The formula for calculating equalization payments was changed from the average per capita yield of the two wealthiest provinces to the national per capita yield. The reduction in payments that this change would have produced was partially countered by extending the formula base to include one-half of the revenues from provincial taxes on natural resources, as well as the three standard taxes. This revised formula did, however, reduce payments to provinces with an above-average natural resource tax base, most notably Alberta. In 1964 the formula was again changed to the average per capita yield of the two richest provinces.

The federal government continued the stabilization concept of earlier agreements by guaranteeing that the revenue of any province from the three standard taxes and equalization would not be permitted to drop below 95 percent of the average that it had received in the previous two years.

The special grants to the Atlantic provinces introduced in 1958 were increased from $25 million to $35 million annually, and the special $8 million grant to Newfoundland was continued. The provinces also continued to receive the statutory subsidies provided at Confederation.

The 1962 arrangements appeared to hold certain advantages for the federal government. They indicated Ottawa's respect for the provinces' autonomy by returning their constitutional taxing rights. They also appeared politically advantageous in that the federal government would no longer be under pressure to raise taxes to meet provincial demands for increased payments. If the provinces required more revenue, they could increase taxes themselves. Provincial demands for larger payments were, however, soon to be replaced by demands for larger abatements and more room for provincial taxes. Moreover, one obvious disadvantage for the federal government was its reduced ability to implement discretionary fiscal policy as it no longer had complete control over the major tax fields.

The provinces were generally dissatisfied with the arrangements. The poorer provinces stood to gain little from the revised equalization formula, and some provinces would actually lose. All provinces maintained that the level of federal abatements was inadequate. In fact, shortly after the agreements were concluded, a number turned to other taxes for increased revenues.[17]

Opting-Out Arrangements: 1965

The early 1960s brought an escalation in the federal government's use of specific-purpose transfers. Several provinces were not particularly pleased with this trend and criticized their use during the 1960 and 1961 federal-provincial conferences; the most vocal was the province of Quebec. It had refused to accept specific-purpose transfers in the past, primarily on constitutional grounds, and in the early 1960s pressured Ottawa to replace these transfers with general-purpose transfers or increased tax abatements. It was primarily as a concession to Quebec that in 1965 an opting-out provision was introduced into the federal-provincial arrangements by which certain specific-purpose transfers were replaced by additional tax abatement points for any province that preferred federal assistance in the latter form.

Under these arrangements, certain programs were designated eligible for opting-out on the basis of equalized abatement points of the personal income tax. Five major programs were designated, for which a total of twenty abatement points were offered as follows:

Program	Equalized abatement points
Hospital insurance	14
Old age assistance, blind and disabled persons allowances	2
Welfare portion of unemployment assistance	2
Health grants	1
Vocational training	1
Total	20

(In 1966, the programs of old age assistance, blind and disabled persons allowances, and unemployment assistance were incorporated into the Canada Assistance Plan, and four abatement points were assigned to the plan.)

To qualify for receipt of these abatements, a province choosing to opt out was required to continue the obligations and conditions of the programs as they existed for an interim or transitional period. More permanent arrangements were to be negotiated for implementation following the interim period.

Provinces were given until October 1965 to determine whether they wished to opt out, but only Quebec chose to do so. Opting out of the programs, together with the Youth Allowances Program, entitled Quebec to twenty-three additional abatement points of the personal income tax. The additional points did not, however, give Quebec any more revenue than it would have received had it accepted the specific-purpose transfers.

Arrangements were also made to permit opting out of federally initiated programs in areas of joint federal-provincial responsibility. The first major program involved was the Canada Pension Plan, introduced by the federal government effective January 1966. Each province was given the option of either permitting Ottawa to occupy the public pension field through federal introduction and administration of the program or introducing and administering a program of its own that adhered to certain general principles. Again, Quebec alone chose the latter alternative.

The short-run effect of the opting-out provision was negligible, since a province choosing to opt out of a shared-cost program was obligated to continue it with no changes during the interim period. It was in the long run that repercussions were expected. In those programs expected to continue following the interim period, an opted-out province would be free to vary its services as it saw fit and still receive the abatement points. The result could be erosion of national standards. It was also argued that the opting-out clause would tend to weaken federation through greater decentralization of power. On the other hand, it could strengthen federation as Quebec would be pacified and be more content to remain part of the Canadian nation.

The sequel to the opting-out arrangement of 1965 appeared in the federal-provincial conference in 1966. In negotiating a new five-year fiscal agreement with the provinces to become effective in 1967, the federal government proposed that they assume full responsibility for shared-cost programs in health and social services in return for seventeen additional abatement points in the personal income tax. Ottawa furthermore proposed that abatements replace specific-purpose transfers for higher education and offered four points in the personal income tax and one point in the corporation income tax for this purpose. The provinces rejected the federal proposals, fearing that with the soaring costs of education, health, and social services the abatements offered would produce less revenue in the future than specific-purpose cash transfers. A compromise was finally reached, and a new five-year agreement was signed to become effective in 1967.

Tax Agreement: 1967-1972

Tax Arrangements. In the new agreements, the provinces were granted four additional abatement points in the personal income tax and one point in the corporation income tax as a partial substitute for specific-purpose transfers in support of post-secondary education. This change increased the abatement in the personal income tax from 24 to 28 percent and in the corporation income tax from 9 to 10 percent. In addition, each province was granted an adjustment payment calculated either to bring the revenue from education abatements up to 50 percent of the operating costs of its post-secondary educational institutions or to equal an amount that started at $15 per capita and would be adjusted annually in accordance with the rate of increase in post-secondary education operating expenditures. Newfoundland, Prince Edward Island, and New Brunswick opted for the latter form of adjustment payment, which brought the federal contribution in these three provinces to more than 50 percent of their total operating costs for post-secondary education.

Equalization. A new formula was established for determining equalization payments. The base for the calculation was extended to sixteen provincial taxes, including the three standard taxes, revenues from natural resources, the retail sales tax, gasoline tax, excises on alcohol, and motor vehicle licence fees. The payment was designed to bring the average per capita yield from these taxes in the poorer provinces up to the national average.

Stabilization was also continued under a revised formula in which the federal government guaranteed the provinces that their total net general revenues would not be allowed to fall below 95 percent of their previous year's revenues.

Opting-Out. The opting-out arrangements of 1965 remained primarily intact, except that the one abatement point granted for the vocational training program was allowed to expire in March 1967 as scheduled. Instead, the federal government assumed full responsibility for adult retraining. Abatements in the personal income tax under the 1967 arrangements were:

Program	Equalized abatement points
General	28
Hospital insurance	14
Canada assistance plan	4
Youth allowances	3
Health grant program	1
Total	50

Tax Agreement: 1972-1977

At the federal-provincial conference of November 1971, held to renegotiate another five-year fiscal agreement, Ontario and Alberta demanded the right to opt out of shared-cost programs as Quebec had in 1965. The federal government refused — an action termed "contradictory and illogical" by Premier Bill Davis of Ontario. The richer provinces also requested a revision of the equalization formula. British Columbia was particularly critical of the formula in force, under which large equalization payments were made to Quebec. Ottawa's response was to propose only minor changes in the equalization formula. Other changes that were introduced stemmed from the federal tax reform of 1972. The result was a new five-year fiscal arrangement.

Tax Arrangements. The tax arrangements were adjusted to conform to the changes that were introduced with tax reform in January 1972. The general abatement system in personal income taxation was abandoned except for the extra abatement points Quebec received under the opting-out agreement. Under the new system, federal tax rates no longer included the provincial abatement. They were reduced by 30.5 percent of the basic federal tax (equivalent to the former 28 percent abatement). Included in this amount were the tax points in lieu of specific-purpose transfers for education arranged in 1967. (The four points for this purpose became 4.357 points.) The provinces that had signed tax collection agreements with Ottawa were free to impose whatever tax rate they desired. It was expressed as a percentage of basic federal tax and could be more or less than 30.5 percent.

The stabilization clause was continued under an amended formula in which the federal government guaranteed each province that its total revenue would not fall below that of the previous year, unless it had changed its taxes.

In addition, the federal government introduced the income tax Revenue Guarantee Program vis-a-vis its significant tax reform of 1972. It guaranteed for a five-year period that the provinces would not suffer a loss of revenues as a result of adopting personal and corporation income tax structures corresponding to the new federal structures. This guarantee program cost the federal government more

than $1.5 billion over the period of the agreement.

The abatement system that had previously applied to the corporation income tax was retained under the 1972 agreement at 10 percent of corporate taxable income. The opting-out arrangements with Quebec were also continued but with an upward adjustment from 22 to 24 points, reflecting the new federal tax base following tax reform.

Another change was prompted by the termination of the federal estate and gift taxes. Ottawa had previously returned 75 percent of the revenues from these taxes to the provinces. A number of provinces now decided to follow the practice of Quebec, Ontario, and British Columbia and impose their own succession duties and gift taxes. It was arranged that Ottawa would collect the two taxes for these provinces for a period of three years.

Equalization. Under the 1972 equalization formula, three taxes were added to the base, bringing the total number of revenue sources in it to nineteen. These additions were race track taxes, health insurance premiums, and the provincial share of taxes on power utilities. In 1973, municipal taxes for school purposes were added to the list. In 1975, revenue from oil and natural gas was redefined, and one-third of the revenue accrued as a result of increased prices of oil and gas was brought into the equalization formula.

As the 1972 fiscal agreement neared its termination, federal proposals for the next agreement included new formulas for financing the major shared-cost programs, the establishment of ceilings on annual increases in equalization payments, and the termination of the revenue guarantee program. The federal proposals for financing shared-cost programs contained various options, all of which included limits to the federal contribution. Ottawa's objective was to transform payments to the provinces from an uncontrollable item in the federal budget to a controllable or at least predictable item.

The provinces with a good tax base favoured larger provincial tax shares as a replacement for specific-purpose transfers but insisted that the taxes in which larger shares were granted be relatively elastic ones, such as the personal income tax. The poorer provinces, on the other hand, preferred to continue with some type of cost-sharing for fear that they would lose revenue in the long run. They also opposed limits on equalization payments. All provinces vigorously opposed the proposal for terminating or changing the terms of the tax revenue guarantee. A compromise was reached, and the next five-year agreement was effected beginning April 1977.

Tax Agreement: 1977-1982

Established Programs Financing. The 1977-1982 federal-provincial agreement centred on a new formula for financing the three major established shared-cost programs: hospital insurance, medicare, and post-secondary education.[18] Federal assistance for these programs was changed from specific-purpose transfers directly related to provincial expenditures to a combination of increased tax room and cash payments — the latter related to the growth of the economy. Under what became known as established programs financing (EPF), the federal government transferred to the provinces 13.5 points of personal income tax and one point of corporation income tax plus the approximate value of these tax points in a cash payment. Since the tax point transfer included the 4.357 points of personal income tax and the one point of corporation income tax that the provinces had been given in 1967 for post-secondary education, the new tax room provided actually was 9.143 points of personal income tax. Moreover, the tax transfer and cash package included one point of personal income tax and its cash equivalent as partial compensation for the termination of the 1972 Revenue Guarantee Program, which was replaced by a limited revenue guarantee. This limited guarantee applied only to the personal income tax and was designed to cover losses in revenue suffered by the provinces as a result of federal tax change, but only if the loss exceeded 1 percent of the basic federal income tax in the provinces. Furthermore, the guarantee applied only to the first year after any federal tax change.

The tax points were equalized to the per capita national average yield with the cash payment to rise with the growth of the economy. Specifically, the basic cash payment to each province was determined by multiplying half of the national average per capita federal payments for the established programs in the base year (1975-96) by the population of the province. This amount was then escalated by a moving average of growth rates for per capita gross national product.

Since the value of tax room made available varied among provinces because of differences in their fiscal capacity, a transitional adjustment payment was provided to ensure that the value of the equalized tax transfer was at least equal to the value of the basic cash contributions.

An additional change involved assistance for extended health-care services, such as nursing-home care, some of which had been included in the Canada Assistance Plan. Under the new agreement, the federal government contributed $20 per capita (to grow in the same fashion as the other cash payment) towards supplementary health-related services.

Because part of the change in the financing of shared-cost programs involved the transfer of tax points, it was also necessary to change the abatement points granted Quebec under the opting-out arrangement. Under the new agreement, Quebec's abatement points were 8.5 points for health insurance, 5 points for the welfare program, and 3 points for the youth allowance, for a total of 16.5 points — a reduction from 24 points. (In 1974, the youth allowances program had been replaced with an extended family allowance plan so that the opting-out provision no longer applied. To avoid disrupting Quebec's tax structure, the 3 percent abatement was continued, but the amount was fully deducted from the cash payments to the province.)

Equalization. In order to reflect more adequately the provincial tax systems and tax potential, the equalization formula was updated by increasing the total number of revenue sources in the equalization base to twenty-nine, including half of all revenues from non-renewable natural resources such as oil and gas. A partial ceiling was built into the formula, however, in that the amount of equalization payable in relation to revenue derived from natural resources could not exceed one-third of the total equalization payments. This provision would apply only if there were large increases in provincial revenue from oil and gas.

Stabilization. A revenue stabilization clause provided protection if a province's total revenue for a particular year was less than its revenue for the previous year: it would receive a payment equal to the difference between the two amounts. A provision protected the federal government, however, from having to make large stabilization payments to resource-rich provinces should their revenues fall as a result of a decline in resource production or prices.

Tax Agreement: 1982-1987

Throughout the 1970s, the federal government continued to view with concern the increasing amounts of federal revenues transferred to the provinces and the effect of these transfers on Ottawa's budget deficit. In an attempt to control its growing debt, the federal government proposed restraint across the range of federal expenditures, including intergovernment transfers when the fiscal arrangements came under review. The "fiscal imbalance" that the provinces had claimed to suffer in earlier years was now, in Ottawa's

view, to the disadvantage of the federal government, not the provinces. As evidence, the finance minister cited the persistent and growing federal deficits compared with the surplus of the provinces in total.

There was general agreement among the provincial governments and the federal government that the principle of equalization was a key element to any successful federal structure. The disagreements concerned what taxes should be included in the base — oil and gas revenues, then very high in Alberta, were particularly controversial — and which province or provinces should be used as the standard.

Established Program Financing. The federal-provincial agreement for 1982-87 brought some changes in the EPF formula. Total per capita EPF compensation was made equal for all provinces by multiplying 100 percent of the national average per capita contributions for the three programs in 1975-76 by provincial population and increasing this amount annually in accordance with the 1977 GNP escalator.[19] In the new agreement, the cash transfer for each province was determined by deducting from the total compensation the equalized value of the 13.5 points of personal income tax and the one point of the corporation income tax. The cash transfers to provinces with above-average tax yields would be reduced by the excess yield.

The limited personal income tax revenue guarantee introduced in 1977 was extended to 1987. The reference to the one percentage point of the personal income tax as compensation for terminating the earlier (1972) income tax revenue guarantee, which had been included in the EPF package, was discarded, but the percentage point was retained in the EPF formula. The personal income tax component in EPF remained at 13.5 percent.

Equalization. The federal-provincial agreement for 1982-87 extended the equalization base from twenty-nine revenue sources to thirty-three, the most significant additions being municipal government property taxes and

the full amount of revenues from natural resources. The standard of equalization was
changed from the national average per capita
yield, which had been used since 1967-68, to
a representative provincial average consisting
of the average per capita yield from the revenues of five provinces: British Columbia,
Saskatchewan, Manitoba, Ontario, and Quebec. (Alberta was excluded because of its
high natural resource revenues, while the Atlantic provinces were omitted as not representative because of their relatively low per
capita revenues.) A national average tax rate
was determined for each revenue source included in the equalization formula. A province's per capita yield for each source was
determined by applying this tax rate to the
province's tax base and dividing by the province's population. The difference between the
province's per capita yield and the stand-
ardized yield from the revenue sources determined the equalization payment.

Although the extension of the revenue source
list in the equalization formula made it a more
comprehensive measure of the provinces' fiscal
capacity, the exclusion of Alberta from the standard tended to diminish the equalization that accrued from the inclusion of full natural resources
revenues. Quebec estimated that the changes in
the equalization program, when applied to the
1977-82 period, would reduce equalization payments to the provinces by more than $700 mil-
lion or 4.4 percent, with the big losers being
Quebec, Manitoba, and Saskatchewan.[20]

It should also be mentioned that during this
year the Constitution Act, 1982, received
royal proclamation. It included a section
committing Ottawa to the principle of equalization payments to the provinces, thereby entrenching the principle in the constitution.

Stabilization. As in the previous fiscal agreements, the stabilization provision was maintained and, in fact, made permanent. This
program protected each province against a
year-to-year decline in the revenues caused
by adverse economic conditions (but not from

lowered tax rates) and was potentially valu-
able to the provinces.

Tax Agreements: 1987-2002

Five-year federal-provincial tax agreements
were concluded in 1987, 1992, and 1997.
Faced with continuing large budgetary deficits, fiscal restraint was an important factor
for Ottawa in its dealings with the provinces.

The basic tax arrangement was maintained
with no change in the tax points conceded to
the provinces. The cash transfer component
of EPF, however, was subjected to further
limitations. A formula had earlier tied the increase in the cash component to the increase
in GDP. The 1987-1992 arrangement limited
the increase in the cash transfer to the rate of
growth of GDP, less 3 percentage points.

In 1990, this cash component of EPF was
frozen at the 1989-90 level, with growth limited to the population increase of each province, or about one percent nationally. In 1994,
the growth in the cash payment was resumed
at the rate of growth in GDP, less 3 percentage points.

A major change in the financial arrangements was effected in 1996 when Established
Program Financing was merged with the Canada Assistance Plan to form a single program
called the Canada Health and Social Transfer
(CHST) program. Under the CHST, federal
financial assistance to the provinces would
consist of the tax points contained in EPF and
a block cash transfer representing the cash
payments of EPF and CAP. The transfers under CHST are not tied to provincial spending
on the programs involved (health, post-secondary education, and social assistance), and the
provinces may allocate the revenues in accordance with their priorities. They are required, however, to continue to adhere to the
conditions established for medicare and to
continue to provide social assistance. The
1996 budget legislated the amount of funding
provided under CHST for each year up to the
year 2003 (outlined in the next chapter).

Equalization was retained with very little change from the earlier agreement. The base formula continues to include thirty-three provincial and local revenue sources as does the standard of the per capita yield in the five representative provinces.

Stabilization, protecting provinces from major revenue declines, was continued, with the change that any federal payment over $60 per capita of provincial population would be viewed as a loan rather than a grant. In 1995 the eligibility threshold of earlier years was restored, providing that stabilization payments would be made when the decline in a provinces' revenue in any one year was greater than 5 percent over the previous year's revenue.

Summary

Taxation issues have been a significant component of federal-provincial relations in Canada since Confederation. The difficulties of achieving a balance between expenditure responsibilities and revenue sources and problems arising from differences in the relative fiscal capacities of the provinces have frequently placed strains on Confederation. Solutions to these problems for the most part have been the product of evolution and negotiation.

Before 1940, each level of government sought additional tax sources as revenue needs increased, with frequent overlapping and complication in tax administration. The tax agreements which began in 1941 were attempts to establish some order in taxation and to cope with the financial problems.

Over time, the federal government granted an increasing amount of tax room to the provinces to enable them to increase their taxes without placing excessive burdens on their taxpayers. At the same time, greater use was made of specific-purpose transfer to assist the provinces to meet their financial obligations until, in 1977, such transfers for major shared-cost programs were replaced by a combination of tax and cash transfers under the Established Program Financing arrangement. In 1996 this program was combined with the grants under the Canada Assistance Plan to form the Canada Health and Social Transfer program.

A significant development in federal and provincial relations was the establishment of equalization to cope with the sharp differences in the fiscal capacities of the provinces. Eventually equalization was entrenched in the Canadian constitution. The details of equalization and federal financial transfers to the provinces is discussed in the next chapter.

NOTES

1   The problems found in Canada are generally characteristic of a federal structure of government.

2   R. MacGregor Dawson, *The Government of Canada*, 4th ed., rev. by Norman Ward (Toronto: University of Toronto Press, 1963), ch.6.

3   The early development of Canada and its impact on government, together with government policy, are outlined in Government of Canada, *Report of the Royal Commission on Dominion-Provincial Relations* (Ottawa: King's Printer, 1940), book 1.

4   J. Harvey Perry, *Taxation in Canada*, 3rd ed. (Toronto: University of Toronto Press, 1961), pp.13-17.

5   *Ibid.*, pp.17-23.

6   *Report of the Royal Commission on Dominion-Provincial Relations*, p.107.

7   *Ibid.*, p.130.

8   The terms "specific-purpose transfers," "specific-purpose grants," and "conditional grants" have frequently been used interchangeably. In Canadian federal-provincial relations in the past, the term most commonly used to describe transfers that had certain conditions attached to them was "conditional grants." Currently, however, the term most commonly used in government and other publications is "specific-purpose transfers," and this is the term most commonly used in this book. The programs that are financed jointly by the provinces and the federal government are referred to as "shared-cost programs."

9   A Milton Moore, J. Harvey Perry, and Donald I. Beach, *The Financing of Canadian Federation* (Toronto: Canadian Tax Foundation, 1966), Tax Paper No. 43, p.8.

10   *Ibid.*, p.11.

11   Perry, *Taxation in Canada*, pp.23-25.

12 Moore, Perry, and Beach, *The Financing of Canadian Federation*, pp.10-14; and *Report of the Royal Commission on Dominion-Provincial Relations*, book 2, pp.269-76.

13 A detailed description of federal-provincial fiscal agreements, and events leading to them, is contained in David B. Perry, *Financing the Canadian Federation, 1867 to 1995: Setting the Stage for Change* (Toronto: Canadian Tax Foundation 1997); Tax Paper No. 102, Moore, Perry, and Beach, *The Financing of Canadian Federation*; and R.M. Burns, *The Acceptable Mean: The Tax Rental Agreements 1941-62* (Toronto: Canadian Tax Foundation, 1980). Sources on various aspects of federal-provincial relations and on specific agreements can be found in House of Commons, Parliamentary Task Force on Federal-Provincial Fiscal Arrangements, *Fiscal Federalism in Canada* (Ottawa; 1981) and Economic Council of Canada, *Financing Confederation: Today and Tomorrow* (Ottawa, 1982), Canadian Tax Foundation, *The National Finances* (Toronto: CTF, various years); Government of Canada, *Statutes of Canada* (Ottawa, various years); David B. Perry, "The Federal-Provincial Fiscal Arrangements for 1982-87," *Canadian Tax Journal* 31 (January/February 1983). Robin Broadway and F. Flatters, *Equalization in a Federal State* (Ottawa: Economic Council of Canada, 1982); Ontario Economic Council, *Intergovernmental Relations: Issues and Alternatives — 1977* (Toronto: OEC, 1979); T. Courchene et al., *Confederation at the Crossroads* (Vancouver: The Fraser Institute, 1978); Economic Council of Canada and the Institute of Intergovernmental Relations, Queen's University *Proceedings of the Workshop on the Political Economy of Confederation* (Ottawa, 1979) R.M. Bird, ed., *Fiscal Dimensions of Canadian Federalism* (Toronto: Canadian Tax Foundation, 1980); George E. Carter, "Established Program Financing: A Critical Review of the Record," *Canadian Tax Journal* 36 (September/October, 1988); and the federal government budget papers of various years.

14 Moore, Perry, and Beach, *The Financing of Canadian Federation*, p.32.

15 Canadian Tax Foundation, *The National Finances*, 1960-1961 (Toronto, 1960), p.114.

16 Canadian Tax Foundation, *The National Finances*, 1962-1963 (Toronto, 1962), pp.25-31.

17 Moore, Perry, and Beach, *The Financing of Canadian Federation*, pp.73-74.

18 For a statement and discussion of the Federal-Provincial Fiscal Agreement of 1977, see Canada, House of Commons, *Minutes of Proceedings and Evidence of the Standing Committee on Finance, Trade and Economic Affairs*, no. 22, March 7, 1977 (Ottawa). For an analysis of the arrangements, see George E. Carter, "Established Program Financing...."

19 In the 1977 agreement, only the cash payments were made equal in per capita terms. The cash payment to each province was determined by multiplying 50 percent of the national average per capita payments for the three EPF programs in 1975-76 by the population of each province and then applying the escalator factor. See Perry, "The Federal-Provincial Fiscal Arrangements for 1982-1987."

20 David D. Perry, "The Federal-Provincial Fiscal Arrangements for 1982-1987," *Canadian Tax Journal* 31 (January February 1983).

CHAPTER 14

Intergovernmental Transfers

Chapter 13 traced the sequence of taxation arrangements between the federal government and the provincial governments and the evolution and entrenchment of equalization as an integral part of these arrangements. A number of other issues relating to federal-provincial fiscal relations are equally significant, and some, such as the use of specific-purpose transfers, are directly related to the tax agreements.

This chapter examines developments regarding transfers in federal-provincial financial relations that were particularly prominent in the last three decades. It also includes a short analysis of provincial transfers to lower governing jurisdictions.

Federal Transfers to Provinces[1]

Federal government transfer payments to the provinces may take a variety of forms. They may be direct transfers of cash in the form of general or specific-purpose grants, or they may take the indirect form of tax transfers that provide increased tax room for the provinces. Table 14-1 shows the estimated amounts that the federal government transferred to the provinces (including the territories and local governments) in 1997-98. As illustrated, equalization and the cash and tax transfers under the Canada Health and Social Transfer (CHST) account for most of the federal transfers.

General-Purpose Transfers: Equalization

General-purpose transfers are made with no conditions attached, and the recipient governments may use the funds for any purpose they wish.

Equalization. In 1997-98, approximately 85 percent of the federal general-purpose transfers to the provinces consisted of equalization payments. These payments are important sources of revenue for the poorer provinces, as indicated in Table 14-2, accounting for about one-quarter of the gross general revenue of the Atlantic provinces.

Equalization grants are designed to bring the per capita revenue of the poorer provinces closer to that of the richer provinces. Equalization was introduced to enable the poorer provinces to provide a level of government services reasonably comparable to those available in the other provinces. All provinces are not equally endowed with resources, and they do not have similar industrial bases. Consequently, the well-endowed provinces have a higher per capita gross domestic product and therefore a greater revenue base from which to finance government-provided goods and services than the less-endowed provinces. For example, in 1995, GDP per capita in the various provinces as a percentage of the Canadian GDP per capita was as follows: Atlantic provinces — 74 percent; Quebec — 90 percent; Manitoba — 88 percent; Saskatchewan — 91 percent; Ontario — 108 percent; Alberta — 118 percent; British Columbia —

TABLE 14-1: Federal Transfers to Provinces, Territories and Local Governments, 1997-98[a]

Transfer	Amount ($ million)	Share (% of total)
General Purpose Transfers		
Equalization	8,292	24.3
Territorial financing	431	1.3
Statutory subsidies	30	0.1
Grants in lieu of property taxes	1,120	3.3
Total	9,873	29.0
Canada Health and Social Transfer		
Specific purpose transfers	12,500	36.6
Tax transfers	11,737	34.4
Total	24,237	71.0
Total Transfers	34,110	100.0

[a] Estimates.

Source: Canada, Department of Finance, Budget 1997, Budget Plan, February 18, 1937, cat. F1-23/1997-1E, p.64; Canadian Tax Foundation, Finances of the Nation, 1997 (Toronto), p.8:2.

104 percent; Yukon and Northwest Territories — 129 percent. Given these interprovincial disparities, the governments of the poorer provinces would be forced to resort to much higher levels of taxation than the richer provinces in order to provide a similar level of services from own-source revenue. The result would be an imbalance between tax burdens and expenditure benefits for residents of the poorer provinces relative to residents of the richer provinces. Not only are such imbalances unjust, but they may also affect factor and industry location choices. Therefore, the federal government engages in fiscal redistribution through an equalization program.

This problem of fiscal imbalance was acknowledged in the early years of Confederation, but it was not until 1957 that the concept of equalization was officially recognized and accepted as a component of federal-provincial relations. It was later entrenched in the Constitution Act, 1982.

The methods of computing the equalization have varied. Equalization payments have been made to bring per capita revenues first up to the level of the two richest provinces, then to the national average, and since 1982 to the average of five representative provinces (Alberta, by virtue of its large natural resource revenues, and the four Atlantic provinces, which have the lowest fiscal capacity in the country, are excluded from the calculations of the average). Since the beginning of equalization transfers, the base for computing entitlements has been increased from three taxes to the current thirty-three, which include almost all provincial and municipal revenue sources. The present formula involves establishing a tax base (that is, what a tax is levied upon) for each revenue source and then calculating how much revenue each province would derive per capita from each base if it levied a national average tax rate. Any province whose calculated total per cap-

TABLE 14-2: Federal Cash Transfers to Provinces 1997-98[a]
Percentage of Provincial Revenue

	Federal Transfers		
	General Purpose[b]	Specific Purpose[c]	Total
Newfoundland	27.9	13.6	41.5
Prince Edward Island	24.1	10.6	34.7
Nova Scotia	27.1	13.2	40.3
New Brunswick	24.2	12.4	36.6
Quebec	10.3	4.9	15.2
Ontario	-----	10.9	10.9
Manitoba	18.9	9.9	28.8
Saskatchewan	2.5	10.3	12.8
Alberta	-----	9.0	9.0
British Columbia	-----	8.8	8.0
Northwest Territories	71.8	8.4	80.2
Yukon	74.8	5.7	80.5

[a] Estimates.
[b] Consist primarily of equalization payments.
[c] Does not include the tax transfers in CHST.
Source: Canadian Tax Foundation, *Finances of the Nation*, 1997 (Toronto), p.8:3.

ita revenue is less than the average of the five standard provinces (Ontario, Quebec, Manitoba, Saskatchewan, and British Columbia) receives a payment equal to the per capita shortfall multiplied by its population.

Methods of computation and the revenue sources to be included in the equalization formula have long been an issue of dispute among the provinces. The poorer provinces favoured alternatives that would increase equalization payments. The wealthier provinces, on the other hand, argued that equalization should be tied to provincial need and that slower developing areas with fewer urban centres had less need for certain government facilities and services. New sources of provincial revenue also posed problems. For example, during the period of large and rapid increases in the prices of oil and gas, the oil- and gas-producing provinces of Alberta and Saskatchewan were reaping massive revenues from these resources. Including the full amount of natural resource revenue in the equalization formulas would have dramatically raised payments to the poorer provinces; in fact, even Ontario would have qualified for equalization payments in some years. A compromise limited the amount of oil and gas revenues that would be included in the equalization base.

Equalization is currently one of the most significant means of intergovernment redistribution of revenues in Canada. It has become an integral component of federal-provincial fiscal relations and has been referred to as the glue that holds the country together.[2]

Other General-Purpose Transfers. Other general-purpose payments from the federal government include: cash payments to the governments of the Yukon and Northwest Territories designed to assist those jurisdictions in financing public services (they do not receive equalization payments); grants to local and provincial governments in lieu of property taxes on federal property, including libraries, historic sites, national parklands, and buildings; a public utilities income tax transfer consisting of payment of 95 percent of the federal income tax collected from investor-owned public utilities engaged in the distribution (or generation for distribution) of electric energy, gas and steam to the public; and statutory subsidies provided in the Constitution Act.

Specific-Purpose Transfers

Specific-purpose transfers, also called conditional grants, must be spent by the recipient government on a specified area of expenditure. The donor government may attach a variety of other conditions to them. For example, a federal matching grant requires provincial governments to spend an amount on the program equal to the federal transfer. Moreover, to be eligible for the federal contribution, the program, although administered by the provincial government, may be required to meet federal standards governing quality of service, accessibility, and so on.

The federal government began to use specific-purpose grants in the early 1900s to encourage spending in areas of provincial jurisdiction in which there was perceived to be a strong national interest. By the 1920s, numerous projects in the areas of vocational training, transportation, health care, and social services were being financed through such grants. These were shared-cost programs, whereby the federal government contributed up to half the total program costs; it also established various conditions that the provinces had to meet in order to qualify for the federal payment.

Trends. Specific-purpose transfers grew more important in the late 1950s, when the federal government launched some major programs involving large expenditures. More programs were introduced in the 1960s, and existing programs were expanded as transfers soared from $76 million in 1953-54 to $9,250 million by 1977-78. As a percentage of provincial expenditures, federal specific-purpose transfers went from about 5 percent in the 1950s to over 15 percent by the 1970s. Most of the transfers were for post-secondary education, health, and social services. In 1967 the federal government assistance to post-secondary education took the form of a tax transfer and a cash adjustment payment. This was followed in 1977 with a package of tax and cash transfers under established programs financing EPF for post-secondary education, hospital insurance, and medicare programs.

Established Program Financing. This new arrangement reduced the significance of the traditional form of specific-transfer as a form of federal assistance to the provinces. Cash transfers under the new formula continued to be considered a form of specific-purpose transfer because the provinces were still required to adhere to certain general conditions established by Ottawa for the health care programs in return for the receipt of these payments. As long as these conditions were adhered to, however, the provinces could split the EPF payments as they desired, like tax transfer, which was unconditional and could be used for any purpose a province desired.

Canada Health and Social Transfer (CHST). Of the remaining shared-cost programs, the Canada Assistance Plan (CAP) was the most costly. It provided federal sharing of costs incurred by the provinces and municipalities in providing social assistance and welfare services to persons in need and in undertaking work activity projects such as job training. The CAP was an open-ended program, and Ottawa was committed to reimbursing each province and territory for 50 percent of eligible costs related to the activities in the program. The open-ended nature of this program was terminated in 1990 for the non-equalization receiving provinces of British Columbia, Alberta, and Ontario when payments to these three provinces were limited to a maximum annual increase of 5 percent.

Effective for the fiscal year 1996-97, the federal government merged its transfers under EPF and for CAP into a single block transfer called the Canada Health and Social Transfer (CHST). The transfer of tax points and cash is not tied to the amounts the provinces spend on post-secondary education, health, and social assistance, and the provinces can allocate the financial resources as they choose. To receive the cash payment under CHST, however, the provinces must continue to provide social assistance and abide by the principles of the Canada Health Act.

The 1996-97 federal budget provided a five year funding arrangement for the period 1998 to 2003. For the first two years, CHST entitlements were frozen at their 1997-98 level of $25.1 billion. The increase in entitlements for the next three years were tied to the growth of GDP at the following rates: the percentage increase in GDP less 2 percent for the year 2000-01, the GDP increase less 1.5 percent for 2001-02, and the GDP increase less 1 percent for 2002-03.[3]

Entitlements under CHST (consisting of EPF tax points and cash plus the cash transfer under CAP) were projected to fall from $29.3 billion in 1994-95 to $25.1 billion in 1997-98. The cash component of CHST was $19.3 billion in 1994-95, projected to decrease to $11.8 billion in 1998-99.[4]

This cash component is the difference between the total entitlement and the value of the tax point transfer and, under the formula, declines as the economy grows.

A growing economy increases the tax base and consequently the value of the tax points, producing a corresponding reduction in the amount of the cash transfer. Ottawa guaranteed, however, that over the five-year period of the arrangement, cash transfers would not fall below $11 billion.

The federal government justified its action in combining EPF and CAP into a single block fund as representing a new approach to federal-provincial relations, marked by greater flexibility for the provinces and more sustainable financing arrangements for the federal government.[5] Provinces would no longer be subject to rules stipulating which expenditures were eligible for cost sharing, they would be free to pursue their own initiatives in social security reform, and the expense of administering cost sharing could be eliminated. For example, there would no longer be a need for the provinces to submit claims for federal approval or draw up lists of welfare agencies. The advantage for the federal government, on the other hand, was that federal expenditures would no longer be driven by provincial decisions on how or to whom to provide social assistance and services.

The federal government could claim that through CHST it was giving to the provinces what they had always demanded, namely, greater flexibility and freedom from the intrusiveness into provincial jurisdictions of previous cost-sharing arrangements. While the provinces welcomed the increased flexibility, they were highly critical of the reductions in federal assistance contained in CHST. The CAP program had brought the provinces increased federal transfers as their expenditures on CAP increased. Not only was this tie eliminated, but Ottawa now intended to reduce the amount of cash transfers in CHST from about $19 billion in 1994-95 to $12 billion by 1998-99, and to do so without meaningful consultation with the provinces. This unilateral action, combined with a history of provincial dissatisfaction with the federal government regarding transfer payments, heightened the frustration of the provincial governments in their dealings with Ottawa.

By 1998 the federal government was projecting budget surpluses, and the provinces sought to restore the earlier federal cuts in cash transfers in CHST to help them restore funding that they had been forced to curtail on post-secondary education, health, and social assistance. Ottawa did not appear to be receptive to these proposals, but instead began to bring forward initiatives for new and expanded social programs such as a National Child Benefit System.

Other Specific-Purpose Transfers. There are numerous specific-purpose transfers or cost-sharing programs in other areas of government activity, although their individual dollar value is relatively small. An inventory for 1995-96 of federal-provincial shared-cost programs listed 148 such programs for which the federal government contributed approximately $4 billion. The largest number of programs and the largest federal transfers were in the areas of agriculture ($497 million), communications and culture ($217 million), human resources ($569 million excluding CAP), Indian affairs and northern development ($228 million), industry ($527 million), justice ($156 million), natural resources ($75 million), transport ($57 million), and public works and government services ($1,182 million).[6] The basis of the federal contribution to these programs varies. For some programs it takes the form of a percentage of costs while for other programs it is a fixed dollar amount.

Provincial Dissatisfaction

The provinces have a history of dissatisfaction with shared-cost programs and Ottawa's use of specific purpose transfers.[7] Their complaints have continued to the present day, and as explained in the next chapter, there were attempts to address these grievances in the constitutional talks in the late 1980s and 1990s. A brief outline of the provinces' problems with specific transfers is presented below.

Planning and Priorities. Some provinces, notably Quebec, opposed specific-purpose transfers on purely constitutional grounds, but the major complaint was that using them enabled the federal government to move into areas of provincial jurisdiction and interfere with provincial planning of expenditure priorities. Provinces complained that they were hampered in the planning of their budgets and the development of programs they judged to be of priority. When the federal government initiated a program and offered to bear the burden of half the cost, the provinces had to participate or forgo the payment. Few provinces have found it politically or economically practical not to participate since the residents of all the provinces would be financing the program in the form of federal taxes. In 1969, Ontario Premier John Robarts expressed the view of his province:

> Massive spending initiatives by the Federal Government, such as medicare, not only rob provincial budgets of any flexibility, but also undermine any real progress towards overall control of expenditures by all governments and fail utterly to recognize provincial priorities... We are being pushed into medicare, which from the point of view of this government is not necessary in the province at this time and is not one of our top priorities, by a level of government that is taxing us for it before we get it.[8]

During the 1960s and 1970s, a period of rapidly increasing government spending, federal priorities were primarily in the areas of health and social services — as is evidenced by the trends in expenditure — whereas a number of provinces wanted to place greater emphasis on economic development. Economic development and diversification were particularly emphasized in the poorer provinces, which, without an adequate economic base, continued to lag in prosperity. They charged that the federal government paid insufficient attention to their needs and that its priorities tended to follow the lines of a more advanced economy in which attention shifted from economic matters (for example, transportation and communications, resource and industrial development, and trade agreements designed to benefit regional industries) to social matters (for example, health, social services, and culture). And the poorer provinces claimed that they could not afford the latter without having established the former.

Many provinces were also very critical of what they claimed was the federal government's apparent eagerness to initiate shared-cost programs without adequate planning or estimation of costs. Ottawa was accused of initiating programs in which provincial studies showed that costs had been grossly underestimated.

A further complaint from the provinces concerned unilateral federal changes of shared-cost programs. They pointed to a number of programs that they claimed were terminated or reduced unilaterally by the federal government.[9] If the program was well-established at the time of termination, the participating provinces might find it difficult to discontinue, or might not desire to do so. They were consequently left to carry the federal share of the program in addition to their own. The provinces argued that they were forced to seek new funds every time the federal government introduced a shared-cost program and to find additional funds whenever it withdrew from a program they wished to continue.

The federal government offered a number of counter-arguments, based on economic, social, and constitutional factors, in support of specific-purpose transfers. First, through these transfers, the federal government was able to support public projects and services that had spill-over effects or external economies and that were in the national interest, such as education, health, and social services. Second, the transfers enabled provinces to provide services that they would be unable to provide through reliance on their own resources. Third, through the transfers, the federal government could ensure national priorities and, to a large degree, a uniform standard of service to all Canadians. Finally, the federal government argued, no province

was constitutionally required to participate in shared-cost programs.

Throughout this period, numerous suggestions for alternatives to specific-purpose transfers were brought forward at federal-provincial fiscal conferences. It was suggested that the provinces be given larger shares of the taxes imposed jointly by the two levels of government or that greater separation of tax sources be arranged, providing the provinces with more of the available tax sources. Another suggested alternative was the replacement of specific-purpose by general transfers with no strings attached. This proposal was, however, unacceptable to the federal government because it viewed its primary responsibility as being to the Canadian public as a whole; it said that it had an obligation to provide all Canadians with an opportunity for an acceptable level of services and national standards. Yet another alternative was to allow provinces to opt out of shared-cost programs in return for the fiscal equivalent — a sum equal to the federal share of the program in a province but a sum it could use in any way it desired. This proposal also met with opposition from the federal government because it would then lose complete control over its payments to the provinces.

Costs and Control. Developments in shared-cost arrangements in the 1970s renewed provincial dissatisfaction with specific-purpose transfers. These developments stemmed from the rapid escalation of the costs of shared-cost programs, particularly in health and education. The federal government was concerned about the open-ended nature of the shared-cost programs, which committed Ottawa to pay its share regardless of the amount of the increase. The uncertainty of future costs and the amount of its contribution caused the federal government to seek to place ceilings on its contributions to shared-cost programs, particularly in the areas of health and education. In 1972, Ottawa limited the increase in its contributions to post-secondary education to

15 percent per year. Another step in this direction was taken in 1976, when the federal government limited the increase in its payments for the medicare program to 13 percent for 1976-77 and 10.5 percent for 1977-78 and established authority to fix limits for subsequent years. The provinces responded that federal ceilings on its contributions effectively destroyed the principle on which shared-cost programs were based and, in turn, requested that they be permitted to opt out of these programs in return for a larger share of the tax fields.

In the next logical step, Ottawa proposed in 1977 to replace cost-sharing for major established programs with the system of tax transfers and cash payments described in chapter 13. This arrangement had both positive and negative aspects for the federal and provincial governments, although the provinces' views varied. On the positive side at the federal level, the move, by severing the link between program costs and the federal contribution, gave Ottawa control over its payments to three major shared-cost programs. On the negative side, it reduced the control that the federal government could exercise over these programs to ensure that they conformed to national standards. The compensation to the provinces represented by tax points goes into provincial revenue to be spent as the provinces choose. There remained, however, some degree of federal surveillance because the cash compensation for the health-care program continued to be conditional upon the provinces' maintaining the basic conditions.

How the federal government could exercise some control became evident in 1983. Some of the provinces began to charge nominal user fees for hospital care in an attempt to hold down the escalating costs of health care. The federal government contended that such action was counter to the spirit and intention of the medicare program — to make health services readily available to all Canadian residents. User fees, argued the federal Minister of Health and Welfare Monique Begin, discriminated against lower-income groups including the elderly. In response to the provinces' actions, the federal government passed the Canada Health Act, in April 1984, reaffirming the earlier established conditions and criteria for federal contributions to health-care services and giving the federal government specific authority to reduce the EPF cash payment to any province that resorted to extra-billing or user charges. The reduction would be $1 for every $1 a province charged patients for health care. The provinces were given three years to comply with the Act, which they did.

The 1977 EPF arrangement was advantageous for the provinces in that it gave them greater flexibility in defining and administering their programs and freed them of detailed federal auditing of provincial expenditures, which had been necessary under the 50 percent cost-sharing formula. They ran the risk, however, that slow economic growth would reduce tax yields and the value of the tax transfer, thereby producing less revenue for the established programs than would have been provided by the previous cost-sharing formula.[10]

Furthermore, the EPF arrangements did not completely alleviate the earlier provincial concern over the possibility of Ottawa's reducing or limiting its contributions to the established programs. The open-ended feature of specific-purpose transfers had been effectively terminated in the 1970s once the federal government began to place ceilings on the rate of increase of its contributions to post-secondary education and medical care. The provinces had vigorously complained that such limits forced them either to seek alternative sources of revenue to maintain the same level of services or to curtail education and medical and other services. As the 1980s drew to a close, this problem reappeared, as outlined in chapter 13. Beginning in 1990, Ottawa unilaterally froze combined cash and tax transfers under EPF until 1994-95, and then limited the increase to the growth of GDP, less 3 percent, for 1995-96.

Payments under CAP to Ontario, Alberta, and British Columbia, the three provinces not in receipt of equalization, were limited to a maximum increase of 5 percent annually. These provinces protested vigorously, and British Columbia, backed by the other two provinces, initiated court action challenging Ottawa's power to unilaterally institute such a change in a joint agreement. In June 1990 the B.C. Court of Appeals ruled in the provinces' favour — that the CAP agreement by which the federal government was to pay 50 percent of the costs of the program could not be changed without the consent of the provinces. Ottawa appealed the decision to the Supreme Court of Canada, which ruled in August 1991 that the federal government's responsibility for national policy justified unilateral actions.

Ottawa's action brought back to the provinces memories of similar federal practices under the earlier shared-cost arrangements and heightened their awareness of continued vulnerability to potential restrictions on federal financial contributions. As outlined earlier, the provinces' frustration with Ottawa continued with the federal government's introduction of CHST in 1996 and its unilateral action to reduce the cash transfer contained in this block fund from $19 billion to $12 billion by 1998-99.

Constitutional Discussions. The general issue of shared-cost programs and the federal government's use of specific-purpose grants in areas of provincial jurisdiction was addressed in the proposals for changes in the Canadian Constitution in the Meech Lake (1987) and Charlottetown Accords (1992). It was proposed to amend the Constitution Act, 1982, with a clause giving provinces the right to opt out of national shared-cost programs initiated by the federal government in areas of exclusive provincial jurisdiction. Provinces choosing to opt out would receive "reasonable compensation" from the federal govern-

ment provided they introduced their own programs "compatible with the national objectives." This highly ambiguous clause did not define "reasonable compensation," or "compatible," or "national objectives," and some interpreted it as an entrenchment of federal spending power to launch new programs in areas of provincial jurisdiction. Controversy over the clause ranged from one extreme position to the other. Some predicted increased federal initiatives in shared-cost programs leading to greater centralization of power, while others predicted the exact opposite. For example, Premier Clyde Wells of Newfoundland contended that the provision would discourage Ottawa from initiating shared-cost programs because opting-out would reduce the federal government's influence in such programs. This, he claimed, would be detrimental to the poorer provinces, which relied heavily on federal financial aid to provide their residents with programs comparable in quality to those provided by the wealthier provinces. Discussion of this and other constitutional issues continued into the 1990s and are examined in the next chapter.

Transfers to Local Governments

Local government consists of the various governing authorities established by the provincial government and vested with specific powers. They include the governments of cities, towns and villages (municipal governments); separate authorities to administer education (school boards); and special boards and commissions to administer some functions. All of these authorities are considered part of local government in the data presented.

The financial burden at the local level of government has become increasingly acute over the last few decades. Increased urbanization means increased local government spending. Furthermore, the deterioration of the city core and the spread of suburbs have

TABLE 14-3: Transfers to Local Governments 1994

Function	Local Expenditure	Specific-Purpose Transfer	Transfers as Percentage of Expenditure
		$ million	
Specific-Purpose Transfers [a]			
General services	3,701	83	2.2
Protection of persons and property	5,750	45	.8
Transportation and communications	6,609	1,330	20.1
Health	3,578	2,875	80.4
Social services	5,571	4,099	73.6
Education	28,341	17,459	61.6
Environment	6,181	649	10.5
Recreation and culture	4,485	290	6.5
Debt charges	4,223	1,077	25.5
Other	7,770	918	11.8
Total	71,987	28,825	40.0
General Purpose Transfers			
Grants in lieu of taxes			
Federal government and enterprises		463	-
Provincial government and enterprises		1093	-
Total		1556	-
Other provincial transfers		1395	-
Total General Purpose Transfers		2950	4.1
Total Transfers		31,775	44.1

[a] Provincial and federal transfers.
Source: Canadian Tax Foundation, *Finances of the Nation*, 1997 (Toronto), pp.8:14; A:11.

added to the strain on finances. Sprawling suburbs require improved and more extensive transportation, sewage, water, recreation, and sanitation facilities, along with new schools, new streets, and new sidewalks. Decay of the city core demands urban renewal. In addition, as people move to cities in search of employment, housing needs increase as does the welfare roll since some are unable to find work.

One of the most important sources of revenue for the local governments is transfers from provincial governments. These transfers, combined with transfers from the federal government and federal and provincial enterprises, amounted to almost $32 billion or 44 percent of local government expenditure in 1994. Of the $32 billion in transfers less than $1 billion came from federal sources.

Of the total transfers to local governments, only about 10 percent were general-purpose transfers. The remainder were for designated purposes or specific-purpose transfers.

The bulk of provincial specific-purpose transfers received by local governments — in recent years, approximately 60 percent of the total — is for primary and secondary education. Of the total expenditure on education, approximately 61 percent is financed by these transfers. Another 24 percent of the specific-purpose transfers the local governments receive are for health and social services. The remainder are allocated to transportation and communications, recreation and culture, the environment, housing, regional development, protection of persons and property, and general services.

The statistics are, however, averages. Transfers to local governments vary considerably from province to province. Some provinces assume direct responsibility for certain functions that other provinces delegate to local authorities and assist in their financing with specific-purpose transfers. For example, the provincial governments of Newfoundland and New Brunswick assume direct responsibility for the administration and financing of education, and both levy and collect property taxes to help finance education. In Ontario, in contrast, education remains largely in the control of local government, financed partly by specific-purpose grants from the province.

Summary

Federal transfers are important sources of revenue for provincial governments, as are provincial transfers to local governments. Federal transfers take the form of general-purpose transfers, specific-purpose transfers, and tax transfers. The primary general-purpose transfers are equalization payments, made to those provinces with poor fiscal capacity for raising revenue. Specific-purpose transfers were designed mainly for cost-sharing programs in the area of health, post-secondary education, and social services. These transfers have gradually been replaced with block transfers consisting of tax points and

cash as represented by the Canada Health and Social Transfer. In the process of changing from specific-purpose transfers to the block transfer, the federal government has cut the ties between cost of programs and its payments, and has also unilaterally reduced the amount of its payments, much to the dissatisfaction of the provincial governments.

NOTES

[1] Sources on federal transfers to the provinces include, David B. Perry, *Financing the Canadian Federation, 1867 to 1995: Setting the Stage for Change* (Toronto: Canadian Tax Foundation, 1997), Tax Paper No. 102; Economic Council of Canada, *Financing Confederation: Today and Tomorrow* (Ottawa: ECC, 1982); and A.M. Moore, J.H. Perry, and D. Beach, *The Financing of Canadian Federation* (Toronto: Canadian Tax Foundation, 1966)

[2] Moore, Perry and Beach, *The Financing of Canadian Federation*, p.108.

[3] Canada, Department of Finance, *Budget Plan*, March 6, 1996, cat.F1-23/1996-1E, p.57.

[4] Canada, Department of Finance, *Budget Plan*, February 18, 1997, cat. F1-23/1997-1E, p.64.

[5] Canada, Department of Finance, *Budget 1995*, February 1995 (Budget White Paper).

[6] Canada, Public Works and Government Services, *Public Accounts of Canada*, 1996, vol. II, part I, cat. P51-1/1996-2-1E, pp.11.1-11.27.

[7] For a more detailed analysis of conditional grants in Canada and provincial government dissatisfaction, see J.C. Strick, "Conditional Grants and Provincial Budgeting," *Canadian Public Administration* 14, no. 2 (Summer 1971). See also George E. Carter, *Canadian Conditional Grants since World War II*, Canadian Tax Foundation, Tax Paper No. 54 (Toronto: CTF, 1971); and R.W. Broadway, *Intergovernmental Transfers in Canada* (Toronto: Canadian Tax Foundation, 1980).

[8] Ontario, *Responsible Taxation: The Ontario Approach* (Toronto, 1969), pp.7, 11.

[9] The shared-cost programs frequently mentioned in this connection included the Winter Works Program, Road to Resources, forestry agreement, resource developments programs, and manpower programs. Federal grants for projects in these areas totalled $150.2 million in 1967-68 and $136.3 million in 1969-70.

[10] A critical analysis of the EPF arrangements is presented in George E. Carter, "Established Programs Financing: A Critical Review of the Record," *Canadian Tax Journal* 36 (September/October 1988).

CHAPTER 15

Constitutional Reform and Related Issues

In March 1982, the British parliament passed the Canada Act, 1982, which was proclaimed by Queen Elizabeth II on April 17, 1982, thus ending a half-century of contentious struggle to bring Canada's Constitution home.[1] The patriated Constitution of Canada contained the original British North America (BNA) Act and amendments, together with changes and additions. The most relevant of these were an amending formula, a charter of rights and freedoms, the formal entrenchment of the principle of federal equalization payments to the provinces, and new guarantees to the provinces regarding jurisdiction over natural resources.

While the patriation of Canada's Constitution was a landmark event in the history of federal-provincial relations, it was only the beginning of a series of events in constitutional reform that threatened to destroy Canadian confederation. The 1982 changes were not satisfactory to the province of Quebec, where a growing proportion of the population continued to support and press for greater autonomy including separation from the rest of Canada.

Early Developments

Serious attempts to sever the Canadian Constitution from Britain began in the 1920s when numerous federal-provincial conferences were held to try to resolve the issue. Britain was generally willing, but the federal government and the provinces could not agree on issues of provincial rights, on language, or on an amending formula. Some of the provinces, particularly Quebec, feared any formula that could potentially enable the federal government to change the Constitution and encroach on provincial rights without provincial consent. The failure to reach an agreement on an amending formula in the 1920s and early 1930s continued Britain's authority over the BNA Act.

Concerns about the Constitution were disrupted by the Depression and by World War II and its aftermath, and although some attempt was made in the 1950s and early 1960s to resolve the issue, it was not until 1967 that constitutional patriation and reform again came to the fore in federal-provincial relations. Beginning in February 1968, a series of federal-provincial conferences examined patriation of the Constitution, the problem of bilingualism, and the question of the distribution of tax and expenditure powers. These sessions were not confined to constitutional issues. They included discussions on a wide variety of economic and social matters: the poorer provinces complained about regional disparities; others expressed concern over federal intrusion into provincial areas of jurisdiction through Ottawa's initiation of shared-cost programs; and all provinces demanded more tax room through increased federal abatements. The fundamental issue, however, remained the constitutional problem of patriation of the BNA Act. Both the federal and provincial governments were anxious to prescribe a formula for amending the act without having to suffer the embarrassment of approaching the British parliament whenever a change was needed.

In 1971, tentative agreement was reached, producing a constitutional charter.[2] It included an amending formula providing for change with the consent of the federal government and of six provinces, which had to include Ontario and Quebec, two Atlantic provinces, and two western provinces representing at least 50 percent of the population of the western region. It also granted the provinces supremacy in all areas of social services except Unemployment Insurance; they would have the right to legislate in these areas along with the federal government, with any conflict in legislation or programs resolved in their favour. (This provision gave Quebec a part of the expanded jurisdiction it sought in the field of social services.) In addition, the charter included proposals to guarantee the equality of the French and English languages, gave provinces a voice in appointments to the Supreme Court of Canada, terminated the federal government's power of disallowing provincial legislation, and changed the title of the British North America Act, 1867, to the Constitution Act, 1867.

This charter was approved by all the provinces except Quebec. Its rejection was based primarily on the fact that, although the document gave the provinces the legislative supremacy in social services that Quebec demanded, there was no corresponding allocation of revenue sources to finance programs in this area. Control over expenditure functions without the necessary sources to finance them produced, in the words of Quebec Premier Robert Bourassa, "the existence of an uncertainty" rather than the complete sovereignty it wanted. Moreover, Quebec was not prepared to accept the continuation of the federal government's power to legislate and use specific-purpose transfers for social services.

The Quebec Issue

Quebec's 1971 concerns were not new (although they may have been heightened by a growing tide of nationalism in the province at that time). It had, from the beginning, opposed what it perceived as federal encroachment on provincial autonomy in both taxation and expenditures. The crisis of World War II did prompt Quebec to sign the 1941 tax rental agreement, but it refused to be party to any further rental agreements. The province feared that the temporary nature of tax rentals would become more permanent over time, and it opposed such centralization of power in Ottawa. Maurice Duplessis, Premier from 1944 to 1959, argued that provincial autonomy in expenditures was meaningless if the province had to depend on the federal government for the necessary funds — a sentiment echoed by successive Quebec premiers to the present day. When Ottawa began to use specific-purpose transfers, Quebec refused to accept them, arguing that through this form of assistance the federal government was interfering with provincial sovereignty in expenditures. In the late 1950s and early 1960s, Quebec did begin to accept these transfers, but only reluctantly, and in the meantime it pressed Ottawa to replace conditional grants with increased tax abatements or general-purpose transfers.

The first step in this direction was taken in 1960 when Quebec was granted an additional 1 percentage point abatement of the corporation income tax in lieu of a specific transfer to universities. When the Liberal party took office in Ottawa in 1963, the federal government began to bend towards Quebec's point of view. In 1964, it offered Quebec a further abatement of three percentage points of the personal income tax for the Youth Allowance Program, a shared-cost program introduced by the federal government to provide allowances for sixteen- and seventeen-year-olds who remained in school. Quebec had earlier instituted its own similar program and wished to continue it. Ottawa agreed to allow the province to receive the federal contribution in the form of additional abatement points rather than as a specific transfer.

These concessions to Quebec were the prelude to the major change in 1965, when the opting-out provision was introduced into the shared-cost arrangements. As outlined in the previous chapter, Quebec was the only province to choose this option.

The specific arrangements were not enough, however. Quebec premiers since the early 1960s have echoed the demand for increased powers for their province through a changed agreement on the sharing of powers and resources. They argue that the division of powers under the Constitution was rendered obsolete by the emergence of the francophone nation and urge a special status for Quebec. This "two-nations" concept of Canada was rejected by the federal government, which under Prime Minister Pierre Trudeau pressed for increased constitutional rights for the French language throughout Canada and the patriation of the BNA Act. Quebec opposed patriation and an amending formula unless they were accompanied by a substantial transfer of powers to the provinces.

Although the roots of Quebec's discontent with federalism can be traced to pre-Confederation times, not until 1976 did its political separation from the rest of Canada seem a real possibility. That year saw the election in Quebec of the Parti Québécois (PQ), a political party committed to separation. Under the PQ's proposed system, Quebec would become an independent country but retain close economic association with the rest of Canada. The Parti Québécois committed itself to a referendum to decide the issue of separation; when it was held in 1980, the PQ lost the referendum with 60 percent of the electorate voting no. Although this loss weakened the separatist movement, it did not eliminate it, and Quebec, under Premier Lévesque, fought long and hard against the constitutional changes finally adopted in the patriated Constitution and the Charter of Rights and Free-

doms in 1982. Moreover, the dream of independence would emerge stronger than ever in the 1990s.

Constitution Act, 1982

In early 1976, Prime Minister Trudeau reopened the constitutional issue by tabling in Parliament proposals for patriating the Constitution and indicating that the federal government was prepared to act unilaterally if the provinces failed to reach an agreement. The provinces objected strenuously to the suggestion of unilateral federal action. They feared that a precedent would be set for further unilateral constitutional changes by the federal government, placing the safeguard of provincial rights in jeopardy.

Ottawa made another attempt at patriation and change in 1978 and 1979. This time its proposal included added resource rights for the provinces and limitations on federal powers; still, the provinces failed to agree. In 1980, following the defeat of the sovereignty referendum in Quebec, the prime minister proposed dividing the constitutional question into two packages: one involving the division of powers, and the other patriation and a charter of rights. This time the federal government was adamant that constitutional change must include a charter of rights and minority-language guarantees.

Federal-provincial conferences and communications on these issues continued throughout 1980 and 1981. The exchanges were frequently bitter, but Ottawa now made a firm public commitment to resolving the issues — by unilateral federal action if necessary. Six provinces filed a court challenge to the federal proposal to act unilaterally, and there was political opposition in Parliament. Following lengthy proceedings, the Supreme Court of Canada ruled in the late summer of 1981 that the federal initiative to patriate the BNA Act was legal in the strict sense but offended convention and the spirit of federalism, which included provincial agreement to constitutional change.

The lack of a clear court victory by either side forced the federal government and the provinces into compromise. A conference in November 1981 considered a variety of proposals, including a federal offer to settle the matter by a national referendum. A last-minute compromise worked out by the provinces formed an agreement that was finally adopted, although Premier Lévesque of Quebec bitterly opposed the arrangement and refused to sign it. Lévesque demanded a veto on constitutional change for Quebec, and when it was refused, he warned of serious consequences for Quebec-Canada relations. The agreement of Ottawa and nine provinces received parliamentary approval in December 1981 and was forwarded to London for the final amendment to the BNA Act by the British parliament.

The amending formula of the Constitution Act, 1982, is two-fold. Some matters require the unanimous consent of the federal Parliament and of the legislative assembly of every province; once the proposal is ratified by one of these governments, the other ten must agree to it within three years. Amending other matters is less stringent; the requirement is the consent of the federal parliament and the legislative assemblies of at least two-thirds of the provinces that have, in the aggregate and according the latest census, at least 50 percent of the country's population of all provinces. (Given the current ten provinces and their relative populations, such a matter would have to have the consent of seven provinces including either Quebec or Ontario.)

The Charter of Rights and Freedoms guarantees the fundamental freedoms of conscience and religion, of the press and other media, of peaceful assembly, and of association. It also guarantees basic legal rights, equality rights, and rights to minority language and education. And it establishes English and French as the official languages of Canada.

The Constitution Act, 1982, also addresses the issue of equalization and regional disparities. Under the act, both Ottawa and the provinces are committed to further economic development to reduce disparity in opportunities and to provide essential public services of reasonable quality to all Canadians. The federal government is to make equalization payments "to ensure that provincial governments have sufficient revenues to provide reasonably comparative levels of public services at reasonably comparative levels of taxation" (subsection 36(2)).

One change from the BNA Act relates to non-renewable natural resources, forestry resources, and electrical energy. Section 92A of the Constitution Act, 1982, grants the provinces exclusive powers to make laws relating to the exploration, development, and management of non-renewable natural resources and forestry resources within their jurisdiction, and to raise money by any mode or system of taxation in respect to non-renewable natural resources, forestry resources, and the generation of electrical energy. In relation to the export from one province to another of the production of non-renewable natural resources, forestry resources, and the generation of electrical energy, the federal and provincial legislatures were given concurrent powers with the proviso that, should federal and provincial laws conflict, federal law would prevail. Furthermore, in exporting these products to another part of Canada, a province cannot apply any discrimination in prices. This section added considerably to the provinces' flexibility in the taxation of natural resources. It removed the restriction limiting their taxing power over natural resources to direct taxation within the province, a clause that had been a major source of federal-provincial conflict (as discussed later in this chapter).

The Meech Lake Accord

The Quebec government had not agreed to the Constitution Act, 1982. Desiring to bring Quebec into the constitutional agreement and to clarify certain federal-provincial issues, Prime Minister Brian Mulroney and the ten provincial premiers held lengthy discussions during April 1987 at a retreat at Meech Lake, Quebec. The resulting proposals for revisions and additions to the Constitution Act, which came to be known as the Meech Lake Accord,[3] were signed by the prime minister and all ten premiers in June 1987. Since the changes were far-reaching, they were judged matters requiring unanimous consent. Thus, the federal and provincial legislatures had to ratify the accord within three years to incorporate it into the Canadian constitution. When Quebec's National Assembly gave assent to the agreement, the deadline became June 23, 1990.

The Meech Lake Accord is examined in some detail in this section because it illustrates Quebec's demands for constitutional change, which are likely to continue into the future, as well as some of the other provinces' positions on constitutional issues.

The Accord. The Meech Lake Accord was designed to meet the minimum basic conditions that Quebec Premier Bourassa argued were necessary to make his province a party to the Constitution Act, 1982. The accord had significance for the distribution of the powers and responsibilities of the federal and provincial governments. The key proposals focussed on the following issues:

- The position of Quebec. Recognition of the right of Quebec to "preserve and promote" its character as a "distinct society."
- The Supreme Court of Canada. Provision for the provinces to provide lists of new Supreme Court nominees, from which the prime minister would make the final selection; as in the BNA Act, three positions on the court reserved for Quebec.

- Senate appointments. Provision for the provinces to submit lists of new senate nominees, from which the prime minister would make the final selection.
- Immigration. New powers for the provinces allowing them to set their own policies within overall targets set by the federal government.
- National shared-cost programs. Requirements of "reasonable compensation" to be paid to a province not wishing to participate in a national shared-cost program established by the federal government in an area of "exclusive provincial jurisdiction, if the province carries on a program or initiative that is compatible with the national objectives."
- Amending formula. Expansion of the types of constitutional changes requiring unanimous consent of the provinces to include senate reform and the creation of new provinces.

The federal Parliament and the legislatures of all provinces except Manitoba and New Brunswick were quick to ratify the accord. Opposition in the two dissenting provinces focussed on the need for further changes and guarantees, particularly with respect to the rights of minorities, including women and Canada's Native peoples.

As debate on the accord continued, opposition widened and stiffened, led by three newly elected provincial premiers, Gary Filmon of Manitoba, Frank McKenna of New Brunswick, and Clyde Wells of Newfoundland. In Newfoundland, Premier Wells led the legislature to rescind its earlier approval of the accord.

In addition to the issue of minority rights, critics argued that the "distinct society" clause implicitly gave Quebec special status within Confederation, with powers that would not be available to the other provinces. The western provinces desired Senate reform — primarily an elected Senate with increased representation from the smaller provinces —

and fears were expressed that the larger provinces of Ontario and Quebec would use the provision of unanimous consent for Senate change to block such changes. Newfoundland, in particular, harboured major concerns about the opting-out feature. Premier Wells argued that it would discourage the federal government from initiating new shared-cost programs, since opting out reduced Ottawa's influence over programs, and this situation would be detrimental to poorer provinces, such as Newfoundland, which relied heavily on federal financial aid. It was also argued that the wording of this clause, which spoke of "national objectives" not "national standards," eroded Ottawa's ability to establish such standards and therefore any degree of uniformity of shared-cost services across Canada.

The Death of Meech Lake. Despite numerous attempts to save the Meech Lake Accord, the June 23, 1990, deadline approached without the required unanimous consent of the provinces. Premier Bourassa, fully supported by the Mulroney government, maintained that the accord met minimum demands and that revisions or additional provisions and issues would be considered only after the agreement was ratified by all provinces. Supporters of the accord argued that to reject it was to reject Quebec as a full partner in Confederation and would serve to strengthen that province's separatist movement. The dissenting provinces and other opponents argued just as strenuously that once the accord was passed, the unanimous consent provision would make it extremely difficult if not impossible to institute senate reforms and other changes requiring unanimity.

In a last-ditch effort to save the accord, a federal-provincial conference of first ministers was finally called on June 3, 1990, three weeks before the deadline. In a week of intense negotiations, amid threats of the breakup of the Canadian federation and much acrimony, the group hammered out a tentative agreement in which the accord remained virtually intact.

The Meech Lake Accord still required passage by three provincial legislatures, however. New Brunswick was quick to approve, but Manitoba legislature regulations required public hearings. The introduction of the legislation to the Manitoba legislature was, however, stalled by Elijah Harper, an Aboriginal member of the legislative assembly, who argued that the accord did not address Native issues. Consequently, Manitoba ran out of time to hold its required public hearings and to obtain legislative approval by the deadline. In Newfoundland, Premier Clyde Wells, rejecting what he termed last-minute "manipulations" and pressure from Ottawa and pointing to the situation in Manitoba, refused on the final day to have the legislature vote as scheduled on the accord. The June 23 deadline passed, and the Meech Lake Accord was declared dead.

Further Consideration. In essence, the controversy over the Meech Lake Accord stemmed mainly from its ambiguity and the uncertainty it created on matters such as Senate reform, minority rights, the status of shared-cost programs and specific-purpose transfers, and the precise meaning of the power granted Quebec to "preserve and promote" its "distinct society." Many opponents viewed the accord as a dilution of federal powers to pursue national goals and as a vehicle for increased fragmentation of the Canadian nation. Some also feared it was only the beginning of more and more demands by the province of Quebec for increased powers to enable it to pursue its particular destiny.

Quebec Premier Bourassa reacted to the failure of the Meech Accord by publicly stating that he would attend no more constitutional conferences but would deal directly with Ottawa to attempt to obtain bilateral agreements between his province and the federal government on issues considered important to Quebec nationalism, such as immigration and communications. The leader of the Parti Québécois, Jacques Parizeau, went much further and charged that the rejection of the Meech Accord was a rejection of Quebec, and he re-emphasized his party's position calling for Quebec's independence from the rest of Canada. Prime Minister Mulroney, however, vowed to continue to seek constitutional reform, believing that the only way to prevent Quebec from separating from Canada was to meet the most pressing demands of Quebec through changes in the constitution.

The Charlottetown Accord

The federal government's post-Meech Lake efforts to renegotiate the Constitution with the provinces came to a climax at a constitutional conference held in Charlottetown, P.E.I., in August 1992. Ottawa and the provincial premiers reached a new agreement which became known as the Charlottetown Accord.[4] This new agreement contained the essential provisions of the Meech Lake Accord plus a number of additional clauses designed to accommodate Quebec as well as the other provinces. The provisions included a Canada clause, clauses on social and economic union, on the Senate, on the Supreme Court and the House of Commons, on constitutional change, and on federal-provincial responsibilities. The main features of these clauses are as follows:

- *Canada clause.* Reaffirms Canada's commitment to democracy, to racial and ethnic equality, and to individual rights and freedoms. Recognition is given to Quebec as a "distinct society" within Canada and to the "role of Quebec's legislative assembly to preserve and promote that distinctiveness."
- *Social and economic union.* The Constitution would identify key social and economic objectives shared by all levels of government, including universal health

care, adequate social services, full employment, environmental protection, and high quality education.
- *The Senate.* An elected Senate of sixty-two members, consisting of six elected senators from each province and one from each territory, with veto power over tax policy relating to natural resources (a prime provincial concern). Legislation affecting French language and culture would require a double majority, meaning approval by a majority of the Senate and a majority of designated Francophone senators.
- *The Supreme Court of Canada.* Composed of nine members, appointed by the federal government from lists submitted by the provinces, with three members from Quebec.
- *House of Commons.* The size of the House increased to 337 members, with 18 additional members from each of Ontario and Quebec, 4 from B.C. and 2 from Alberta, to better reflect the principle of representation by population.
- *Aboriginal peoples.* Recognition that the Aboriginal peoples of Canada have an inherent right of self-government within Canada.
- *Amending formula.* Unanimous consent of the federal Parliament and the provincial legislatures to amend the Constitution to include changes in the Senate, the supreme court, and the creation of new provinces.
- *Federal-provincial roles and responsibilities.* More clearly defined roles and responsibilities of the governments to eliminate or reduce overlapping of jurisdictions and duplication of services as follows:
  - forestry, mining, tourism, housing, recreation, and municipal and urban affairs recognized as exclusive provincial matters;
  - labour-market development and training, since they are closely related to

the provincial responsibility of education, recognized as exclusively in the provincial domain, with the federal government continuing to be responsible for Employment Insurance; cultural matters within provincial boundaries established as provincial responsibilities, but Ottawa continue its existing role regarding national cultural agencies such as the CBC;

- the federal government commit to negotiate agreements with the provinces on immigration giving the provinces greater voice on immigration policy;

- establish a mechanism to protect federal-provincial agreements from unilateral change;

- develop a framework that would limit federal spending power in areas of exclusive provincial jurisdiction, along with a provision that a province could opt out of a Canada-wide shared-cost program and receive reasonable federal compensation as long as it established a similar program compatible with national objectives.

- the federal government commit to meaningful consultation with the provinces before making changes in equalization payments.

The amendments to the Constitution proposed in the new accord went beyond the Meech Lake Accord in several areas, including an elected Senate, an enlarged House of Commons, and an extension of provincial powers with a reduction in duplication of jurisdictions and federal intrusion into areas of provincial jurisdiction.

The governments had committed to a national referendum on the Charlottetown Accord. If approved by Canadians, the proposals would become law upon ratification by Parliament and the provincial legislatures. In the referendum, held on October 26, 1992, the Charlottetown Accord was defeated.

On the national level, 45 percent of the voters approved the Accord, 55 percent voted against it. The greatest opposition was polled in the western provinces, Ontario voters split evenly, Quebec voted against it, while voters in the Atlantic region favoured the agreement. The recorded percentages of yes-no votes by region were as follows: P.E.I., 74-26; Nfld. 63-37; N.S. 49-51; N.B. 62-38; Qu. 42-56; Ont. 50-50; Man. 38-62; Sask. 45-55; Alta. 40-60; B.C. 32-68; Yukon 44-56; Canada 45-55.

The defeat of the Charlottetown Accord was attributed to a combination of a number of factors. Many Canadians outside of Quebec believed that it gave too much to Quebec. Quebecers, on the other hand, believed that the accord did not adequately meet their demands, while staunch separatists could only be satisfied with complete independence. Aboriginal people were not satisfied that their rights were clearly enough defined. Many Canadians feared that the accord provided for too much decentralization of power, severely weakening the federal government. Various observers argued that the referendum was an anti-Mulroney vote. The Conservative Mulroney government had become very unpopular, with gallop polls showing the government holding a mere 12 percent approval rating. The electorate, it was contended, identified the Charlottetown Accord with Mulroney and took the referendum as an opportunity to vote against him. And finally, it was argued that the negative vote reflected public disillusionment with the entire constitutional issue and process. Outside of Quebec the issue of constitutional reform did not appear to be a high priority and people wanted their governments and representatives to start devoting more attention to more urgent matters such as the severe recession and high unemployment the economy was suffering.

In the subsequent federal election in the autumn of 1993, the Conservative government went down to an overwhelming defeat, succeeding in capturing only two parliamentary seats. The new Liberal government, under Prime Minister Jean Chretien, stated that it had no interest in reopening constitutional talks with the provinces. Chretien took the public position that separatism was not a serious problem.

Support for sovereignty within Quebec, however, had continued to grow. A newly formed federal political party called the Bloc Québécois had been organized by Lucien Bouchard, a former Cabinet minister in the Mulroney government, and captured enough House of Commons seats in the 1993 federal election to form the official opposition in Parliament. The Bloc was committed to promoting the sovereignty cause for Quebec in Parliament. The cause was furthered with the election to power in Quebec in 1994 of the Parti Québécois under the premiership of Jacques Parizeau. Parizeau promised the people of Quebec a referendum on sovereignty in 1995.

Separatism in Quebec was not a unified movement. Hard-line separatists pressed for complete independence while more moderate sovereignists preferred some economic and political ties with the rest of Canada. The referendum on sovereignty was set for October 30, 1995, and the question Quebecers were asked to consider reflected a compromise. The question voted on was as follows: "Do you agree that Quebec should become sovereign, after having made a formal offer to Canada for a new economic and political union...." The question raised considerable confusion. Surveys found that one-quarter to one-third of Quebecers thought that a sovereign Quebec would remain a province of Canada, that they would continue to hold Canadian citizenship, and use Canada's currency.

The referendum campaign pitted the separatist forces led by Parizeau and Bouchard against the federalist forces led by Daniel Johnson, leader of the opposition Liberal party in the Quebec legislature. Prime Minister Chretien and the federal politicians remained largely outside the fray until the eleventh hour when public opinion polls showed that the separatist forces were slightly ahead. Panicked federal politicians and groups from across Canada rallied in support of anti-separation, with the prime minister promising flexibility on the constitution. The vote produced a slim victory for the "no" side. In the referendum, 49.6 percent voted against the question and 48.6 percent voted in favour, with 1.8 percent of the ballots rejected.

In a bitter speech immediately after the results were announced, Jacques Parizeau claimed that it was "money and the ethnic vote" that led to the defeat and vowed that there would soon be another referendum. Parizeau's remarks, hinting at an intolerant form of nationalism, led to his resignation as premier and he was succeeded by the Bloc Québécois leader Lucien Bouchard. Bouchard promised to continue to work to achieve a sovereign Quebec and another referendum on the issue in due time.

Since the referendum, the issue of Quebec separation has continued to smoulder. The Liberal federal government has attempted to forge new power-sharing arrangements with the provinces, and negotiate a "distinct society" clause for Quebec in the constitution. The provinces have indicated that they would favour a new partnership with the federal government but maintain that all provinces must have equal status. While they generally concede that Quebec should be able to protect its language, heritage, culture and laws — those features that make it a unique part of the nation's character — they oppose any measure or change that would given Quebec any powers not available to other provinces.

The federal government finally decided to take the issue of the legality of unilateral secession of Quebec to the Supreme Court of Canada. The Court was asked for its opinion on three questions: (1) can the Quebec government secede unilaterally from Canada under the Constitution?; (2) does it have the right to secede unilaterally under international law?; (3) if there is a conflict between international and Canadian law on the issue of the right to secede, which takes precedence in Canada? The court began its deliberations in early 1998. The federal government's position was that the Constitution does not permit unilateral secession. Canada is a federal state based on constitutional government. Secession would affect the structure and scope of the Constitution, therefore it would require constitutional amendments applying the amending formula from the Constitution Act, 1982. Consequently, since constitutional amendments require the consent of Ottawa and the assemblies of two-thirds of the provinces, unilateral secession is unconstitutional. The separatist government of Quebec under Premier Lucien Bouchard refused to participate in the case, contending that the judiciary could not determine the political future of Quebec. It was argued that Quebec had the right to self-determination and only the people of Quebec could determine Quebec's future.

The Supreme Court rendered its decision in August, 1998. It ruled that Quebec could not secede from Canada unilaterally within the framework of the Constitution, that international law did not give Quebec this right, and in the light of these answers there was no conflict between domestic and international law to be addressed. However, in the court's judgement, the federal government and the provinces would be obligated to negotiate with Quebec if a clear majority voted in favour of secession in a referendum in the province. The terms negotiated for separation would have to meet the needs, and protect the rights, of all concerned, and the court acknowledged that it would not be an easy set of negotiations. Both federalists and sovereignists claimed satisfaction from the judgement.

Confrontation over Natural Resources

The Constitution Act, 1867, divided the responsibility for natural resources, giving the federal government jurisdiction over Native people's lands and national parks and the provinces jurisdiction over forests, minerals, oil, and natural gas and providing shared jurisdiction over agriculture, fisheries, and water resources. In addition, Ottawa claimed certain kinds of jurisdiction as stemming from its constitutional power to regulate trade and commerce and imports and exports and, in times of emergency, from the "peace, order, and good government" provision. Jurisdictional conflicts between the two levels of government have simmered and occasionally flared, as in the 1970s and 1980s when major confrontations developed over the issue of energy.[5]

The Two-Price System. To assist the development of Canada's petroleum industry in the 1950s, a national policy was instituted by which western Canadian crude oil was supplied as far east as the Ottawa Valley. The part of the country east of this line was supplied with imported oil, which could then be obtained at a lower price. This policy established a domestic market for approximately half of the Canadian oil produced; the remainder was exported to the United States.

In October 1973, the Arab-Israeli conflict and the formation of the Organization of Petroleum Exporting Countries (OPEC) resulted in a reduction in Arab oil exports and a drastic increase in the international price of oil. The price of oil imported into eastern Canada jumped from $3.75 to $10.50 per barrel. The Canadian government, desiring a uniform price for oil across the country and wishing both to protect consumers from large price increases and to control the export of oil, temporarily froze the price of domestic oil (at $4.10 per barrel) and imposed an export tax on oil exported to the United States. One-half of the proceeds of this tax was paid to the producing provinces, and the other half was used, under the Oil Import Compensation Program, to subsidize refiners processing imported oil in eastern Canada so as to reduce their costs to the level of refiners using domestic oil. In turn, Alberta, which produced 85 percent of Canada's oil, and Saskatchewan increased royalty charges on oil and gas. Ottawa responded by making royalty payments a non-deductible business expense for income tax purposes.

Alberta and Saskatchewan vigorously protested the various federal actions, contending that Ottawa was intruding into provincial jurisdiction over natural resources and demanding the full benefits of rising oil prices. The eastern provinces, in turn, complained that the federal subsidy was insufficient because it left their consumers with oil and gasoline prices higher than those of their western counterparts. In addition, the provinces receiving equalization payments demanded that the new natural resource revenues be included in the equalization formula.

After much discussion and debate, a series of federal-provincial agreements on oil and gas pricing were negotiated in the middle and late 1970s. The price of domestic oil and gas was to rise gradually, but it was to remain substantially below the international prices. As the price of domestic oil increased, the oil export charge was changed correspondingly to reflect the difference between domestic and international prices.

The National Energy Program. It was in this environment that the federal government introduced its National Energy Program (NEP) in late 1980.[6] The NEP was a long-term plan for managing Canada's energy resources. It had three primary objectives: (1) to achieve security of supply and independence from the world oil market by the end of the decade; (2) to offer Canadians an opportunity for increased participation in the development of the industry and to achieve 50 percent Canadian ownership of oil and gas production by 1990 (compared to 27 percent in 1980); and (3) to ensure fairness in petroleum pricing and revenue distribution among producers, consumers, and the levels of government.

The NEP included various tax incentives and grants for oil and gas exploration and the development of energy alternatives. It also specified additional taxes, such as an oil and gas revenue tax of 8 percent of the income related to the production of oil and gas; a tax on natural gas and gas liquids, including gas for export; and an oil compensation charge. In addition, it continued the oil export charge.

The vehicle for increasing Canadian ownership and participation in petroleum development was to be Petro Canada, a Crown corporation, created in 1976 for the purpose of undertaking oil and gas exploration and of ensuring security of supply. It had become involved in the tar sands development as well as in Arctic and Atlantic offshore exploration; it had also began to purchase interests in other petroleum companies. (For example, it had earlier purchased Atlantic Richfields Canada Ltd. and Pacific Petroleum Ltd., and in 1981, it paid approximately $1.5 billion to acquire Petro-Fina, a large foreign-owned oil company involved in both exploration and retail distribution.) Under the NEP, Petro Canada was to play a major role in Canadianizing the petroleum industry through the purchase of foreign-controlled petroleum companies.

In essence, the NEP considerably extended the federal government's authority and participation in natural resource development. Consequently, it was bitterly opposed by the oil- and gas-producing provinces as an intrusion on provincial ownership rights and a resource "revenue grab" by Ottawa. Alberta, Saskatchewan, and British Columbia objected to Ottawa's unilateral fixing of prices and to the new taxes. The petroleum industry also reacted negatively, arguing that the revenue left to its firms after they deducted royalties, charges, and taxes was insufficient to finance new investment and exploration.

Premier Peter Lougheed of Alberta announced that, until provincial concerns were resolved, his province would reduce oil production by 15 percent in stages and withhold approval of two huge tar sands projects, as well as initiate a legal challenge to the proposed federal excise tax on natural gas. The confrontation between Ottawa and Alberta was in essence a struggle for the control of Canada's natural resource policy, including issues of resource ownership, pricing, the distribution of revenues from oil and gas, and the overall direction of development.

The impasse continued for almost a year. In September 1981, after intensive negotiations, the two governments signed the Canada-Alberta Energy Pricing and Taxation Agreement, which was to continue until 1986. Similar agreements followed with the governments of British Columbia and Saskatchewan. These agreements, together with the provisions relating to the jurisdiction and taxation of natural resources introduced in the Constitution Act, 1982 (discussed earlier in this chapter), effectively put an end to the political conflict between Ottawa and the western provinces. The agreements left the central thrust of the NEP intact but significantly changed the pricing and tax proposals it contained to meet provincial concerns. Under the new agreements, the price of oil and gas was to continue to be regulated and increased. But this schedule was soon disrupted. The international prices of petroleum began to fall, depressing the energy sector. The petroleum-producing provinces were forced to change their royalty structures and Ottawa postponed and reduced certain resource taxes.

The Western Accord. The weakening of the OPEC cartel, increased oil production, falling prices at the international level, and the election of a Conservative government in 1984 prompted the dismantling of the National Energy Program and restructuring of federal energy policy during the mid-1980s. In 1985, the federal government and the three oil- and gas-producing provinces of Alberta, British Columbia, and Saskatchewan signed the Western Accord, an agreement to replace the NEP. It removed many of the special federal taxes that had been imposed on oil and gas under the NEP and left prices to be determined by the marketplace.

At the same time, Petro Canada was mandated to operate as a commercial corporation in a competitive environment. Then, in the February 1990 federal budget, Finance Minister Wilson announced plans to privatize Petro Canada by selling shares in the company to the public. The minister rationalized that the role of Petro Canada as an instrument of public policy was becoming increasingly limited because of changes in the nature of the industry and the international energy environment. Ottawa had, by 1990, invested more than $4 billion in the company, but it still needed large capital resources for its frontier exploration and development program. A privatized Petro Canada, the minister argued, would have access to the full range of financing opportunities available to shareholder-owned corporations in the private sector.

The sale of Petro Canada was part of the Conservative's government's continuing program of privatizing Crown corporations. As well, it appealed to a government anxious to control its expenditures and in need of revenues to reduce huge annual deficits. The minister made no claims that Petro Canada had achieved the government's objectives. It had by no means attained a dominant position in the Canadian petroleum industry. By 1988, its asset base had accounted for about 5.5 percent of Canadian domestic oil production and 6 percent of natural gas production, and its refining activities used about 22 percent of Canada's refining capacity.

The Offshore. The struggle over natural resources was not confined to Ottawa and the western provinces. Offshore resource rights became a heated issue in the Atlantic region. Although an agreement was reached between the federal government and Nova Scotia in

March 1982, a prolonged, bitter dispute continued between Ottawa and Newfoundland.

Newfoundland claimed jurisdiction and ownership of offshore minerals by virtue of having been an entity with its own territory before joining Canada in 1949 and of not having surrendered its extraterritorial powers to the federal government when it became a province. Various attempts at negotiation and compromise ended in failure, and early in 1983 the governments sought a constitutional ruling from the Supreme Court of Canada. In March 1984, the Supreme Court ruled that offshore mineral rights came under the jurisdiction of the federal government. Newfoundland Premier Brian Peckford responded that he would continue the fight for significant provincial control of offshore oil development.

The legal matter of ownership was settled, but there remained questions of the extent of provincial control of the offshore resources and what share of revenues from these resources it would draw. Intensive negotiations culminated in the signing of the Canada-Newfoundland Atlantic Accord in 1985. The terms of the accord gave the province the power to control the method and pace of offshore oil and gas development and the right to impose royalties and taxes on the resources as if they were on land. In a further spirit of co-operation, the two governments entered an agreement in 1988 on the development of the Hibernia oil field off the coast of Newfoundland. The terms of the agreement provided that from 1989 to 1995 the federal government would contribute 25 percent of specified pre-production capital costs of the project to a maximum of $1.04 billion and would guarantee loans for 40 percent of the capital costs to a maximum guarantee of $1.66 billion.[7]

Co-ordination of Economic and Social Policies

The general trend in Canada over the last four decades has been a gradual decentralization of power in terms of the relative shares of federal and provincial expenditure constituting the public sector. Along with such decentralization comes an increasing need for co-operation between the two levels of government and for co-ordination of policies. Without co-operation, fiscal policy becomes difficult to implement, taxation may produce inequities and adverse economic effects, waste and inefficiency may creep into overlapping government expenditure functions, and uncertainty may characterize areas under jurisdictional dispute. The term "co-operative federalism" has been frequently used to describe the situation in Canada, and numerous formal, informal, and ad hoc avenues for co-operation have been employed.

The most publicized method of bringing together the federal and provincial governments to discuss problems and co-ordinate policies has been the federal-provincial conference of premiers and the prime minister. These conferences are generally reserved for discussion of relatively general principles and issues, and because the meetings draw extensive media coverage, they frequently tend to serve as a political forum. The interests and opinions of the participants have been as varied as the regions of Canada themselves, with much controversy and conflict and only occasional consensus. The Charlottetown Accord had proposed that a provision be added to the Constitution requiring the prime minister to convene a meeting with the provincial premiers at least once a year.

Regular discussions are also held among federal and provincial ministers of the various departments of government, such as the meetings of the federal minister of finance and provincial treasurers to discuss fiscal policies and tax and expenditure issues. In addition, liaison between the two levels of government is provided by numerous ad hoc committees at the public service level, supplemented by day-to-day contacts in the ordinary process of administering government affairs.

In 1975 the federal government established the Federal-Provincial Relations Office (FPRO), replacing a previous federal-provincial unit within the Privy Council Office. In 1986, a Minister of State for Federal-Provincial Relations was established. The FPRO serves this minister and provides assistance to other federal ministers, departments and agencies in the conduct of their relations with provincial governments. It consists of five secretariats: one responsible for liaison with the provinces, a second responsible for policy development, a third dealing with economic policy and programs, a fourth dealing with social policy and programs, and finally one handling constitutional affairs.

Offices counterpart to the FPRO exist at the provincial level. Examples are Ontario's Ministry of Intergovernmental Affairs and Manitoba's Federal-Provincial Relations and Research Division of the Finance Department.

In addition, the Canada Intergovernmental Conference Secretariat, created, funded, and staffed by both the federal and the provincial governments, serves federal-provincial and interprovincial meetings of first ministers and ministers and officials of departments. It provides secretarial, translation, and printing services along with various assistance in arranging conferences.

A number of intergovernmental agencies have been established between the federal government and the provinces, between the federal government and certain provinces, and between provinces.[8] Their functions vary from co-ordinating government activities to providing services directly to the public.

Various economic development agreements between the federal and provincial governments provide for consultation and co-operation as well as financial assistance. In 1984, the ten-year Economic and Regional Development Agreements (ERDAs) were signed between Ottawa and each province. The ERDA was a mechanism to facilitate consultation on and co-ordination of economic and regional development policies, programs, and activities of the two levels of government; the Department of Regional Industrial Expansion was the primary federal agency involved. In the area of environmental protection, most provinces have entered into agreements with Ottawa for a more co-ordinated approach to protecting the environment and to eliminate duplication of programs. While forest resources fall primarily under provisional jurisdiction, the federal government and the provinces have negotiated a variety of shared-cost programs aimed at improving forestry management and conservation and regenerating depleted forests.

Despite this extensive co-operation between the two levels of government on economic and social policies, disagreements, conflicts, and confrontations are common. The confrontations over shared-cost programs, medicare, oil and gas pricing, and offshore mineral rights were discussed earlier. Other recent areas of dispute concern the regulation of telecommunications and the federal imposition of the Goods and Services Tax (GST). A decision of the Supreme Court of Canada in 1989 determined that the activities of the provincially owned telephone companies in Alberta, Saskatchewan, and Manitoba were interprovincial and therefore subject to federal, rather than provincial, regulation,. Those three provinces petitioned that regulatory jurisdiction be legislated back to the provinces, but the federal government refused, arguing that jurisdiction over all telephone service would enable Ottawa to establish a national telecommunications policy.

When the federal government first introduced its proposal for a Goods and Services Tax in 1987, the Minister of Finance outlined, as an option, a joint federal-provincial sales tax. The arrangements suggested were similar to those in place for the personal and corporate tax system; the tax would be legislated separately by the federal government and the provinces, with flexibility for the latter to determine their own rates. Ottawa contended that a joint tax would simplify administration and compliance and avoid a complex, double layer of sales tax. The provinces, however, were not prepared to co-operate and negotiations aimed at a joint tax failed. Indeed, the provinces were highly critical of the federal decision to impose the GST. The retail sales tax, levied by all provinces except Alberta, had been a major source of provincial revenue for years, and they viewed the federal GST as an intrusion into provincial tax territory. The provinces also refused to help Ottawa collect its tax, a course that would have avoided some duplication in administration and reduced collection costs. The federal Minister of Finance, however, left the door open for provinces to join the GST after it came into effect, and as discussed earlier, the provinces of Quebec, Nova Scotia, New Brunswick, and Newfoundland have since harmonized their sales tax with the GST.

Another area of recent federal-provincial dispute has been the coastal fisheries. British Columbia, in particular, has been extremely critical of the federal government, charging that its policies were inadequate in protecting and managing west coast salmon stocks and that the province should have greater responsibility for managing this resource and protecting the salmon from overfishing by the Alaska industry.

Summary

In 1982 Canada finally succeeded in patriating the British North America Act, which along with some amendments, became the Constitution Act 1982. The new Constitution, however, was not supported by the Quebec government, and as a result the federal government began a series of attempted constitutional reforms which would satisfy that province and stem the tide of growing

separatism within Quebec. The first attempt was the Meech Lake Accord of 1987 which failed to receive unanimous ratification by the provincial legislatures and consequently died in 1990. Undiscouraged in 1992 the federal government brought the provinces together again and obtained agreement on a constitutional reform package called the Charlottetown Accord, which was an expansion of Meech Lake. It more clearly defined federal and provincial roles and responsibilities, gave the provinces exclusive jurisdiction in some overlapping jurisdictional areas, established a mechanism to protect federal-provincial agreements from unilateral change, and limited federal spending power in areas of provincial jurisdiction.

The governments brought the accord before the Canadian electorate in a referendum in late 1992. It was defeated nationally, as well as in Quebec and the western provinces.

Continuing to pursue its policy of gaining sovereignty for Quebec, the governing Parti Québécois called a referendum on sovereignty in 1995 which was defeated by the narrowest of margins. Undeterred, the government promised another referendum on the issue in the near future.

In addition to confrontation between Ottawa and the provinces over the Constitution during this period, there was also confrontation in other areas, most notably natural resources and communications. In attempts to avoid such confrontations, Ottawa and the provinces have established formal agencies and offices and strive to maintain close contacts and consultations to co-operate in matters of mutual interest, and co-ordinate policies and programs to reduce duplication and waste.

NOTES

1 For a detailed presentation of the developments leading to the patriated Constitution, see Edward McWhinney, *Canada and the Constitution 1979-1982* (Toronto: University of Toronto Press, 1982); and J.M. Beck and I. Bernier, eds., *Canada and the New Constitution* (Toronto: Institute for Research on Public Policy, 1983), vol. 1 and 2.

2 Canada, *Proceedings of the Constitutional Conference*, Victoria, June 14-16, 1971.

3   For a discussion of various aspects of the Meech Lake Accord, see, "The Meech Lake Accord," *Canadian Public Policy* 14, supplement (September 1988).

4   The full text of the Charlottetown agreement, together with a summary, is presented in Canada, *Your Guide to Canada's Proposed Constitutional Changes* (Ottawa, 1992).

5   A discussion of this conflict can be found in J. Harvey Perry, *Background of Current Fiscal Problems*, Tax Paper No. 8 (Toronto: Canadian Tax Foundation, 1982) ch.7 and 8; and E.A. Carmichael and J.K. Stewart, *Lessons from the National Energy Program* (Toronto: C.D. Howe Institute, 1983).

6   Canada, Ministry of Mines and Resources, *The National Energy Program* (Ottawa, 1980).

7   Canada, Federal-Provincial Relations Office, *Federal-Provincial Programs and Activities, A Descriptive Inventory, 1988-89* (Ottawa: June 1989), p.10-9.

8   Canada, *Federal-Provincial Programs and Activities*, 1994-95 (Ottawa: June 1995).

PART FIVE

FISCAL POLICY

CHAPTER 16

The Budget as an Instrument of Fiscal Policy

The objectives of fiscal policy are generally identified as full employment, stable prices, and economic growth. Traditional fiscal policy concentrates on government management of aggregate demand through discretionary application of tax and expenditure measures, which are primarily introduced through the budget. A period of economic decline and unemployment calls for tax and/or expenditure changes, producing a budget deficit. In a period of excessive aggregate demand and inflation, a budget surplus would be the appropriate discretionary policy.

Fiscal policy first came to prominence with the Depression of the 1930s and the publication of the *General Theory of Employment, Interest and Money* by J.M. Keynes in 1936.[1] Keynes argued that the key to ending the Depression and maintaining high levels of economic growth and full employment was a high level of aggregate demand. If private demand was insufficient to achieve this, then government should step in with expansionary tax and expenditure policies. In the Keynesian theory, aggregate demand in a closed economy (one without imports and exports) consists of the demand of consumers, business, and government. The sum of consumption (C), investment (I), and government expenditure (G) constitutes gross national expenditure (Y), or $C + I + G = Y$.[2] In an open economy, exports (ex) and imports (im) are introduced into this identity to produce $Y = C + I + G + $ ex - im. A change in any of the components will affect aggregate demand.

According to traditional Keynesian theory, an increase in aggregate demand in a period of unemployment should raise production and employment, assuming the supply of goods and services expands to meet the demand. Consequently, if the government budget is balanced to begin with, an increase in government expenditure with taxes held constant will produce a budget deficit but will also raise aggregate demand and provide a stimulus to economic activity and employment. Similarly a reduction in taxes for consumers and business will provide increased incomes for expenditure on consumption and investment. A tax reduction with government expenditure held constant will also produce a budget deficit. A budget surplus, on the other hand, will have a contractionary effect on aggregate demand and economic activity. The impact on the economy from a budget surplus or deficit will exceed the size of the surplus or deficit by a multiple amount, through the multiplier process.[3]

More recent developments in macroeconomics and in fiscal theory focus on the management of aggregate supply as well as demand. In fact, the term "supply-side economics" was used to describe this approach to fiscal policy during the 1980s. This theory emphasizes the effects of tax changes on incentives, such as the incentive to work and to invest. Positive incentives for work or investment will increase the supply of labour and capital and may have a positive impact on productivity and economic growth. An increase in aggregate supply may moderate inflation in a period of rising prices caused by large increases in demand.[4]

The budget as a tool for implementing and analyzing fiscal policy, together with the objectives of fiscal policy, are examined in this chapter. This will provide a framework for the analysis of Canadian fiscal policy that is presented in chapter 17.

The Budget Accounts

The federal government uses three different measures to show its fiscal position. In effect, it presents three budgets, each with a different balance. The three budgets are the administrative budget, the consolidated cash budget, and the national income and expenditure accounts budget. The first two are based on the public accounts, an accounting system designed to facilitate parliamentary control over expenditures; the third is based on the national accounts.[5] Each serves a different purpose, and the three are not equally appropriate for the analysis of fiscal policy.

Administrative Budget. The administrative budget reflects government department and agency operations, incorporating their estimates of expenditure for the fiscal year with estimates of tax proceeds and certain other revenues. The financial transactions in this budget are called budgetary transactions.

This document is commonly referred to as "The Budget," and its transactions and balance are the focus of the annual budget speech by the Minister of Finance. Its balance is the one highlighted by government and by the news media as the indicator of the state of government budgetary affairs and the extent to which the government is operating in the red or the black. The accumulated deficits in this budget since Confederation form the total net government debt, which consists of gross government debt minus the value of recorded government assets.

The administrative budget serves the administrative and financial control purposes described in the earlier chapter on the budgetary process.

Consolidated Cash Budget. The consolidated cash budget includes all government financial transactions — the administrative budget and all other payments and receipts — and is a comprehensive measure of cash flows. It is broken into three main categories of financial transactions: budgetary transactions, non-budgetary transactions, and foreign exchange transactions. Non-budgetary transactions consist of loans, investments, and advances; transactions related to specified-purpose accounts; and other transactions. The distinguishing feature between budgetary and non-budgetary transactions is that the former change the net indebtedness of the government, while the latter do not since they involve the creation of offsetting financial assets or liabilities.

Non-budgetary transactions have in the past provided a net source of funds to the government and consequently have reduced the extent to which the government has had to borrow on financial markets. Loans and advances are primarily those made to Crown corporations; a loan by the government increases its financial assets since the recipient incurs an obligation to repay. The specified purpose accounts in non-budgetary transactions include the Canada Pension Plan and the superannuation accounts (federal government employee's pension accounts). Accounts that are held in trust for third parties are self-financing. For many years, the non-budgetary accounts included three other major funds: the Unemployment Insurance Fund, the Foreign Exchange Fund Account, and the Grain Stabilization Account. In 1985, on the recommendation of the Auditor General of Canada, these three funds, along with loans to developing countries, were reclassified from non-budgetary to budgetary transactions.

Foreign exchange transactions record the purchase and sale of foreign currencies, used to stabilize the Canadian dollar in international money markets, and include a reserve of borrowed funds to provide for flexibility.

The consolidated cash budget is the most comprehensive of the three budgets and is useful for internal cash management purposes. It shows the net amount of borrowing on the financial markets the federal government requires for a fiscal year. For example, in 1995-96 the administrative budget deficit was estimated at $28.6 billion. Non-budgetary transactions were a surplus of $11.4 billion, while the deficit in foreign exchange transactions totalled $4.7 billion. Thus, the total borrowing required amounted to approximately $22 billion. This budget, therefore, has relevance to the analysis of the effect of government on the economy in terms of its impact on the money or capital market and on interest rates.

National Accounts Budget. First presented in 1964, the national accounts budget employs the national income and expenditure accounting system developed by Statistics Canada to measure current economic activity and serves, among other things, to measure the interaction between the public sector and other sectors of the economy. The national accounts concepts are similar to those used internationally and permit comparisons from one nation to another.

The national accounts budget serves economic analysis. It is more comprehensive than the administrative budget but excludes some items found in the consolidated cash budget. Government pension and social security transactions are included, but government borrowing and lending operations are excluded, as are transactions of a purely book-keeping nature that have no impact on the economy. The national accounts budget concentrates on income-creating and resource-absorbing transactions and therefore includes only those operations that have a direct effect on the flow of incomes in the economy. Furthermore, it is based on the accrual method of accounting in which revenues are accounted when earned rather than received and expenditures are recorded when liabilities are in-

curred rather than when actually paid; therefore, it measures the timing of the impact of government operations of the economy.

The system of national income and expenditure accounts employed by Statistics Canada, on which the government's national accounts budget is based, defines output as currently produced goods and services; consequently, it excludes both transactions on used goods and financial transactions that do not involve the production of new goods and services. Thus, government loan transaction are omitted, an exclusion that does limit the usefulness of this budget for analyzing the impact of the government on the economy. Some government loans have significant economic effects, and if they were incorporated into the budget, it would present a more complete picture. For example, a government loan to an industry that uses the proceeds to purchase domestically produced machinery and equipment affects economic activity and output. Although the expenditure of the loan by the recipient is reflected in the national accounts, the fact that it came from the government is not.

The difference between the administrative budget balance and the national accounts budget balance can be substantial. Usually, a large part of this difference results from the manner in which the two budgets treat transactions in the government employees' pension accounts. National accounts revenues include employer and employee contributions, as well as interest earnings, and expenditures include all benefits and interest payments. The budgetary transactions, in contrast, exclude all revenues recorded by these pension accounts and include as expenditures only the government's contribution as an employer and interest paid on surplus funds (included as interest on the public debt). Thus, the national accounts deficit is usually lower than the budgetary deficit. For example, in 1992-93 the budgetary deficit was $41 billion while the national accounts budget deficit was $31 billion. In 1995-96 the difference was smaller, $28.6 billion compared to $25.4 billion. Despite the frequent substantial differences between the two deficit measures, it should be noted that they have tended, for the most part, to move symmetrically (the trends are broadly similar).

Although the budget based on the national income and expenditure accounts has some limitations, it is generally considered the most appropriate of the three budgets for analyzing fiscal policy and is used in the next chapter for the analysis of Canadian policy. Some reference is also made there to the balances on the administrative budget and the consolidated cash budget — the former because it affects the net national debt and the latter because it presents the government's borrowing requirements in the financial market and may affect this market and interest rates.

Fiscal Impulse Measures

The actual budget balance is generally viewed as a summary indicator of the government's fiscal policy stance. In any analysis of fiscal policy, it must be recognized that the budget can affect the economy and that the economy can affect the budget. Variations in government revenues and expenditures, and therefore in the budget balance, may result from discretionary changes in tax and expenditure policies or from changes in economic conditions. The actual budgetary surplus or deficit, therefore, can be viewed as consisting of two components: a structural component produced by discretionary policy changes, and a cyclical component produced by a fluctuating economy.

The structural budget balance is defined as the balance that would occur, given the existing structure of taxes, tax rates, and expenditure programs, if the economy were operating at its potential level of activity. It is based on estimates of revenues that would be generated at this level of activity and of the amounts that government would be spending on its existing programs.

The cyclical budget balance shows surpluses and deficits that are produced by the state of the economy. They result from the operation of the stabilizers built into the government budget. Built-in stabilizers respond automatically to changing economic conditions or cyclical fluctuations in the economy. Assume the starting point is a balanced budget. In a period of rapid economic growth, stabilizers will increase revenues and reduce expenditures, producing a budget surplus; the fiscal restraint will help to combat inflation. In a period of economic decline, stabilizers will cause revenues to fall and expenditures to rise, producing a budget deficit that will stimulate a declining economy. Automatic stabilizers are found on both the tax and expenditure sides of the budget. Within a given tax structure, revenues from personal and corporation taxes and from sales taxes depend on income, profit, and sales levels and will change as these variables change. Similarly, certain expenditures, such as unemployment insurance payments and the unemployment component of welfare payments, vary automatically with the state of health of the economy, increasing in a recession and decreasing in periods of rapid growth and falling unemployment.

The removal of the cyclical component from the actual budget balance leaves the structural budget balance, which is also referred to as the cyclically adjusted budget balance. This exercise is undertaken by the Department of Finance using a particular methodology it has developed. The department first determines the output gap, which is the difference between the potential and observed output. It identifies the government revenues and expenditures which are sensitive to cyclical changes in the economy, calculates the elasticities of each, and then applies the elasticities to determine revenues and expenditures at potential GDP.[6]

FIGURE 16-1: Actual and Structural[a] Budget Balance

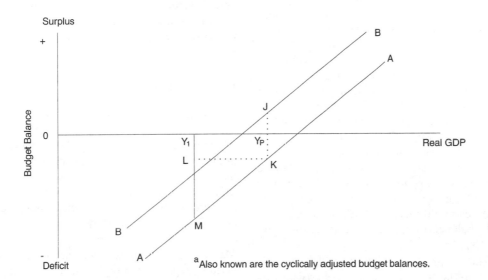

[a]Also known are the cyclically adjusted budget balances.

The structural balance does contain some non-discretionary elements. Changes in agricultural prices, for example, will change the amount of subsidies paid and affect the structural balance although they are clearly non-discretionary. Similarly, interest rate changes produce non-discretionary changes in public debt charges and affect the structural balance. The federal Department of Finance, therefore, views the structural balance excluding public debt charges as a more appropriate measure of the component of the budget over which the government exerts discretionary influence, particularly in the short run. The structural budget balance minus public debt charges is called the primary structural balance. This balance is considered to be the most appropriate measure of discretionary fiscal policy.

Figure 16-1 illustrates the concepts of cyclical, structural, and primary structural budget balances. In the diagram, Y_P measures the potential real GDP in any given period. The line AA represents a given government expenditure and tax structure (or budget structure) that produces a budget deficit of Y_PK when the economy is operating at its potential level. This is the structural budget balance. Ideally it should be zero when the economy reaches its potential, indicating a neutral impact of the budget on the economy (i.e., AA in that case would pass through Y_P). If the economy is in a recession, or is operating below its potential at Y_1, the total budget deficit will be Y_1M, of which LM is the cyclical component produced by the automatic stabilizers. Discretionary fiscal policy to combat the recession might consist of tax reductions, which would reduce revenues and increase the structural deficit. This would be illustrated as a downward shift in AA.

The line BB represents the budget structure when public debt charges are deducted from budget expenditures. At Y_P, therefore, the primary structural balance is shown as a surplus of Y_PJ. As explained earlier, the change in the primary structural balance is viewed as the most appropriate measure of discretionary fiscal policy.

Goals of Fiscal Policy

The general objective of fiscal policy is to manage supply and demand in the economy, using discretionary tax and expenditure measures, to prevent or to reduce the severity of fluctuations producing periods of economic decline and unemployment and periods of excessive demand and inflation. Fiscal policy tends to focus on three main indicators of the state of health of the economy: unemployment, inflation, and economic growth. The goals of fiscal policy are usually given as a high rate of employment, reasonably stable prices, and an adequate rate of economic growth. In an open economy, fiscal policy may also be directed towards achieving a viable balance of international trade and payments.

The commitment of the Canadian government to the achievement of these goals is evident from various statements found in budget speeches and position papers throughout the aftermath of World War II and the following decades. Attempts were made to determine the economy's potential for full employment, price stability, and economic growth and to establish specific levels for these goals. Such an attempt was made by the Economic Council of Canada in 1964. The council determined that, on the basis of the Canadian economy's potential, reasonable fiscal goals for the rest of the decade included an unemployment rate of 3 percent of the labour force, an increase in consumer price index of less than 2 percent, and an average annual increase in real GNP of 5 to 6 percent.[7]

Over the years, actual unemployment, price, and economic growth levels have fluctuated widely and have deviated significantly from the levels established earlier by the Economic Council of Canada. There has been considerable debate on the issue of achievable rates of employment and economic growth and degrees of price stability, and the expectations of feasible goals have tended to change over time as factors affecting the economy changed. For example, the Economic Council of Canada determined in 1989 that reasonable fiscal targets for the 1989-93 period were an unemployment rate of 5 to 7 percent, an inflation rate of 4 percent, and an increase in real gross domestic product of 3 to 4 percent.[8]

Employment

Full employment was an early goal of fiscal policy, spurred by the very high unemployment rates generated by the Depression of the 1930s. In fact, the aggregate unemployment rate came to be viewed as the leading indicator of economic conditions and the measure of the hardship inflicted upon society by a depressed economy.

Measuring Unemployment. Information on various aspects of employment and unemployment in the country are obtained from monthly surveys.[9] Employed persons are those who, during the survey period, did any work at all and therefore includes part-time workers. Unemployed persons are those who were without work, were looking for work, and were available for work. The unemployment rate represents the number of unemployed as a percentage of the labour force. The labour force consists of those members of the civilian population fifteen years of age and over who are employed or unemployed. Not included in the labour force are housewives, full-time students, and most retired people.

This measure may underestimate the extent of unemployment in the country because it does not include those who may have become discouraged by the lack of employment opportunities and are no longer seeking work. Another problem with this measure is under employment (also known as disguised or hidden unemployment). This concept covers those people who are employed, but are working at jobs below their skill qualifications because they cannot find work that makes full use of their skills (i.e., a trained economist working as a waiter in a restaurant).

In the early 1990s the official unemployment rate stood at about 11 percent. Statistics Canada estimated that if discouraged workers were included, the jobless rate would be one percentage point higher. If those working part-time because they could not find full-time jobs were considered unemployed, another 1.9 percent could be added to the official unemployment rate. And finally, if employees whose working-time was cut back temporarily (due to economic slowdown) were included, another .7 percent would be added. Combined, these measures of hidden unemployment would have made the official unemployment rate significantly higher than the official rate.[01]

Types of Unemployment. Unemployment may be classified into different types, reflecting the causes of unemployment. These classes are: cyclical unemployment, frictional unemployment, structural unemployment, seasonal unemployment, and voluntary unemployment. The need for, or design of, fiscal policy should be determined in accordance with the nature of the problem.

Cyclical unemployment is the product of inadequate aggregate demand during a recession, the downward phase of the business cycle. During periods of economic slowdown or decline, workers are laid off and new members entering the labour force have difficulties finding jobs. Fiscal measures to combat this type of unemployment should focus on stimulating aggregate demand and pulling the economy out of the recession.

Frictional unemployment includes those unemployed workers who are in the process of charging jobs and those who may have been fired and are looking for a new job. It is usually of short-run duration and can exist whether the economy is prospering or is in a slump. Such job turnover is viewed as part of the dynamics of the labour force and the economy and not a concern for fiscal policy.

Structural unemployment is the product of changes in the structure of the economy. It is of a long-term nature. Over time, consumers' tastes may change and consumer demands may shift. Unemployment is not caused by insufficient demand for goods and services, and therefore labour, but by shifts in demand. Furthermore, changes in technology and innovation bring new products and changes in the production process. Industries decline and new industries spring up producing changes in the demand for labour. Workers losing their jobs in declining industries may not be readily absorbed by new industries because they may not have the necessary skills. Advancements in technology may result in less labour intensive production and therefore job loss. Structural unemployment calls for specific fiscal measures, such as worker retraining to improve worker mobility and education and technical training to help prepare potential new entrants into the labour force for the changing job market.

Seasonal unemployment, as the term suggests, is the product of the seasonal nature of certain industries and occupations. These include farming, fishing, and some types of construction. Demand for workers in these industries tends to fluctuate with the climate, with peak employment in the summer months, and lower levels of employment during the winter. Fiscal measures to cope with seasonal unemployment could include short-term public or winter work programs which would provide employment for those temporarily laid off during the low employment season.

Voluntary unemployment consists of people who may claim to be seeking work but have no desire to work, and those who could find work but choose not to accept a job either because of low pay or location, or because it would leave them underemployed. As outlined in an earlier chapter, generous employment insurance benefits may contribute to voluntary and frictional unemployment.

The Natural Rate of Unemployment. The fiscal goal of full employment does not mean 100 percent of the labour force is employed. There will always be some voluntary, seasonal, frictional, or structural unemployment in an economy. The objective of fiscal policy is therefore not to try to reduce the unemployment rate to zero. Instead the objective should be to achieve some level that is judged to be consistent with a healthy economy and that can be achieved without aggravating inflation. This rate has been called the natural rate of unemployment or the non-accelerating inflation rate of unemployment (NAIRU).

Considerable attention had been devoted in the economic literature to the issue of a possible unemployment-inflation trade-off. The Phillips curve, developed by the economist A.W. Phillips, illustrates this trade-off as an inverse relationship between changes in unemployment and changes in prices. Phillips and his followers contended that when economic activity declines, producing an increase in unemployment, the rate of increase in prices falls as pressure on prices is reduced. A rapidly expanding economy with declining unemployment, on the other hand, builds inflationary pressures and prices spiral upward. According to the "accelerationalist theory," attempts to use expansionary fiscal policy to reduce unemployment below some minimum rate can succeed only in producing an accelerating rise in prices. Some estimates in the early 1980s placed the NAIRU for Canada in the range of 6.5 to 7.0 percent.[11]

The experience of the 1970s and the 1980s casts doubts on the existence of an unemployment-inflation trade-off as both unemployment and inflation moved together rather than inversely, to unprecedented high levels. Some argued that the trade-off continued to exist but that over time the Phillip's curve was shifting, indicating a trade-off at higher levels of both unemployment and inflation and a gradually increasing natural rate of unemployment.

The Unemployment Rate as an Economic Barometer. Unemployment has two primary adverse impacts: a production effect and a welfare impact. Their severity depends not only on the number of the unemployed but also on who they are. An increase in the unemployment of part-time and occasional workers will not have as severe an effect on either production or welfare as an increase in the unemployment of full-time workers. The welfare impact is also affected by the duration of unemployment, the number of wage-earners in the household, and their eligibility for employment insurance and other public welfare benefits. For instance, the unemployment of a worker in a multi-earner household will likely not be as drastic for household maintenance as the unemployment of the sole wage-earner in a family. In addition, unemployment may place serious social and psychological stress on the unemployed workers and their families. For all these reasons, high or increasing rates of unemployment continue to be of major concern, winning headlines in the news media and inspiring calls for government action.

Over the last two decades, however, a growing number of economists have been questioning whether the aggregate unemployment rate is a sensitive barometer of the state of the economy and of the economic stress of society. Reservations have also been expressed over using the unemployment rate as a measure of the degree of unused labour capacity. These questions and reservations have their foundations in a variety of factors and developments, ranging from the dynamics of technology and demography to the methods of measuring the labour force and unemployment.

Since World War II, each decade has witnessed a higher actual average unemployment rate than the one before. The average unemployment rate was 4.2 percent during the 1950-59 decade; 5.0 percent for 1960-69; 6.7 percent for 1970-79; 9.3 percent for 1980-89; and 10 percent for the period 1990-97. The unemployment rate reached double digit levels (up to 11.9 percent) in the early 1980s, fell to 7.5 percent by 1989 and then began to increase to reach 11.3 percent in 1992. It has not dropped below 7 percent since 1975. These figures seem to indicate a long-term upward drift in Canada's unemployment rate, part of which may be explained by institutional and demographic factors. Analysts argue that it is increasingly difficult for the economy to absorb the labour force and achieve a low unemployment rate because of several developments: rapid expansion of the labour force brought about by population growth and increasing participation rates; the changing composition of the work force with an increasing proportion of the female population and more part-time and occasional workers entering the labour market; and capital-intensive production.

The dynamics of the labour force, it has been argued, have reduced the significance traditionally placed on the aggregate unemployment rate as an economic indicator. A high unemployment rate does not necessarily signal job loss from economic decline. It may also reflect, in part, an increase in voluntary unemployment or a rapid influx of full-time or part-time workers stemming from population growth, an increase in the participation rate, or both. On the other hand, a decline in the unemployment rate does not necessarily indicate economic improvement. During periods of prolonged recession, some workers give up looking for work. This "discouraged worker" phenomenon is reflected in a reduction in the participation rate and tempers the unemployment rate as an indicator of unused labour capacity. In addition, some workers may work part-time only because they cannot find full-time jobs, so their numbers may really represent disguised unemployment. Some analysts contend that the unemployment rate remains relatively high even when the economy recovers from a slump and enters a period of prosperity because although workers who are only marginally attached to the labour force (part-time and occasional workers) are slow to leave it when economic conditions deteriorate, they are quick to join when the economy begins to improve. Therefore, as the business cycle swings upward, job creation is required not only to absorb those who could not find work during the recession but also to take up new labour force entrants and the marginally attached who re-enter the labour market.

Another consideration in using the unemployment rate as an economic barometer is that regional unemployment is a serious problem in Canada. A high national unemployment rate does not necessarily suggest that the entire economy is in a slump and is in need of national or across-the-board expansionary fiscal policies. When unemployment is mainly regional, it is more appropriate to direct fiscal measures to those areas experiencing the highest rates of unemployment.

Given these various developments, it is becoming increasingly difficult to define some aggregate rate of unemployment as a numerical goal for fiscal policy over the longer term. Changing technology, institutional and demographic factors, and the dynamics of the labour market suggest that no single magic number exists for guiding fiscal policy.

Therefore, in addition to the official unemployment rate, Statistics Canada calculates and publishes a number of supplemental unemployment rates and measures of unemployment, as well as participation rates, and changes in unemployment and productivity, or output per worker. These include unemployment rates by province, age, gender, industry, and occupation. Other statistics show unemployment by duration, by type of work sought, by job-search methods, and by reason for leaving the last job. Such data can be helpful for designing strategies and developing programs to increase employment. In addition, an official employment rate, which measures the percentage of the population fifteen years and over who actually have jobs is also calculated. The Department of Finance, in its analysis of the labour market as an indicator of economic conditions, examines these variables along with the unemployment rate, with particular emphasis on employment growth and the rate of increase in employment, or number of jobs created by the economy. While a high and persistent unemployment rate would indicate an inadequately performing economy, in other aspects such as growth of employment and output per worker the economy could be performing reasonably well.

Prices

Inflation is defined as an increase in the general level of prices of goods and services. Price increases may be small, moderate, or severe; they may be abrupt or develop slowly; they may be short term or prolonged. A small annual increase in the general price level is usually acceptable, as it is extremely difficult in a dynamic, complex, and open economy to have stable prices in the sense of a fixed general price level. The changing structures of supply and demand, along with inflexibility and imperfection in the market, contribute to fluctuations and a general upward movement in prices. Traditionally, economists interpreted the fiscal policy objective of reasonable stable prices to mean an annual increase in the general price level of less than 2 percent. But, as in the case of full employment, the minimum rate of inflation achievable appeared to have moved upwards during the 1970s and 1980s decades.

Measuring Inflation. Statistics Canada compiles several measures of price changes; some relate to specific categories of items, while others are more comprehensive. They include the industrial product price index, the raw materials price index, the farm input price index, the construction price index, the gross domestic product deflator, and the consumer price index. Although none of these measures purports to be a cost of living index, the one most commonly used as a general indicator of

inflation and implicitly as a measure of changes in the purchasing power of a dollar is the consumer price index (CPI).[12]

The CPI is defined as a measure of price change obtained by comparing through time the cost of a basket of goods and services purchased by a target population. The basket contains commodities of unchanging quality and quantity, and therefore the index reflects only the price movement. Statistics Canada collects data on the prices of most of the commodities in this basket on a monthly basis. The basket reflects consumer spending patterns based on surveys, which are periodically updated. To calculate the index, prices in any given period are compared to prices in an earlier year or base year. Current prices of goods and services are expressed as a percentage of the base year prices. For example, if the base year price of a good was $1.50 and the current price is $1.80, the price index for that good would be $(1.80 \div 1.50)\ 100$ or 120, indicating that the price has risen 20 percent. The base year would be designated as equal to 100. Besides an all-item index or general CPI, Statistics Canada calculates a price index for major groups of items including food, housing, clothing, transportation, health care, recreation, and tobacco and alcohol products.

Types of Inflation. Inflation may be classified by type, reflecting the factors which cause increases in the general level of prices. Inflation may be identified as demand-pull, cost-push, structural, sellers, imported, or government induced, or may result from a combination of these factors.

Demand-pull inflation may result as demand increases when the economy is at or near full employment, and it is not possible to increase supply to meet the increasing demand. Prices will consequently rise in response to the excess demand. Rising prices may lead to workers and their unions demanding higher wages, which leads to rising costs of production and further pressure on prices. Or the initiative for increased wages may come from the labour market, as labour shortages appear at or near full employment, or unions pursue higher wages for their members, resulting in cost-push inflation. The rising costs of production are passed to the consumer as higher prices (unless absorbed by productivity increases). Once prices and/or wages begin to rise, an inflationary wage-price spiral becomes self-perpetuating.

Structural inflation may result from changes in the structure of demand. If the shifts in demand are more rapid than the rate at which resources can be shifted from one industry to another, bottlenecks may appear where the demand exceeds the supply of various goods and services and prices begin to rise. Some economists have argued that firms frequently increase prices in a period of shortages, and if the commodity is a primary input in the production of many goods and services (i.e., petroleum), their costs of production and prices may rise. This is a form of sellers' or administered price increase.

An open economy, relying heavily on foreign trade, could import inflation. If prices of imports of consumer goods rise, this will be reflected in an increase in the consumer price index. If the imports consist of inputs for production, costs of producing domestic goods will rise producing cost-push inflation.

The government itself might induce an inflationary spiral through taxation or by raising the prices of public goods subjected to user charges. An increase in sales and excise taxes is generally shifted to the consumer in the form of higher prices. The resulting price increase, along with increases in the personal income tax, results in lower real income for the consumer/worker, who in turn may press for higher wages and salaries initiating cost-push inflation.

Price Stability. Although some members and groups of society may benefit from inflation, there is a general public fear of it for the costs it is perceived to inflict upon individuals, so-ciety, and the economy. A high rate of inflation may have serious and inequitable effects on the distribution of income and wealth. People with fixed income and assets suffer more than those whose income and asset values increase along with prices. Inflation benefits debtors at the expense of creditors, discourages saving, and affects contracts and investments. It contributes to stress and confrontation in industrial relations as workers seek wage increases in order to maintain their real income levels. It may have adverse consequences on a country's trade and balance of payments, producing speculative behaviour that leads to a further acceleration of prices — galloping inflation — and threatening a country's social and economic stability.

Concern over inflation goes back many centuries, and history attests to the devastating effects of hyperinflation on national economies. Until recently, industrialized countries, such as Canada and the United States, experienced relative price stability. Direct wage and price regulation provided price stability during World War II, and fiscal policies of increased taxes tended to dampen the inflation that might otherwise have arisen with the outbreak of the Korean War in the early 1950s. Between 1952 and 1965, the annual average increase in the Canadian CPI was 1.4 percent, and in only four years during that period did it exceed 2 percent. Beginning in the late 1960s, however, the annual increase in the inflation rate began to accelerate, and it reached double-digit levels in 1974, 1975, 1980, 1981, and 1982. Having peaked at 12.4 percent in 1981, the inflation rate fell to 5.7 percent in 1983 and remained in the 4 to 5 percent range for the remainder of the decade. In 1992 it fell to 1.5 percent and remained at the traditional goal level of less than 2 percent into 1998.[13] During the 1970s and 1980s when inflation was high, the goal of price stability like that of unemployment was subject to re-examination and redefinition. It was suggested that an acceptable rate of inflation be determined in relation to price performance in other countries. Such an inflation goal would be based on a relative standard, comparing price changes in Canada with those in other industrial countries, particularly its major trading partners. An acceptable rate of inflation, it was contended, would be a rate comparable with that of those partners. But as the rate of inflation dropped during the 1990s, the traditionally accepted goal of a rate of increase in prices of less than 2 percent annually appeared to again become the standard.

Many economists and policymakers contend that inflation is acceptable if it is maintained at a low or moderate rate. A notable exception was John Crow, the Governor of the Bank of Canada in the 1980s. In 1988, Mr. Crow announced that the goal of the Bank's monetary policy was price stability defined as a zero rate of inflation. Mr. Crow argued that accepting a specified level of inflation only entrenches inflation and that any increase beyond a set target requires considerably more effort and cost to pull back than would be the case if zero inflation, or true price stability, was the target. In his words, "a commitment to a steady inflation rate is ultimately not credible."[14] Throughout 1989 and 1990, Mr. Crow consistently voiced this view and continued to maintain high interest rates in the face of severe criticism that his policies would drive the economy into recession. But despite Crow's pronouncements and corresponding anti-inflationary monetary policy, the rate of inflation began to increase in 1989 and 1990, raising questions about the attainability of zero inflation. Furthermore, it was difficult to understand Crow's insistence on a zero inflation target in a period when federal taxes on goods were themselves causing prices to increase. For example, in 1989 the government increased excises on alcohol, tobacco, and gasoline and raised the manufacturers' sales tax from 12 to 13.5 percent. These taxes are all reflected in the CPI.

The high inflation rate in the 1970s and early 1980s in Canada, as well as in other countries, arose partly from traditional inflation-producing factors, such as low productivity and rising production costs, but even more from new influences, such as shortages of energy and minerals. The creation of international cartels for the sale of energy and basic materials produced rapidly escalating costs and prices in spite of depressed economic conditions. A realistic goal in this situation was to prevent an already high rate of inflation from rising further and gradually to reduce it from the double-digit level that had been reached. This goal was achieved, in part by a monetary policy of very high interest rates and in part by the easing of international causes of inflation. The annual increase in the CPI declined to 4.4 percent in 1984 and remained in the 4 percent range for the next four years, suggesting that a 4 percent inflation target was a realistic target for Canada going into the 1990s. A severe recession from 1990 to 1994, however, combined with international price stability and increasing global competition, exemplified by the Canada-United States Free Trade Agreement, helped reduce the rate of inflation to between .2 and 2.1 percent during the period 1992-1997.

Economic Growth

One of the features in the evolution of fiscal policy was the turn from preoccupation with short-run fluctuations — cycles — in economic activity to long-run economic growth. It was expected that the maintenance of economic growth at a relatively stable rate would preclude wide cyclical fluctuations.

Measures of Economic Growth. The general measure of economic growth is real gross domestic product (GDP). The traditional goal of fiscal policy was to maintain a balance between the actual rate of economic growth and the potential rate of growth. Potential economic growth is described as the increase in the capacity of the economy to produce goods and services and is the maximum production of goods and services the economy can sustain. The potential growth rate or supply capacity is determined by a number of factors, including the rate of technological development, the rate of capital formation, and the quantity and quality of the labour force and natural resources. Actual growth can exceed potential, but only temporarily. When demand and production persistently exceed the economy's potential, pressures leading to inflation are created in the goods and services market and the labour market.

The method of balancing actual with potential growth is to maintain a level of aggregate demand that matches supply capacity. A balance ensures full utilization of resources. Excess demand generates inflationary pressures, while insufficient demand results in unemployment and idle capacity. In addition to matching actual and potential growth, it is equally important to attempt to promote and expand potential growth, without which the economy would be stagnant with depressed levels of per capita output and income. Policies designed to stimulate research and development, technological innovation, capital formation, and education and training of the labour force contribute to the expansion of the growth potential of the economy.

The Goals for Economic Growth. In the early 1960s, the Economic Council of Canada — based on its projections of the determinants of economic growth and given 3 percent unemployment as a goal — estimated Canada's potential annual growth rate for the decade to be between 5 and 6 percent increase in real GDP. During the 1970s, the potential growth rate was established at 4 to 5 percent. The actual rate of economic growth in the 1960 decade averaged 5.5 percent per year, while during the 1970 decade the annual average rate of increase was 4.7 percent. These actual rates were close to the estimated potential rates of growth. For the period 1981 to 1990, the council estimated annual poten-

tial growth from 2.7 percent (low potential estimate) to 3 percent (high potential estimate) with a non-inflationary level of unemployment of 4 to 5 percent.[15] The decline in the projection for the 1980s compared to that of the previous decade was attributed to an expected slow growth in population, productivity, and investment. The Canadian economy however, exceeded the projections for growth during the latter part of the 1980s, following the earlier recession, and the gap between the potential and actual figures disappeared. The average annual increase in real GDP from 1983 to 1988 was 4.5 percent. This rise produced a decline in the unemployment rate, from 11.8 to 7.8 percent, and a relatively constant rate of inflation of between 4 and 5 percent. The 1990 budget projected the potential growth of the economy for 1990-95 period to average 3.4 percent per year, aided by the Canada-U.S. Free Trade Agreement, by deregulation of the economy, and by tax reform, all of which were expected to create increased investment opportunities in Canada.[16] In effect, however, the recession beginning in 1990 produced a fall in real GDP in 1990 and 1991 and then it began to increase. The average rate of increase in real GDP for the six-year period of 1992-97 was 2.4 percent. The actual growth rate of the economy was therefore well below its estimated potential during the 1990s.

Summary

The federal government's fiscal position is presented in three different budgets. The administrative budget and the consolidated cash budget are based on the public accounts and serve financial administrative purposes. The national accounts budget is used for fiscal policy analysis. The surplus or deficit in this budget can be separated into a cyclical component and a structural component. The former shows the balance on the budget produced by the state of the economy. The latter shows the budget balance that would prevail if the economy was healthy and operating at an average level of activity. It is through the national accounts budget and the structural balance that the budget and budget policy may be analyzed for their effects on employment, prices, and economic growth.

The pursuit of the fiscal policy goals of full employment, stable prices, and economic growth requires a definition of these goals. Over time, however, the levels of employment, price stability, and growth attainable appear to vary. The rate of unemployment (the natural rate of unemployment) deemed acceptable as full employment has been increasing with each decade since the 1950s from 3 percent to anywhere between 5 and 8 percent by the 1990s. Traditionally, the rate of inflation defined as an acceptable level of price stability was set at 2 percent or less per year. Double-digit inflation in the 1970s and 1980s appeared to place the traditional level of price stability out of reach. Developments during the 1990 decade, however, have returned the annual inflation rate to less than 2 percent.

The goal of economic growth is viewed in terms of the actual rate of growth and the potential rate of growth of the economy. The fiscal objective is to attempt to balance the actual with the potential, as well as to raise the potential growth rate.

NOTES

[1] J.M. Keynes, *General Theory of Employment, Interest and Money* (1936; reprint, London: Macmillan and Co. 1960).

[2] The fundamentals of macroeconomic theory can be found in introductory macroeconomic textbooks. A more advanced analysis of macroeconomics and various developments in the theory, including supply-side economics and rational expectations theory, is presented in most intermediate macroeconomics texts.

[3] The multiplier is given as $1/(1 - b)$ where b is the marginal propensity to consume (defined as the change in consumption from an additional dollar of disposable income). For any given change in government expenditures, the change in total expenditures will be $1/(1 - b)$ times the change in expenditure. The tax multiplier is smaller and is shown as $b/(1 - b)$. For a change in government expenditures matched by a change in taxes, the multiplier equals one. This is known as the balanced budget theorem. A discussion of various multipliers is contained in most macroeconomics texts.

[4] For a discussion of supply-side economics, see E. Raboy, ed., Essays in *Supply-Side Economics* (Washington, D.C.: Institute for Research on the Economics of Taxation, 1982); M. Evans, *Truth about Supply-Side Economics* (New York: Basic Books, 1983); and P.C. Roberts, *The Supply-Side Revolution* (Cambridge: Harvard University Press, 1984).

[5] For an explanation of the difference between the budget on a national accounts basis and the public accounts budget, see Canada, Department of Finance, *Budget Plan*, February 18, 1997, pp.121-124.

[6] An explanation of the methodology employed by the Department of Finance to calculate structural balances can be obtained from the Fiscal Policy Division, Department of Finance, Ottawa.

[7] Economic Council of Canada, *First Annual Review, Economic Goals for Canada to 1970* (Ottawa, 1964). For other early discussions of fiscal policy goals, see T.N. Brewis, et al., *Canadian Economic Policy* (Toronto: MacMillan of Canada, 1961); Canada, The Royal Commission on Canada's Economic Prospects, *Final Report* (Ottawa, 1957); and John J. Deutsch, et al., *The Canadian Economy: Selected Readings* (Toronto: MacMillan of Canada, 1962).

[8] Economic Council of Canada, Legacies, *Twenty-Sixth Annual Review 1989* (Ottawa: Supply and Services, 1989), p.67.

[9] For a description of labour market concepts and of the labour force survey, see Statistics Canada, *The Labour Force* (cat. 71-001, monthly).

[10] Statistics Canada, *Perspectives on Labour and Income*, Winter, 1992.

[11] Economic Council of Canada, *Lean Times, Policies and Constraints, Nineteenth Annual Review 1982* (Ottawa: Supply and Services, 1982), pp.11-13.

[12] For a description of the Canadian consumer price index, see Statistics Canada, *The Consumer Price Index* (cat.62-001, monthly).

[13] Canada, Department of Finance, *Economic Reference Tables*, August 1996.

[14] John Crow, *The Work of Canadian Monetary Policy*, Eric J. Hanson Memorial Lecture University of Alberta, January 18, 1988.

[15] Economic Council of Canada, *Seventeenth Annual Review* (Ottawa, 1980), pp.49-55.

[16] Canada, Department of Finance, *The Budget*, February 20, 1990 (Ottawa), pp.51-55.

CHAPTER 17

Application of Fiscal Policy in Canada

The Keynesian approach to economic stabilization was formally accepted by Canada in 1945 with the issue of a policy paper committing the government to the maintenance of high levels of employment and income in the economy. This chapter examines the federal government's application of discretionary fiscal policy for economic stabilization. The examination is from both a macroeconomic and a microeconomic perspective.

The macroeconomic indicator of fiscal policy is the budget balance on a national accounts basis, employing the three budget balance concepts discussed in the previous chapter:

- The actual budget balance;
- The structural budget balance, also called the cyclically adjusted budget balance, which is the actual budget balance with the cyclical component removed; in other words, it is the balance that would occur, given the existing structure of taxes, tax rates, and expenditure programs, if the economy were operating at its potential level of activity;
- The primary structural budget balance, which is the structural balance minus public debt charges. This balance, and changes therein, is viewed as the most appropriate indicator of discretionary fiscal policy.

Actual, structural, and primary structural balances are presented in dollar amounts and as percentages of gross domestic product. The actual budget balance as a percentage of GDP provides an indication of the impact of the fiscal system on the economy. The differences between the actual budget balance and the structural budget balance suggests the effects of automatic stabilizers. The direction of discretionary fiscal policy is signified by the change in the primary structural balance between adjacent years, and the size of the movement provides a gauge of the relative strength of the impact on the economy of discretionary fiscal policy. Movement towards a higher surplus or lower deficit implies a contractionary or restraining impact on the economy, while a movement towards a lower surplus or a higher deficit means an expansionary stance in discretionary policy. (Keep in mind, however, that structural balances are used only as rough indicators of the shifts in the government's fiscal stance.)

The microeconomic approach to fiscal policy analysis involves an examination of specific fiscal measures, such as the introduction of new taxes, changes in existing taxes, and changes in expenditure programs. This approach is used to supplement the macroeconomic indicators in the analysis of fiscal policy in recognition of the fact that fiscal impact is not independent of the mix of discretionary tax and expenditure changes.

Two periods are identified for purposes of analysis, namely the period from 1953 to 1974 and the period since 1975 as illustrated in Figures 17-1 to 17-4. The first period featured attempts to apply discretionary Keynesian-based fiscal policies to counter the business cycle and promote economic growth.

The second period commenced with the first of a continuous string of fiscal deficits, regardless of the state of the economy, which eventually left the government with little or no flexibility to pursue counter-cyclical fiscal policy. Before analyzing the economic conditions and government policies during these two periods, a brief background of the development and use of Keynesian fiscal policy is presented.

Background

Before 1930, the doctrine of annually balanced budgets was firmly entrenched in Canadian economic thought. Taxes were regarded as a means of financing expenditure, and as expenditure changed, they were adjusted to balance the budget. There was no recognition of the possibility of the discretionary use of government expenditure and taxation to stabilize the economy. From the period 1935 to 1939, however, under the influence of the leading economists of the time, Canadian governments began to experiment with policies to stimulate economic activity and employment to end the Depression.[1]

Thus, at the beginning of the Depression, government policy was to attempt to maintain a balanced budget. Despite tax increases, government revenues fell as income and production declined. Accordingly, attempts were made to hold down expenditures. Federal, provincial, and municipal governments reduced their spending between 1930 and 1933, and this move, coupled with high taxes, served to aggravate the economic decline. Even after the emergence of fiscal policy theory in the latter part of the decade, there appeared to be some reluctance on the part of the Canadian federal government to pursue expansionary fiscal measures actively.

At the outbreak of World War II in 1939, Canada was still experiencing a relatively high unemployment rate (12 percent). But the problems of unemployment and idle productive facilities disappeared in the war econ-

omy. As productive factors and materials were diverted to the war effort, the shortage of consumer goods and materials began to place pressure on prices. The CPI increased by 18 percent between 1939 and late 1941. The Canadian government's answer to the rising prices was a wage and price freeze, which succeeded in containing inflation.[2]

Concern about the problems of the wartime economy did not, however, reduce concern about the problems that had plagued pre-war Canada. It was anticipated that when the hostilities ended, the difficulties of the Depression would return and added to them would be the dislocations the war had created in the economy. In 1945, in a policy white paper entitled *Employment and Income*, the Canadian government officially accepted "a high and stable level of employment and income, and thereby higher standards of living, as a major aim of government policy."[3] The white paper implicitly embraced Keynesian philosophy, proposed the use of the budget for purposes of fiscal policy, and subscribed to planned budgetary surpluses and deficits.

The difficulties of the post-war reconstruction period did not arise with the severity that had been envisaged. Reconversion took place rapidly, and the demand for consumer and durable goods that had been repressed during the war period not only kept productive facilities operating at capacity but provided for rapid expansion and a high level of employment.[4]

The primary concern in the immediate post-war period was inflation as consumer demand that had been pent up during the war was released and tended to outstrip supply.

The government's response to these inflationary pressures was to remove wartime price controls only gradually. Taxes were reduced during this period. Although tax reduction during a period of inflation may appear contrary to accepted fiscal policy doctrine, taxes during the war had been exceedingly high relative to pre-war levels and there was considerable public pressure to have them re-

TABLE 17-1: Budget Balances 1962-1996 (National Accounts Basis)

Year	Actual	Structural	Primary-Structural
	($ million)		
1962	-528	-444	30
1963	-303	-263	222
1964	330	233	721
1965	517	264	789
1966	201	-161	373
1967	-108	-177	344
1968	-36	-163	437
1969	994	739	1,236
1970	247	554	1,157
1971	-139	58	594
1972	-530	-323	268
1973	434	99	1,187
1974	1,268	1,579	2,852
1975	-3,823	-3,930	-2,250
1976	-3,337	-3,970	-1,826
1977	-7,343	-8,179	-5,772
1978	-10,854	-11,400	-8,114
1979	-9,383	-9,950	-5,233
1980	-10,000	-10,748	-4,618
1981	-7,315	-7,670	1,564
1982	-20,281	-15,429	-3,754
1983	-24,993	-21,017	-9,000
1984	-30,024	-27,014	-11,840
1985	-31,424	-30,810	-12,356
1986	23,617	-23,707	-4,114
1987	-20,704	-23,306	-2,493
1988	-19,166	-23,927	252
1989	-21,055	-26,049	3,174
1990	-25,947	-26,960	6,041
1991	-30,398	-24,290	7,185
1992	-29,217	-21,313	7,964
1993	-35,131	-29,169	-654
1994	-28,442	-26,115	2,755
1995	-26,566	-24,239	10,204
1996	-15,938	-12,892	20,003

Source: Canada, Department of Finance, Fiscal Reference Tables, October 1997, p.46.

duced once hostilities had ended. Government policy was to gradually reduce those taxes considered to be impeding work and production but otherwise to maintain taxes as high as reasonably practical in attempts to dampen aggregate demand. Combined with large reductions in defence spending, this policy produced large budgetary surpluses. Given the economic conditions during this period of reconstruction and adjustment, the government's fiscal policy can be considered appropriate.

The beginning of the Korean War brought rapidly rising prices. The CPI jumped 10.6 percent during 1951, partly because of the increase in government defence spending and partly because of public fear of wartime shortages, which brought a large increase in demand for consumer durables. The government responded with a policy of retrenchment in non-defence expenditure and substantial tax increases to finance the defence build-up. The tax changes included extension of the excise tax to a large number of commodities and an increase in existing excises; a 20 percent defence surcharge on corporate and personal income taxes; an increase in the manufacturers' sales tax from 8 to 10 percent; and deference of depreciation on capital expenditures. In addition, the government attempted to restrain the buying public with a policy restricting consumer credit. These measures can be viewed as textbook fiscal policy to combat demand-pull inflationary pressures. These discretionary measures combined with the automatic stabilizers to produce budget surpluses and a contractionary fiscal tone, contributing to bringing inflation under control.

After the Korean War, following a short period of adjustment, the Canadian economy prospered. Large actual surpluses were recorded, but they were primarily cyclical, produced by a rapidly growing economy.

Fiscal Policy 1955-1974

The macroeconomic indicator of the direction and strength of discretionary fiscal policy is the primary structural balance expressed as a percentage of potential GDP.[5] Movements in this indicator are illustrated in Figure 17-1 along with the actual budget balance and the structural budget balance. Figure 17-2 plots the trends in the main economic indicators — the increase in real GDP, the inflation rate (changes in the consumer price index), and the unemployment rate. An analysis of the trends in Figure 17-1 in conjunction with the trends in Figure 17-2 serve to indicate the appropriateness of discretionary, anti-cyclical fiscal policy within the context of economic conditions.

The 1955-1974 period was characterized by major fluctuations in real GDP, unemployment, and prices. The two periods of most concern, however, were the recession from 1957 to 1962 and the period of rising unemployment and inflation beginning in the late 1960s. As illustrated in Figure 17-2, economic growth dropped dramatically in 1957 and remained low until 1961, while unemployment reached 7 percent. Price increases remained relatively low, and to a degree the recession produced the Phillips curve trade-off between prices and unemployment.

Recession: 1957-1962

The government's first major challenge in anti-recession fiscal policy occurred with the recession that began in 1957 and was to continue into the 1960s. The recession featured a major decline in the rate of increase in real GDP and a rate of unemployment that climbed to 7 percent, a comparatively high rate for the period.

Fiscal policy fluctuated during this recession, partly because of a misreading of economic conditions. The structural balance (as a percentage of GNP) tended to exert an expansionary effect, then a contractionary one, and then another expansionary influence (see Fig-

FIGURE 17-1: Budget Balances, 1953-1974
Percentage of GDP[a]

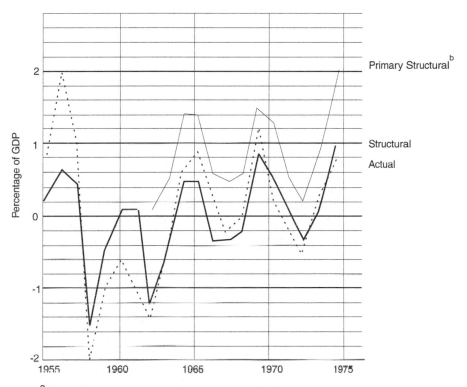

a Actual balances are shown as a percentage of actual GDP. Structural
and primary structural balances are shown as percentages of potential GDP.

b Primary structural balances are not avoidable prior to 1962.

Source: Canada, Department of Finance, *Economic Review,* April 1980; and
Quarterly Economic Review, Annual Reference Tables, June 1990.

ure 17-1). This tone of fiscal policy can also be observed in the specific measures that were introduced. In 1958, discretionary measures consisted mostly of expenditure increases for social security, economic development, housing and community works, and a winter works employment program. Restrictive fiscal measures were introduced in 1959 with an increase in personal and corporation taxes of 2 percent. It was clearly the wrong policy for a relatively stagnant economy with an unemployment rate of 7 percent. The return to expansionary measures in 1960 included a reduction in the corporate income tax, a repeal of the 4 percent surtax on investment income and of the 7.5 percent excise tax on automobiles, a policy of double depreciation for new industry locating in areas of chronic unemployment, and incentives for scientific research and productivity improve-

FIGURE 17-2: Economic Indicators, 1953-1974

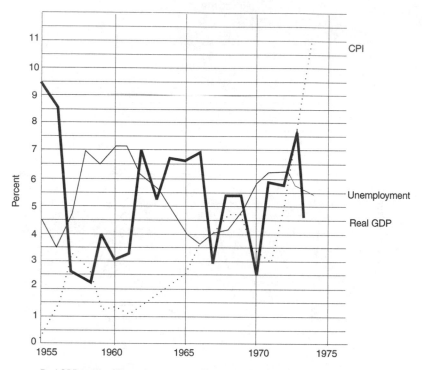

Real GDP and the CPI are shown as annual percentage changes.
Unemployment is shown as the unemployment rate.

Source: Canada, Department of Finance, *Economic Review,* August 1980;
and *Quarterly Economic Review, Annual References Tables,* June 1990.

ment. It should be noted that towards the end of this period, rather than relying primarily on expenditure policies in its fiscal policy mix, the government began to place greater stress on taxation, particularly in the form of tax incentives to industry.

Unemployment and Inflation

Following the recession, the economy entered a period of prosperity, when the increase in real GDP reached levels of 6 and 7 percent. Problems began to appear in 1968 as unemployment rose over 4 percent and climbed to over 6 percent by 1972. Price increases reached 4.5 percent annually between 1968 and 1969, dropped over the next two years, and then shot up dramatically to almost 11 percent in 1974. The reduction in the primary structural balance from 1969 to 1972 reflects expansionary fiscal policy. The government decided to place priority on unemployment with its fiscal policy, as indicated by the fall in the primary structural balance, and to fight inflation with a program of voluntary wage-price controls. During the period of these controls, inflation was reduced but returned with a vengeance in 1972. The government responded with anti-inflationary measures which produced large increases in the primary structural balance as shown in Table 17-1 and Figure 17-1.

The selective expansionary measures between 1969 and 1972 included removal of the 3 percent surtax on the personal and corporate income taxes; reduction of the personal income tax by 3 percent and the corporate income tax by 7 percent for 1972; removal of the 15 percent excise tax on radios, television sets, and stereos; and elimination of the income tax on persons with taxable incomes of $500 or less. Expenditure programs that were expanded included personnel training, housing, grants and loans to provincial and municipal governments to finance job-creating public works programs, and grants and incentives to industry to locate in depressed areas to alleviate regional unemployment problems. By 1973, the employment growth rate had reached 5 percent and unemployment had begun to fall, but serious inflation loomed on the horizon and the government turned to restrictive anti-inflationary measures.

The inflationary surge that began in 1973 pushed the CPI up by 10.9 percent in 1974. Inflation, which was practically worldwide, was rooted in international developments including rapid increases in aggregate demand for many primary products, shortages caused by supply disruptions in agricultural markets, and the decision of the international oil cartel to raise prices substantially.[6] As the effects of these developments began to be reflected in rising consumer prices, inflationary expectations strengthened. Workers expecting persistent price increases were demanding higher and higher wages and salaries in attempts to protect their real incomes.

The government's announced policy in 1973 was to attempt to combat both unemployment and inflation. Emphasis was placed on tax reductions designed to stimulate output and employment and, at the same time, to

ease the pressures on prices. Personal exemptions were increased, the personal income tax was reduced by 5 percent, the manufacturers' sales tax on children's clothing and footwear was abolished, and tariffs on a wide range of imports were reduced by an average of 5 percent. The Minister of Finance expressed the hope that the tax reductions would be taken into account as representing increases in disposable income during negotiations on wage settlements.

Despite the announced tax reductions in 1973, the actual and structural budgets showed increased surpluses by the end of 1973 and 1974. They were partly the result of the tax reform introduced in 1972. It had broadened the income tax base (including a tax on capital gains), and certain tax increases did not come into effect until 1973 and 1974. While the selective tax changes may have contributed to the drop in unemployment in 1973 and 1974, the drag of the increased budgetary surpluses did little to stem inflation.

Overall, the Canadian government's application of fiscal policy during 1947 to 1974 followed the Keynesian remedy and can be viewed as reasonably appropriate, given the economic conditions that prevailed. In terms of achieving stated fiscal goals, the economy's overall performance for this period proved much better than the record for the years following 1974, albeit the problems of the later period were considerably more complex. It could be contended that the economy of 1947 to 1974 more closely resembled the trade-off pattern illustrated by the Phillips curve, characterized by periods of unemployment or inflationary pressures and periods of reasonably low unemployment coupled with reasonably stable prices. Traditional fiscal policy is more readily applicable in such a pattern as compared to the economic conditions that prevailed during the later 1970s and the early 1980s. Indeed, although the actual federal budget balance fluctuated between surpluses and deficits during the 1947-72 period, the net balance was close to zero over the period as a whole. This pattern was to change after 1974 when the government began incurring continuous and substantial budgetary deficits as recorded by the actual and structural budget balances.

Fiscal Policy 1975-1998

The economy of this period was characterized by two major recessions at the beginning of the 1980 and 1990 decades and a high rate of unemployment. The first recession also featured a high rate of inflation and unemployment, which was contrary to the Phillips theory of a trade-off between the two.

The implementation of fiscal policy proved to be difficult during this period.[7] The year 1974 saw the last actual budgetary surplus until 1998, and the continuous deficits that followed hampered the government's ability and flexibility to actively pursue discretionary fiscal policy.

Inflation and Wage-Price Controls: 1975-1978

The year 1976 witnessed the beginning of a declining economy as the rate of increase in real GDP began a downward trend which bottomed out in 1982. At the same time the rise in the consumer price index of 10.8 percent in 1974 and 1975, along with rising unemployment, brought a major dilemma for fiscal policy. The government analyzed the inflation as being of the cost-push variety, arising from escalating domestic costs of production in an underemployed economy. Low productivity gains combined with relatively high labour compensation tended to put pressure on prices.

The focus of discretionary fiscal policy was on supply and featured tax incentives to stimulate output and employment. They included an investment tax credit against the corporation income tax equal to 5 percent of investment in new buildings, machinery, and equipment (increased to 7.5 percent and 10

percent in designated areas of chronically high unemployment); a 3 percent deduction on inventories held at the beginning of a corporation's fiscal year for profit calculation; and a reduction in the manufacturers' sales tax from 12 to 9 percent. The substantial drop in the primary structural balance between 1976 and 1978 was partly attributable to these discretionary tax reductions and partly to major increases in government program spending, which averaged 12.4 percent annually. (Recall that only program spending appears in the primary structural budget.)

While fiscal policy was geared to unemployment, the government attempted to cope with inflation with wage-price controls. In late 1975 the government adopted a program of mandatory wage and price regulation to bring inflation under control. (See appendix to this chapter.) It was expected that continued efforts to stimulate output, combined with an improving world economy, would gradually reduce unemployment, while wage and price regulations, which would continue for three years, would bring inflation under control. From 1975 to 1976, inflation was reduced from 10.8 to approximately 7.5 percent. Despite this reduction, the government continued the wage-price control program and resisted pressures to introduce massive temporary expenditure programs to combat unemployment, which began to reach postwar highs exceeding 8 percent.

Stagflation: 1979-1983

Faced with slow economic growth, high unemployment, and double-digit inflation — a combination called stagflation — the government announced a fiscal policy of balancing restraint to combat inflation with measures to promote economic growth to reduce unemployment. Successive budget speeches also hammered at the need to bring government expenditure growth under control and to reduce the size of the deficit. Revenue-raising measures included a corporate income surtax and a tax on petroleum, natural gas,

FIGURE 17-3: Budget Balances, 1975-1996
Percentage of GDP[a]

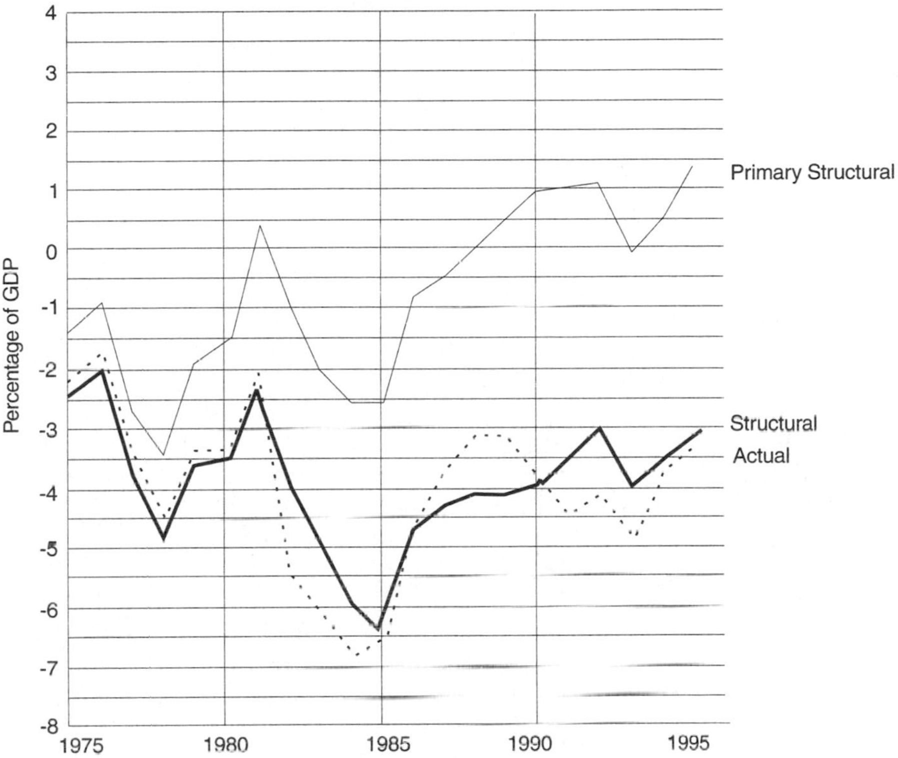

[a] Actual balances are percentage of actual GDP. Structural and primary structural balances are percentage of potential GDP.

Source: Canada, Department of Finance, *Fiscal References Tables,* October 1997, p.47.

and gas liquids. The latter tax was to yield almost $3 billion in annual revenues and contributed to the substantial reduction recorded in the primary structural deficit by 1981. The restrictive impact had little effect on prices as inflation rose to over 12 percent, while unemployment remained at 7.5 percent.

A dramatic fall in real GDP by over 3 percent in 1982, combined with a pay restraint on the federal public service, finally broke the inflationary spiral but pushed unemployment to over 12 percent by 1983. Increases in pub-

lic servants' wages were limited to 6 percent in 1983 and 5 percent in 1984. (Many provincial governments followed suit.) This "6 and 5" pay restraint was expected not only to save the federal government about $500 million, but also to lead the private sector to restrain wage demands voluntarily and help control cost-push inflation pressures. (See appendix to this chapter.) At the same time, the government announced expenditure initiatives and tax reductions to stimulate employment. A special recovery program planned over four

FIGURE 17-4: Economic Indicators, 1975-1995

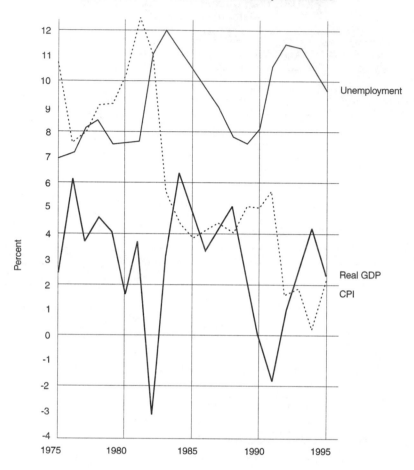

Real GDP and the CPI are shown as annual percentage change.
Unemployment is shown as the unemployment rate.

Source: Canada, Department of Finance, *Economic References Tables*, August 1996.

years offered $2.2 billion for capital projects and $2.4 billion of special incentives for private investment. Other discretionary measures included more attractive depletion provisions for the mining industry; lower energy taxes; additional funds to spur housing construction; an additional $710 million over two years for new expanded employment initiatives, including retraining programs and student sum-

mer employment; and increased support for research and development. These expansionary measures increased the primary structural deficit to almost $12 billion or 2.5 percent of GDP by 1984 and, combined with rising public debt charges and automatic stabilizers, increased the actual budget deficit to more than $30 billion.

Continuing Deficits: 1984-1990

By 1984, the economy was on the road to recovery from the recession of the early years of the decade. Economic growth produced a steady increase in job creation, and unemployment began to fall. Inflation stabilized at between 4 and 5 percent, and the economy averaged a rate of growth of 4 to 5 percent.

The main problem the government faced in its budgets during this period was the continuation of large budget deficits. Despite the strong economy, discretionary tax increases almost annually, and attempts at expenditure restraint, the government was unable to bring its actual budget deficit to less than $20 billion. The tone of discretionary fiscal policy was contractionary as the primary structural budget changed from a deficit to a surplus position by 1989.

The general election of September 1984 brought to power a Conservative government with a huge majority, and fiscal policy came under the direction of Minister of Finance Michael Wilson for the remainder of the decade. The new government immediately embarked on a program of "economic renewal" highlighted by three major objectives: control the national debt, manage government more effectively, and invest in productive activities to promote economic growth and job creation. The focus of budgetary policy was to control the trend of rising debt, but the Finance Minister cautioned that this goal had to be balanced with the other fiscal goals of maintaining economic growth and reducing unemployment.[8]

Federal budgets from 1985 through 1990 contained numerous measures designed to achieve the stated fiscal goals. Government announcements kept reasserting the need for reduction in the growth of government spending, coupled with selective tax changes to stimulate sectors of the economy and numerous tax increases designed to raise additional revenues for deficit reduction. Table 17-2 outlines the tax changes made during this period.

Only in his February 1990 budget did Finance Minister Wilson proudly announce that there would be no new taxes in his budget, undoubtedly much to the relief of most taxpaying Canadians.

As part of its expenditure control program and its pledge to manage government more effectively, the government in late 1984 appointed the Ministerial Task Force on Program Review to undertake a detailed examination of government expenditure programs with the purpose of eliminating unnecessary and obsolete programs, increasing the efficiency of the remainder, and reducing the size of the public service. Regulations that hampered business efficiency were to be streamlined or eliminated if possible. Crown corporations with no public policy purpose were to be sold in a program of privatization of government enterprise. Subsidies to agriculture, transportation, and other businesses were also to be reduced.

The government was reasonably successful in reducing the rate of growth of its program expenditures (defined as total expenditures less public debt charges). As shown in Table 17-3, the average annual increase in program expenditures had been 12 percent during the 1974-84 period. This figure was reduced to 4.8 percent for the 1984-89 period. Despite the revenue increases from higher taxes and a buoyant economy, the reduction in the rate of increase in spending was insufficient to make major inroads in deficit reduction. Only in 1985-86 were program expenditures actually reduced.

The expenditure restraints that stirred up the most controversy were those placed on federal transfer payments to the provinces. Transfers under the Canada Assistance Plan (CAP), which had been based on 50-50 cost-sharing of eligible provincial spending, were limited to a 5 percent increase per year in the three wealthiest provinces of Ontario, British Columbia, and Alberta. Transfers under Established Program Financing were frozen to the 1989-90 level for a two-year period.

TABLE 17-2: Federal Tax Changes, 1985-1989

1985
A lifetime capital gains exemption of $500,000.
A 1 percent increase in the manufacturers' sales tax to 11 percent.
Increases in excises on cigarettes, tobacco, alcohol, and gasoline.
A tax on the capital of banks and trust companies.
A surtax on higher income individuals.
A surtax on larger corporations.

1986
Replacement of the 1985 surtaxes with a 3 percent surtax on federal personal income taxes and on corporation income taxes.
An increase in the manufacturers' sales tax to 12 percent.
Reductions in the general corporation income tax rate from 36 to 33 percent.
A reduction in the investment tax credit from one-half to one-third of the cash dividends received from Canadian companies.
A 4 percent increase in excises on alcohol.
A 6 percent increase in excises on tobacco.
Reduction in indexation of the personal income tax: tax brackets and exemption to be increased only by the amount that inflation exceeds 3 percent.

1987
Increases in the excises on gasoline, cigarettes, and tobacco products.
Extension of the manufacturers' sales tax to cover snack foods.

1988
Reform of the personal income tax, estimated to reduce revenues from it by $2.4 billion by 1992.
Reform of the corporation income tax, estimated to increase revenues from it by $1.5 billion by 1992.

1989
Increase in the personal income surtax from 3 to 5 percent with an additional 3 percent new surtax for high-income individuals.
Increases in the excise on alcohol, tobacco, and gasoline.
An increase in the manufacturers' sales tax to 13.5 percent.
Imposition of a large corporations tax.
Impostiion of the "clawback tax" on family allowances and Old Age Security payments received by higher-income individuals.

These measures were expected to save Ottawa about $2 billion in 1991-92. The Minister of Finance justified his actions by saying that the deficit was a national problem demanding a national solution, and provincial governments had to do their part.

The Deficit Problem

Deficits were recorded in the federal government budget every year from 1975 to 1997. The actual deficits in the earlier part of this period resulted from a combination of automatic stabilizers and deliberate expan-sionary fiscal policy measures. Beginning in 1984, however, the newly elected Mulroney government committed itself to a policy of deficit reduction. Yet the primary structural deficit was not eliminated until 1988, and there was only modest success in reducing the actual budgetary deficit. The deficit was reduced from a high of $31.4 billion in 1985 to $19.2 billion by 1998, and then began to rise. By 1993, the last year of the Conservative government's mandate, the actual deficit had reached over $35 billion.

Why was the deficit so difficult to eradicate? The question takes on more urgency when one realizes that the government made some serious attempts to balance revenue and expenditure with significant tax increases and cuts in various expenditure programs. Total federal revenues increased by an average of 9.5 percent annually over the 1984-90 period. The rate of spending increases was down but by an insufficient amount. While the government had no control over public debt charges, it could control program spending. The rate of increase in program spending was reduced but expenditures were not reduced in the absolute and continued to feed the deficit.

The government placed the source of the deficit problem on public debt charges.[9] For example, in 1989-90 those charges rose an estimated $6.4 billion from the previous year, absorbing approximately 80 percent of the forecast $8 billion increase in budgetary revenues. The cumulative deficits correspondingly increased the total public debt, absorbing an increasing proportion of total budgetary revenues. Finance Minister Wilson pointed out that in 1969, just 12 cents of the taxpayer's dollar went to interest payments on the public debt, but by 1989, it took more than 35 cents of each tax dollar to finance a net public debt of $352 billion.[10]

Deficit reduction was hampered by the drain of financing the deficits themselves. Each year that a deficit was incurred meant a substantial increase in the revenue required just to cover interest charges. For example, an average interest rate of 10.5 percent on the $30 billion budgetary deficit in 1984 added $3.2 billion to the government's revenue requirements for that fiscal year alone. While interest rates declined in the first few years of the Conservative government administration, helping to reduce the deficit, they rose between 1987 and 1990 (the bank rate rose from 8.4 percent to 13 percent). Approximately 60 percent of the government's total outstanding debt (primarily Treasury bills and Canada Savings Bonds) has to be refinanced or re-priced each year. If a year is characterized by rising interest rates, revenue requirements are raised further because part of the public debt issued earlier at lower interest rates matures and has to be refinanced at the new, higher rates. In 1990-91, with unmatured debt at about the $300 billion level, refinancing 60 percent of it with a 1 percent increase in interest rates would require an additional $1.8 billion.

The significance of the government's failure to make substantial inroads on the size of the deficit is magnified by the fact that the economy enjoyed relative prosperity during most of the period. From 1984 to 1988, the average annual real GDP growth was 4.7 percent, prices stabilized at roughly a 4 percent annual increase, employment grew, and unemployment fell from 11.2 to 7.8 percent. At the same time, as shown in Table 17-3, budgetary revenues increased at an average annual rate of over 10 percent.

The failure to reduce the deficit during the period of relative prosperity in the 1980s placed the government in a difficult position with respect to fiscal policy when the economy went into a recession in the latter part of 1990 and early 1991.

Recession: 1990-1993

The economy began to decline in 1989 and by 1990 was in a major recession. Unemployment, which had been steadily falling since 1983, began to increase as did prices. In this economic environment the government re-iterated its standing position since the mid-1980s — the need for reducing the federal deficit. This precluded any major increases in government spending or reductions in taxation to combat the recession. The tone of fiscal policy was mildly contractionary as the primary structural balance slowly increased, but the government's focus continued to be on deficit reduction.

In 1991 the government introduced two major initiatives for deficit reduction. The

TABLE 17-3: Budgetary Expenditures, Revenues and Public Debt Charges, 1984-1997

Year	Program Expenditures	Public Debt Charges	Total Budgetary Expenditures	Total Budgetary Revenue
		(percentage change)		
1974-84[a]	12.0	21.4	13.4	11.3
1984-85	10.3	23.9	12.8	10.7
1985-86	1.1	13.5	1.9	8.2
1986-87	4.5	4.9	4.6	11.7
1987-88	7.2	8.6	7.5	13.6
1988-89	3.4	14.5	5.9	6.7
1989-90	4.2	17.0	7.4	9.2
1990-91	4.7	9.8	6.1	4.0
1991-92	5.9	-3.3	3.3	2.3
1992-93	6.4	-5.7	3.2	-1.3
1993-94	-2.1	-2.2	-2.1	-3.7
1994-95	-1.1	10.7	-1.8	6.3
1995-96	-5.7	11.6	-1.2	5.7
1996-97	-6.4	-4.1	-5.7	8.1

[a] Average annual change.

Source: Canada, Department of Finance, Fiscal Reference Tables, October 1997, cat. F1-26/1997E.

Spending Control Act of 1992 legislated spending limits for a five-year period. The act limited annual increases in program spending to 3 percent between 1991-92 and 1995-96. The government also established a Debt-Servicing and Reduction Fund to be used to pay the interest on the national debt. The fund was to be financed with revenues from the Goods and Services Tax as well as revenue raised from the sale of Crown corporations.

Instead of falling, the actual budgetary deficit rose from $25.9 billion in 1990 to $35.1 billion in 1993. This increase was fuelled by an average annual increase in program spending of almost 6 percent (including increases of 5.9 percent in 1991-92 and 6.4 percent in 1992-93, the first two years of the Spending Control Act). A fall in interest rates, however, brought a reduction in public debt charges during this period, which contributed to a reduction in the increase in total budgetary expenditure. A contributing factor to the rise in the deficit was the fall in revenues due to the poor performance of the economy. Real GDP fell by .2 percent in 1990 and by 1.8 percent in 1991. It grew only .8 in 1992, and 2.2 percent in 1993. As a result, budgetary revenues declined from $122 billion in 1991-92 to $116 billion in 1993-94.

The budgets of 1991, 1992, and 1993 contained few discretionary fiscal measures to combat the recession and the increasing unemployment rate. There were some minor tax concessions in 1992 with a reduction in the personal income surtax from 5 percent to 3 percent, and the corporation income tax on manufacturing and processing from 23 percent to 20 percent. On the expenditure side of the budget, program spending was estimated to increase by less than 3 percent in accordance with the Spending Control Act.

In his earlier budgets the Minister of Finance submitted five-year projections on the budgetary deficit. The 1985 budget had projected a balanced budget by 1990; a reduction in the $30 billion deficit to zero. In 1990 the deficit stood at almost $26 billion. In his February 1990 budget the Minister projected a decline in the deficit to $9 billion by 1992-93 and a budget surplus by 1994-95.[11] In fact, however, during 1993, the last year of the Mulroney Conservative government, the budget deficit on a national accounts basis reached its highest post-war level at $35.1 billion. By this time, the government's deficit projections had lost all credibility.

Deficit Elimination: 1994-1998

Following its election in the fall of 1993, the Liberal government under Prime Minister Jean Chretien and Finance Minister Paul Martin embarked on a program to eliminate the budgetary deficit. The government's strategy for achieving its fiscal objectives was based on two-year rolling deficit targets. Deficit reduction was to be achieved by reducing program spending and maintaining the high tax rates established by the previous government. Given these taxes, a growing economy was expected to produce substantial annual increases in revenues. Indeed between 1993-94 and 1996-97, the level of budgetary revenues increased from $116 billion to $149 billion (a 22 percent increase) while program expenditures fell from $120 billion to $104.8 billion (a 13 percent reduction). Falling interest rates held the increase in public debt charges to 9 percent over the 1993-98 period despite the increase in the public debt from continuing deficits. As illustrated in Figure 17-3, the actual and structural budget deficits began to fall beginning in 1994. By 1996-97 the actual deficit had been reduced to $7.5 billion, and for 1997-98 the Finance Minister announced a budget surplus.

The period following 1992 featured an inflation rate of less than 2 percent. The unemployment rate, however, remained at a high level. In 1994 it stood at about 10.5 percent, falling very slowly to 9.2 percent by 1997 and to 8.6 percent by early 1998. The annual increase in real GDP from 1994 to 1997 averaged approximately 2.8 percent. With a reasonable rate of economic growth, low inflation rates, and falling unemployment, the government could devote its full attention to the deficit.

The first step in the deficit reduction program was a comprehensive Program Review, designed to reduce program spending by identifying lower priority programs and reallocating reduced resources among the higher priority programs. The Finance Minister projected a reduction in program spending of $17 billion over a three year period, with total federal spending declining about $25 billion. Discretionary tax increases were expected to add about $4 billion towards deficit reduction. The Finance Minister projected seven dollars in spending reductions for every dollar of revenue accruing from tax increases in his strategy for reducing the deficit.[12]

The rate at which program spending and revenues increased is shown in Table 17-3. By 1996-97, the high taxes set in earlier years, plus additional taxes in 1994 and 1995, combined with a growing economy to increase budgetary revenues from about $116 billion in 1993-94 to $141 billion. The tax increases included an increase in the Large Corporations tax by 12.5 percent, the corporate surtax was raised from 3 to 4 percent, and the gasoline excise tax raised by 1.5 cents per litre. In addition, a temporary surtax was imposed on the capital of banks and other deposit-taking institutions.

Of the reduced program expenditure, about $7 billion consisted of reduced cash payments to the provinces under the Canada Health and Social Transfer program. Predictably the provincial governments expressed outrage at what they viewed as the transfer to them of a large portion of the burden of federal debt reduction. Other expenditure reductions included: defence, $1.6 billion; transport, $1.4 billion; foreign aid, $550 million; natural resources, $600 million; agriculture, $450 million; industry, $900 million; and human resources development, $900 million.[13] At the same time, the salaries of public servants were frozen until 1997. Reductions in Employment Insurance benefits and lower payments as unemployment fell combined to reduce spending in the Employment Insurance program from $17.6 billion in 1993-94 to $12.4 billion by 1996-97.

As illustrated in Figure 17-3 and Table 17-1, the fiscal tone of government policy from 1994 was contractionary as the primary structural deficit moved from a deficit position in 1993 to a surplus of $20 billion in 1996. The contractionary impact of the large increase in the surplus, brought about by expenditure reductions and increased taxes on top of existing high tax rates, most likely contributed to the relatively low rate of economic growth of 2.3 percent in 1995 and 1.5 percent in 1996, and prevented unemployment from decreasing more rapidly.

Why was the Liberal government able to eliminate the deficit between 1994 and 1998 while the Conservative government was unsuccessful, particularly during the period of economic prosperity from 1984 to 1988? Indeed the Mulroney government was operating in a stronger economic environment in 1984-88 in comparison to the 1994-98 economic climate. As illustrated in Figure 17-4 and Table 17-3, the economy grew at a more rapid rate during 1984-88 than during 1994-98 while revenues rose more rapidly. The unemployment rate was declining in both periods. The governments of both periods put fiscal policy on hold and focussed on an announced objective of deficit reduction and elimination. The Conservative government managed to reduce the national accounts budget deficit from $30.0 billion in 1984 to $19.2 billion in 1988. The deficit then increased to peak at $35.1 billion in 1993. Taking office in October 1993, the Liberal government managed to balance the budget by the end of the 1997-98 fiscal year. The different results stem primarily from the failure of the earlier government to control program spending compared to the success of the later government in actually reducing expenditures. Under the Conservative government, program expenditures increased from $78.9 billion in 1983-84 to $96.4 billion in 1987-88, an increase of $17.5 billion, while from 1993-94 to 1996-97, program expenditures were reduced from $120.6 billion to $104.8 billion, a decrease of $15.2 billion.

The continuous deficits not only tied the government's hands in the application of fiscal policy during the recessions in the early 1980s and again in the early 1990s, but also placed a large public debt burden on Canadians. As discussed in an earlier chapter, the federal gross public debt increased from $54 billion in 1974-75 (the first year of the deficits) to $204 billion by 1983-84. The inability of the Conservative government to eliminate deficit financing pushed the debt to $546 billion by 1993-94, and it increased to $640 billion by 1996-97. At the same time public debt charges increased from $3.2 billion or 8.5 percent of budgetary expenditures to $45 billion or 30 percent of budgetary expenditures, severely reducing the proportion of the budget available for public goods and services such as education, health, and other social services.

Implications for Future Counter-Cyclical Fiscal Policy

Events over the last two decades have raised questions about the applicability of

Keynesian economics in a changing economic world.[14] Counter-cyclical fiscal policy of budget deficits and surpluses was based on the premise of a Phillips trade-off between unemployment and inflation. Beginning in 1973 and continuing into the 1980s, the economy was characterized by both high rates of unemployment and inflation (Figures 17-2 and 17-4). Deficits to stimulate the economy and fight unemployment threatened to aggravate inflation, while anti-inflationary measures threatened to contribute to unemployment. Simultaneous unemployment and inflation is inconsistent with traditional counter-cyclical Keynesian fiscal policy.

The trend towards a more global economy has repercussions in a government's ability to influence domestic economic activity. In a highly open economy, heavily dependent on international trade, the economy becomes very susceptible to outside factors and economic conditions. Inflation may be imported; recessions abroad or devaluation of foreign currencies could harm exports and contribute to unemployment; large budgetary deficits might affect foreign investor confidence and scare off needed foreign investment; and higher taxes in an inflationary period might contribute to factory relocation. Governments have to consider potential foreign repercussions to their policies, while external developments could potentially work to counter the impacts of domestic policies.

Difficulties of implementing fiscal policy in the past have also contributed to disillusionment with the concept. The problems of correctly forecasting changes in the economy to apply timely policy, the time lags before the impact of the policy takes effect, the unpredictable reaction of consumers and business to tax policy changes, and the reduced impact of the multiplier in an open economy all combine to reduce the effectiveness of fiscal policy.

Probably the one most important factor contributing to the disillusionment with traditional fiscal policy has been governments' financial mismanagement and misuse of the Keynesian formula. The Keynesian formula called for budget deficits to stimulate the economy during the downward portion of the business cycle, and budget surpluses to dampen economic growth in the upward portion when inflation threatened. Over the course of the business cycle, the deficits and surpluses would cancel each other, producing a balanced budget. During the early post-war period, the federal government in Canada was reasonably successful in implementing this formula. Beginning in 1974, however, the government appears to have forgotten the surplus side of the fiscal policy formula, and produced continuous deficits, including deficits in the absence of cyclical economic downturns (and the absence of shocks to the economy such as wars or natural disasters). It appears that governments, when faced with the decision to finance increased spending by raising taxes or using debt finance, are biased towards the more politically expedient route of deficit financing. One might argue that governments simply cannot be trusted to apply responsible finance, and too easily tend to fall into a habit of deficit financing and financial mismanagement. An indication of the recognition of this lack of confidence in the fiscal discipline of governments is the trend of governments to consider, and to enact, balanced budget laws.

In the United States, virtually every state has some type of balanced budget requirement. Approximately one-half of the states have stringent anti-deficit rules which apply to the general budget as well as to any special non-budgetary funds. Many states also have tax limitation laws, limitations on borrowing, or requirements that debt be approved by voters.[15] At the federal level the United States Congress in 1995 narrowly defeated a proposal for a constitutional amendment requiring a balanced budget, but the goal continued to be pursued.

In Europe, the Maastricht Treaty on European Monetary Union (EMU) included rules which limited the size of deficits and the national debt of member countries. Government deficits were limited to less than 3 percent of GDP, while the public debt was not to exceed 60 percent of GDP.[16] This requirement provides some flexibility to the budget balance in comparison to a requirement of a zero deficit.

In Canada, some of the provincial governments, including Alberta, Manitoba, New Brunswick and Nova Scotia, passed laws during the 1990s mandating balanced budgets. The government of Ontario under Premier Harris outlined plans for balanced budget legislation, and in 1997 a legislative committee recommended a law requiring a referendum to approve new Ontario tax measures unless they were revenue neutral. The announced objective was to keep politicians accountable to the taxpayer.

In 1992 the federal government attempted to legislate fiscal discipline upon itself by passing the Spending Control Act, limiting annual expenditure increases to 3 percent over the 1991-92 to 1995-96 period. The new Liberal government declined to extend the act beyond 1996. Finance Minister Martin contended that the restraints on spending that he was exercising made the act redundant. While the Finance Minister rejected the concept of entrenching a balanced budget law, his 1998 budget committed his government to a new fiscal era of balanced budgets, with a reserve fund dedicated to steadily reducing the public debt.[17]

The implications for future fiscal policy are unclear. Governments which have enacted balanced budgets laws will be precluded from using counter-cyclical budget deficits and surpluses, unless of course the law is changed or the accounts are manipulated by excluding certain financial transactions from the budget. (i.e., non-budgetary special funds). Governments which have gone through a difficult period in attempting to balance their budgets, and have accumulated a huge debt in the process, such as the Canadian government, may be very reluctant to return to deficit financing as in a recession, in fear of triggering another string of deficits or in political fear of an electorate backlash. Governments may opt to rely primarily on monetary measures for counter-cyclical effects.

Summary

Economic conditions from the end of World War II to about the mid-1970s tended to follow a cyclical pattern of economic prosperity and economic slowdown, featuring the traditional unemployment-inflation trade-off illustrated by the Phillips curve. The federal government attempted to employ counter-cyclical fiscal measures during this period when unemployment or inflation threatened. Anti-inflationary measures were introduced in the early 1950s during the Korean War, and anti-recessionary measures and budgetary deficits were employed during the severe recession in the late 1950s. The movement of the structural and primary structural budget balances, within the context of prevailing economic conditions, indicate that, in general, fiscal policy was reasonably appropriate.

Following 1970, however, both inflation and unemployment began to increase simultaneously, posing a major problem for traditional fiscal policy. The situation was complicated by a string of consecutive budget deficits beginning in 1975 and lasting until 1997. A large budget deficit at the beginning of the recession in the early 1980s left the government little flexibility for effective fiscal measures. This was repeated when another recession began in 1990.

For the last two decades the federal government has been preoccupied with deficit reduction. Despite a rapidly growing economy and large revenue increases during the mid-1980s, the government made little inroads in deficit reduction. The 1990s recession aggravated the deficit problem. It was not until after 1994, with the election of the Liberal government of Jean Chretien, that the deficit began to fall and by 1998 a balanced budget was achieved. By this time the accumulated deficits had pushed the federal public debt to over $600 billion dollars.

Over this latter period of continuous deficits there developed a degree of disillusionment with Keynesian fiscal policy and the government's ability to employ it prudently. Some governments enacted balanced budget laws which effectively prohibited budget deficits and therefore the active employment of traditional fiscal policy. The Canadian government committed to a balanced budget, with reserve funds to steadily reduce the public debt.

NOTES

1   For an account of the attitude of the government of Canada towards fiscal policy prior to 1940, see Irving Brecher, *Monetary and Fiscal Thought in Policy in Canada, 1919-1937* (Toronto: University of Toronto Press, 1957).

2   Price and wage controls in Canada during World War II are described in K.W. Taylor, "Canadian War-Time Price Controls, 1914-1946, *Canadian Journal of Economics and Political Science* XIII, no. 1 (1947).

3   Government of Canada, Department of Reconstruction, *Employment and Income* (Ottawa: King's Printer, 1945). The federal government had earlier enacted statutes, such as the Unemployment Insurance Act, 1940, and the Family Allowance Act, 1944, which, it was believed, would partly meet future problems of declining incomes.

4   Of the plants that faced a reconversion problem following the termination of the war, more than half had completed the reconversion process by March 1946. Of the remainder, 75 percent completed the process before the end of the year. Approximately 45 percent of the plants had completed or were undertaking modernization or expansion programs, and a large number of new establishments were coming into operation to produce for the peacetime market. Of the 1,000,000 people who gave up their wartime occupations in the fall of 1945, close to 800,000 had found employment by March 1946. See the statement by C.D. Howe in Government of Canada, *House of Commons Debates*, 1946 (Ottawa: King's Printer, 1946), pp.112-120.

5   Analysis of the 1947-63 period can use some but not all of the methodology described at the beginning of the chapter. Information on the structural budget balance is available beginning only in 1953, and information on the primary structural balance is unavailable. Indications of the direction of fiscal policy are obtained from examining the actual and structural balances and from the specific measures that were introduced.
The major sources of information and the data on economic conditions and federal government fiscal policy from 1947 to the present are the budget speeches of the Minister of Finance, the various accompanying budget papers and reports prepared by the Department of Finance, and publications of Statistics Canada and the Department of Finance.

6   For an analysis of inflation in Canada during the 1970s, see Canada, Department of Finance, *Canada's Recent Inflation Experience*, November 1978 (Ottawa).

7   For a systematic application of macroeconometric modelling techniques analyzing fiscal policy between 1980 and 1990, see Thomas A. Wilson and D. Peter Dungan *Fiscal Policy In Canada: An Appraisal* (Toronto: Canadian Tax Foundation, 1993), Tax Paper No. 94.

8   Canada, Department of Finance, *Budget Speech*, May 23, 1985 (Ottawa), p.5.

9   Canada, Department of Finance, *The Fiscal Plan, Controlling the Public Debt*, April 27, 1989 (Ottawa), p.52.

10   Canada, Department of Finance, *The Budget Speech*, April 27, 1989 (Ottawa), p.1.

11   Canada, Department of Finance, *The Budget*, February 20, 1990, p.111.

12   Canada, Department of Finance, *Budget Speech*, February 27, 1995, p.4.

13   *Ibid.*, p.8.

14   See, for example, Donald W. Kiefer, "Whatever Happened to Counter-cyclical Fiscal Policy?" National Tax Association — Tax Institute of America, Proceedings of the Eighty-Fifth Annual Conference, 1992.

15   James M. Poterba, "Budget Institutions and Fiscal Policy in the U.S. States," *The American Economic Review, Papers and Proceedings*, May 1996, vol. 86, no. 2.

16   G. Corsetti and N. Roubini, "European vs. American Perspectives on Balanced Budget Rules," *The American Economic Review*, vol. 86, no. 12.

17   Canada, Department of Finance, *The Budget Plan 1998*, February 24, 1998, p.9.

WAGE AND PRICE REGULATIONS

Traditional fiscal policy to combat inflation in Canada has several times been supplemented by experiments with wage and price controls. The first application of controls occurred during World War II, and they almost certainly contributed to relative price stability in that period. This appendix briefly describes the three following attempts: the Prices and Incomes Commission of 1969 and 1970; the wage and price controls of 1975 through 1978, and the "6 and 5" restraint program of 1983 and 1984.

Prices and Incomes Commission

Canada's first post-war experiment with wage and price controls began in 1969 with a program of voluntary guidelines administered by a Prices and Incomes Commission. The guideline for annual wage increases was 6 percent; the guideline for prices was that increases were to be less than the amount needed to cover all increases in costs.

In February 1970, the commission succeeded in bringing together approximately 250 business and professional representatives at a conference on price restraints and obtained from them a commitment to follow the price guidelines it recommended. Organized labour, however, refused to attend the conference or to co-operate with the commission. The Canadian Labour Congress said that it was not in a position to make commitments for its member unions. Labour in general argued that a wage ceiling would hold the status quo on income distribution, a situation that would be inequitable as labour had considerable catching up to do on profits and other forms of income. Labour also refused to accept wage controls on the grounds that other forms of income, such as rents, profits, and interest, were not subject to restraints.

During the early months of 1970, the Prices and Incomes Commission did manage to persuade various industries to agree to a moratorium on price increases, and between January and March a number of announced and intended price increases were postponed. Without the co-operation of labour, however, the commission's task was ex-tremely difficult, for it was apparent that business was not prepared to maintain price freezes for any length of time if costs continued to rise. By late 1970, business declared that it no longer could co-operate with the commission, and in December, the government announced that it was abandoning its program of voluntary price restraints. The commission would continue to function but only as a research agency to study the causes and processes of inflation and to promote public understanding of the problem.

How successful was the commission in controlling inflation? The rate of inflation decreased during the latter months of 1970 — the consumer price index (CPI) increased from 127.9 in December 1969 to 130.5 in July 1970 and then stabilized, falling slightly to 129.8 by December 1970. But it is difficult to determine to what extent the work of the commission contributed to this moderation. The rate of economic growth declined in 1970, and aggregate demand levelled off; both factors could be expected to have some moderating influence. Moreover, in October, a price war broke out among the major grocery chains, resulting in a three-point decline in the food price index (food is a major component of the basket of goods used to determine price changes). One can only speculate on what the degree of price increases would have been in 1970 if aggregate demand had not become depressed or if food prices had not declined.

Mandatory Controls

Canada's second experiment in wage and price regulation began in 1975. The Liberal government had rejected mandatory controls in the autumn of 1974 and even waged an election campaign denouncing the wage and price control proposals of the Conservative party. When in power, the Liberal government at first argued that controls had been attempted and abandoned by most Western nations over the past decade and cited the various traditional argument against controls, such as difficulties of administration and distortions caused in the allocation of resources.[1]

TABLE A17-1: Anti-Inflation Board and Wages: Summary of Effective Rates of Increase in Compensation and Relationship to Wage Guidelines by Program Years

	No. of employees	Average effective increase[a]	Average guideline
	(000s)	(%)	(%)
Immediate preprogram	183	12.5	10.6
First program year (1975/6)[b]	3,019	9.3	9.7
Second program year (1976/7)[b]	3,406	7.3	7.6
Third program year (1977/8)[c]	471	5.2	5.6
All program years	7,079	8.2	8.4

[a] Weighted average of settlements within guidelines and after board decisions.
[b] October of one year to October of the following year.
[c] October 1977 to February 1978. Employee groups began to be freed from the guidelines in early 1978.

Source: Department of Finance, *Economic Review*, April 1978 (Ottawa), p. 36.

By October 1975, however, with prices increasing at an annual rate of approximately 11 percent, wage settlements exceeding 14 percent per year, and productivity stagnant, the government reversed its position and introduced an anti-inflationary program of wage and price controls.[2]

It was announced that the program would continue for three years. Inflation rate targets were set at 8, 6, and 4 percent for the first, second, and third years respectively. Wage guidelines were based on the inflation target factor plus a productivity and experience adjustment factor, with a maximum annual increase of $2,400. For 1976, the guideline could vary between 8 and 12 percent; it would decline for each of the subsequent years, although provisions were included to permit additional flexibility if necessary to maintain historic relationships between income groups.

The government established three administrative bodies to administer the program: the Anti-Inflationary Board to establish guidelines, to review wage settlements and income increases, and to monitor prices and profits; an administrator to investigate contraventions of the guidelines and to enforce compliance where necessary; and the Anti-Inflation Appeal Tribunal to consider appeals on the rulings of the administrator.

During the first program year (October 14, 1975, to October 13, 1976), compensations plans covering approximately 3 million employees in the public and private sectors were submitted to the Anti-Inflation Board. Plans covering over one-third of these employees contained increases beyond the guidelines and required a decision by the board. Some compensation increases approved early in the program exceeded the guidelines, primarily to maintain historical relationships. As the program continued, compensation plans showed a continued deceleration in the rate of wage increases being sought and being approved (see Table A17-1). During the second program year, for example, approximately 70 percent of employees sought increases within or below the guidelines, while the remaining 30 percent sought increases averaging 1.8 percent above the guidelines. The effective rate of increase in the average of settlements was reduced steadily in each year of the program. It is estimated that the average wage rollback by the Anti-Inflation Board was 2 percent in the first year and 1.2 percent in the second year. The increase in the first-year wage settlements of large bargaining units was reduced from 21.1 percent in 1975 to 8 percent in 1977, and by the end of the second quarter of 1978, the first-year wage settlement in collective agreements of bargaining units of 500 or more employees had fallen to 6.6 percent.[3]

The wage and price controls were gradually phased out during 1978 and expired at the end of the year. During the regulation period, the increase in the CPI moderated from 10.9 percent in 1974 to 7.5 percent in 1976, but it then began to move upward gradually, reaching 8.9 percent by 1978. Although the country beat the inflation rate target set for 1976 (8 percent), the targets for the second and third years were not achieved.

Wage and price regulation is extremely difficult to evaluate for its effectiveness in controlling inflation because one does not know what would have occurred in its absence. As in 1970, part of the improvement in the rate of change in the Canadian CPI reflected factors beyond the direct control of the program. During the first year of the experiment, unemployment increased and international inflation abated to a degree, which may have had a moderating impact on the rate of inflation in Canada. Then there were variables, such as food prices, which increased by only 2.7 percent in 1976 compared to an increase of 12.9 percent a year earlier; this falloff helped to moderate the increase in the CPI, yet food at the producer level was exempt from the controls of the anti-inflation program. Moreover, the food component of the shopping basket became a factor contributing to inflation in 1977 and 1978 when rising food prices refuelled inflation.

Fear was expressed that, with aggregate inflation again on the rise, inflationary expectations would also be raised and lead in the post-control period to higher wage and salary demands and to a renewed wage and price spiral. This did indeed occur. The average negotiated wage settlement, which had declined considerably between 1975 and 1978, began to increase in 1979 and, with consumer prices, continued to rise into 1982.

The "6 and 5" Program

Fearing a renewed surge in the wage and price spiral, the government again turned to wage restraints in June 1982. In his budget of that month, Finance Minister Allan MacEachen introduced a pay restraint policy for the federal public sector and expressed hope that the other levels of government and the private sector would follow Ottawa's example. Under this program, increases in the public employees' wages were limited to 6 percent in 1983 and 5 percent in 1984. The same limits were applied to the indexation factor for a number of federal transfer payments. Some provinces had already announced measures to limit the pay increases of some categories of their employees, and other were quick to introduce restraints similar to the federal program.

The momentum of rising wage settlements and earnings began to break in 1982 and continued to decline into 1983. Combining with the "6 and 5" program to contribute to the decline were numerous factors, including a high rate of unemployment, a serious recession, and a moderation in international inflationary forces.

NOTES

[1] For a summary of various arguments against wage and price controls, see R.G. Lipsey, "Wage-Price Controls: How yo Do a Lot of Harm by Trying yo Do a Little Good," *Canadian Public Policy* 3 (Winter 1977).

[2] A detailed description of the wage and price control program and the decisions of the Anti-Inflation Board is presented in the board's technical bulletins and reports. Wages were controlled directly. Prices were controlled by a complex system of monitoring corporation profit margins. In addition, a list was established of some 500 companies that were required to give advance notice of planned price increases. The controls also covered dividends, the incomes of professionals, and the federal public service, and under agreements with eight provinces, the regulations also applied to their employees.

[3] For one analysis of the effectiveness of the anti-inflationary board in restraining wages, see D.A.L. Auld et al., "The Impact of the Anti-Inflation Board on Negotiated Wage Settlements," *Canadian Journal of Economics* XII, no. 2 (May 1979).

Index

ability to pay, 116-17
administrative budget, 250
Alberta
  budget balance, 193
  natural resources confrontation,
    240-41
  revenues, 158
  taxation, 157
alcohol, taxes on, 151, 161
allocation of resources, 12-14, 19-42
alternative minimum tax, 140-41
alternative program delivery
  systems, 75-83
Anti-Inflation Board, 283-84
assessment, property, 163-64
Auditor General, 87-88, 99-101, 145
Auditor General Act, 100
Auld, Douglas, 42n, 284n
automatic stabilizers, 252

Ballentine, J.G., 126n
Bank of Canada, 181-83
Baumol, W., 126n
Beach, Donald I., 126n, 216n, 229n
Beck, J.M., 245n
Begin, Health and Welfare Minister,
  226
benefit approach to taxation, 116-17
benefit-cost analysis, 108
Bernier, I., 245n
Bird, Richard M., 74n, 177n, 217n
Bloc Québécois, 239
Blum, W.J., 126n
bonds, 181-82
Borcherding, Thomas E., 73n, 74n
borrowing
  effects of, 186-88
  federal, 179-82
  provincial/local, 179-80, 182-83
  rationale for, 179
  types of securities, 180-82
Bouchard, Lucien, 239-40
Bourassa, Premier Robert, 232,
  235-36
Brecher, Irving, 281n
Brewis, T.N., 262n
Broadway, Robin, 217n, 229n
British Columbia
  budget balance, 193
  revenues, 158
  taxation, 157, 159-61
British North America Act (BNA Act),
  See Constitution Act
Brownlee, O., 126n
Buck, A.E., 126n
budget accounts

administrative, 250
consolidated cash, 250-51
national accounts, 251-52
budget balance
  actual, 265
  cyclically adjusted, 252-53
  legislation, 192, 194, 279-80
  primary structural, 253, 265
  structural, 252-53, 265
  trends in, 193, 265
budget deficits, See also fiscal policy
  190-94, 265, 273-75
budget, federal government
  audit, 99-101
  budget cycle, 89-91
  budget plan, 91
  expenditure estimates, 90-99
  Parliament approval, 94-96
  secrecy, 98-99
  speech, 97
  Treasury Board review, 93-94
  types of, 250-52
budget, instrument of fiscal policy,
  250-53
budget systems, 104-108
budgeting
  federal, 85-101
  local, 101-102
  provincial, 101
budgets, provincial balances, 192-94
bureaucratic behaviour, 62
Burns, R.M., 217n
business taxes, 143, 164

Canada Act, 231
Canada Assistance Plan, 47, 211,
  215
Canada Health Act, 31, 226
Canada Health and Social Transfer
  (CHST), 206, 215, 222
Canada Pension Plan, 52-53, 210
Canada Savings Bonds, 182
Canadian Millennium Scholarship
  Foundation, 36
capital budgets, 102
capital gains tax, 139-40
capital taxes, 143, 159
Carmichael, E.A., 245n
Carter, George E., 217n, 229n
casinos, 173-76
charitable donations, tax credit, 136
Charlottetown Accord, 227, 237-38
Charter of Rights and Freedoms,
  234
child care expenses, tax deduction,
  133

child tax benefit, 48-49
Chrétien, Prime Minister Jean, 104,
  109, 196, 239, 277
Clark, C., 74n
Coase, R., 26n
Combines Investigation Act, 21
commercialization, in government,
  81
commodity taxes, See also Goods
  and Services Tax, excise
  duties, excise taxes,
  manufacturers' sales tax, and
  retail sales tax
  federal, 144-52
  provincial, 159-60
common property, 22-23
communications, 39, 244
Competition Act, 21
Comptroller General, 87, 94
conditional grants, See specific
  purpose transfers
Confederation Bridge, 80
consolidated cash budget, 250-51
Consolidated Revenue Fund, 87,
  95-98
Constitution Act, 85, 94, 121, 155,
  201-202, 232-34
constitutional reform, 231-45
consumer price index (CPI)
  changes in, 259-60
  measurement, 258
consumer services, 19-20
consumer sovereignty, 25
consumption taxes, See specific
  taxes
Corak, Miles, 55
corporation income tax, federal
  revenue from 128-29
  structure, 142-43
corporation income tax, provincial
  revenue form, 156, 158
  structure, 159
Corsetti, G., 281n
Courchene, T., 217n
Crow, John, 260, 262n
crowding out, 186
Crown corporations, 41, 69-72, 81
customs duties (tariffs), 151-52
Cuyler, A.Y., 42n
cyclical deficits, 252
cyclically-adjusted budget balance,
  252-53

Dawson, R. MacGregor, 216n
death taxes, See estate tax and
  successions duties

debt finance, See borrowing
debt, public
  burden of, 187-89
  charges, 188, 276
  external, 183, 186, 189-90
  features, 183
  federal, 183-92
  growth, 191-92
  holders of, 185
  international comparisons, 195-96
  local government, 184
  management, 183-84
  percentage of GDP, 190-91
  provincial, 184, 192-94
  retirement, 194
deficits, See also fiscal policy,
    190-94, 265, 273-75
depreciation (capital cost)
    allowances, 142
depression in the 1930s, 203-204
deregulation, 81-82
Deutsch, John, 262n
devolution, of government services,
    81
direct taxes, 121, 155, 159, 202-203
distribution of income, 11-15, 43-51
dividend tax credit, 136
Downs, Anthony, 62
Dungan, Peter D., 281n
Duplessis, Premier Maurice, 232

Economic Council of Canada,
    economic targets, 254, 261
economic indicators, 268, 272
economic growth
  fiscal policy goal, 15-16, 260-61
  measures of, 260-61
economic policy, See fiscal policy
education
  expenditures, 32
  financing, 36-37
  systems, 35-36
  tax credits, 135
elasticity, expenditure, 62-63
employment expenses, tax
    deduction, 132-33
employment insurance, 53-54
energy policy, 240-42
envelope system, 106
environment protection, 39-40
equalization
  Constitution Act and, 215, 220,
    234
  formulas, 206-207, 209, 212-16,
    220-21
  payments, 220
  rationale for, 207, 219-21
equity
  income distribution and, 14-15
  taxation and, 116-17
established programs financing
    (EPF), 206, 213-15, 222
estate tax, 115, 140
Evans, M., 262n
excise duties, 151
excise taxes, 115, 151
exemptions, See specific taxes
Expenditure Management System,
    89, 92, 106-108
expenditure, public sector
  composition and trends, 64-72
  Crown corporations and, 69-72

factors influencing, 59-62
GDP and, 12, 64-65
growth theories, 62-64
external diseconomies, 13, 22-23,
    27-28
external economies, 13, 22, 27-28

family allowance, 48, 139
federal government
  borrowing and debt, 179-92,
    194-96
  budgeting, 85-101
  expenditures, 65-68, 276
  fiscal policy, 263-81
  programs, 19-25, 31-55
  revenues, 127-29, 276
  taxation, 121-25, 127-54
  transfers to provinces, 219-27
federal-provincial fiscal relations
  Canada Health and Social
    Transfer (CHST), 206, 215, 222
  constitutional reform and, 231-35
  co-ordination of policies, 243-45
  equalization, 206-207, 209,
    212-16, 220-21
  established program financing,
    206, 213-15, 222
  historical development, 201-15
  natural resources, 240-43
  opting-out arrangements, 210-12,
    227, 233, 236
  revenue stabilization, 207, 209,
    211-12, 214-16
  tax rental agreements, 205-207
  tax sharing agreements, 207-208
  transfers and, See
    intergovernmental transfers
Federal-Provincial Relations Office,
    243
Feldstein, Martin, 126n
Filmon, Premier Gary, 235
Financial Administration Act, 87,
    94-96, 100
financial management systems,
    104-109
financial structure of government,
    85-89
Finley, Lawrence, 83n
fiscal balance, 201-202
fiscal capacity, 201, 213
fiscal impulse measures, 252-53
fiscal policy, federal
  application through budget, 15-16,
    249-53, 263-80
  deficit dilemma, 274-75
  early development, 264-65
  from 1955-1974, 266-70
  goals of, 254-62
  since 1974, 270-78
  future of, 278-80
Flatters, F., 217n
foreign tax credit, 136
functions of government, 11-18

Gagnon, Julie, 177n
gaming, 171-76
gasoline taxes, 160
general purpose transfers, See
    intergovernmental transfers
gift tax, 116, 140, 212
gifts to government, tax treatment,
    136

Gillespie, Irwin W., 126n
Gini coefficient, 44-45
Goods and Services Tax
  assessment of, 150
  harmonization with retail tax,
    149-50, 244-45
  introduction, 145-46
  structure, 146-49
  tax revolt, 64
  value-added tax, 114
government, See public sector and
    specific levels of government
Governor General's Warrants, 96
grants, See intergovernmental
    transfers
gross domestic product
  changes in, 261, 168, 271
  government expenditures and, 12,
    65
  price index, 60
guaranteed income supplement,
    47-48

Haig-Simons, definition of income,
    113
Hansen, Alvin, 15
Harmonized Sales Tax, 149-50, 160
Harper, Elijah, 236
Harris, M., 61, 280
Hartle, D.G., 74n
Hausman, Jerry A., 126n
health care
  crises in, 33-35
  expenditures, 32-33
  finance, 33-34
  medicare, 31-33
health care premiums, 160-61
Hemming, R., 83n
Henrikson, Lennart E., 177n
Herber, Bernard P., 74n
Highway 407 control, 80
House of Commons
  Auditor General and, 87, 99-100
  budgeting and, 94-98, 106
  committees, 90, 95-96
  control of expenditures, 96, 106
housing subsidies, 49
Howe, C.D., 281n
Hyman, David N., 18n, 126n, 197n

imperfections in competition, 13-14,
    19-21
income distribution
  in Canada, 44
  goal of government, 14-15
  limits to redistribution, 50-51
  measurement, 43-45
  poverty and, 43-46
  programs for redistribution, 46-50
income security programs, 14, 51-55
income tax, See personal income
    tax and corporation income tax
indexation, of income tax, 138-40
indirect taxes, 159, 202, 203
Industry Canada, 19-20
inflation
  accelerationist theory, 256
  fiscal policy and, 264-65, 268-70
  goals, 259-60
  indexing for, 138-40
  measurement of, 258
  types of, 258-59

unemployment and, 256, 268-69
zero rate, 260
inheritance tax, See estate tax and
succession duties
insurance premium taxes, 161
interest rates, 180, 182, 184-86
intergovernmental fiscal relations,
See federal-provincial fiscal
relations and provincial-local
government relations
intergovernmental transfers
general purpose, 162, 202, 204,
219-22
limitations on, 215, 225-27
provincial dissatisfaction, 224-25,
227
specific purpose, 162, 203-204,
208, 222-24
to local government, 227-29
interim supply, 95
investment tax credit, 143

Johnson, Daniel, 239

Kalven, H., 126n
Keynes, J.M., 15, 249, 262n
Keynesian theory, 15-16, 60, 249,
264, 279
Kiefer, Donald W., 281n
Kitchen, Harry, 42n, 166n

La Porta, Rafael, 83n
Lalonde, Finance Minister, 98
large corporation tax, 143
Lévesque, Premier, 233-34
Lipsey, R.G., 284n
liquor taxes, See also excise duties
and excise taxes
federal, 151
provincial, 160
local government
borrowing and debt, 102, 165
budgeting, 101-102
expenditures, 67-68, 70
provincial-local relations, 227-29
revenues, 162-65
taxation, 163-65
transfers to, 165
log rolling model, 62
Lopez-de-Silanes, Florencio, 83n
lotteries, 171-73
Lougheed, Premier Peter, 241
low-income cut-offs, 45-46

MacEachern, Finance Minister
Allan, 284
Manitoba
budget balance, 193
Meech Lake Accord and, 236
revenues, 158
taxation, 157-58, 161
Mansoor, A., 83n
manufacturers' sales tax, 114,
144-45
market system, 12-18
marketing boards, 55-56
Martin, Paul., 54, 277, 280
McKenna, Premier Frank, 235
McWhinney, Edward, 245n
measures of effectiveness and
efficiency, 108-109

medical expense, tax credit, 135
medicare, See health
Meech Lake Accord, 227, 235-36
merit good, 25, 27
minimum wage laws, 49-50
monopoly, natural, 21
monopoly regulation, 20-21
Moore, A. Milton, 126n, 216n, 229n
moral hazard, 54
Mulroney, Prime Minister Brian, 99,
235-38
multiplier, 249, 262n
municipal government, See local
government
Musgrave, R.A., 18n, 63, 73n, 74n

national accounts budget, 251-52
national defense, 37-38
National Energy Program, 71,
241-42
National Policy 1879, 16, 202
natural resources
constitution and, 234, 240
federal-provincial confrontation,
240-43
revenues, 162, 167
NAV Canada, 77-78
New Brunswick
budget balance, 193
revenues, 158
taxation, 157-61
Newfoundland
budget balance, 193
Meech Lake Accord and, 236
off-shore resources, 242-43
revenues, 158
taxation, 157-61
Niskanen, William, 62, 74n
non-residents, taxation of, 137
non-tax revenue, 167-70
Nova Scotia
budget balance, 193
revenues, 158
taxation, 157-59, 161
Nutter, G. Warren, 74n

oil and gas, See natural resources
Old Age Security, 51-52, 139
Ontario
budget balance, 193
revenues, 158
taxation, 157-59, 161
opting out, 210-12, 227, 233, 236

Pareto optimum, 13-14, 18n, 19
Parizeau, Jacques, 237, 239
parliament, See House of Commons
Parti Québécois, 233, 237
partnerships, government and
private enterprise, 79-80
payroll taxes, 152, 161
Peacock-Wiseman theory, 63
Peckford, Premier Brian, 242
pensions, See Canada Pension
Plan and Old Age Security
perfect competition, conditions of, 13
performance measurement, 108-109
Perry, David, 217n
Perry, G.L., 126n, 229n
Perry, J. Harvey, 74n, 126n, 216n,
229n, 245n

personal income tax, federal
administration, 141
alternative minimum, 140-41
base, 128-32
calculation, 130-31
capital gains, 139-40
credits, 133-37
deductions and exemptions,
132-33
indexation, 138-39
rates, 137-38
reform, 123-25, 133-34
revenues, 128-29
surtax, 138
personal income tax, provincial,
157-58
PetroCanada, 17, 71, 78, 241-42
Phillips, A.W., 256
Phillips curve, 256
Planning-Programming-Budgeting
System (PBBS), 104-105
Policy and Expenditure
Management System (PEMS),
104, 106
political process, and expenditures,
61-62
pollution, 22-24, 39-40
Poterba, James M., 281n
poverty
anti-poverty programs, 46-51
measures and incidence, 45
premiums, medical, 160-61
price controls, 282-84
price level, See consumer price
index
Prices and Incomes Commission,
282
primary structural budget balance,
253, 263, 265, 267
Prince Edward Island
budget balance, 193
revenues, 158
taxation, 157-59, 161
principles of taxation, 116-19
privatization, 76-78
program delivery
traditional, 75-76
alternatives, 76-83
program expenditure trends, 276
property tax, 115, 163-64
provincial government, See also
individual provinces
borrowing and debt, 192-94
budget balances, 193
budgeting, 101
enterprises, 162
expenditures, 67, 69
non-tax revenue, 156, 161-62
programs, 32-36, 38-41, 46-47,
49-50
revenues, 128, 156, 158
taxation, 155-61
transfers to, 156, 161-62
provincial-local government
relations, 227-29
public accounts, 97, 100
public choice theories, 61-62
public debt, See debt
public enterprises, 69-72
public sector
growth, 59-73

programs, 31-55
  role in the economy, 11-18
pure public goods, 24-25, 30

Quebec
  budget balance, 193
  Constitution Act and, 231-34
  pension plan, 52
  revenues, 158
  sovereignty referendum, 239
  separatism, 17, 233, 239
  taxation, 157-61

Raboy, E., 262n
Rae, Bob, 61, 192
Reagan, Ronald, 61
Receiver General, 87, 97
redistribution of income, 14-15,
  50-51
Registered Retirement Savings
  Plans (RRSP), 132
regulation, 16-17, 39, 75-76, 81-82
rent controls, 49
resource allocation
  economic efficiency in, 12-14,
  19-30
  programs, 31-42
resource conservation, 40-41
retail sales tax, 114, 159-60
retirement plans, 53
revenue sharing, 207-208
Revenue Canada, 87, 98
Revenue Guarantee Program, 212
revenues, government
  federal, 127-30
  local, 162-65
  provincial, 128, 156, 158
Robarts, Premier John, 224
Roberts, P.C., 262n
Roubini, N., 281n
Royal Commission on
  Dominion-Provincial Relations
  (Rowell-Sirois Commission),
  204-205
Royal commission on Financial
  Organization and
  Accountability (Lambert
  Commission), 105
Royal Commission on Government
  Organization (Glasco
  Commission), 105, 109n
Royal Commission on Taxation,
  123, 139, 144
royalties, 143

sales tax, See Goods and Services
  Tax, harmonized sales tax,
  manufacturers' sales tax and
  retail sales tax
Sarlo, Christopher A., 55
Saskatchewan
  budget balance, 193
  revenues, 158
  taxation, 157-61
Savoie, Donald J., 74n
Seniors Benefit program, 48
shared-cost programs, See
  intergovernmental transfers
six and five program, 271, 284
Small, Doug, 99

Smith, Adam, 12
social benefits repayment, 139
social goals, 12-18
social service expenditure, 67-69
social welfare programs, 46-47
specific purpose transfers, See
  intergovernmental transfers
Spiro, Peter S., 154n
stabilization policy, See fiscal policy
stagflation, 270-71
statutory appropriations, 92
Stewart, J.K., 245n
Strick, J.D., 18n, 26n, 42n, 74n,
  103n, 109n, 126n, 197n, 229n
structural budget balance, 252-53,
  263, 265, 267
succession duties, 206-207, 212
supplementary estimates, 95
supply, "business of", 95
supply side economics, 249
Supreme Court of Canada
  communications jurisdiction and,
  244
  mineral rights and, 242
  Quebec separation issue and,
  239-40
surtax, 138

tax abatements, 206-208, 210, 212
tax administration, 118-19, 141
tax bases, 113-16
tax capacity, See fiscal capacity
tax credits, 113, 124, 133-37
tax deductions and exemptions,
  113, 130, 132-33
tax efficiency, 117-18
tax equity, 116-17
tax evasion, 141, 153-54
tax events in Canada, 122, 124
tax expenditures, 73
tax incidence, 119-21
tax neutrality, 118
tax principles, 116-19
tax rates, 117, 124
  See also individual taxes
tax reform, 123-25, 133-34
tax rental, 205-206
tax revenues, 128-31
tax revolts, 64
tax shifting, 119-21
tax tolerance, 64
taxable income, 113-14
taxation
  constitutional provisions, 121
  development of, 121-25
  principles of, 116-19
  taxes, See also specific taxes
  alternative minimum tax, 140-41
  capital gains, 116
  corporation income, 113-14,
  119-20
  estate, 115, 140
  excise, 115, 151
  gift, 116, 140
  goods and service, 114, 145-50,
  244-45
  inheritance, 115
  large corporation, 143
  lump sum, 116
  luxury, 115

natural resources, 162
payroll, 114
personal income, 113, 119,
  123-25, 128-41, 157-58
poll, 116
property, 115, 163-64
sales, 114-15, 120-21, 145-50,
  244-45
spending, 114
wealth, 115-16
withholding, 139
Taylor, K.W., 281n
technological change, effects on
  government, 59-60
Thatcher, Margaret, 61
tobacco taxes, 151, 153-54
transfers between governments,
  See intergovernmental transfers
transfers to persons, See income
  distribution
transportation, 38-39
transport Canada, 92-93, 107-109
treasury bills, 181
Treasury Board, 87, 93-94
Triest, Robert K., 126n
Trudeau, Prime Minister Pierre, 233
Tsiopoulos, Thomas, 177n
tuition fees, tax treatment, 135
turnover tax, 114

unconditional grants, See
  intergovernmental transfers
underground economy, 153-54
unemployment
  economic barometer, as an,
  256-57
  inflation trade-off, 256, 268-69
  measurement, 254-55
  natural rate, 256
  rates, 256-58
  types, 255
United States, deficit control, 279
urbanization, 60
user charges, 167-71

Vaillancourt, Francois, 126n, 177n
value-added tax, 114
value-for-money audit, 100
video lottery terminals, 176
voluntary codes, 81-82
vote trading, 62

wage-price regulation, 16, 270,
  282-84
Wagner's Law, 62-63
Ward, Norman, 103n, 216n
wars, effect on expenditures, 59, 63,
  123
welfare, See social welfare
Wells, Premier Clyde, 227, 236
Western Accord, 242
White Paper on Employment and
  Income, 264
White, W.L., 103n
Wilson, Finance Minister Michael,
  99, 122, 191, 242, 273, 275
Wilson, Thomas A., 281n
withholding tax, 139

zero rate inflation, 260